LAW, RHETORIC, AND IRONY IN THE FORMATION OF CANADIAN CIVIL CULTURE

In *Law, Rhetoric, and Irony in the Formation of Canadian Civil Culture*, Michael Dorland and Maurice Charland examine how, in the approximately four hundred years since the encounter of the First Nations with Europeans, rhetorical or discursive fields developed in politics and constitution making, in the formation of a public sphere, and in education and language. They discuss the ways in which these fields changed over time within the French regime, the British regime, and in Canada since 1867, and how they converged through trial and error into a Canadian civil culture.

The authors establish a triangulation of fields of discourse formed by law (as a technical discourse system), rhetoric (as a public discourse system), and irony (as a means of accessing the public realm) in order to scrutinize the process of creating a civil culture. By presenting case studies on historical themes such as the legal implications of the transition from French to English law and the continued importance of the Louis Riel case and trial, the authors provide detailed analyses of how communication practices form a common institutional culture.

As scholars of communication and rhetoric, Dorland and Charland have written a challenging examination of the history of Canadian governance and the central role played by legal and other discourses in the formation of civil culture.

MICHAEL DORLAND is a professor in the School of Journalism and Communication at Carleton University.

MAURICE CHARLAND is a professor of Communication Studies at Concordia University.

MICHAEL DORLAND and MAURICE CHARLAND

Law, Rhetoric, and Irony
in the Formation of
Canadian Civil Culture

UNIVERSITY OF TORONTO PRESS
Toronto Buffalo London

© University of Toronto Press Incorporated 2002
Toronto Buffalo London
Printed in Canada

ISBN 0-8020-4283-X (cloth)
ISBN 0-8020-8119-3 (paper)

Printed on acid-free paper

National Library of Canada Cataloguing in Publication Data

Dorland, Michael, 1948–
Law, rhetoric, and irony in the formation of Canadian civil culture

Includes bibliographical references and index.
ISBN 0-8020-4283-X (bound)   ISBN 0-8020-8119-3 (pbk.)

1. Canada – Politics and government.   2. Civil society – Canada.
3. Law – Canada – History.   I. Charland, Maurice René   II. Title.

FC95.D67 2002   971   C2002-900962-6
F1021.D67 2002

University of Toronto Press acknowledges the financial assistance to its publishing program of the Canada Council for the Arts and the Ontario Arts Council.

This book has been published with the help of a grant from the Humanities and Social Sciences Federation of Canada, using funds provided by the Social Sciences and Humanities Research Council of Canada.

University of Toronto Press acknowledges the financial support for its publishing activities of the Government of Canada through the Book Publishing Industry Development Program (BPIDP).

A country, after all, is not something you build as the pharaohs built the pyramids, and then leave standing there to defy eternity. A country is something that is built every day out of certain basic shared values. And so it is in the hands of every Canadian to determine how well and wisely we shall build the country ...

Pierre-Elliott Trudeau, *Memoirs*

Contents

List of Illustrations

Acknowledgments

In March 1996, Michael Dorland was invited by Will Straw, director of the Graduate Program in Communication at McGill, to give a talk on what he imagined cultural studies to be concerned with in the context of Canada. The suggestion he came up with was cultural studies of law; as Rosemary J. Coombe has put it, a field of academic inquiry that will emerge 'when scholars stop reifying law and start analysing it as culture' (2001: 1). It seemed that one of the traits that was especially striking of the 'deep structures' of Canadian culture was that here was a site of complex and prolonged attempts to make very different conceptions of law, those of First Nations, those of the ancien régimes of pre-revolutionary France and late eighteenth-century Britain, and their subsequent mutations into modern Canadian law, enter into conversation with each other as well as with the new environments of their New World contexts. Maurice Charland, whose work on the rhetoric of constitution is better known by his American colleagues than at home in Canada, was spending his sabbatical at McGill and heard Dorland's talk. Charland was working on the problems of rhetoric, constitution, and political theory, and some of what Dorland said piqued his interest. A year later, the authors sat down together to begin planning this book.

In the interim year, Dorland had spent part of a sabbatical at Duke University, immersing himself in legal studies, and taking some amusement from working in the law library where Richard Nixon had earned his law degree while supposedly surviving on Mars bars. He thanks John H. Thompson, director of the then Center for Canadian-American Studies, as well as the late Ted Davidson and his wife, Judith Harrow, for their hospitality both at Duke and in Durham. Thanks also to Margaret Brill at the Perkins Library and Janet Sinder at the Law Library for their advice, assistance, and direction. Dorland's time at Duke had generated a plan for a history of Western law. Charland thought that such a task was too daunting, and suggested we not reinvent the wheel but concentrate instead on what we both felt were the ambivalences of law and its attendant political culture in Canada, a topic that in itself seemed sufficiently complex for the both of us. In 1997 the Social Sciences and Humanities Research Council of Canada granted the authors a three-year Standard Research Grant that made subsequent research possible. Appreciation is extended to SSHRCC and its reviewers for their invaluable support.

At Carleton University, that support was initially made possible through internal grants from the Faculty of Graduate Studies and Research under the successive Deanships of John ApSimon and Roger Blockley. Then Dean of Arts Stuart Adam, Dean of the Faculty of Public Affairs and Management Allan Maslove and Vice-President Feridun Hamdullahpur also provided invaluable support. Dorland's two chairs, Paul Attallah, Associate Director, and Chris Dornan, Director of the School of Journalism and Communication, as usual gave of themselves unstintingly in backing his research endeavours.

Still at Carleton, three of Dorland's PhD students, Peter Hodgins, Anne-Marie Kinahan, and Charlene Elliott were active co-collaborators in the research: Peter working on late eighteenth-century newspapers, Anne-Marie on aspects of woman's suffrage, and Charlene for being such a careful reader of an earlier version of the manuscript, and for doing the index. We thank the Kesterton Endowment of the School of Journalism and Communication for supporting Charlene's work on the index. At Concordia, Sheryl Hamilton, a former MA student at Carleton and later doctoral candidate at Concordia, now an assistant professor of communication at McGill, assisted Charland, both in collecting materials and in commenting upon various versions of what became our manuscript. Also at Concordia, Charland was assisted by Yon Hsu, Tricia Bell, Alana Baskind, Fabio Josgrilberg, and James Hill.

In other locations where researching this study took us, the authors would like to thank Christine Veilleux, archivist of the Literary and Historical Society of Quebec. In England, the reference staff at the Public Records Office, Kew, provided a haven of air-conditioned comfort. The archival staff of the old British Library were patient in response to many queries. And the Senate House Library at the University of London, while sorely lacking in air-conditioning, was a treasure trove of texts in British imperial history. In Paris, archivists and staff at the old Bibliothèque Nationale, rue Richelieu, turned out to be much kinder than their fearsome reputations would have one believe. The staff of the CARAN not only provided the excellence of their archival resources to the Archives Nationales but also fine coin-operated espresso coffee machines! Back home again, the staff responsible for the Manuscript Groups at the

National Archives in Ottawa offered their usual gracious assistance; Carleton University's MacOdrum Library staff are to be saluted for the marvels they have accomplished in electronic access under hard budgetary times; and thanks too to the staff at the Université d'Ottawa's Morissette Library as well as the Centre de recherche en civilisation canadienne-française.

Parts of the chapters that follow were presented in different forms at conferences in a number of countries. Portions of chapter 1 were presented at the International Popular Culture Conference at the University of York in July 1997 and also at the Social Moves Conference, Tulane University, in November 1997. Parts of chapter 3 were presented at the National Communication Association annual conference in New York City in November 1998, at the Canadian Communication Association annual conference at the University of Sherbrooke in June 1999, and at the National University of Ireland, Galway, also in June 1999. Portions of chapter 5 were presented at Indiana University, Northwestern University, and the Annual Meeting of the Working Group on Law and Humanities at the Georgetown Law Center in Washington DC in 1999. Elements of chapter 6 were presented at Northern Illinois University's Women's Studies Center and the Wake Forest Conference on Argumentation in Venice in 2000. A shorter version of chapter 9 was presented at the International Conference on Constitution-Rhetoric-Agency at Concordia University in September 2000. All translations, unless otherwise noted, are our own.

Thanks are especially due to Robert Hariman, John Lucaites, Lois Self, James McDaniel, Jim Jasinski, Thomas Farrell, and Philippe Salazar for their enthusiasm and helpful comments. Charland also thanks his wife, Ellie DiRusso, without whose love, enthusiasm, and encouragement he would have given up long ago. Dorland thanks his partner, Percy Walton, for her love, support, and keen critical interest in our project.

The process of getting the manuscript into the capable hands of the University of Toronto Press also occasioned numerous obligations. First to Gerald Hallowell, who until his retirement was the project's first editor, a job taken over by Siobhan McMenemy, who undertook all those many necessary things authors tend to be oblivious to; and to Frances Mundy, our top-notch managing editor. Thanks to the two fine readers for the Aid to Scholarly Publications Program of the Humanities and Social Sciences Federation of Canada, as well as an anonymous internal reader for the University of Toronto Press for responding to the project so favourably. Special appreciation is due to Dr Miriam Skey for the delicate job of copy-editing the manuscript. Finally, thanks to the National Gallery of Canada and the Musée du Québec, as well as to artist Robert Houle, for kind permission to reproduce the five paintings that form the iconographic armature of the study. We regret only that we were not able to reproduce them in their original colour.

Despite all the obligations we have incurred in realizing this study, the work of interpretation remains ultimately that of its authors; as that of judgment befalls to its readers. It is to them that we offer up this work in a gesture of mutual self-understanding oriented toward communication.

MD & MC
Ottawa and Montreal,
Summer 2001

LAW, RHETORIC, AND IRONY IN THE FORMATION OF
CANADIAN CIVIL CULTURE

Envoi

The phrase 'Peace, Order, and Good Government' is to Canada what 'Life, Liberty, and the Pursuit of Happiness' is to the United States, a *project* of the authority of governance. But more than that, the phrase speaks to the arts and manners of governance; the styles or *mentalités* that both inform and perform how governance gets acted out. To be sure, there are obvious differences in emphasis between the two; where the first specifically emphasizes 'government' (as in the State), the second does so indirectly, suggesting 'government' more in the sense of a self-governing civil society. Yet the two phrases do not stand in contradiction to one another; they both reflect a common historical discourse that permeated such discussions in the early modern period. The difference between the two is that the Canadian one derives from an *earlier* period in the discussion; the American phrase appears at its end, an end that will be forever ruptured by political revolution and revolutionary war, inaugurating a 'new order of the ages.' In the Canadian case, while there will be breaks and ruptures in modes of governance, which the following study details, these will not be clothed in the language of revolutionary discourse. On the contrary, and this is vital to the following study, Canada stumbles into the modern age without having recourse to the facilities revolutionary language provides (e.g., Before and After; the End of History, and its radical New Beginning, etc.). With the onset of an age that self-consciously defines itself as 'revolutionary' (politically, industrially, socially, and so on, down to the trivial 'revolutions' of consumer products of all kinds), it is difficult, to put it mildly, if one has to negotiate all these passages without being able to recur to the language that supports revolutionary transformations. The resulting inarticulateness has been one of the principal problems that Canadian political and civil culture has faced, as we discuss below in detail. Without having recourse to revolutionary befores and afters, one becomes historically disoriented, especially in generally revolutionary times. Such notions as 'the past,' in which, as both Karl Marx and Thomas Jefferson remarked, the living in their pursuit of happiness are already heavily mortgaged through prior social relations and arrangements that they cannot see, weigh upon them like a nightmare. Haunted by ghosts that they do not necessarily believe in, and tongue-tied by not being able to speak the violent language that wipes the historical slate clean and allows one to begin anew, one not only faces considerable problems, but is ill-equipped to cope with them. One is not at a total loss, however; speech does not come to a sudden end; there are still events, befores and afterwards, though not of the revolutionary kind. There were the French discoverers; then there was 'the Conquest,' a form of historical calamity with wide-ranging ramifications throughout the non-English-speaking Americas; then came the English, who eventually transmuted into the fictitious monolith of 'English Canada' or 'the Rest of Canada.' In short, there are still signposts by which to mark far-reaching changes, and no end of Others to blame them for. And always in an age of writing and recording observations, there is no shortage of explorers and the like to describe the New Lands, the aboriginal inhabitants and their mores and customs; no shortage of missionaries to preach the ways of Christ and pass judgment on the state of people's souls; and soon enough no shortage of historians, writing in French and in English, to explain in two languages that do not speak to each other the whys and hows of the order of things natural, political, and social. Even without the language of Revolution, discourses abounded.

The problem, rather, concerns the fit of these many discourses – those that were there 'in the beginning' (as in John Locke's 'in the beginning, all the world was America') and the various discursive waves that followed; from the France of the ancien régime to that of 1789 and after; from the Thirteen Colonies to the new United States of America; from an England wracked by the immense transformations of the Industrial Revolution and political and colonial reform, and so on. The study that follows attempts to make organized sense of these waves of discourse, especially those that make up 'the law,' which is understood largely in John Conway's sense of 'politics, culture and the writing of constitutions' (1969). These discourses are to a great degree rhetorical: strategic and agonistic in character, directed towards forging consensus among some and challenging the authority of others, and ultimately resting upon the convictions that they seek to create. These are three fields of discourse to which Canadians, in French and in English, have devoted considerable effort, much heat, and too often little light. In part, this stems from an oft-repeated belief (e.g., Conway 13) that Canadians, being English and so 'pragmatic,' are deeply scornful of abstract ideas. One can see right away how misleading such a belief can be, especially given that, in historical terms, as we argue below, Canadians are at least as French as they are English in the sedimentation of political and legal institutions – and everybody knows how fond the French are of 'abstract ideas.'

But as we shall have more to say about this in the pages that follow, let us return briefly to 'peace, order, and good government.' There is in the end little common agreement about the phrase itself. For some historians and jurists, it constitutes the very essence of a Canadian political and social project. Its political incarnation is found in the powers of the central government to steer into being a form of civil belongingness that has sometimes been referred to as 'the Peaceable Kingdom' (Kilbourn 1970) – institutional forms of civility and civil society that have been highly valued (e.g., Griffiths 1996) or condemned as mere 'deference to authority' (Friedenberg 1980).

For other historians and jurists, 'peace, order, and good government' – that specific clause of the British North America Act (1867), the preamble to section 91, which enumerates the powers of the general government and which lawyers refer to as 'the POgG clause' – is nothing more than a meaningless, throwaway phrase used conventionally by the constitutional drafting officials of the Colonial Office and committees of the Houses of Parliament in London. Among those who argue against giving undue importance to words that do not especially mean anything, Eggleston (1996–7) notes, for instance, that it was originally drafted as 'peace, welfare, and good government' (81). He goes on to remark that the 'POgG' phrase had been used routinely by the Imperial authorities since 1689 – ironically, he notes, the year after the Glorious Revolution and the year of publication of Locke's *Treatises on Government* – as a signifier for the general authority of colonial legislatures. Eggleston also asks why, if the phrase holds the importance to Canadian political discourse that some have claimed, does it so seldom appear in the Confederation Debates that lasted for weeks, and filled over a thousand double-columned pages (85)?

Finally, Eggleston goes on to note that at a time in the Imperial Parliament when 'all eyes were focused on the Reform Bill,' the BNA Act sailed through the House of Lords in fifteen days and the Commons in eleven and was treated 'with all the indifference of "a private bill uniting two or three English parishes"' (91–2). He concludes that the POgG debate is another marker of Canadians' alienation from a Constitution less of their own making than of 'the terminological preferences of a British aristocrat and his bureaucratic underling' (93). We will hear more about this below. Suffice it for now to say that this debate in large measure has missed the point, for the significance of POgG rests not with the intentions of drafters or founders, but with the uses to which it is put – in its practical and strategic interpretations in Parliament, in the courts, and in the often noisy agonistic sites known as the public sphere .

As much of the discussion in this book is concerned with words and their various and possible meanings, it might prove useful to spend some time instead with some paintings. There are five in number and have been chosen because each represents an aspect of the five principal forms of discourse that have historically configured Canadian civil culture.

Two we discovered in Quebec City, hanging in the Musée du Québec's exposition of historical paintings. The other three are in the National Gallery in Ottawa, two of which – Benjamin West's *The Death of General Wolfe* (1770) and a Robert Harris preparatory drawing of his now-destroyed *The Fathers of Confederation* – have become clichés of Canadian history and its attendant myths. West's *Death of Wolfe* is a bathetically grandiose, battlefield painting from the end of the eighteenth century. It is a real tear-jerker, full of tragic irony: the pale, mortally wounded general dying at the very moment of his triumphant victory over Montcalm on the Plains of Abraham, with his officers in distress surrounding him beneath the looming clouds of the battle behind still raging. Jarring this bodice-ripper's bathos is the foregrounded figure of an Indian warrior, kneeling like Rodin's *The Thinker* and staring closely and silently at the scene. This same figure is key to Robert Houle's *Kanata* (1992), which plays with and rests upon West's rendition, but does so in ways that profoundly disrupt and ironize the historical original. Houle's is the only painting among our five that is not primarily a cliché. Why, then, this visible fondness for clichéed – that is, non-ironic renditions of Canadian history? In part, the answer has to do with predominant styles at the time of execution; but, more importantly for us, it has much more to do with how 'history' has been understood, written, and codified.

Harris's *Fathers of Confederation*, an image familiar to every Canadian youth who has been subjected to the tedium of learning Canadian history in high school, is almost breathtaking in its banality. A bunch of dead, nineteenth-century, white guys stand or sit about at some meeting: nobody is saying anything at all, some are reading, others just look bored. It is by itself a depiction of the utterly insignificant. It could be the corporate board of some firm. Obviously, it was important enough to *them* to have the scene sketched, but as to what possible importance this scene might possess for others is anybody's guess. Like a strange abstraction, one has to read the words of the title to begin to get a sense that, politically, this gathering was a big deal. Otherwise, the image of these fathers of confederation serves only to explain why schoolchildren find Canadian history among the most boring of many

The fondness for non-ironic renditions of Canadian History has to do with how history has been understood, written, and codified. Benjamin West (1728–1820), *The Death of General Wolfe*, 1770. 152.6 × 214.5 cm, oil on canvas. Reproduced by permission of the National Gallery of Canada, Ottawa. Transfer from the Canadian War Memorials, 1921 (Gift of the 2nd Duke of Westminster, Eaton Hall, Cheshire, 1918).

Houle's *Kanata*, the only painting here that is not a cliché, disrupts and ironizes the historical original by highlighting the Amerindian with some colour, thus making him the most conspicuous part of a scene otherwise all rendered in a tan monochrome. Robert Houle (1947–), *Kanata*, 1992. 228.7 × 732.0 cm, acrylic and conté crayon on canvas, National Gallery of Canada, Ottawa. Reproduced by permission of the artist.

Like a strange abstraction, the title of Harris's cartoon has to be read for one to get a sense that, politically, the gathering depicted was an event of some portent for the country. Robert Harris (1849–1919), Cartoon for *Meeting of the Delegates of British North America to Settle the Terms of Confederation, Quebec, October 1864,* 1883. 160 × 362 cm, charcoal and red chalk on woven paper. Reproduced by permission of the National Gallery of Canada, Ottawa. Transfer from the House of Commons of the Parliament of Canada, 1981.

dull subjects to which they are exposed. Again, why is this? And what does this say about the style of writing of Canadian history? Why the preference here for the dullest possible rendition of what was, after all, supposedly an historical event – Confederation and what led up to it – of some matter to this country?

Now if, by contrast, we turn to the two other paintings that will concern us both directly and indirectly in these pages, we find some interesting variations on the clichéed. Charles Huot's *Esquisse de la première séance de la Chambre d'Assemblée* (1910) visually says: History in the Making. Largely this is because it is recognizably in the familiar style of representations of Significant Moments in History, like Washington's crossing of the Delaware, say; in fact, Huot's is almost, with minor differences, identical to representations of the debates over the U.S. Constitution at Philadelphia from 1787–8. Still, while we can see that important stuff is going on, major speeches are being made, listeners press in closely to listen to the orator, we do not know (yet) what all the excitement is about. That we will discover in the chapters that follow, but this painting is saying something of import about the nature of public speech, in sharp contrast to the others that, from a speech perspective, are just solemnly *dumb*.

Finally, we come to a stunning, if still clichéed, work by Napoléon Bourassa, a turn-of-the-century Quebec artist whose paintings tended generally toward the religious. This large, never-completed canvas is roughly four meters by seven and took up almost the entire wall in the room where it was hanging. It is entitled *L'Apothéose de Christophe Colomb* and is utterly marvellous in its baroque absurdity, its bizarre mixture of angelic, heavenly creatures floating about on clouds, and (to the bottom-right, standing on more solid ground) a lineage of historical persons, beginning with Jacques Cartier and ending with Sir John A. Macdonald, who is holding the 'Mosaic tablets' of the BNA Act.

In all, in this work that Bourassa began in 1859–60 and never completed (he died in 1916), there are sixty-two human and mythic figures. The mythic figures represent the geniuses of seafaring, poetry, glory, the Furies, and the like. The human figures form an odd constellation of philosophers (Socrates and Plato), rhetoricians (Cicero and Plutarch), classical statesmen (Demosthenes), discoverers, both scientific and geographical (Archimedes, Galileo, Amerigo Vespucci, and Columbus, of course), poets (Dante, Milton), painters (Michelangelo, Raphael), inventors (da Vinci, Gutenberg). But, to our way of seeing, buried among these and other figures, there runs a continuum of greater significance, from Numa, the founder of Roman law, to the sixteenth-century Dominican priest and jurist Bartolomé de las Casas, and the nineteenth-century Canadian lawyer-politicians who will preoccupy us at greater length below. As

Obviously a Significant Moment in History, but whose history and what is going on is harder to decipher. Charles Huot (n.d.), *Esquisse de la première séance de la Chambre d'Assemblée*, c. 1910. 90.2 × 183 cm, oil on canvas. Accession no. 57.23. Photograph by Jean-Guy Kérouac. Reproduced by permission of the Musée du Québec.

Bourassa's uncompleted fresco depicts a genealogy of the law from Numa, the legend-
ary founder of Roman law, to the sixteenth-century Dominican jurist Bartolomeo de las
Casas, and including the lawyer-politicians of nineteenth-century Canada. Napoléon
Bourassa (1827–1916), *Apothéose de Christophe Colomb*, c.1906–12. 484 × 734 cm,
oil on canvas, unsigned. Accession no. 65.174. Photograph by Patrick Altman 1992.
Reproduced by permission of the Musée du Québec.

we will argue in due course, what matters to us about Bourassa's uncompleted fresco is that it depicts *a genealogy of the law*, from the classical age through to the sixteenth- and seventeenth-century debates in Spain and the Spanish Americas over whether the 'Indians' were human and had souls, and on through to the processes of the constitution of Canada as an entity *in* law and *of* law.

The paintings, then, tell us, or appear to tell us, things about words and the absence of words; about history – specific stylizations of words, which are, it could be well argued, forms of rhetoric; and, finally, of the relation of rhetoric to the law over what constitutes political and civil authority. The following study devotes itself to making these relations clearer.

1

Situating Canada's Civil Culture

It is our sense of loss that brings us together.

David Young, *Glenn*

... the past was never just the past, it was what made the present able to live with itself.

Julian Barnes, *England, England*

United in grief.

Globe and Mail headline on the death of Trudeau

The Canadian Question

To say that Canada as a political and discursive entity exists in a condition of constant, latent symbolic crisis is as much a truism as it is a cliché. From Voltaire's dismissive 'forty arpents of snow,' if not before – Jacques Cartier had initially compared his discovery to the land God gave Cain – Canadian self-definitions have laboured alternatively between a pervasive sense of generalized inferiority and wishful aspirations to grandiosity. If such sentiments of inferiority emerged often in contrast to the more flamboyant self-definitions and dynamic continental expansion of the republic south of the 49th parallel, the United States was not the only source of invidious comparisons; the aspiration to greatness set standards equally impossible to achieve. Thus, the *Globe* newspaper at the time of Confederation (1867) compared the political union of the four Canadian provinces to the founding of a new Rome; similarly, the turn-of-the-century prime minister, Wilfrid Laurier, would claim that the twentieth century 'belongs to Canada.'

This dialectic of superiority-inferiority continues to be a characteristic of contemporary Canadian civil culture, in the form of agonistic preoccupation with defining a stabilized self-understanding of Canadian political and/or cultural 'identity' and, with this, the seemingly interminable pursuit of issues of constitutional reform, to the point of having reached what some observers see as the final impasse for the Quebec sovereigntist project (see Dubuc 2000: 8–28). In turn, concerns about the soundness of the polity alternate with boostering claims by federal politicians, drawing upon UNESCO quality of life survey data as of the 1990s and annually thereafter, that Canada is globally deemed to be the best place on earth in which to live.

However, it is the darker side of such a civil culture that constitutes the more striking aspects of its better-known historical analyses. In contradistinction to Almond and Verba's classic contribution to the study of democratic cultures, *The Civic Culture* (1963, 1989), we prefer the term 'civil culture' because it is our view that the latter better brings out the ambivalences of what they were trying to define, namely, 'a pluralistic culture based on communication and persuasion, a culture of consensus and diversity' (1989: 6). Thus, Canada's equivalent to de Tocqueville, Lord ('Radical Jack') Durham, in his *Report on the Affairs of British North America* (1839), spoke of the conflict of two nations warring within the bosom of a single state. Half a century later, French political scientist André Siegfried's *The Race Question in Canada* (1907) found Canada to be above all 'a land of fears and jealousies and conflicts' whose politicians 'stand in fear of great movements of public opinion ... [and] seek to lull them rather than ... bring them to fruition' (141–3, cited in Underhill 1960: 10). James Bryce, a former British ambassador to Washington and author of a classic study of the American commonwealth, remarked generally of Canada's civil culture in his *Modern Democracies* (1921), that the predominance of party spirit in pursuit of material interests 'so far from being a measure of the volume of political thinking, may even be a substitute for thinking' (1921, 1: 505). Similar diagnoses of the peculiarities of the civil culture of Canada – petty, anti-intellectual, overly deferential to authority, yet perpetually quarrelsome – have become staples of contemporary comparative sociological analyses (see Lipset 1990, for one example among many).

The pervasiveness of such observations would soon imprint itself on Canadian-born historians; thus, Frank Underhill, in a notable article first published in 1946, commented on the apparent paradox of Canadian political culture: namely, that it was marked by an almost complete intellectual poverty, while, at the same time, 'we were the pioneers in one of the great liberal achievements of the nineteenth century,' the advent of responsible government (Underhill 1960: 7–8). And, of course, philosopher George Grant's *Lament for a Nation* (1965) still maintains classic status among Canadian self-reflections –

as the impossible project of attempting to establish a conservative polity in a sea of liberal technological modernity.

The historical debate over the nature of Canada's political culture thus continues into the present day. But what was formerly viewed as a kernel of Toryism – conservative and communitarian in a hierarchical conception of the social obligations of noblesse oblige – enveloped by a majoritarian liberal constitutionalism has, under the influence of the work of revisionist historians like John Pocock (1975) and Bernard Bailyn (1967), become a more complex model, acknowledging a greater presence than earlier Canadian historiography had granted to the continuity of the eighteenth-century 'civic humanist' or republican tradition (see Ajzenstat and Smith, 1995; also Smith 1999), and in turn to their corresponding rhetorical tropes. Particularly among academic analysts, however, as opposed to alternative arguments proffered by non-professional historians (such as, most recently, Saul [1997] or Moore [1997]), the analytical framework for the discussion of Canadian civil culture, if it exists at all, remains largely within the terms of the translation, into a Canadianized idiom, of findings often developed from the generalization of largely American or English conditions.

This interpretive tension, itself another version of the dialectic of inferiority-superiority, is the subject of a complex history, going back to the 1920s and 1930s and the initial attempts by Canadian-born academics, particularly in the human sciences, to articulate the epistemological bases of Canadian schools of economic history, geography, and communications (Melody, Salter, A. Smith 1994; and Heyer 1981; Acland & Buxton 1999; Babe 2000). In turn, the efforts to bring governance within the purview of social sciences better adapted to local conditions would find their cultural science equivalents, especially in the 1960s, in the literary fields, particularly criticism, in the definition and subse-quent canonization of Canadian literature (see esp. Klinck 1976). But the development of Canadian studies carried within itself the self-fulfilling risk of subsuming emerging fields of knowledge in narrowly nationalistic self-understandings; another great risk was of fetishizing the autochthonous. Ironi-cally this initially entailed the erasure of the country's First Peoples and their history and cultures (see e.g., Goldie, Lambert, and Lorimer 1994).

Attempts at nationalistic revisionism, however, remained relatively mar-ginal, restricted to certain, largely artistic or imaginative, fields of knowledge. While subject to recent criticism and admissions of the 'paradigmatic failure' of a dominant left nationalist academic consensus (e.g., Angus 1997), they have led to calls for perspectival repositionings, although still within the same dialectic of inferiority-superiority. Thus, for instance, while sociologist Ian Angus finds that the preoccupation with questions of identity has been as much a characteristic of Mexican, Central American, and Latin American intellectuality as it has been of the Canadian, the resulting problem, for Angus, is that of the Eurocentric biases of social and historical analysis. Reversing the bias, he accordingly claims that innovation in civilization, in fact, comes from the margins and peripheries of empire, and not from the so-called civilized centres (Angus 1997: 107–11). This is itself an echo of Harold Innis's earlier attempt in the 1930s to recentre economic, and in the early 1950s communications, history so as to situate the locuses of social change in the frontier zones of empire where greater experimentation becomes possible (see Innis 1972).[1]

Attempting to move beyond the Eurocentric dialectic of inferiority-superiority, although now from the perspective of the margins of Europe, a recent analysis of the Canadian identity, by an Irish sociologist, situates the problem of Canada still more broadly. 'The problem of Canada is fundamental and universal. It is an expression of Hegel's question: how to cancel the opposition while preserving the difference. It is the problem of the spirit of the collective: the desire for the elusive synthetic moment of social solidarity where we glimpse the "I" that is "We" and the "We" that is "I" ' (Keohane 1997: 3). That claim advanced, however, Keohane readily admits that such an attempt is virtually impossible, because 'the nation' is itself an impossibility – or at best an imagined community (B. Anderson 1986) – because, in Keohane's Lacanian formulation, 'the nation exists only as symptoms of its lack' (13).

But even if one claims that contemporary social life has become utterly fragmented into an infinity of antagonistic 'ideolects,' the analyst is still confronted at a minimum with a problem of sociological particularity; in this case, that of *nonetheless* attempting to understand the 'impossible' idioms that make up Canada, this imaginary place. As Keohane puts it: 'We must search for the difference, for what is particularly "Canadian," in the symptoms of the nonexistence of Canada' (1997: 13–14). And yet, interesting as his interpretive symptomatology is, Keohane only scratches at the idiomatic surface: the analysis of beer commercials, while revealing of the representations attachable to the production of a widely imbibed beverage and no doubt semiotically rewarding, is as superficial a method of sociological observation as Jean Baudrillard's equally glib remark that all one needs know about American society can be learned by driving across the country (cited in Keohane 1997: 17).

More substantively, Keohane's central insight – that Canada represents a particular case of the inability of the '*enjoyment* of a historical identity – that is, the innumerable social practices, languages, signs, codes that animate a particular identity' (23, emphasis added) because it 'is constantly under threat of being stolen away by the necessary coexistence of Otherness' (23) is, he argues, itself symptomatic of the anxiety-laden transition between the breakdown of an old symbolic order and the emergence of a new one.

In response, might one not wonder, however striking the 'Canadian' lack, whether these conditions are, in fact, particular only to Canada, or are they not rather dimensions of larger sets of processes – call them postcolonialism, globalization, or postmodernism – of sociological transformation and symbolic breakdown that have come to affect all nations, all imagined communities, in various ways and to varying degrees?

Complicating Factors

Before discussing the effects of globalization, some additional predisposing characteristics first need to be considered. For one, Canada's inability to derive enjoyment from its symbolic order – its pervasive 'culture of *ressentiment*' (Dorland 1988) – is a socio-cultural trait also observable in small countries, many of them former British colonies or dependencies. Despite its huge geographic size, Canada, with a population today of some thirty million people, is a relatively small country demographically. Ireland, for instance, offers strikingly comparable cultural similarities to Canada. In a recent review of David Lowenthal's *The Heritage Crusade and the Spoils of History* (1997), Richard Jenkyns (1998) makes the point that the preservation of Irish culture would necessitate giving recognition equally to the *ressentiment* that forms one of its constitutive traits. 'Ireland provides a lesson in how to get heritage wrong. A relaxed, open, and charming society in most respects, and now blessed with an enviably dynamic economy, it ought to be the model of a modern small nation, but it is wounded by a damaging idea of itself. As Lowenthal says, "A culture of victimhood haunts the classroom." Where there should be self-confidence, the rhetoric of grievance lingers on' (cited in Jenkyns, 50). Jenkyns goes on to note parallels with Pakistan, which also 'suffers from a similar uneasiness ... a deep impulse to think ill [both of oneself and] of one's larger neighbor.' Similarly, V.S. Naipaul in his essay 'The Return of Eva Perón' (1980) remarked on the many resentment-filled aspects of Argentine culture, sentiments that could be reproduced in the Canada context verbatim and for many of the same reasons. Quoting a musing by Borges on Argentina's problematic semi-colonial relationship to Britain ('I wonder whether being a colony does any good – so provincial and dull'), Naipaul observes that 'to be European in Argentina was to be colonial in the most damaging way. It was to be parasitic. It was to claim – as the white communities in the Caribbean colonies claimed – the achievements and authority of Europe as one's own ... It was to accept, out of a false security, a second-ratedness for one's own society,' and, along with this, an underlying, accompanying terror of being thought 'mediocre' (1980: 116–17).

Another factor to take into account, therefore, related to the formation of cultures of *ressentiment*, concerns the imaginary community's self-perception of the timeline of its entry into modernity. Drawing upon examples as varied as nineteenth-century Greece and Bismarckian Germany, cultures whose entry into modernity was viewed by contemporary nationalist observers as 'belated' (see Jusdanis 1991), some analysts have suggested that this oppressive sense of belatedness influenced particularly sociological self-reflection in specific ways. Thus, for instance, Max Weber's gloomy view of modernity as an 'iron cage' of rationalization can be correlated to a diagnosis of having arrived too late to fully benefit from the optimal, normative conditions of modernity; this led others to see a special trajectory of German exceptionalism – the so-called *Sonderweg*. As a consequence their resulting, resentment-filled view of Germany's development, particularly in contrast to England and France, would indirectly contribute to two world wars in the first half of the twentieth century (Liebersohn 1988; Stern 1961). In other words, a culture of symbolic disenchantment, significant as it may be, as Keohane claims distinguishes Canada's, is not by itself a sufficient explanation; other elements come into play as well, such as the course of economic development, or more precisely, local theories of economic development and how they have marked the respective cultures from which they have come.

Here again, Canadian political economists provide a store of particularly bleak narratives – in one analyst's words, 'a nightmarish vision ... stuck in a perpetual trap of resource-exporting, foreign ownership and economic and political dependence' (Laxer 1989; see also Bodemann 1984). In the Canadian context, much subtlety has been deployed by political economists and also by literary critics to deal with the implications of these problems. In a version of Canadian exceptionalism, particularly as expounded by literary critics, Canada would have skipped over modernity entirely to offer a model of the world's first postmodern nation (Hutcheon 1988; Elder 1989: 30–1, 84–5). This is not dissimilar, if rather differently inflected, to historian Frank Underhill's remark that Canadian political thought had entirely missed the eighteenth-century, with its preoccupation with the appropriate forms and language of polity, to better devote itself to the merely muscular, nineteenth-century tasks of 'nation-building' (1960).

A further complicating factor thus concerns the weight to be accorded to the colonial heritage. As has been noted many times, Canada, unlike the United States most notably, or India within the British Empire, did not self-constitute as a polity through a process of revolutionary struggle, rhetoric, and rupture, leading to a definably declaratory moment of the proclamation of political independence. On the contrary, nineteenth-century British Canada saw itself, in marked contrast to the dangerous experiment in mob rule of the American Republic, as a consciously counterrevolutionary project, loyally ensconced within the millenial mythology of English monarchical constitutionalism, and incrementally acceding to the progressive benefits of English liberty under the indivisible sovereignty of the British Crown (see e.g., Wise 1993; Mills 1988). If Canada's political separation from Britain as a result entailed a long, slow process – the 1867 British North America Act that served as Canada's constitution was finally removed from the aegis of Westminster only by the Constitution Act of 1982 – Canada's antecedent separation from France's eighteenth-century empire was, after the latter's loss of the Seven Years' War, a more wrenching affair, particularly for the small fraction of the former ruling class that elected to remain in Canada after New France's cession to Britain. Thus, depending on the linguistic group, cultural background, and the resulting historiographic interpretations, two versions of the institutional origins of modern Canada emerged: in English, a counterrevolutionary and yet progressive loyalty to the British Crown; and, in French, the developing black legend of 'the Conquest' with its symptomatic inscriptions, as on contemporary Quebec vehicle licence plates, of the mnemonic injunction never to forget the past: 'Je me souviens.'

Extending an argument about the continuity of institutions from de Tocqueville's *L'Ancien régime et la révolution française* (1840), the late Quebec sociologist Fernand Dumont granted enormous salience not only to the lasting consequences of the trauma of the Conquest, but also to the extent to which the transitional period following the cession, 1759–91, profoundly influenced the subsequent course of institutional development in its formative, not to say determinative, influence of the orientations of Quebec civil culture (Dumont 1993). In the same vein of the determining imprint of the formative colonial culture, two other Quebec political scientists, Gérald Bernier and Daniel Salée, in a study of the formation of nineteenth-century Quebec politics and society, have put forth what they term 'the theory of *ancien régime* domination' (1992: 65–98) to explain the underlying influence of ancien régime continuity in the shaping of contemporary Canadian institutions. Ironically perhaps, analysts from both sides of the major Canadian linguistic divide more often than not have tended to argue strongly *for* the continuity of a determining influence of the past upon the present, although they differ over which and whose 'past' is to be determining, an English past or a French past, each providing an additional imagined community to draw upon. But while there are differing degrees of inflection to all this and much depends upon the context of writing, among historians Harold Innis, particularly in articles of the late 1940s period (see Dorland 1997: 7–21), tended to be the exception for scholars writing in English in his insistence that it was France's history which provided the normative model for understanding Canadian institutional development, more so than England's, which was, as French prime minister Georges Clémenceau once remarked, only the history of 'a French colony gone wrong' (Innis 1956: 384).

Such ongoing debates – in short, the difficulties of evaluating the past – have been further complicated by the rise of the field of studies that goes loosely by the name of postcolonialism. And however problematic the term, postcolonial studies have considerably enriched our understanding of the complexity of the processes of European colonization on the one hand and on the other hand of the difficulties of the subsequent 'de-colonization' undergone by former colonies. The work of such scholars as Anthony Pagden (1995) on the ideologies of the empires of Spain, France, and Britain, of Renaissance historian Walter D. Mignolo (1995) on the interplay of literacy, territoriality, and colonization in Meso-America, of Bernard Cohn (1996) on the relations between knowledge and the British colonization of India, or Denys Delâge (1991) on the differential economic and social effects of imperial rivalries in North America, remind us to tread cautiously; we are dealing here with phenomena far more complicated than mere brute force or crude symbols. We are dealing profoundly with epistemic encounters in the fully Foucauldian sense (see Foucault 1970). The term 'postcoloniality' can too readily suggest a rupture with colonial practices that on the contrary remain far more deeply imbedded than the prefix 'post' implies. In a context such as Canada's, in part because of the absence of a revolutionary tradition with its rhetorical capability to proclaim a *novus ordo seclorum*, but also because of the interwoven continuities stemming from a dual colonial heritage, we suggest that the embeddedness of the past remains not only more problematic, but also more subtle. As a result, a more probing diagnostic conceptualization, perhaps, is called for than the mere analysis of symptoms, although, as the above discussion has suggested, these are certainly plentiful.

Global Postmodernity

In addition to such factors, we should also acknowledge the contemporary preoccupation with the uncertain implications of economic globalization, particularly as these concern policy analysts who have suffered a presumed erosion in the decision-making capacities of the formerly sovereign nation-state. This is reflected in the symbolic, cultural, or literary sciences in the form of a variety of theories under the rubric of 'postmodernity.' Thus a further level of complexity follows in which to frame our discussion of Canada's civil culture.

In both perspectives of globalization and postmodernity, analysts are confronted with the problems of two processes of breakdown: 1) the supposed loss of autonomy of a limitlessly independent actor, the modern state; and 2) the equivalent dissolution or blurring at the cultural level of the key symbols – 'grand narratives' in Jean-François Lyotard's well-known phrase (Lyotard 1979) – of the unity of consciousness of mind, self, and society (God, Ego, and History in their upper-case versions), thought to give coherence to the project of Western civilization (or European modernity, depending on the grand narrative). At the same time, analysts as well as actors are also confronted with an additional set of problems, reconstructing the articulations of systems of power. This may be in the form of a 'new' world economic order with larger zones of political, trading, or cultural integration such as the European Union, the North American Free Trade Agreement, or regional equivalents such as Mercosur in Latin America. Along with the expansion of international trade pacts dealing with global financial and other services, intellectual property rights and so on, come the often violent reconfigurations of political boundaries, such as those of the former Soviet Union or the former Yugoslavia. The attempt to manage large-scale changes, on the one hand, within ever larger systems, notably of the regulation of international commerce, has also been accompanied by, on the other hand, the re-emergence of virulent particularisms, as well as unforeseen and catastrophic economic disturbances within widely divergent geographic regions, such as the recent collapse of the Southeast Asian 'Tigers,' just yesterday alleged models of economic performance, in what financier George Soros has termed the first serious threat to the contemporary global economy, a massive market failure with ramifications that spread almost instantaneously from Southeast Asia to Russia and to Brazil (1988: 21–6; see also Friedman 2000). In other words, globalization of the world economy would appear to go hand-in-hand with equivalent powerful processes of symbolic disturbance, ranging from the explosion of lingering ethnic or tribal antagonisms, to the emergence of global cultures of instantaneous communications or hybrid forms combining elements of so-called global and local cultures ('glocalization'), along with attendant processes of generalized symbolic disenchantment, such as the loss of faith in political institutions and the rise of a public culture of cynicism (Goldfarb 1991; Chaloupka 1999).

Trying to trace a navigable path through such a complex range and scale of transformations is obviously no easy affair. The Portuguese sociologist Boaventura de Sousa Santos in *Toward a New Common Sense: Law, Science and Politics in the Paradigmatic Transition* (1995) has proposed approaches that are profoundly insightful in understanding the paradoxes of the present and their complex relationship to the past. As suggested above, globalization is not a single process; it is, if not multi-faceted, at the very least the combination of both economic and symbolic transformations working in tandem but also at cross-purposes. As de Sousa Santos argues, globalization, beginning with the extension of European power beyond Europe itself, with the thirteenth-century *Reconquista* of Iberia, was both conquest (in fact, always recursively, the 're-capture' of lands and peoples) and the (re)conversion (of souls). In other words, European expansion involved the spread of economies *and* the extension of human rights simultaneously. This dual process, with its roots in the Christian division of temporal and spiritual powers, would, in time, unleash one document, the Declaration of the Rights of Man and the Citizen *and* Napoleon, 'world history on horseback,' as Hegel called him. Or, as Marx stated the paradox of bourgeois civilization: 'The bourgeoisie, by the rapid improve-ment of all instruments of production, by the immensely facilitated means of communication, draws all, even the most barbarian, nations into civilization. The cheap prices of its commodities are the heavy artillery with which it batters down all Chinese walls ... [and] compels all nations, on pain of extinction ... to introduce what it calls civilization into their midst' ([1848] 1998: 39–40).

For his part, de Sousa Santos thus distinguishes four dimensions of globali-zation, one of which (arguably the most important one for our purposes in this study) is that of the transnationalization of the legal field. For de Sousa Santos, there are four 'passes of entry into modernity: the European gate; the New Worlds; the colonial zone; [and] modernization in the face of modernity as an external threat' (1995: 271). If the European gate was asymetrical to all the others for reasons of power, this calls all the more strongly today for 'a genuinely de-Westernized conception of the global process of modernization,' as a partial and painful experience of unequal contact and exchange, but as an encounter nonetheless, in a sea of contingent variables. Some of these vari-ables, however, would include, besides knowledge of the hierarchies in the political economy of the world system, 'the knowledge of the historical trajec-tories of the different routes to and through modernity ... [as well as] knowledge of the different historical legal cultures and styles prevalent in the different regions and countries of the world system,' because while some legal cultures were part of Western modernity itself, others had existed long before the contact period, whereas others developed in conjunction, conflict, or complementarity with the Western ones (1995: 271–2).

In de Sousa Santos's analysis, the processes of the transnationalization of the legal field are the most significant because it is these that push the implications of globalization to their furthest limits, as they entail the possibility of the emergence of a *jus humanitatis* that clashes with the dominant legal concep-tions of property upon which the world capitalist system is based, and of the conceptions of sovereignty upon which the interstate system is based. In short, according to de Sousa Santos, the paradigmatic transition we are experiencing is potentially that of an emerging global *ecumene*. Or to invoke other authors in the same vein, the more significant dimension of contemporary globalization, as opposed to its more *visible* manifestations, consists in 'the global expansion of judicial power' (Tate and Vallinder 1995). If, as Sally E. Merry writes, 'law has been described as the cutting edge of colonialism' (Merry 1991: 889), a cutting edge is also one that cuts two ways.

Colonialism and the Translation of Institutions

Colonialism is the spatial extension of a given system of political power for purposes of the resettlement of surplus populations (which implies the reduction of the aboriginal inhabitants) and/or the establishment of local mechanisms for the extraction of resources for the benefit of the metropole. It is also equally the attempt to reproduce, to varying degrees, the institutions, symbolic and real, of the metropole in a different environment. The latter processes – the reproduction of institutions – will most directly concern us in this book in coming to grips with the rhetorical forms of Canadian civil culture. While the use of outright violence is obviously a factor of undeniable and major importance (see e.g., Giddens 1981–5; Hughes 1986), as are the various stages of the penetration of economic colonization (such as the use of the new territory initially as a *comptoir* for trade and later as an entrepôt for the stockage of staples, for example), these aspects will take second place to our primary focus on how the symbolic dimensions that constitute the realms of civil society come into play and are reconfigured by their transfer to new contexts.

Processes of symbolic interplay have many ramifications. It is striking, for instance, that the French Jesuits' concern for the conversion of the souls of the 'savages' of New France stemmed not only from a self-evident missionary imperative; their concern was also an extension to the New World of contemporary debates among sixteenth-century European rhetoricians seeking to find living exemplars of the rhetorical tradition of the Ciceronian orator. Here was a figure which the Jesuit *Relations* claimed to have discovered reincarnated in the elaborate rhetorical performances of the Iroquois, the Hurons, and the Montagnais (see Doiron 1991: 375–402). If the 'nobility' of the 'Noble Savage' initially derived from the fact that the figure seemed to reincarnate the virtues of classical, Mediterranean antiquity, that same figure would, by the time of Rousseau's writings in the mid-eighteenth century, begin to serve as the exemplary ground for the developing Enlightenment critique of European corruption. From the figure of the 'Noble Savage' as the reincarnation of classicism, it would be but a short step to the extension of a notion of novel civilizational purity to the continent as a whole, as in Locke's 'in the beginning, all the world was America' (1924: 140) or, later, in the nineteenth century, Hegel's baroque view of 'America' as the source of the global unleashing of monstrous, new historical fabulations (Hegel 1965).

In other words, the process of symbolic exchange is not a unilateral one; it rapidly leads to reconfigurations, imagistic and historical criss-crossings, in a kind of early postmodern blurring of temporalities as the new environment acts not only as a site of reception, but serves as well for the reinscription of key cultural tropes and other symbolic re-imaginings. Thus, for instance, the seventeenth-century Jesuit project to recreate in New France a theocracy that would replicate not only the history but the actual living conditions and holy community of the early Church of the Martyrs (Dumont 1993). Likewise, the Massachussetts Pilgrims' project to recreate in the New World a 'community of saints' far from the corruptions of religion in England (E. Morgan 1958; Walzer 1965).

Thus, in addition to the domination of superior military, economic, or political power, one is also dealing with what we will broadly term processes of symbolic 'translation' in the movement of the reproduction of social institutions from one context to another. Our use of the concept of 'translation' draws upon a growing body of scholarly literature that recentres the understanding of translation in relation not only to literary but also to scientific discourse – in short, that foregrounds 'translation' as integral to the workings of modernity.[2] As Lydia H. Liu writes: 'The problem of translation has become increasingly central to critical reflection on modernity. What it means is that we can no longer talk about translation as if it were purely a linguistic or literary matter ... The universalizing tendencies of modernity have always called upon the service of the translator to spread its gospel elsewhere' (1999: 1). Liu goes on to remark that 'translation has been indispensable to the processes of global circulation of colonial language theories, universal history, scientific discourse, material culture, and international law for the past few hundred years' (3). Not the least of these processes of global circulation has entailed the role played by translation in the history of colonialism, because it was in the context of colonial encounters between European and 'other' languages that 'the unique intellectual contour of Western philosophical thinking about language, difference, culture and alterity' (3) came to be defined.

Within the lexicography of Western languages themselves, as Barbara Godard has noted, the Latin '*translatere* refers to the displacement of people as well as to the physical transportation of objects and to the transfer of legal jurisdiction as well as of ideas,' while the French *traduction* that emerged from Italian in the sixteenth century carried within itself the meaning of 'to lead across, to transform, or to bring before justice' (Godard 1997: 56). The concept of translation thus entails multiple levels of semantics that include an idea of law as well as an idea of justice as a regulatory mechanism, or metaphor for the circulation of both people and goods. In this sense, while colonialism undoubtedly constituted domination, and as part of that domination included the large-scale transfer of laws and legal institutions from one society to another – as Sally Merry notes, 'European law was central to the colonizing process' – it was so 'in a curiously ambiguous way' (Merry 1991: 890).

The ambiguity between law and justice, as Harold Berman has shown, forms one of the great tensions – and particularities – of 'the Western legal tradition' (Berman 1983). On the one hand, law in the metropole, as well as in the colonial context, had the power to transform conceptions of time, space, property, work, marriage, and the political sphere – that is, to reshape not only social institutions, but also culture and consciousness. On the other hand, in colonial contexts in particular, it also

provided a way for [peasant and subsistence producers] to mobilize the ideology of the colonizers to protect lands and to resist some of the more excessive demands of the settlers ... Moreover, the law provided a way for the colonial state to restrain the more brutal aspects of settlers' exploitation of land and labor. Thus, the legal arena became a place of contest among the diverse interest groups in colonial society. The contest included struggles between traditional leaders and new educated elites of the colonized population, as well as colonial officials, missionaries and settler populations. It was an unequal contest, however. (Merry 1991: 890)

And yet there would be considerable gradations within the unequal contest: the case of the Thirteen Colonies, for instance, provides a particularly significant example of the turning by colonial lawyers of colonial law against the colonizer,[3] whereas, as will be seen below, Canadian circumstances would offer rather different problems in translating one colonial legal system into another. Furthermore, the conceptualization of law as 'translation' – as the dialectic of law and justice – entails as well keeping to the fore a third dimension in the translatability of colonial institutions, and law in particular, and that is their stylistic, rhetorical, and communicative aspects, a field of study that has emerged under the name of 'law as communication' (see Nelken 1996). Such an approach stresses (as Peter Goodrich has argued in the common law context and Pierre Legendre in the Roman law context) the extent to which the language of law is more than 'mere' language, but forms instead the core of what Legendre terms 'the dogmatic order' in (particularly Western) social thought and organization. In Goodrich's strongly stated formulation, the language of law is 'a model for all other forms of language' (1990: vi). The language of law 'founds the legitimacy of social speech; it institutes an order of lawful discourse and prohibits those heterodoxies of speech or writing that are deemed to threaten the security of legal meaning of the order of legal and political reason.' In this sense, law forms nothing less than 'the basis of *all social forms* [and] so of *all communication*'(1990: 7–8, emphases added; also Legendre, 1988). This is because, as James Boyd White explains, 'At the center of law is the activity of translation.' And this work of translation is neither a merely mechanical nor a solely technical process; for White, it is 'a kind of pushing forward of what was written in one context into another,' that creates a paradoxical interpretive 'space of uncertainty' open to both understanding and misunderstanding. In his sense, the law 'is a discourse that mediates among virtually all the discourses of our world, all ways of talking, and it does this not on the premise that meaning can be translated from one discourse directly into a different one, but by the creation of texts that are new compositions,' at the same time that it is also a discourse of power (1990: 246, 261–2). In the light of these perspectives, then, the language and rhetoric of law constitutes nothing less than the basis of all forms of social communication legitimizing social speech, and also the conditions of possibility of future speech. The role it plays in the definition of what constitutes the realms of the social, and particularly so in contexts of colonial translation, demands closer examination.

Law and the Public Sphere

The explosion in legal studies over the past twenty years has been a near-global phenomenon occasioned by the far-reaching changes mentioned above. The expansion of the legal field has ranged from the rewriting of the constitutions of the countries of the former Soviet sphere of influence, to the 'privatization' of economic sectors formerly the property of the state in numerous areas, most spectacularly perhaps in telecommunications and broadcasting, to the reassertion (and contestation) of the terms of the land-treaties signed by the former European empires (and their nation-state successors) and native populations, to the elaboration of refugee rights and the legal problems posed by large-scale displaced populations, and related redefinitions of the rights of community and citizenship, to mention just a few examples. Paralleling these changes, the academic study of law – as history, as semiotic systems, as social theory – has moved from the law-schools to form an interdisciplinary area of investigation striving to actualize the claims advanced above as to the centrality of law to understanding the complexity of social communication. From these perspectives, the widely perceived 'crises,' economic and symbolic, of modern society seen to be in an uncertain state of transition toward a new order of articulation vaguely signified by the addition of the word 'post,' are not only related to theories of the deep transformations of society itself, but also to crises in the forms of modern political thought that accompanied the emergence of the liberal capitalist state. Related to this has been a corresponding crisis of the ability of the social sciences – classical sociology in particular – to satisfactorily explain 'in thought and language the relationship among social facts' (Unger 1976: 7). This has resulted in a turn, or return, to legal theory, to deal with some of these and related problems in particular. The writings of Jürgen Habermas and Niklas Luhmann reveal the increasingly cavernous gaps between the highly technicized ('autotelic,' in Luhmann's perspective) steering systems that allow complex industrialized societies to 'function' and the existentially barren or symbolically ever-more fragmented dimensions of the lifeworld in which we dwell subjectively. The turn to legal theory can thus be seen, in part, as a return to older corpuses of thought, and so to a re-examination of the questions of governance, politics, and civility, from perspectives with longer and more complex narratives than those offered up by macro-economics or the sociology of the nineteenth century to the dilemmas of social co-existence. As Thurman Arnold put it in the mid-1930s: 'Far older than economics as a way of thinking about society, stands the "Law"' (1935: 31), although he also pointed out, as would Daniel Boorstin some years later (1973), that 'the Law' is 'perhaps the most mysterious and most occult of all branches of learning' (1935: 31). As we shall return to this point below, suffice it for now to say that the law is, as Arnold writes, 'a great reservoir of social symbols' for thinking about the character of governance.

Law's complexity, however, warns us not to fall too easily into the belief that one need only look to the history of an older knowledge-formation for more adequate explanations. The risk of succumbing to the relativisms of historicism is as great as the risk of falling back into the mode of explanation it attempted to replace – rationalism – which was itself overly subject to the temptations of overdetermined causality (see Unger 1976: 8ff). It has been widely argued (Gouldner 1970; Unger 1976; Habermas 1974) that some of the overriding dilemmas of modernity include an inability to any longer satisfactorily answer the question of what constitutes social order, an inability to reconcile system-level actions and the actions of individuals, and third an inability to accept that 'society' is a differential as opposed to a homogenizing conceptualization – the whole forming what Habermas has tellingly termed a 'legitimation crisis' (1973), with implications for the technicization of law as well. It is striking, therefore, how many contemporary social theorists have turned to, 'an examination of law's place in modern society' (Unger 1976: 44) as a site of possible reconciliation of macro-level and micro-level explanations. Or, also in Unger's terms, between historiography and generalizing social theory (see as well Wallerstein 1991, 1999). It is, in short, precisely the 'translatory' dimensions of law's ability to enfold within itself both rules (order) and the changing of rules (justice), to be both highly abstract and also historically concrete, and finally to be able to change from one form of social life to another ('each society reveals through its law the innermost secrets of the manner in which it holds [human groups] together' [Unger 1976: 47]), that have made it in recent years such a widespread object of renewed scholarly interest.

Emblematic among contemporary social theorists for whom law has become increasingly the central structure by which to think through the problems of late-modern conditions of association has been Jürgen Habermas. He has long been preoccupied with the problems of, and conditions for, deliberative democracy, and the institutionalized forms of critical discussion of public matters of general interest. From the time of the German-language publication (1962; English ed. 1989) of his highly influential study of the structural transformation of the public sphere to his recent contribution to a discourse theory of law and democracy (German 1992; English 1996), Habermas's work has centred upon elaborating the communicative structures of social coordination. Indeed, in his translator's introduction to *Between Facts and Norms* (1996), Wilhem Rehg remarks that the latter is '[in] many respects the culminating effort' of the project that began with *The Structural Transformation of the Public Sphere*, a project that culminates 'with a bold proposal for a new paradigm of law that goes beyond the dichotomies that have afflicted modern political theory ... and that ... underlie current controversies between ... liberals and civic republicans' (1996: ix–x). It is precisely the law's bridging 'functions' between lifeworlds and power-systems, between the normative and facticity, that permits 'the language of law, unlike the moral communication restricted to the lifeworld, [to] function as a transformer in the society-wide communication circulating between system and lifeworld' (Habermas 1996: 81). The two principal perspectives by which modern law has been analysed since the late nineteenth century – what Habermas terms 'sociological disenchantment' on the one hand, and its philosophical obverse in a (Rawlsian) liberal version of the social contract unconcerned with the institutional dimensions of law (1996: 56) – have only led to a deepening of the crises of legitimacy. Habermas argues therefore that, 'the sole ideas that can justify modern law' are those of human rights and the principle of popular sovereignty, perspectives which do not so much complement as compete with each other (99). Given that 'discourses (and ... bargaining processes ... whose procedures are discursively grounded) are the site where a rational will can take shape, then the legitimacy of law ultimately depends on a communicative arrangement' (103–4). But *other* than a discourse-principle built into the conditions of association in general and the law itself in particular (whether as entitlements to the public use of communicative freedom, the legal institutionalization of various forms of communication, or the implementation of democratic procedures meant to guarantee that formally and procedurally correct outcomes enjoy a presumption of legitimacy), 'nothing [else] is given prior to the citizen's practice of self-determination' (127–8).

Not only does such a formulation place enormous theoretical and practical weight upon the citizens' own practices of self-determination, it also makes the struggle for the democratic establishment of a public sphere that much more concrete and pragmatic an endeavour; in a word, these struggles are, among other things, much about talk. As Thomas McCarthy put it in the introduction to the English translation of *The Structural Transformations of the Public Sphere*, that process of struggle could be presented causally (and casually) as 'the emergent bourgeoisie's gradually replac[ing] a public sphere in which the ruler's power was merely represented before the people with a sphere in which state authority was publicly monitored through informed and critical discourse by the people' (1991: xi). *Between Facts and Norms*, at a high level of abstraction, makes clearer the actual difficulties this would represent for empirical actors. The Canadian context, as one version of 'the clash with the arcane and bureaucratic practices of the absolutist state' (McCarthy 1991: xi) in first its French and then its British variations, will provide the site we will examine in more detail to ascertain what was actually involved.

Conditions of Possibility for Public Speech

Under the French ancien régime (ca. 1535–1759), in the context of the partial transfer of French institutions to New France and within a regime of law that will be discussed at greater length in chapter 3, some of the conditions established for public speech included certain types of representative assemblies (see Reid 1946), but not the reproduction of the estates of the metropole – and especially not their legal embodiment in *parlements* (literally, places for speech). The French regime, and particularly so under Louis XIV and the royal government that would see New France directly incorporated into the central governing structures emanating from Versailles, was still very much one in which 'publicness' consisted of representations of the ruler's power before the people (see Habermas 1989: 9–12). Beyond such manifestations of aristocratic publicness, and the pulpit, there was no public sphere as such, but rather official or quasi-official gathering points, such as the parvis of the churches for the reading of proclamations (and conversations among parishioners), and places of execution, not to mention less official gathering places for conversation such as clubs, hotels, and cafés (see Massicotte 1928). Repeated requests were made by the various religious orders for the establishment of a printing shop in the colony, but these were turned down both by their superiors in Paris and by the royal government. The Minister of Marine in a letter of 4 May 1749 to the Governor General (Jonquière) did agree that the establishment of a printing press in the colony would be 'of great utility for the publication of proclamations and police regulations ... the king did not consider the expense of such an establishment to be appropriate'; one could only wait for 'some printer to present himself' in which case the possibility of granting him a printing privilege would be evaluated (cited in de Lagrave 1993: 92n2). Peter Kalm, the noted contemporary Dutch observer of mid-eighteenth-century colonial conditions in North America, thought that the absence of a printing press in Canada stemmed probably from the desire to prevent the publication of any book or text harmful to religion, kingdom, or good mores and their dissemination among the people; it was as well a way for France to enhance Canada's dependence (in de Lagrave 1993: 92n2). It would not be until the British regime that the colony could produce its first newspaper, and not until the American Revolution that the city of Montreal (with a population of only 5733 at the time) saw the arrival of its first public printer; before then, other than the personal libraries of the educated elites there was neither print shop nor book store nor public library nor journalism.

It is under such conditions of the initial, non-existence of a public sphere – or, more accurately, the existence of 'a public sphere in apolitical form' (Habermas 1991: 29) – that the debates over the law, and the prolonged discussion of the nature of the transition of legal regimes that would hold sway from the time of the cession to Britain (1759–60) until well into the middle of the nineteenth century, take on such paramount importance in the Canadian context. The resulting debates over 'the law,' whose law, its extent and applicability, and the rapid acquisition by the former French colonials – the so-called 'new' subjects of the British Crown – of the language and politics of British colonial parliamentary practices, contributed to the creation of a public sphere, in Habermassian terms, of the 'parliamentarization' of state power.

Towards a Public Sphere

The ensuing struggles, discussed below, over the laws (ranging from land tenure to legislative institutions; that is, forming the matrix of the social relations of the colony's civil cultures) and involving various practices of knowledge-acquisition and formation (for example, rhetorical and political education), thus situate themselves within a continuum of struggle in the context of Canadian colonial history. This is a history going back to the contact period with the continent's first inhabitants, and, within the French chapter, to the period of colonization itself, and it involves the delimitation, definition, and control of *the symbolic order*. Was the symbolic order, then, ultimately to be defined by the religious orders as the reproduction in a new land of a theocracy, or by the economic interests of the fur trade with its expansive territorial drive further into the continent in search of pelts and with it of ever more extensive contact with, contamination of, and ultimately absorption of the cultures of the Amerindians within destructive European imperial rivalries? Or, was the symbolic order to be established by the attempted reproduction by the centralized French state of a settled, village-based peasantry on the metropolitan model, to be ruled according to the dictates of 'good police,' to be taxed and *corvée'd* appropriately in response to the needs of the absolutist state? None of these struggles was resolved by the time New France fell to the British; indeed, Delâge has argued (1991) that the French empire in America was, in contrast to the British or the Dutch, a particular model of economic inefficiency that therefore required the ideological apparatus of the missionaries to survive without the symbiotic interrelationship of fur trade and religious conversion. Unlike the Dutch or the ultimately victorious British, whose economic take-off toward greater capitalization of land and with it extensive reproduction (certainly within the Thirteen Colonies) of the political and legal forms of English liberty offered a more competitive model of the self-governance of civil society, the French empire in North America was in a state of symbolic breakdown, as the outbreak of the French Revolution would soon confirm. In North America, however, and British North America in particular, the ancien régime would, on the contrary, discover a second life.[4]

That second life would be signified in the paradoxical statement that Francis Parkman gave in the conclusion to his *The Old Régime in Canada*: 'A happier calamity never befell a people than the conquest of Canada by the British arms' (1887: 401). Or, to take an example that might fall within Keohane's 'interpretive symptomatology,' Canada's eventual self-definition as a project of governance would be the Dominion's power (1867) to legislate for 'Peace, Order and Good Government' – an impeccably ancien régime telos. And whatever the subsequent (and changing) interpretation by constitutional scholars of the extent of section 91 of the BNA Act (see e.g., Laskin 1947; Gold 1985; Risk 1996), those words, associated with figures such as the North West Mounted Police and later the Mounties, have served as cultural signifiers not only of the supposedly more 'peaceful' colonization of the Canadian West under the rule of law (as compared to the 'wild west' of American expansion), but also of the formation of a civil culture characterized largely by premodern (or 'classical' as Pocock terms it [1976]) deference. In this sense, before the patriation of the Constitution in 1982 and, along with it, the increased juridicalization of state power resulting from the application of the Charter of Rights and Freedoms, the forms of Canadian governance remained more within a continuum of ancien régime domination than not .

In other words, the self-characterization of governance as 'Peace, Order and Good Government' falls directly in line with both Colbertian notions of governance as *une bonne police* and with what seventeenth-century German administrative thought would designate by the term *Polizei*. Foucault would subsequently rename this substantial seventeenth- and eighteenth-century pan-European body of literature under the rubric of 'governmentality.' This was a model of governance 'which mean[t] exercising towards its inhabitants, and the wealth and behaviour of each and all, a form of surveillance and control' through the regulation of 'communication'; that is, the regulation by the state of the common activities of individuals, particularly in labour and production, within a physical infrastructure of connection and mobility (Foucault 1979 in Burchell et al. 1991). Thus, the image of settlement, as reported by travellers to British North America in the early nineteenth-century, particularly along the St Lawrence River between Quebec City and Montreal, the central artery of Canada's communication infrastructure, was *not* one of colonial wilderness and dispersion but, on the contrary, it was part of a city, 'almost a continued street.' In another traveller's account, 'this extensive chain of farms exhibits along the ... shores of the St. Lawrence for more than 400 miles ... the appearance of one immense town' (both cited in Paquet and Wallot 1974: 547). However, such a model of 'police,' with the objective of organizing the entire royal territory like one great city by the regulation of public spaces, roads, bridges, and rivers, was, as Keith Tribe observes, 'unlike a legal order which defines transgressions and prescribes punishments.' Instead, '*Polizei* remained a prescriptive model of social order' (Tribe 1988: 31). The great change that the British Conquest would bring in its wake was to superimpose on this prescriptive model a new mode of social interraction, that of British law. As then lieutenant-governor (later governor and subsequently Lord Dorchester) Guy Carleton remarked in 1767: 'So short sighted are Men, that ... yet I have met with only one Canadian who sees this great Revolution in its full influence.' As one contemporary legal scholar has observed, what is striking is the extent to which, two centuries later, this 'great revolution' remains still so little understood (cited in Brisson 1986: 6). It is the aim of the chapters below to better understand the implications of this 'revolution' in law.

Law and the Rhetorical Violence of Authority

In an influential text that encapsulates the spread of 'critical legal studies' beyond the confines of especially American law schools, Jacques Derrida, probing the distinction between law and justice that, as was mentioned above, constitutes one of the profound ambiguities of the Western tradition of law, cites an observation of Montaigne's. The 'laws keep up their good standing, not because they are just, but because they are laws: that is the mystical foundation of their authority, they have no other' (Derrida in Cornell et al. 1992: 12). And while numerous other scholars could also be cited as regards 'the mystical foundations of authority' (e.g., Arnold 1935, Kantorowicz 1955; Boorstin 1973; Legendre 1988; Goodrich 1990; Conklin 1996), Derrida's point is more concerned with establishing 'the basis for a modern critical philosophy, indeed for a critique of juridical ideology, a desedimentation of the superstructures of law that both hide and reflect the economic and political interests of the dominant force of society' (1992: 13). However concerned with social violence, and much of Derrida's text is a gloss on this point through a discussion of Walter Benjamin's 'Critique of Violence' (1921), he is just as concerned with identifying the extent to which 'the very emergence of justice and law, the founding and justifying moment that institutes law' is itself 'a performative and therefore interpretive violence,' a *coup de force* that operates on its own terms – 'not in the service of a social force or power, for example an economic, political, ideological power that would exist outside or before it and which it would have to accommodate' (13). 'Since the origin of authority, the foundation or ground, the position of the law can't by definition rest on anything but themselves, they are themselves a violence without ground' (14).

The laws, in other words, constitute their own form of figurative and rhetorical violence by the imposition of a language. 'Here the best paradigm is the founding of the nation-states or the institutive act of a constitution that establishes what one calls in French *l'état de droit*' (23–4). Law's violence 'belongs to the symbolic order': in this sense, 'the foundation of all states occurs in a situation that we can thus call revolutionary' because '"the successful foundation of a state" (in somewhat the same sense that one speaks of a "felicitous performative speech act") will produce *après coup* what it was destined in advance to produce, namely, proper interpretive models to read in return, to give sense, necessity and above all legitimacy to the violence that has produced, among others, the interpretive model in question, that is, the discourse of its self-legitimation' (31, 35, 36).

In a curious postscript to what Derrida himself terms a 'strange text' (57), he offers some additional reflections on the Nazi 'Final Solution' as an example of 'the most pervasive figure of media violence and of political exploitation of the modern techniques of communicative language, of industrial language and the language of industry' (58). He goes on to discuss 'the radical but also fatal corruption of parliamentary and representative government through a modern police that is inseparable from it, that becomes the true legislative power and whose phantom commands the totality of the political space' (59). If as some have argued (Bauman 1989; Adorno and Horkheimer [1944] 1982), the Final Solution is the logical terminus of Enlightenment modernity that culminates in the towering phantom of the figure of a totalitarian Police, this apparent return to a modernized, updated form of the governmental regime of the eighteenth-century conception of 'police' introduces additional dimensions to the figuration of authority and the transition to the rule of law that Derrida does *not* discuss.

As Jean Starobinski has shown, the concept of 'police,' with its derivations from the Greek words *polis* and *politeia*, and the Latin *polire* (polishing), had in seventeenth- and eighteenth-century French dictionaries formed a complex of meanings in which the governmental notion of 'police' was closely related to notions of cleansing, polishing and, in the figurative sense, of civilizing, of discourse and style (as in 'polir un discours') (1989: 26–7). As Starobinski notes, citing Trévoux's 1743 dictionary, the verb *policer* meant: 'Faire des lois, des règlements de police pour entretenir la tranquillité publique' (29) – to make laws and police regulations to maintain public tranquility. 'Police' and 'politeia,' then, are regimes of law, in contrast (in Trévoux's example) to 'the savages of America who had neither laws nor police, at the time of their discovery' (30). In turn, the notion of police was itself also closely related to those of civilization and civility; a number of mid-to-late eighteenth-century dictionaries Starobinski cites are themselves derived from jurisprudential terminology. This is to understand the *cives,* from which notions such as civility, civilization, or what we term civil culture derive, as, foremost, an act of justice, as a process of decriminalization or, more broadly, as the equivalent to sociability (12–13). Over time, however, Starobinski notes that the term 'civilization' – in Turgot, for instance – loses its initial association with juridical terminology and becomes increasingly a lay substitute for the concept of religion (14), a turn of meaning that is itself perhaps more germane to the violence of the subsequent dialectic of Enlightenment, especially the violent transformations of language effect by the French Revolution (see Gordon 1994).

Derrida is useful in drawing greater attention to the figurative characteristics of law and its discourses of self-legitimation, but only up to a point. It is equally important to bear in mind that the transition from a regime of police to one that explicitly derives its self-justification from a conception of the rule of law is more gradual than it might first seem. Indeed, it is profoundly relevant to an understanding of law as part of the processes of civility that writers of the Scottish Enlightenment, like Adam Smith, Adam Ferguson, and James Millar, begin to form the basis of social science's theories of stages of social development, and in particular, that they explain the transition from landed to commercial societies as an integral part of the civilizing (and so rhetorical) process, and not as an aberration. We propose to study this process.

Synopsis of the Study

As the present chapter has suggested, such large-scale struggles over the definitions of the symbolic order – over the changing understanding of *dominium* in the transition from the French Empire to the British, from the old colonial system of the first British Empire to the Second British Empire, and of the republican and democratic struggles against despotism radiating from the influence of the American and then the French Revolutions – form the background for our study. Broadly, we are concerned with the symbolic dimensions of the transition from aristocratic, landed power to the democratic and bourgeois forms of an emerging public sphere as this was experienced in the Canadian colonial context. As has been suggested above, if it is indeed the legal sphere that serves as the conduit not only for the redefinition of social relations but even more so for the circuits of communication between specialized subsystems of power-knowledge and the lifeworld, it will be appropriate, beginning in chapter 3, to examine in some detail what Evelyn Kolish has termed 'the judicial nightmare' (Kolish 1987: 327) that faced the British, as well as the colonists, old and new, in the transition from one legal regime to another. The resulting vacuum of contested legitimacy ranged from passive resistance to English law by otherwise litigious *Canadiens* to their rapid mastery of the practices of parliamentary politics and the problems resulting from the domination by francophone elites of control of the local legislative assembly. If rhetoric is, in fact, the medium of a civil culture's self-reflection, that reflection is both conditioned by law and conditions law itself, as will be shown in chapter 3 and subsequently.

Given the ensuing protracted battles over questions of political representation and how to incorporate 'the Other' within the polity, the struggles over constitutional forms – indeed, the very question of how constitutions are *constituting* – will be the subject of chapter 4. The development of local rhetorical and parliamentary practices was not, it will be argued, an accident of administration but was anticipated in the British model of law and constitution instantiated in founding speech acts. Thus British law can be seen as fundamentally prudential *and* rhetorical and dependent upon a reciprocity between Crown and subject. It differs from the French ancien régime model of the recovery of logos through a conception of communicative yet non-political sociability (Habermas 1991; Gordon 1994). If the new regime is still concerned with 'police' – it is after all imperial and colonizing – the British technology of governance recognizes the colony's antecedent corporate character and that it requires a corporate voice. Britain does not ignore but recognizes its 'new subjects,' albeit painfully. As will be seen in chapter 4, the manner in which the laws are implemented ambiguously permits the emergence of local practices not anticipated in the law as understood only as a closed coding and regulation of the lifeworld. This ambiguity, for reasons of language, legal *différance*, and the slippages inherent in translation (both linguistic and spatial), allows for the emergence of irony as a coping strategy, a theme that will also recur in subsequent chapters.

Because the difficult process of the 'recognition of Others' in law is a constant and ongoing one in the Canadian context, the problem will be taken up in chapter 5 in a detailed discussion of the Northwest Rebellion and its aftermath as a case study that in many ways replays aspects of the transition from the French regime of law to the British one. If governance in the tradition of peace, order, and good government is, to a large extent, a technical operation, the resulting dialectic of POgG and a metaphysics of legal continuity is compounded by the 'double sovereignty' identified in chapter 3, inherited from the French regime and recognized by the British. These difficulties will be replayed over again with Canada's expansion following the cession of Rupert's Land to the Dominion, in the same manner that trying to cope with these problems had led to responsible government in the 1840s and the BNA Act in the 1860s. The process is thus both a project and a strategy. The project was directed, soon after the cession of New France, toward the creation of a new (mercantile and political – indeed, almost republican) nationality. As a strategy, however, it also seeks to contain identity and particularity within each province. This was certainly the case as regards Quebec, and it will be revisited in the wake of the Riel rebellions with the debates over the legality of the post-Manitoba Act of 1870 legislation in chapter 7.

Chapter 6 will further take up some of these debates and themes over how the law both contains and produces identity crises, as seen particularly in the strategies utilizing irony adopted by the struggle for Canadian women's suffrage at the turn of the century. As with the transition from French to English law, and as with the problem of incorporating new subjects into a regime of law seen as 'foreign' that the rebellions in the Northwest represented, this chapter focuses upon what happens when gender becomes the topic for the public figuration of 'difference.' This case study of the women's suffrage movement provides a prototype for a civil style effective in what we call a monarchical republic characterized by resigned or philosophical irony.

At the same time, however, the dialectic of expansion and containment creates wounds, linguistic, cultural, and *identitaire* (ranging from the black legend of 'the Conquest' to the execution of Louis Riel). Probing the rhetoric of these wounds will be the task of chapter 7 as we contrast the different responses to these continuing problems in contemporary Quebec legal and social thought with the legal crisis that Manitoba faced in the 1980s when the Supreme Court of Canada threatened to render unconstitutional all laws passed in the province since 1870. Here, we see on the one hand how the law seeks to contain or ultimately mend the breach left by Riel's execution, but on the other hand how a skillful rhetoric of legal interpretation only serves to reinforce Quebec's sense of its legal uniqueness. In chapters 6 and 7, we encounter again the crucial role played by irony in the Canadian context as a strategy for dealing with the contradictions inherent to the apparently self-contained metaphysics of law, and its rhetorical limits.

If chapter 6 illustrates how what Linda Hutcheon has termed 'irony's edge' (1994) provides a template for an ironizing form of civil style in a rhetorical culture not characterized, as in the U.S., by 'rights' talk,' then chapter 8 broadens the discussion of a stylistics of civility to the split, notably in early-modern France and in England, between *civilité* and its relation to the *cives* and civil law, and a more ironic, or mannered British view of the variability of social appearance appropriate to the fluidity of social roles in commercial societies. Returning to a debate begun by Norbert Elias (1939) on the role of civility and manners as 'the glue' that holds together a rhetorical community, chapter 8 looks at the challenges that the rights-based Charter of Rights and Freedoms (1982) as well as Canadian multiculturalism policies pose to civility, or at least to the pious, homogenizing, and class-based view that a rhetorically-oriented civic education was a viable basis for holding a community together. From a discussion of manners, chapter 8 moves to the rhetorical category of decorum (which includes the idea of occasionally violating manners), and looks instead at what could be loosely termed alternative or postmodern versions of impious or ironic decorum, that range here from the mock parliaments of the Canadian suffrage movement to more recent calls in the Quebec context to forget the Quiet Revolution. If our studies of the rhetorics of Canadian civil discourse are heavily imprinted by an existential 'unhappy consciousness,' chapter 8's analysis of the stylistics of civility proposes that a focus on the *agon* of the political is itself a never-ending rhetorical process, in the light of which neither Canada – nor any polity – should expect to be 'a Peaceable Kingdom.'

The concluding chapter (chapter 9) returns to the paintings mentioned in the Envoi and sees them as representative of the five principal rhetorical styles that have historically formed Canada's civil culture. In particular, we wish to highlight that Canada has to be understood above all as a noisy and talkative place, and indeed has been so since the Jesuits encountered native eloquence. The problem, rather, has been one of locating the appropriate idioms and audiences for all this talk. This is not a matter of exposing the right idiom; there is no *right* idiom; but there is a complex layering of discourses that it is the purpose of this study to bring out.

The attentive reader will have noticed perhaps that we have not yet mentioned chapter 2. This has been deliberate since it is the chapter we turn to next, and one that concerns itself with the fundamental importance of a parallel system of interpretation – namely, historiography. Chapter 2 focuses upon key debates in the historiography of Canadian history, since the practices of the writing of history are inseparable from the self-understanding of an imagined community. If pre-Bismarck Germany thought of itself as a land of poets and philosophers, it is no less an exaggeration to say that Canada has thought of itself as a land of historians. It is no accident that, in that most Canadian of cities, the ancient capital, Quebec City, a monument to the historian F.-X. Garneau prominently figures on the Grande Allée. But just as the law is part of the symbolic order and as such is intertwined with symbolic violence, historical interpretation as well forms a field of knowledge that bases itself upon what Susan Stewart has termed 'crimes of writing' (1991). As we will investigate the nature of these crimes shortly, suffice it to say that the study of the role of law makes a very late – and only recent – appearance on the Canadian historiographical scene. What preoccupied Canadian historiography instead, and why this has been the case, will be our concern in chapter 2; the writing of Canadian history has been characterized more by what has been left out and left unsaid than not. We see one of our tasks as filling in these *aporias* and bringing out their latent meanings and implications. This is why, in the history we propose in this study, we offer an account of the intersection of discourses as discourses. The 'object' of these discourses is 'Canada,' or rather those parts of Canada that self-consciously referred to themselves as such – whether the Native peoples who just referred to themselves as 'the people'; or French Canada; Upper and Lower Canada; or Western Canada, as historian George Stanley referred to Manitoba (1961). Ours is not, however, a study in regionalism or its ideologies. If readers feel slighted that we have not sufficiently attended either to their particular region or to all regions equally, we can only apologize beforehand. On the contrary, the 'subject' of our history is discourse, and in particular the discourses relative to the constitutive language of the law; how this language has figured as a problem facilitating or complicating communication; its historical sedimentations; and the continuing tension between law and rhetoric in understanding our contemporary civil condition.

2

'Who Killed Canadian History?'[1] The Uses and Abuses of Canadian Historiography

There seems to be considerable unease in Canadian historiography of late, at least in its more public manifestations. Some of this stems from the transformations in historical studies over the past three decades, in the light of revisionist perspectives emphasizing the arbitrariness of the objects, topics, and categories of history, so-called national history in particular, and even of the notion of history itself. The result has been the attempt to include, within new ways of historical narration, previously absent or insufficiently foregrounded factors, such as economic and social determinants, social class, and regionalism, and, at the actor-level, class fractions, social movements, state formation, and the redefinitions of civil society that ought to follow from reconsiderations of gender, sexuality, and race. These debates, or versions thereof, had already been rehearsed in various forms in a number of countries, beginning in France, in particular, around the turn of the century over the emphases to be accorded to economic and social factors, and formalized with the publication of the first issue of the *Annales ESC* in 1929. The Annales School subsequently became the dominant force in postwar French historiography until the encounter with structuralism from the mid-1960s to the mid-1970s (see Revel and Hunt 1995; Dosse 1987). But while the French example is no doubt exemplary by its richness, similar upheavals in historiography also occurred in England in the late 1960s (see as emblematic P. Anderson 1969; R. Williams 1977; Thompson 1963); and in the United States of the same period, especially in the historiography of Cold War diplomacy (e.g., W.A. Williams [1959] 1988; Kolko 1968), but also in the analysis of race and class relations (e.g., Myrdal [1944] 1964, Elkins 1976; Genovese 1967; Harrington 1965). One could no doubt offer up numerous other examples from countries the world over, but let us stress here, because of its acuity, the late 1980s *Historikerstreit*, or historians' struggle, in Germany over the enduring problems of the historiography of the Final Solution (see

Habermas 1989; Maier 1988). All of which underscores that historiography is by definition a contentious field of intellectual activity at the best of times, and has long been so. To expect that Canadian historiography should be spared from similar debates is naive – or, on the contrary, attests to the presumption of a consensus that is in itself problematic and worth examining further.

But before doing so, let us turn to a definition of historiography by one of the pre-eminent historiographers of Canadian history, Carl Berger. Written over thirty years ago, it has not lost any of its pertinence:

The history of historiography, properly conceived, fulfils a dual role. Its primary purpose is to make the reader and writer of history aware of the subtle and unconscious ways in which the very forces the historian seeks to interpret shape his [*sic*] own thought. 'There are,' as Herbert Butterfield put it, 'hidden factors behind any national tradition of historical interpretation, and these need to be raised as far as possible to the level of consciousness, so that they can be neutralised or brought under control.' ... History has never been written with complete detachment; invariably it reflects and incorporates the ideological climate of the period in which it was conceived and composed. By studying the assumptions and guiding ideas which influenced the writing of history, one is really assessing the values and aspirations of the culture which produced it. (Berger 1967: vii)

In this light, then, historiography encodes not only the 'unconscious' of the historian, but also that of the culture, broadly or narrowly understood, in which the historian is writing. It is significant, therefore, in the paragraph that followed the quotation above, that Berger went on to remark that 'Canadian historians have remained reticent concerning the philosophy of historical knowledge' (vii), a trait which the accompanying essays in that collection, reprinted from the 1920s to the late 1950s, all comment upon in one form or another. For instance, Frank Underhill, in his oft-quoted reflections on the liberal tradition in Canada (1946, repr. 1960), observes that the form of intellectual inferiority he termed 'colonialism' had particularly marked the Canadian (historical) imagination, as a result of which the 'guild of Canadian historians confine their activities ... to ... local national history' (in Berger 1967: 31). Similarly, although with a differing emphasis, W.L. Morton, in perhaps the first attempt at a meta-level reflection upon 'Clio in Canada' (1946), offers the remarkable proposition that 'history is peculiarly the consolations of the conquered,' for whom the memory of past freedom gives hope to 'present despair,' and points to Ireland, India, and French Canada as illustrative (in Berger 1967: 43). Whether reticently expressed or not, these few remarks already indicate that Canadian historiography, as much as any other, would not be without acrimonious debates. In the following pages, we propose to examine in more detail what these have been and in particular what they reveal about the culture in which and of which historians are writing.

Changes over Time in Canadian Historiography, 1964–94

In a review of changes in recent Canadian historiography published in 1995, historian Jean-Paul Bernard provides an explanation of the transformations that have occurred in Canadian historiography of the past three decades. For Bernard, the central question concerns the shift from a dominant and widely consensual interpretation of Canadian historiography – in English-Canadian historiography, that of nation-building; and in French-Canadian historiography, that of 'national' *survivance* – that endured roughly until the 1960s, and then changed to 'a more open historiography that, for lack of a better term, has been termed "social history"' (321–2). He observes quite correctly that the transition to 'social history' was not an abrupt change: English-Canadian economic historians, such as Harold Innis, Donald Creighton, and W.A. Mackintosh, for example, had throughout the 1920s literally created a Canadian economic history, based on the effects of geographic determinants within the North American continent; nor had historiographical interpretation solely focused upon individual actors (the so-called great white males). Creighton (1937), for one, had made the commercial class, or fractions thereof, the heroes of the empire of the St Lawrence. For Bernard, the dominance of the national development/national survival perspective had not arisen out of the blue, but had served rather as the predominant 'organizing theme that articulated all the others' (323). The shift in historiography from the mid-1960s on, then, was less a matter of an *Ürsprung* of pure creation than one of the reordering of priorities and of professional concerns.

As Bernard also rightly notes, a tradition of Canadian historiography developed, based on the cataloguing of the federal archives in the late nineteenth century, the establishment of a chair in Canadian History at the University of Toronto in 1894, a first 'scientific' journal in 1897, and the founding of the *Canadian Historical Review* in 1920. The history of this solidly entrenched tradition is explored in Carl Berger's *The Writing of Canadian History* (1976). In French Canada, Bernard observes, the institutionalization of historical studies, in terms of research institutes and a professional journal, did not take equivalent shape until just after the Second World War, although he feels that Groulx's *Histoire du Canada français depuis la découverte* (4 vols, 1950–2) offers both a scope and a documentary basis as solid as anything produced by the 'Toronto School' (322–4).

He notes further that the existence of history departments in English-speaking Canada, initially limited to Toronto, Montreal, and Kingston, greatly favoured a historiography centred upon the Canada of the Laurentian Shield, to the exclusion of other regions. This would not change until the mid-1950s with Morton's history of Manitoba (1957), Ormsby's on British Columbia (1958), and MacNutt's on the Atlantic Provinces (1965), with the resulting tilt towards a balance of region and nation, followed by Careless's positing of a 'metropolitan-hinterland relationship' (1954) tilted toward the metropolis, and his later even more resonant article on 'limited identities' (1969). Similar debates and repositionings rocked French-Canadian historiography, ranging from Maurice Séguin's famed 1956 paper on the idea of independence to Brunet's scathing denunciation in 1959 of the 'amateurism and romanticism' of Canadian historians of both languages, and the call for social science 'to approach the study of society with more scientific methods' (Berger 1967: 97; for Brunet, see 84–98).

If, broadly speaking, a nationalist perspective was the dominant one in the historiographies of both linguistic groups until the mid-1960s, Bernard distinguishes four aspects to this. First, it was by definition selective, and so allowed historians to grasp only three further levels of belongingness: regions, ethnic groups, and social class. Second, it was linked to a preoccupation with national politics over either economics or demographics. Third, there was no encompassing historical approach emphasizing economic and social factors. Finally, it entertained suspect relations with nationalist ideologies (325–6). In short, the 'revolution' in post-1960s historiography decried by Granatstein (1998) was less a result of the importation of 'foreign' methodologies brought in from the United States (or from French graduate schools), or a wholesale repudiation of Canadian national history, as it was a reordering within the already established terms of twentieth-century Canadian historiography. To these internal repositionings, Bernard also draws attention to a range of factors external to the historians' profession, but nonetheless significant in their impact upon it. These include, between 1964–94, a 50 per cent increase in population largely through immigration; the expansion of the role of the state in the economic, social, and cultural domains in the mid-1960s, and its subsequent withdrawal from these fields in the 1980s; the establishment of the Consultative Committee on the Status of Women; the Free Trade Agreement with the United States, and so on. But perhaps most significant within this period initially were the perturbations between Canada and Quebec in the wake of the Quiet Revolution, Quebec's passage of restrictive language legislation, and at the federal level, the rise of multicultural policies in the early 1970s: in other words, the development of divergent national identity policies, one centred upon a Canadian identity, the other upon *l'identité québécoise*, and the resulting contests over economic development strategies; the modernization of education, culture, and communications; and their constitutional ramifications and renegotiations. If this was indeed a period of the fracturing of the former bilingual consensus over 'national' identity, it was also, not surprisingly a period of growing affirmation of gender identity and difference, of the return of issues of autochtonous identity, and of the problems of the integration of Canada's ever-increasing 'visible communities.'

Returning to the historians' profession, Bernard notes the six-fold increase of university students between 1962–85, the resulting expansion of graduate studies and, in Canadian history alone, the increase of PhDs from 130 in 1967 to 212 in 1985 (for data, see 332–3). In turn, the period would see as well a proliferation of new journals, from the *Journal of Canadian Studies* (1966), *Social History* (1968), and so on, through to the creation of the *International Journal of Canadian History* (1990). These developments entailed a corresponding expansion of bibliographical materials on Quebec and Canadian history, from some 1395 pages between 1946–65, to 2073 pages in the 1981–5 period alone (334). If this enormous proliferation was at first loosely termed 'social history,' the category itself disappeared from bibliographical repertories by 1994, replaced by such themes as women's history, the history of First Peoples, intellectual history of culture, and other more focused categories.

At the level of the so-called major themes of Canadian history itself, an equivalent fracturing of formerly 'monolithic' groupings also occurred. If there was once considerable agreement over the fundamental Canadian duality (the French-English 'two solitudes'), the dualisms themselves subsequently stratified internally. Thus, for example, according to Jean-Claude Robert (1990), while Canadian historiography continues to be written in two languages, it is increasingly differentiated within each linguistic division, with notably the least divergence between the two concerning the historiography of New France (337, 339). Contemporary Quebec historiography, for instance, has moved far from the *doléances* of its nineteenth-century predecessors; *conquêtisme* has been considered an ideology for some twenty years now (341); even federal/provincial preoccupations have given way to a more global approach concerning the advent of modernity as a complex of long-term social processes, rather than the myth-based earlier tradition of seeing Quebec as a traditional (agricultural and clerical) society abruptly dragged into the modern era (Bernard 1995: 341).

In other words, the basic commonplaces of traditional Canadian history have themselves been changed. Internal factors, such as a changing profession, the arrival of immigrant populations with differing historical memories, and in the case of the First Nations, historical memories antecedent to the coming of the Europeans, have influenced the change, as have external factors, such as the diversity of North America itself, and a distancing from a once-near unanimous ideological investment in the validity of state policies to more critical and comparatively-based perspectives on historical state formation. 'Historians,' as Berger put it in the second edition (1986) of *Writing*, 'no longer see themselves as the interpreters of national characters and purposes' (cited in Bernard, 352).

As Bernard concludes, the very notion of 'national history' itself thus turns out to be a far more redoubtable enterprise than its earlier proponents assumed, less a multidimensional totalization of everything that was or happened, and more one of understanding what French historian Pierre Nora, writing about French national history, terms a process of 'crystallization' (Bernard, 352). We are left, then, with two very differing images of Canadian history. In Granatstein's view, an overweening and tyrannical presentism has 'killed' Canadian national history. In Bernard's view, the very category of 'national history' is a problematic one, or at least one that changes over time, given internal and external transformations that affect both historians and the environments in which they work. The first view laments and accuses; the second recognizes that the present does weigh upon what historians do; how can it not? Is it possible to reconcile these divergent views? Should one even attempt to?

The Narrow Circles of Canadian Historiography

As Underhill noted (see above), Canadian historians, even those whom Granatstein might approve of as 'proper' national historians, practised 'local national history.' The question is taken up again, some fifty years later, by one of the new generation of contemporary historians, Doug Owram, who might be considered Granatsteinian. He wrote a key article on the narrowness of recent Canadian historiography in the first issue of *National History* (1997), the new journal founded by members of the National Organization of Historians, a group that broke away from the Canadian Historical Association over the divergences encountered above.

Owram's historiographical review combines the calls of Granatstein, Bliss, and others for a new synthetic framework of interpretation of Canadian national history with an analysis of many of the changes covered by Bernard's 1995 article. He uses somewhat different data, however, with respect to the growth of the professional infrastructure: for example, he says that by the mid-1970s there were nineteen Canadian universities with doctoral programs in Canadian history producing nearly 300 dissertations (8). Like Underhill or W.L. Morton in his 'Clio in Canada' article of 1946, Owram points to a long-standing malaise in Canadian historiography, one that Morton first drew attention to, but that was largely concealed by the gender-and-class homogeneity and smallness of the profession at the time. The malaise concerned the bindingness of nationalism, the preponderance of the Toronto School's influence, and the thematic uniformity of the basic interpretations of Canadian history (French survival, Ontario dominance, and Western subordination), none of which elements came seriously into question until the late 1960s. Interestingly, however, Owram offers a contrasting grid for the analysis of Canadian history, depending upon whether one approaches it through methodology or interpretively. On the methodology axis, twentieth-century Canadian history falls into four phases: 1) the constitutional school of the 1920s; 2) the economic interpretations of the 1930s; 3) the biographical approaches of the 1940s and 50s; and 4) the fragmentation of the 1960s and thereafter (6). The interpretive axis, on the other hand, reveals 'two long phases' and a possible third phase: 1) the Laurentian thesis in the 1920s; 2) a second phase marked by Maurice Careless's 'Limited Identities' article of 1969; and 3) the recent beginnings of a third phase calling for 'a return to a nationally coherent vision' (7), but also accompanied by uncertainty in the profession as a whole as to how to effect such a reintegration.

If Morton's 1946 article marked the beginning of the critique of the Laurentian thesis, a critique that culminated in Careless (1969) and the resulting dominance of subdisciplines (labour history, regional history, etc.) and subassociations within the Canadian Historical Association, this leads Owram to write: 'It is only a slight exaggeration to say that Canadian history collapsed in the 1970s and was replaced by groups of Canadian histories and ... the Canadian historical profession was ... supplanted by regional and subdisciplinary history' (11). While Owram sees a similar fragmentation among American historians, he views the Canadian case as the result of the simultaneous breakdown of two specific aspects of Canadian historical writing: the loss of faith in the Laurentian model and the lack of an alternative nationalist model to replace it, combined with structural changes in the post-1960s profession (13). The resulting fragmentation, over-specialization, and lack of synthesis between the subdisciplines has entailed heavy costs, not the least being the withdrawal of the public's interest in Canadian history as written by professional historians, an interest seemingly better met by the writings of former journalists like Pierre Berton or Peter C. Newman (17). Owram's own call for a return to synthesis does not mean, he says, a return to consensual nationalism or to some mythical past where a small elite doled out patriotism; rather, 'Canadian historians need to broaden their outlook,' and he argues that there is no reason why academic historians cannot have 'a significant impact on the public' (17).

Unfortunately, Owram does not go much beyond this sort of appeal for greater breadth. 'There have been many attempts to define what it is that makes

Canada unique. Metropolitanism, the frontier thesis, Hartzian fragments, tory touches, multiculturalism, violence and redress, even victimization have been used over the years in attempts to explain what was unique about Canada' (18), but none of these attempts, he feels, 'have reached the level where we can talk about a school of interpretation.' At the same time, he does at least sketch out the skeleton of such an interpretation: 'this nation, supposedly so fragmented and "limited," has had a common historical experience of considerable duration ... [W]e may now have to look at the reverse side of limited identities' (19). Or at least, 'we must try.' However, as Owram suggests (18), the professional historians have seemingly boxed themselves 'into an unnecessary corner.' Perhaps, then, it is simply time to leave them to their agonies, and look instead at the appeal of the non-professionals. After all, as the American historian Crane Brinton once put it: 'History has many mansions [and] it would now seem that History has suburbs and shantytowns, trailer parks and condominiums as well' (cited in Owram, 10–11). Since it is still uncertain what sort of habitation Canadian historians dwell in, other than that many of its occupants consider the place cramped, let us look awhile at the amateurs.

The 'Amateur' Historiographers

Not surprisingly, given the contentiousness of the twentieth-century Canadian academic historical profession, the writing of Canadian history has had a far longer tradition of amateurism, going back to the sixteenth- and seventeenth-century narratives of exploration (see Warkentin 1995). The great French-Canadian historians of the nineteenth century (Garneau, Chapais, Sulte) were not professional historians in the academic sense of the term; and in the twentieth century, like Gustave Lanctôt, they might be archivists, or in the case of Maheu in Quebec City or Groulx and Rumilly in Montreal, they often occupied academically precarious positions (see Bernard 1995: 323; Gagnon 1978; Rudin 1997). As well, the historical writings of journalists like Bruce Hutchison in the 1950s and, in the 1960s and subsequently, Pierre Berton's histories of the building of the CPR, of Canadian movie-making, or of the War of 1812, and Peter C. Newman's book-length studies putting faces to otherwise faceless politicians and chronicling Canada's corporate elites, both contemporary finance capitalists and the 'lords' of the fur trade, have consistently proven popular with general readers. Here, however, we will look at recent contributions to Canadian history by two other well-known popularizers, specifically Christopher Moore and his 1997 account of the making of Confederation, and John Ralston Saul with his best-selling *Reflections of a Siamese Twin* (1997). The choice of these two authors is not totally arbitrary, given that Moore's work is, in part, a chastisement of professional historians' supposed neglect of a crucial event in Canadian history – he notes proudly on the book jacket that he 'is not a professor.' Saul, on the other hand, does hold a PhD in history, but this former oil-company executive turned best-selling novelist (and in his personal life, since 1999 husband of the current Governor General of Canada) has, in his more recent works, abandoned fiction to wage war against the tyranny of reason in Western intellectual history since the Enlightenment (1993, 1995). *Siamese Twin* contains his equally sweeping reflections on Canada at the end of the twentieth century and, because of this, we will turn to it first.

A word of caution, however. The response of the academic world to Saul's reflections was hardly friendly. University of Calgary political philosopher Barry Cooper, in a sneering article published in *The Literary Review of Canada*, pretty much summed up the gravamen of his response in the title of his review: 'Shoddy Pamphlet or Great Man's Thesis?' (November 1998, 16–18). That noted, it is more difficult to tell exactly why Cooper so passionately hated Saul's book: one point, much belaboured, seems to be that he does not like some of the things Saul says about Canada's West and its resentments of central Canada, a form of betrayal of regional loyalty compounded by the fact that Saul should know better, having once worked in the Calgary head offices of the Alberta oil patch. The other central charge concerns what Cooper terms Saul's 'rhetoric of certainty. He pronounces on Quebec poetry and the nature of referendums, on the differences between Plato and Socrates, between true and false populism, and much, much more' (16). Not only does Saul's rhetorical 'portentousness' exercise Cooper; the book itself, he says, is nothing but 'a portent of the exhaustion of analytic skills among leftist intellectuals' (16). Now it seems somewhat unfair on Cooper's part to be sneaking into the discussion another bugbear altogether – that of the alienation of intellectuals on the left in their 'uniform hostility to liberal, commercial society,' a hostility that drives them to pump out 'ideology' aimed at destroying 'the political and economic order that has sustained them' (18). This *querelle des intellectuels* might best be reserved for another discussion. Suffice it to say that Cooper thinks not only that Saul's book is thoroughly 'counterfeit scholarship' (18), but also that 'leftist' intellectuals are too alienated from the surrounding society to be able to say anything worthwhile about it.

One interesting point that Cooper does make is that 'Saul begins where Margaret Atwood left off in *Survival*, more than a quarter century ago, with the imagery of victims and the task of overcoming victimhood' (16). This observation is a good place to begin from; it reminds us of the more general problematic of the near-universal predilection of many communities the world over for accounts of victimhood as a principal form of self-identification. As Cooper implies, since Atwood's *Survival* (1972), if not long before (see Dorland 1988), accounts of victimhood have been a highly prevalent trait of Canadian historiography (and literature and the visual arts as well). If the emphasis on the tasks of *survivance* had long been a driving ideology of French-Canadian historiography, one particularly reinforced with the reaction that set in after the Rebellions of 1837–8, the importance of Atwood's book lay in its identification of a similar element in (some of) the literature of (some portions) of English Canada. Secondly, it is also worth remarking that the methodological framework that pays attention to narratives of victimization, in Atwood, in Saul, or in another recent book of popularizing Canadian history (see Francis 1997) is not anything we might understand by the term 'historical,' but rather draws upon a much more nebulous enframing concept, that of the mythological. It is not surprising, then, that Saul devotes most of his 500-page text to revisiting the mythological in the Canadian context.

'Canada, like other nation-states,' Saul writes in his opening paragraph, 'suffers from a contradiction between its public mythologies and its reality. Perhaps we suffer more than most. Perhaps the explanation is that, while all countries are complex, the central characteristic of the Canadian state is its complexity' (1997: 3). This immediately calls for three brief remarks: for one, by 'the Canadian state' he presumably means not the central apparatus of governance but an existential condition; for another, we note once again, as we have seen repeatedly in the historiography of the national, and stressed by Owram above, the leitmotif of the search for *the* unique, *the* distinguishing trait, and *the* explanation of it – e.g., that perhaps Canada has suffered more than any other nation (but what about Poland, Russia, or any number of other possible claimants?) from the contradictions of its public culture. Third, that Saul opts for complexity as an explanatory framework is fine but hardly a distinguishing trait of anything, other than the self-evident recognition that the worlds we inhabit, both physically and symbolically, are, indeed, complex.

If other nation-states managed to produce the appearance of simplicity (a single language, a single culture, a single or dominant race) and by the use of force to centralize government and, more importantly, to produce 'the writing of a centralized justificatory history' (8), Canada, while no innocent in these matters, has been, by general consensus, more of a failure at this than a success. But, argues Saul, this is precisely its uniqueness: what is distinctive of Canadian 'public mythology' is its complexity, and to accept this complexity is to undertake 'a revolutionary reversal of the ... nation-state myth'; it is to 'live out of step with most other nations' in a daring act of nonconformity (9). Or so Saul attempts to argue; namely, instead of bemoaning our lack of conformity to the centralized nation-state ideal, we should, on the contrary, embrace it by accepting that the Canadian experience constitutes a complex, open-ended, and still ongoing experiment in the 'translation' of democratic practices whose 'reality' is, in fact, the complete observe of our official public culture.

Now while this is an intriguing tack to pursue, there are a number of problems with it. First, if the predominant characteristic of Canadian public life, as others like Richard Collins (1990) have attempted to argue, is its near-total disconnect between the official discourses and the lived realities of the citizenry (see also Saul, 15), either this disjunction is a matter of complete indifference to the citizens, who know better anyway and just get on with their lives regardless, or it isn't. And if the first is indeed the case, why bother to write about it? Since Saul *does* bother, we must assume that the disjunction between public 'lies' and private lives is of some import to him, as of course it should be.

The problem is that this disjunction has created a vacuum of publicness which has been filled with 'fear, frustration, passivity and anger' (15), which the citizenry cannot just shrug off; they are, on the contrary, drawn into its vortices with the resulting poisoning and embitterment of public life and culture. Most of the blame for this rests with Canada's 'elites' who, although 'fact-driven and power-dependent,' and armed with 'ever more deformed [and powerful] machinery of communications,' are nonetheless 'frightened by the citizenry and by the idea of non-corporatist participation [in democratic life]' (15). 'At the heart of Canadian leadership lies a need to blame ... Toronto blames the United States. The West blames the East. Francophones blame anglophones. Northern Ontario blames Toronto ... I could fill pages with this network of fear ... at the core of [which] is a refusal to assume responsibility' (17).

The refusal by Canada's elites to accept the responsibility that devolves from being elites is because they are still 'colonial-minded.' 'In spreading fear among the citizenry ... the elites are exporting their own sense of being victims ... [thus] expressing their own fear that they are inferior' (16–17). Crippled by their disbelief in their own worth and of that of the country they are responsible for, the dominance of the colonial-minded elites has meant that 'the history of Canada is filled with waves of recurring insecurity among those who lead us' (17), current and recent manifestations of this being evident in the widespread belief among the state and financial elites of the inevitable and irresistible consequences of technological and economic globalization, and the corresponding devolution of national sovereignty. In a rather cursory way, Saul traces this elite insecurity back to a psychology of abandonment that took root along the banks of the St Lawrence with the cession of New France, a crippling psychology of leadership that maintained itself thereafter and has accompanied each phase of the subsequent territorial growth of Canada from Atlantic to Pacific (see 18–54), and has also profoundly marked provincial politics, especially of Quebec and the Western provinces.

'It is difficult to think of another country – except perhaps Australia – so consistently populated by the abandoned and the defeated,' Saul writes (128). This is the basis not only of governmental policies of the management of economic and social poverty, but also of Canada's cultural traits: its anti-utopianism (140); its antiheroism and lack of heroic war literature (143); its paintings, that are not about heroes or war but about the natural landscapes of the Group of Seven (143); and the *coureur de bois – habitant* tension between mobility and settlement, a tension in patterns of habitation that is also reflected in popular sports, particularly in the difference between hockey (constant motion) and baseball (static) (152). This is also manifested at the continental level, by the tension between East-West and North-South, in which 'the natural flow in Canada is East-West' (155), a claim which Saul extrapolates from fur-trading patterns as well as more recent studies on trading patterns by economist John Helliwell (168). Bit by bit, Saul thus composes a picture of the 'strategic acts' that have constituted Canada as 'above all *an idea of what a country could be*, a place of the imagination ... based on the dominance of constant movement' (171, emphasis added). In Saul's view, Canada is the result of eight strategic 'acts' that were unplanned but grew out of 'the practical metaphysics' of an 'equilibrium between an individualism of unstructured risk and an individualism of the public good' (182). The eight strategic acts were these: 'the reformers' alliance, the Maritime dash, the railroad, the National Policy, the immigration flood, the refusal of imperial engagement, the social revolution, [and] the cultural engagement' (182), a 'foundation' which the resurgence of the 'colonial' elites (e.g., the two Mulroney prime-ministerships and thereafter) have, since the 1980s, attempted to dismantle, and successfully enough apparently to warrant Saul's writing this book.

One could go on, but it is hoped that his general argument is by now as clear as it is going to get, as Saul hops breezily from one topic to another, the Danes here, Catalonia there, but always meanders back to his central point that 'Canada' is about the attempted realization of an Idea. This is the idea of 'a constant rebalancing act' (506), 'a balanced equality, created and maintained by a reasonably effective social-democratic system,' and it is a commitment that, he claims, has lain at the centre of Canada's evolution. 'That was the meaning of the Mackenzie-Papineau cooperation, as it was of Lafontaine and Baldwin's belief ... in the idea of a country built on the conception of ongoing reform. The railway was a redistribution device, just as public broadcasting has been ... just as Medicare and transfer payments have been ... the unending application of ever-evolving methods of redistribution [based on] ... reconciliation and reform' (506–7).

So how do we evaluate all this? One could dismiss it outright, as Barry Cooper does, as portentous nonsense, and retreat to one's ivory tower. One could also say with Granatstein that Saul's *Reflections* are an appalling illustration of what happens when rampant presentism totally takes over historical writing. One could further add that this isn't historical writing at all but rather 'mythological' musings by one now Ottawa-based, public intellectual on the topic of *his* idea of Canada, formed by idiosyncratic reading. And all of these possibilities are likely. On the other hand, the Granatsteins and Owrams mentioned above complain that the professional historians, for various reasons, cannot get it together sufficiently to propose to a reading public an idea of Canada they can agree upon (never mind that it is unlikely that there is *an* idea of Canada anyway). So Saul girds himself to the task and writes a book that gets onto Canadian best-selling non-fiction lists: in so doing, has he committed some great harm, or are there mitigating aspects to his writerly deed?

Instead of just reverting back to Red Toryism, Saul wants to insist, more than the historiographical tradition has done until recently, on a *democratic* conception of Canada, one that might, or should, be more attentive of its citizenry. Red Tory nevertheless, Saul stresses again and again the responsibilities of governing and financial elites towards both the country and its peoples, a tune which, if it smacks somewhat of noblesse oblige, is not so unpleasant as to not bear repetition. Owram stresses that historians should make a greater effort to concern themselves with the fact that this country's history reveals more commonalities than the contrary. This is what Saul attempts to do with his *Reflections*. One may complain that he might have done a better job of it, but he has at least taken a stab at it.

For a different and less sweeping, or perhaps differently sweeping, attempt to generalize about the characteristics of the Canadian experience overall, we now turn to another non-academic popularizer of Canadian history, Toronto writer Christopher Moore's study of the making of Confederation. Somewhat like John Ralston Saul, Moore in his *1867: How the Fathers Made a Deal* (1997) emphasizes several broad points, although his study is far more focused on the political strategies and coalitions of alliances that went into bringing Confederation about. The first of his most general points, as if building upon Saul's suggestion that there is more to be said about the processes of 'translation' to better understand the complexities of Canada's cultural cross-effects, is the belief that it is possible to 'translate' nineteenth-century constitutionalism into present-day terms that would serve as a lesson to contemporary politicians about the importance of the 1867 'deal' (Moore, x). Second, his re-examination of the processes that lead to Confederation reveals the enormous importance given to, and legitimating authority conferred by, the ideals of British parliamentary government upon the Canadian actors. These beliefs for Moore clearly 'translate' into the idea of the supremacy of the legislatures and accordingly of a far more democratic conception of political authority derived from 'the people' than Canadian historiography has traditionally allowed (see 234 ff.). Third, the view of Confederation presented by academic constitutional historians (e.g., Peter Russell of the University of Toronto) is, as Moore puts it, that Confederation was 'something imposed on cringing colonial Canadians by the reactionary local agents of Imperial dictate' (234). Quoting Russell, in turn quoting the 'deferential' view, that Confederation would 'not profess to be derived from the people but would be the constitution provided by the imperial parliament' (quoted in Moore, 234), Moore goes on to argue, on the contrary, and based rather surprisingly on a reading of Bagehot (1867), that 'Britain and British North America were disguised republics – in disguise certainly, but certainly republics, if republic meant a government derived from the people' (235). Now this is a topic which, if presented in somewhat exaggerated form by Moore, has recently been reopened in academic historical and political theoretical debates concerning the persistent underlying influence of republican currents in seventeenth-century British political thought, and in particular their translation to British colonies such as Canada (see Ajzenstat and Smith 1995; D.E. Smith 1999). Moore's own view of the historiography of Confederation and its baleful contribution to the misunderstanding of Confederation's 'real' significance is that the professional historians wrote a lot about Confederation until 1967, and then, he claims, they suddenly stopped. 'In the last thirty years, there has scarcely been a single new book about how confederation was made in the 1860s. Nineteenth-century high politics has vanished almost entirely from the agenda of the Canadian historical profession and the historical popularizers. The books are out of print, the documents almost unavailable, and the issues undebated' (ix). Oddly, however, Moore has read such recent academic historians writing about the politics of Confederation as Phillip Buckner (1985), Ged Martin (1995), and Gordon Stewart (1986). As well, Moore is not beyond a nod to presentism, when he remarks, in spite his attempt to rescue Confederation from the alleged harm done it by the neglect of historians and the lack of historical understanding of present-day political elites, that 'the ratification of confederation ... was a deeply imperfect process. An electoral system ... excluded women for their gender and men for their lack of property ... Substantial, politically active minorities, such as the Acadians ... and the Catholics of several provinces, were shockingly under-represented ... Aboriginal nations and racial minorities ... were almost completely disenfranchised ... No one spoke of a charter of rights' (227).

Moore ends up, in his conclusion, wondering 'if it was simply perverse to be offering a book that gave close and often respectful attention to the ways responsible government and parliamentary democracy had made possible the constitution-making of the 1860s' (250–1), and he wonders this because of his present-day conviction that 'parliamentary government ... has ceased to function in Canada.' His proposal, then, is for a return to these now-abandoned ideals, a proposal that, like Saul's, he feels is 'a very modest, unambitious, and anti-utopian notion' because, instead of a call for spectacular transformations, it has 'the great advantage of being possible' (252). All it needs is 'a change of mind' and 'an act of will' by elected members of Parliament to once more shoulder the responsibilities of 'responsible government' (252).

Again, if one reverts to Owram's list above of the key interpretations of Canadian history proffered by professional historians, Moore, like Saul, does not offer anything broader or significantly different. Indeed, 'responsible government' does not even make Owram's list, perhaps because, as Underhill once remarked, it was nothing more than 'a mild British liberal Whiggism' (Underhill 1960: 257). Or, in the same spirit, as Creighton remarked in 1948, complaining that a recent series of biographies were really only examinations of political teleology in a biographical framework: 'Are there really biographies or Baldwin, Hinks and Laurier, or are these merely lives of Robert Responsible-Government and Francis Responsible-Government, and Wilfrid Responsible- Government?' (cited in Berger 1967: 218).

But this would be too rapidly dismissive of both Moore and Saul, for there are differences between the amateurs and the professionals worth noting. Among the amateurs is the recurrence of several themes not noticeably dealt with by the professionals: to mention but three, these concern an emphasis on processes of translation (a recurring theme in our book); an emphasis on the mind-set that Saul calls 'practical metaphysics,' a concern with the concrete, not immediately dismissed as anti-intellectual as, say, Underhill does in his reflections on the stunted Canadian liberal tradition (1970: 31); and the emphasis by both Saul and Moore on a democratic basis for Canadian politics, that is, one that derives its authority from a conception of 'the people,' a reminder to present-day elites stemming from the conviction that the actions of the latter appear to have utterly lost sight of this 'fact.' Now this democratic bias may be wishfulness on their part, or creeping presentism, a backwards rereading of contemporary concerns into the established historical consensus. On the other hand, the professionals have debated aspects of such questions, as well as the validity of *the* so-called historical record itself. The process of writing history, precisely because it is a process of writing, is thus also a constant rewriting. It must be, both because the past can never be fully known and because the present itself is ever-changing, in certain ways. The amateurs, one might say, are perhaps less rigorous in their views of what constitutes 'change' and thus more prone to discovering apparent novelties than the professionals. But the amateurs, or here Saul and Moore, both make a point that the professionals often seem to have lost sight of. Moore prefaces his book with some thoughts on the following phrase: 'As If Confederation Mattered.' Saul's *Reflections* might just as well have been subtitled: 'As If Canada Mattered.' Again and again, they want to remind the political and economic elites that it matters to be charged with the governance of a country; Moore, for his part, returns to the venerable, if decidedly old-fashioned, view of the significance for Canada of the attainment of responsible government, emphasizing the responsibility that the latter entails.

In the end, perhaps, what the whole discussion amounts to is that the professionals, or some of them, accuse their colleagues of having forgotten that they ought to write, not in the ideolects of the profession, but 'as if history mattered.' To which the accused reply that they write the way they do, precisely because what they do *does* matter; and, being academics, they then battle over the meaning of '*what* matters.' Perhaps the contribution of the amateurs to the discussion is less one over historiography per se, then, but rather to offer a more modest reminder that 'it' (however so defined) matters, and that this should not be lost sight of, as there are 'real' consequences to neglecting 'it.'

Recent Debates about Canada's Founding

And yet, even if indirectly, Moore's injunction to write as if Confederation mattered has had an impact upon the concerns of the professionals. Here, we focus upon recent academic debates over Confederation and inquire in some detail into the process that brought together six of the seven territories of British North America in the years 1864–73 to form a new country and perhaps a new nationality. The issue is examined once more because it continues to constitute a source of fundamental preoccupation and remains a problem that has never been satisfactorily settled – or, if one prefers, has been discussed differently at different times.

We are, in other words, and as Saul argued above, within a discursive terrain still enveloped in 'myth,' as a number of the professionals have also remarked (most recently Romney 1999; Ajzenstat et al. 1999). But by 'myth' here, we will follow Romney who characterizes it as 'a story that embodies a certain idea of the order of things – the natural or the political order' (1999: 13); in this case, the story of Canada's 'creation,' about which there has never been more than a degree of periodic agreement, if that, as the story has changed with circumstances and times.

The story has many versions. One, that John A. Macdonald and Georges-Etienne Cartier, respectively representing the two founding 'races,' compacted together to form a larger political union in which the sectional differences of previous political arrangements would have a larger (continental) context in which to work themselves out better. This version soon ran aground over the events in the North-West, Riel's execution, and the separation, or lack thereof, of church and state regarding schools in Manitoba. Another version is that, repelled by the American Civil War attributed to the weakness of the U.S. federal government, Canada's founding fathers opted for a sterner mode of federalism, characterized by a strong central government. A third version, paralleling Charles Beard's *Economic Interpretation of the Constitution* (1913), makes of Confederation a business deal by lawyers representing railway interests and London merchant bankers (see Innis 1923; Ryerson 1968; Naylor 1975). Variants of this version, but now applied to the realm of political thought – or more precisely, the absence of political thought – see Confederation as a purely pragmatic affair, devoid of any political ideas whatsoever, and cobbled together by political fixers who hammered out a structure whose content would somehow be filled by whatever. This view, as Janet Azjenstat and her coeditors of a recent collection of documents on Canada's founding debates have laboured mightily to dispell, is 'pernicious nonsense, because it purges political values from Canada's founding' (1999: 1). Yet another version, and probably the predominant one, since it represents, as Paul Romney points out, 'a commitment to a certain ideal of Canadian nationality,' is that the 'Fathers of Confederation set out to found a great nation with a strong central government having dominion from sea to sea and with provincial governments of subordinate stature, exercising merely municipal powers' (1999: 5). Then, there are the Quebec-centred versions of this, in which the Quebec government constitutes the only political force strong enough to defend the French national language and civil identity that, outside of Quebec, have fallen victim to the ever-present assimilationist anglophone menace. And finally there are the additional regional variants, from British Columbia to Newfoundland, that have arisen from time to time, expressing degrees of disenchantment with the federation and what it has done or, most of all, *not* done for the particular region, in economic and political terms. All of these stories, as Romney notes, have some basis in lived experience, or at least in other stories 'based on real events,' as screenwriters might put it.

More important, however, is the extent to which such stories almost invariably draw upon the work of historians to inspire loyalty to a homeland usually by the creation of an external threat. The U.S. has both in fact and in imagination played a major role in cohering Canada against various waves of 'Americanization,' just as English Canada has served as both a comparable threat and a stabilizer for Quebec's sense of identity. Romney argues in his 1999 *Getting It Wrong: How Canadians Forgot Their Past and Imperilled Confederation*, that equally the role performed by Canadian nationalist and centralizing historians and jurists in the 1920s and 1930s – Donald Creighton's work representing an especially powerful example of the centralizing historian – has been crucial in the ability to write and rewrite history. This involves more than merely reflecting the bêtes noires and personal prejudices of particular historians; even more significantly, it concerns the ability to (ab)use the writing of history as a hegemonic form of discourse that possesses the power to obliterate living memory (which in any event degrades on its own through time, age, and forgetfulness), and substitutes for living memory an altogether different 'story.'

If a Granatstein can bewail the 'killing' of Canadian history, Romney, in *Getting It Wrong*, proposes an analysis somewhat less dramatic than outright murder, but on other levels more frightening – as the gradual slipping away of one version of history and its replacement by another, a kind of historical Alzheimer's disease that slowly effaces the possibility of one account for another, leading to blackouts and near-complete forgetfulness.

As Romney tells it, he had 'set out to examine what was wrong with the account of Canadian history that I learned at the University of Toronto some twenty years ago' (1999: 3). What he found – or, rather, stumbled upon – was 'an entirely different way of thinking about Canada and its history of which the entire canon of scholarly writing offered scarcely an inkling' (12). This 'new way' of thinking was actually an older way of thinking about Canada that revealed 'a lost middle ground between French- and English-Canadian ideas of Canada' (3). This was, in effect, the rediscovery of a deeply rooted Québécois belief (and as we shall see, not just a Québécois belief) that Confederation was a *pacte solennel* between two nations that guaranteed Quebec's special status within Confederation as well as that of individual francophones within Canada, an understanding apparently dating from the British Conquest of 1760. As Romney notes, the specific idea and wording of the *pacte solennel* can be traced back in the documentary record to a petition of 1823; that is, more than forty years before Confederation itself. This is, in effect, a version of comedian Yvon Deschamps's quip about 'un Québec indépendant dans un Canada fort et uni'; except here it is no longer a saw, but corresponds to profoundly held beliefs about how Quebecers, or those directly involved, envisaged Confederation. As Romney goes on to show, however, since his study is in fact more about Upper Canadian views of Confederation, very similar perceptions were held by political reformers in what became Ontario. Namely, that Confederation was, in addition to the recognition of Quebec's special status, also a theory of radical provincial sovereignty.

Needless to say, the 'compact theory' of Confederation would be roundly denounced and rejected by the centralizing historians and lawyers of the 1930s seeking to make of the central government the basis of the Canadian welfare state's power to undertake exercises in social engineering. The compact was rejected at two levels: first, as a national compact between French and English and second, as a compact between the provinces, granting them far greater independence than the later strongly centralized model would allow (5). Both of these ideas, which had French- and English-language antecedents that preceded Confederation, were, Romney argues, accommodated by the Confederation settlement without contradiction (6). Both ideas were at the forefront of the late nineteenth-century struggle for provincial rights, led by Ontario premier Oliver Mowat. Over time, the compact theory weakened in English-Canadian thought, and the 'resulting void was filled by that centralist, nation-building idea of Confederation which still prevails in English-Canadian minds' (6).

There are several aspects to Romney's argument that need to be examined further, particularly as they pertain to a revisionist political theory of Confederation, rooted in a heightened sense of democracy and the relationships between civil society and law. The nature of governance under the French regime had been, as it were, proconsular: the governor and the *intendant* constituted the two principal pillars of the extension of absolutist monarchical power radiating out of Versailles. Under the British initially, the mode of governance was at first that of the military governors, with the balance of power gradually tilting away from the military apex toward the cautious establishment of civilian rule, but destabilized in part by pressures from the newly arrived Protestant and mercantile interests for the establishment of a legislative assembly that they could control. This was balanced against the concerns of the political governors amid the shifting sands of colonial policy, after the loss of the Thirteen Colonies, over how much to accommodate the 'new subjects' of the Crown; for example, what concessions should be made to them, notably regarding Catholicism, which was illegal in the England of the period. Here too there were contending pressures from the new subjects for the establishment of an elected, or quasi-elected, assembly that they might control. The resulting compromises led to a bit of everything, added to rapidly by émigré influxes from the former Thirteen Colonies, bringing with them, in part, a revanchist mindset that the calamity that had taken place in the newly created United States of America should never be allowed to repeat itself in British North America. At the same time these émigrés brought elements of that very sense of colonial British liberty that had contributed to the American Revolution. The result would be the establishment of ruling oligarchies, the so-called family compacts and *châteaux cliques* in the respective Canadas; the former attempted to reproduce a version of the late eighteenth-century English and Anglican landed gentry, and the latter fused a continuation of seigneurial rule with aspects of pre-reform British parliamentarianism. Rule by oligarchy, thus, anticipated the preferred mode of Canadian governance that Robert Presthus in 1973 would term 'elite accommodation.'

The problems of governance, then, and in particular from the perspective of a democractic (liberal or Reform) tradition that runs from Mackenzie and Lafontaine, to the reform governments of the late 1840s and early 1850s, and beyond to Blake, Laurier, and Mackenzie King, were those of freeing themselves from the heritages of oligarchical rule and its various subsequent manifestations in the centralizing structures of the United Canadas, and from the centralizers' version of what Confederation was about.

As Romney argues, part of the difficulty of sorting all this through is that the democratic perspective turns the familiar stories about Canada and its founding upside down.

For English-speaking Canadians today, their country's history is largely an account of the formation of a distinctly un-American English-speaking society in North America, a great nation stretching from sea to sea. From this perspective, Upper Canada appears first and foremost as a rampart of embattled loyalism, beset by American military power and weakened within by a horde of less-than-loyal American settlers. It figures, secondly, as a seedbed of responsible government, but here too the emphasis falls on the invention of a British-style solution to the problem of colonial self-government in preference to the American remedies favoured by the radicals of the 1830s and their ... successors. (1999: 30)

Inversing this narrative, and focusing on Upper Canada, one gets a different story (Romney is analysing an 1872 speech by Oliver Mowat [see 21–31]). And this is one whose central theme is the unceasing struggle of the people of Upper Canada for liberty. In this perspective, the related theme of anti-Americanism, so prominent in the conservative narrative, 'runs a poor second' (30), and the overprivileged theme of nation-building in that same discourse 'comes last and least' (30). The promise of Confederation lay in its belated granting of self-government for Upper Canada. It follows from this that the much-vaunted advent of responsible government was not a triumph, but a failure. It follows as well that the thrust of Upper Canadian politics was its resistance to 'despotic and unaccountable government. Treason lurks not on the left ... but on the right. Where, in the standard story, a loyal garrison "stands on guard" ... against the American menace, [here] "the people must ever be standing on the watch" against oppression and betrayal from above' (30).

As Romney notes, both stories have a similar structure: in the one, Canadians struggle to preserve their autonomy against an alien aggressor – the Americans; in the other, the Upper Canadian people struggle to assert their autonomy against an alien oppressor – first the British, then the French of Lower Canada. 'In each case, the alien foe is aided by domestic traitors' (31).

But there is a difference, Romney notes. Mowat's 'story' is addressed to the Upper Canadian people 'first seen groaning under the domination not of Lower Canada but of the Family Compact, an oligarchic elite.' What distinguishes Mowat's story 'is its populist character' (31), and its de-emphasizing the external American threat for an internal, antidemocratic one. Mowat's story embodies a populist counterhistory to the creed of loyalism 'that preferred an orderly, hierarchical society to the anarchic democracy that supposedly typified American republicanism. The rejection of republicanism became an excuse for the authoritarian political system that prevailed ... [and] justified that centralization which – as Creighton rightly contended – was an essential feature of monarchical government in the British style, as opposed to the devolved and elective government favoured by populists' (32).

For Romney, Mowat's story is neither more true nor more false than the loyalist one; it is a different story, but one that, whatever its mythic dimensions, unsettles other Canadian political myths, such as 'responsible government,' the story of Confederation, and subsequent interpretations of the British North America Act by the Judicial Committee of the British Privy Council, all of which he subjects to scrutiny. For, as we shall see, these differences do add up to something more than a collection of myths and their revision; they end up touching upon the fundamental principles of political existence.

Civil Society and Legality

As we have seen, 'responsible government' has been celebrated by liberal historians from Underhill to Chris Moore as a distinctive Canadian contribution to liberalism. One of the problems faced eventually head-on and violently by the American colonists had concerned the question of devolving Westminster's legislative sovereignty to that of the colonial assemblies. The inability to satisfactorily negotiate such a devolution had led to the Revolution itself. In the Canadas, the rebellions of 1836–7 were repressed. The Canadian reformers had to press their demands for great independence through argument, not force of arms, and had to do so in the face of the political ascendency of Loyalism on the one hand and, on the other, slippery legal doctrine that too readily could make the demand for responsible government appear as 'a frank insistence on colonial sovereignty' (Romney 1999: 57).

As Romney points out, they negotiated a course between these obstacles by 'accentuat[ing] certain aspects of their ideology and play[ing] down others' (57). Since responsible government was itself a British principle, 'they managed by the 1840s to assimilate their colonial heresies to the imperial orthodoxy' (58). This they did *rhetorically*, by insisting on the villainy of the Family Compact in a discourse in which 'the British government normally figured ... as a benign but ill-informed ruler, misled by governors who had fallen under the influence of the oligarchy' (58). The strategy of stealth allowed for some significant successes in the late 1820s, followed by major reversals in the 1830s and early 1840s. The problems with the Reformers' insistence on the evils of the Family Compact and the assimilation of their own constitutionalism to British orthodoxy were many: they disregarded the fact that the Compact itself was a creature of British rule; the Reform discourse all too readily collapsed into a version of the English Whig myth of the gradual victory of parliamentary government over absolute monarchy (see Romney, 58–69). In other words, the autonomy that the Upper Canadian Reformers had expected of responsible government was spurious to the extent that it buried the problem of the distortions to colonial politics caused by imperial control beneath a Whig version of incremental parliamentary progress. And this would be confirmed by the Act of Union of 1841 in which the two Canadas were reunited, bringing with it the old problem of Lower Canadian dominance of the united legislature (and the displacement of the Family Compact by the 'French clique'). As Romney puts it:

In 1859 Upper Canadian Reformers embraced the idea of Canadian federation, somewhat gingerly, as a way of securing the autonomy which they had expected from responsible government but which the union of 1841 had denied them ... But no one advocated confederation as a substitute for Upper Canadian autonomy; no one argued that local autonomy was worth sacrificing to achieve the wider union. (87)

These perspectives accord completely with A.I. Silver's 1982 study of French-Canadian newspaper opinion regarding Confederation. As the *Journal des Trois-Rivières* stated it in July 1866: 'For us, French Canadians, w[e] are only entering Confederation on the condition of having our own legislature as a guarantee of our autonomy ... The deeper we can make the demarcation line between ourselves and the other provinces, the more guarantee we'll have for the conservation of our special character as a people' (cited by Silver 1982: 41). Silver goes on to note that this was 'the very heart and essence' of the pro-Confederation argument in French Lower Canada – 'a province with an enormous degree of autonomy: in effect, *separation* (from Upper Canada) and *independence* (of Quebec) within its jurisdictions. 'As a distinct and separate nationality,' said *La Minerve*, 'we form a state within the state. We enjoy the full exercise of our rights and the formal recognition of our national independence' (quoted in Silver, 41).

So what happened to this version of Confederation? How did an agreement which, as seen in the above, clearly had 'its origin in the need to gratify the yearnings of French-Canadians and Upper Canadians alike to be masters in their own house' (Romney 1999: 88), come instead to be seen first as an exercise in nation-building, second as the degradation of the federal structure of the new union into a subsidiary feature 'designed ... to accommodate the cultural peculiarity of French Canadians' (88), and third as a much more centralized version of the classic model presented by the United States?

Here, other than a series of only partially explained reversals, Romney's account falls upon shakier ground. In part, the Quebec Resolutions of 1864 proposed a far more centralized scheme than that which the Reformers had discussed in 1859. While Romney displays much analytical subtlety in trying to show elements of ambiguity over the division of powers between the provinces, the federal government, the uncertain status of the residual powers, and the recentralization in Canadian form of the U.S. federal model (see 88–100), in the end, matters remain unclear – and not helped by the silence of his hero, Oliver Mowat, who accepted a federal judgeship soon after the Quebec Conference.

The recent edition of the Confederation debates by Ajzenstat, Romney, Gentles, and Gairdner, which publishes new documents for the first time, reveals debates that often seem to verge on the anarchic. To wit, D'Arcy McGee stated in the Quebec Legislative Assembly, February 9, 1865: 'We have had liberty enough – too much perhaps in some respects ... We need in these provinces ... a large infusion of authority' (Ajzenstat et al. 1999: 16).

For his part, Romney in *Getting It Wrong* goes on to observe that the circumstances of the drafting of the British North America Act early in 1867 'are still unclear,' but in his view bear evidence of 'a determined effort on the part of British officials to overbear the colonial will and centralize the scheme of confederation' (100). He notes that drafting was delayed for two years by Maritime opposition to the Quebec scheme: not until December 1866 did a delegation from Nova Scotia and New Brunswick meet a Canadian delegation in London to work out revisions. It was the British, according to Romney, in drafting the confederation bill, who caused the local residuary power to disappear, moved the federal residue to the head of the section dealing with the powers of the federal parliament, invested the federal parliament with the power to make laws for the peace, order, and good government of the united colony in all matters not exclusively confined to the local legislatures, and went on to enumerate 'the Generality' of certain federal powers, including such matters that it might, from time to time, see fit to transfer to the local jurdisdiction (see 100–1).

If, as Romney claims, 'British officials had little understanding of [Canadian] federalism ... and had colluded with Macdonald at the London conference to centralize the proposed confederation beyond the Fathers' intentions' (109), the officials of the Colonial Office would, by the 1870s and 1880s, be out-flanked by British judges – the Judicial Committee of the Privy Council in particular – in the first juridical efforts to define more exactly the division of powers in the BNA Act. The centralizers' version of Confederation has long vilified the Judicial Committee's interference in Canadian constitutionalism by making the law lords champions of Canadian provincial autonomy. Here the Judicial Committee in the centralizing story plays an equivalent role of behind-the-scenes Colonial Office officials in changing the course of the decentralizers' story of Confederation, but now more in accord with the decentralizers' script. In Romney's story, it is his hero, Oliver Mowat, premier of Ontario at the time, who leads the legal struggle, who 'fought long and hard' (111) to educate the Privy Council in the nuances of an emerging Canadian legal culture. Romney credits Mowat with teaching the Privy Council the essential differences of Canadian constitutionalism: namely, that the provinces were not subordinate to the Dominion but 'its sovereign equals' (111); that provincial lieutenant-governors could exercise the prerogative powers of the Crown (e.g., appoint queen's counsel, pardon convicts and receive escheated estates). These are 'matters of little practical significance,' he adds, 'but ... vital as symbols of the provinces' sovereign status and constitutional equality to the Dominion' (111).

We disagree and, as we shall see, so does Romney ultimately, for these are not matters of little practical significance; on the contrary, they are hugely significant precisely because of their symbolic content. At issue in the struggle for provincial autonomy, led by Mowat and his Quebec counterpart, Honoré Mercier, was a shared view that the 1867 settlement had guaranteed that autonomy.

Both men knew that Canada had been created by the founding provinces. Confederation had emerged from an intercolonial agreement to form a federal government and devolve part of the provincial powers on it, while retaining the sovereignty that was inherent in internally self-governing colonies of the British empire. The imperial government was represented in Canada not by the governor-general alone but by the governor-general for federal purposes and the lieutenant-governors for provincial purposes. This fact symbolized the essential equality of the two orders of government. (137–8)

Second, that equality and the sovereignty of the provinces in turn rested upon a shared Upper- and Lower-Canadian Reformer perspective going back to the Constitutional Act of 1791, and in the latter case the Quebec Act of 1774, and forward to the compact theory of Confederation as a *pacte solennel* that had given French Lower Canada a permanent and legal guarantee of the preservation of its liberty, property, and civil culture, not just by the creation of a legislature but, in effect, the creation of 'a country belonging especially to its French-speaking inhabitants' (139). The difference, as Romney sees it, between the Lower-Canadian and Upper-Canadian Reformer sense of self-definition as 'a country belonging to its inhabitants' lies in its legal sourcing: in the case of Lower Canada, in international law and, in particular, the promises supposedly made by an imperial conqueror to a conquered people, and in the case of Upper-Canada, from the common law rights of British subjects. And this compact or treaty between peoples was further seen as constitutionally and legally binding upon the Imperial Parliament.

Now, as Romney also recognizes: 'All this talk of compacts may seem fanciful' (140). No British statesman ever said or wrote anything along these lines. Neither the texts of the Quebec Act nor the Constitutional Act spell any of this out in so many words. The situation parallels the long debates over the words of texts of the treaties signed by the Crown with First Peoples' oral and cosmological understanding of these compacts, a debate in which the Supreme Court of Canada recently recognized the validity of the latter (see 1997 3 *SCR*, *Delgamuukw* v. *British Columbia*). As Romney puts it of the 'compact' theory of Canada: 'It was nonetheless a valid conception of the relationship between Britain and the Canadian colonies. It was so because it expressed a *fundamental principle of civil society*: the rule of law' (140, emphasis added).

Obviously, there are a number of ways by which to understand the rule of law. In order not to wander too far afield, we will stick mainly with Romney's usage, which is basically the principle that the framework of legal rules by which we live our lives cannot be casually disrupted (see 140 ff). R.D. Winfield (1995), however, adds the complicating proviso that 'the rule of law will be fair *provided* the founders of the state are concerned with the *common good*' (4, emphases added). Both of these conditions are difficult to guarantee or define. Romney divides the principle of the rule of law into two aspects: in the case of ordinary laws, the requirement for due process in legislation and adjudication (and the attendant elaborate procedures); in the case of fundamental laws, the 'culture of restraint' of British constitutionalism in the exercise of political power, of which the idea of the rule of law is an expression, together with the system of unwritten conventions that inform the British constitution. He goes on to remark that, in the case of these fundamental laws, it is one thing to have a country's constitution left to the mercies of its own legislature, and another to leave it to the disposal of the legislature of another country. Ultimately, he argues *via negativa* that, for these reasons, the Canadian colonial legislatures would never have agreed to constitutional modifications that would have diminished the provinces' ability to control their cultural autonomy. He cites here the nineteenth-century Quebec jurist T.J.J. Loranger:

Why should the province of Quebec, for example, have, on an inauspicious day, with utter want of thought, abandoned its rights the most sacred, guaranteed by treaties and preserved by secular contests, and sacrificed its language, its institutions and its laws, to enter into an insane union, which, contracted under these conditions, would have been the cause of its national and political annihilation? *And why should the other provinces, any more than Quebec, have consented to lose their national existence and consummate this political suicide?* (cited 142–3, emphasis Romney's)

Now Romney's argument, interesting as it is, however, in our view, tables a set of problems that beg further questions namely, how then did the opposite (or centralizing) view of Confederation come to be that which prevailed in English Canada? We could blame historians like Creighton, jurists like F.R. Scott, the British, etc. – there is rarely a shortage of possible scoundrels.

Rather, it seems more important and more productive to us to return to probe further the key point concerning the relationship between civil society and the rule of law. If we turn by contrast to *Canada's Founding Debates*, a new collection of materials from sea to sea that importantly adds to previous collections, and is edited by Ajzenstat, Romney, Gentles, and Gairdner (1999), we find that the editors argue for a view of the Fathers as 'thinkers about politics – men consciously acting within a tradition of political thought' (1999: 1). We sympathize with their argument that the founding debates were serious ones.

[The founders] bring to the enterprise broad knowledge of law, history, political science, and modern political thought. They cite British, American, and French authorities; they study European constitutions and compare federal systems. They readily refer to the founding of the United States and to American constitutions ... [T]hey are clearly steeped in the thought of Thomas Hobbes, John Locke, Montesquieu, and Rousseau ... The debates represent political deliberation at a high level. (2)

And while this is no doubt the case, why do the editors then qualify their remarks? 'It is true that speakers sometimes fall back on very human and not always admirable emotions. They boast ...; they mock ...; they quibble and

equivocate. Some of them are very angry; some are confused' (2). But fair
enough; these are human beings, not angels, as James Madison fully recognized
in the scheme of governance he proposed for the United States. Given this,
given as well the editors' heavy thematic editing (and very useful notes) and the
general brevity of the excerpts they reproduce – few speeches (except for those
of the lead players: Macdonald, Tupper, Brown, Cartier, etc.) get more than a
few paragraphs – the net effect appears to be that it is the editors themselves
who have attempted to give the material a coherence it does not possess.
Canada's Founding Debates, in other words, are not *The Federalist Papers*,
and for good reason: the first are oral debates; the second are a brilliantly
crafted series of written texts. The Canadian debates may very well articulate
traditions of political thought; they do not do so, however, in a sustained
manner.

It is precisely the absence of those sustained traditions of argumentation that
preoccupy us in this study, and that are just beginning to manifest themselves in
this very period. There are, as it were, too many influences, too many differences to be reconciled, for such traditions to lastingly take hold. Significantly,
however, as Jan Swearingen observes, it is precisely at such periods of profound transition (e.g., potential democratization) that rhetoric emerges: 'Rhetoric can be understood as a replacement of one kind of opinion with another, in a
context of *new discourse structures and new modes of authority* where there
was as yet no weight of tradition to ground or check its substance' (1991: 68,
emphasis added). But the ensuing difficulties are major ones. Let us take an
example from *Canada's Founding Debates*. It is from the excerpt of D'Arcy
McGee, quoted earlier, in which he says that the provinces have had too much
liberty, and goes on to add that this is because there is 'not on the face of the
earth a freer people than the inhabitants of these colonies' (16). More important
– and this returns to the relationship of civil society to law – he goes on to state
that the problem is precisely one of the absence of a shared understanding of the
rule of law. 'It is necessary that there should be respect for the law, a high
central authority, the virtue of civil obedience, obeying the law for the law's
sake; even when a man's private conscience may convince him sufficiently that
the law in some cases may be wrong, he is not to set up his individual will
against the will of the country expressed through its recognized constitutional
organs. We need in these provinces ... a large infusion of authority' (16).

This is tantamount to asking what is the law, where is it located, and whose
law is it to be? In *Getting It Wrong*, Romney seems to answer unproblematically:
the law lies in civil society or the local community and extends outwards and
upwards from there into a compact. But McGee offers the countervision of an
Ür-Recht, a kind of Kantian categorical imperative that embodies the legal

'will of the nation' and from which derive the collective virtues of civil obedience that constitute civil society from above. The point – and the problem – is that Canada's history answers to such questions of the location of legality and civil society multivocally: 'All of the above.'

The problem, of course, is, as Richard D. Winfield remarks, that there is no question 'more central to legal philosophy than this: does legality fall exclusively within the scope of politics, or is there law in civil society?' (1995: 70). The dimensions of the conundrum are, briefly, as follows: to a great extent, much depends on the strength of the society's prepolitical institutions (e.g., the freedoms of property relations, morality, the family, and civil society itself) and where these are adequately preserved and consummated within the constitutional, and democratic, state. Even so, while this would seem at first glance to support Romney's line of argument, it does not resolve the question of where legality finally resides. For, as Winfield notes, although the law will have to conform to the pre-existing civil society, this suggests that legality lies elsewhere, notably in the state (see 1995: 68–70). In turn, this raises the problem of the relation of politics and legality, since 'politics cannot help but be preoccupied with legal affairs if law has any place in valid conduct' (69). But then does not legality itself risk becoming as a result essentially political, in that no aspect of law could be conceived or realized apart from political institutions? On the other hand, the 'just' state's rule over prepolitical institutions means that there have to be some legal institutions over which government does preside, but which, because it cannot simply take over property ownership, moral striving, the home, or the market, 'must fall within the only other field available, the universal community of interest of civil society as it extends beyond mere commodity relations' (69–70).

Can politics or political associations even be conceivable if legality does not have an antecedent in civil society, 'this one remaining prepolitical sphere in which it might have a home' (70)? And the final problem that arises here is that, if law's positing of right, in the end, is nonpolitical, this reflects the global (or potentially so) dimensions of civil society. In the end, the conception of legality within civil society effaces the legal authority within a particular state as well as the distinction between domestic and international law (Winfield, 98). This speaks to the radical implications of Romney's point about the legal differences between Upper- and Lower-Canadian aspirations to being countries, a difference that ceases to be one, if law resides in civil society.

We raise these questions, not in order to answer them (although Winfield's 1995 line of inquiry is a suggestive one), but in order to provide a better grasp of their complexity. For these are not problems that would be settled easily, and in this sense Ajzenstat et al. are quite right in arguing for the seriousness of the questions underlying the Confederation debates, the questions that the Canadian 'founders' were attempting to answer. But these were also, as we will see in the following chapter, the very questions that faced the British over how to administer justice in the newly acquired former New France, not only for the British but for the 'new subjects' as well.

The Promises of Legal History for Canadian Historiography

The historians we have considered so far, amateurs as well as professional academics, all draw attention to the problem of complexity, especially as it involved the intellectual division of labour. This is a time of increasingly narrow specialization and heightened professionalization. Thus we have an intensified production of historical knowledge with the resulting delays in reviewing publications and disseminating results, paradoxically combined with a broadened, mass-mediated, global, and near-instantaneous dissemination of rapidly circulating but superficial information, the 'economy' of knowledge, so to speak. Some say this has also become increasingly knowledge-based and capable of generating entirely new social formations, the so-called knowledge-based, or information, society. As a result, issues of literacy, education, and curriculum reform – in particular, regarding the introduction of new information technologies in the classroom, the growing gap between the information rich and the information poor, etc. – have become topics of public concern and of controversial policies at all levels of governance. In such a context of accelerated transformation affecting 'knowledge,' it may well be that the fissures in the old economy of knowledge, already prefigured in discussions in the 1950s over the growing split between 'scientific' and 'humanistic' cultures, have since become so broad that the hopes of mere historians (i.e., one professional grouping out of many thousands of 'knowledge' workers) for maintaining a monopoly on knowledge outside the immediate professional enclave that they might one have held, or imagined they did, is simply a pipe-dream. Never mind historians; the very category of what was once termed 'intellectuals' may also have become so fragmented as to have lost whatever relevance it might once have had in the capacity to table general topics of broad public discussion (see, e.g., Gouldner 1979; Jacoby 1987; Robbins 1993), a capacity by and large now widely assumed to have been taken over by the mass media.

In such a light, then, the debates among Canadian historians surely seem to have taken place, in Doug Owram's phrase, in 'narrow circles.' However, as McGill historian Desmond Morton recently reported, at the end of January 1999: 'Montreal saw the biggest conference ever on the teaching and learning of history in Canada' ('How Should Canadians Learn Their History? *Conflu-*

ences 1:1, April/May 1999, 6). Gathered together in part in response to books such as Granatstein's, the widely-attended conference, Morton noted, was, if nothing else, at least, 'proof that Canadian history is a lively-looking corpse.' So whether dead, cleverly embalmed, or on the contrary alive and well, there still appears to be sufficient continuing discussion of Canadian history, by the professionals and the amateurs, to warrant some further discussion.

Returning to Owram's point above that there may be, in fact, more commonalities to Canadian history than not (such as 'a common historical experience of considerable duration ... common laws, social programs, and ... cultural and social ties that have national as well as local characteristics' [1997: 18]), we turn to some aspects of these commonalities, in particular as they regard the development of the study of Canadian legal history over the past two decades.

Rather than succumbing to the call for a new grand synthesis of Canadian history, we argue that 'law' is surely one of the great commonalities of social organization: in Habermas's view (1996), it is the central, remaining site of interface between the lifeworld in which we dwell existentially and the highly technical 'steering systems' that regulate lifeworlds in complex societies. Law is, in other words, one of the principal communicative channels by which societies organize the continuing contact between ordinary lives and systems of regulation which, if these were totally severed, would reanimate such dire prognoses as Adorno's notion of the 'totally administered life' (Adorno [1951] 1974).

As we shall see in the next chapter, the processes of establishing communicative commonality in the case of Canadian law have been especially difficult. Translations, both literally and figuratively, must occur as part of the transfer of European legal systems to the different environment of the New World. Then the linguistic and conceptual difficulties of effecting the translation between the French pre- and postrevolutionary civil law tradition and the English common law tradition must be addressed – a set of protocols that socio-linguists term 'code-switching.' Last we must consider the resulting cultural ambilingualism, as opposed to the more traditional and official conception of bilingualism, that pertains both to the governance and legal regimens of the Canadian federation. Ambilingualism here is to be understood not in the sense of ambidexterity but, on the contrary, as its complete opposite: as a deeply embedded sense of ambivalence as regards the forms of belongingness ('Who are we?' 'What are we?' or 'Where is here?' in Northrop Frye's famed question about the Canadian literary imagination).

This ambivalent world view came especially into the foreground as legal historians, in English Canada in particular, began, in the 1980s, to seriously examine Canada's legal history. In one of the first attempts at mapping out the contours of Canadian legal culture, Graham Parker drew heavily upon the model of intellectual colonialism so influential in Underhill (see Parker 1986). For Parker, Canada's legal culture was so deeply marked by 'the colonial mentality' (4) and 'the cultural cringe' (18), that it was an exaggeration to describe the Canadian obsession with law and order as a legal culture; rather, it was instead 'a smug, self-righteous criticism of the dynamic, violent, and lawless republic to the south' (12). Born not of revolution but accommodation, Canada was an 'unimportant' colony (and would maintain that status well into the twentieth century), populated not by successful rebels but by 'defeated peoples' (10) – a 'remnant society' of 'stoic north-minded people' dominated by an economy of staples and natural resources extracted by a 'few giant organizations ... and the government [who] have kept the country in the thraldom of a feudalism of complacency' (10–11). This 'strange brand of Toryism' had authorized overly high degrees of government interference in people's lives; 'a clear preference for order and authority ... over freedom and liberty'; the (ab)use of the constitution 'as an administrative device'; and 'an exaggerated reverence in private law and its institutions for English legal ... precedents' (11); a legal culture, in short, marked by inferior high Tory judges determined to preserve the status quo at any cost, thus heavily favouring discretionary justice and the thorough permeation of a legal philosophy emphasizing social control (25). All this, Parker argued, was not merely symptomatic of either party politics or crude reaction. It was, above all, an effect of 'the external influences on the country [that] have always exceeded the power of its own past' (27), and to such an extent that Canadian legal scholars 'do not have a ... clear concept of Canadian law as distinct from English or American models. We need to do some basic work in Canadian legal history and historiography' (28).

Some of that 'basic work' was already in print by the time Louis Knafla's collection, in which Parker's article appeared, saw publication. As editor David Flaherty remarked in the first volume of a continuing series of essays in the history of Canadian law, the various 'grand hypotheses' advanced by twentieth-century Canadian historians from the 1930s through the 1970s to explain the origins of Canada had 'essentially ignore[d] the legal dimension' (1981: 9). (While highly significant, this was not unique to Canada: the same could be said of the lack of impact of U.S. legal history, up to a slightly earlier time, on American historical scholarship in general, with the exception of the work of Willard Hurst and Daniel Boorstin as of the early 1950s.) In Canada, Flaherty goes on, aside from early twentieth-century constitutional historians such as Chester Martin and W.P.M. Kennedy, 'the role of law and the legal system in Canadian development seems either to have been entirely ignored or treated simply as a pale reflection of what the dominant commercial elites wanted' (9–10). If the major Canadian historians had merely treated the legal system as a second-order and passive set of phenomena, legal historians, by stressing instead that law was both instrumental and dynamic in historical development, surely had their work cut out for them – especially 'given the well-known deference in this country to peace, order and good government' (10).

For Flaherty, a more comprehensive approach to Canadian legal history meant that it had to be highly comparative. As for Parker but with greater nuance, the most outstanding trait of Canadian legal history for Flaherty was that it functioned 'under a heavy weight of external influence, whether *de facto* or *de jure*' (10). This has been evidenced in the dominating influences of both the jurisprudence and the legal practices of France, Britain, and the United States; in the subordination of the Supreme Court of Canada to the British Privy Council until the late 1940s; in the doctrine of *stare decisis*, which cloaked innovative decisions in adherence to precedent; in the lack of explicitness of rationale in judicial decisions that made legal interpretation 'a sensitive enter-prise' (10), and so on.

Some of the consequences of the stifling weight of external influences have depended, of course, on the time period and area of law in question. If we focus here on nineteenth-century Ontario in particular, as R.C.B. Risk and others have done, we find that, in Risk's words, 'the organization and structure of law and most of the terms of doctrine were substantially the same in Ontario and the United States' (cited in Flaherty, 11). As Blaine Baker has found (1985), Upper Canadian (i.e., Ontario) legal thought in the late Victorian period was predomi-nantly part of a North American legal culture, the result of 'the richness and diversity of the particular processes by which European law and custom were transplanted to this side of the Atlantic' (219) in myriad, complex networks of 'cultural cross-effects' (Saul), or what we term processes of translation. A second consequence of all this criss-crossing was a kind of legal 'three-card Monte': what, then, was distinctive about Upper Canadian legal thought? Baker reverts, in part, to an iceberg metaphor (222–3), in which the 'deep structures' remained largely hidden from view, the major premises unarticulated or contained in 'invisible discourse[s]' (222). Paradoxically as well, the 'dis-tinctiveness' of Upper Canadian legal culture often hid itself defensively in 'imperial legal symbolism' (219), a paradox also discernible in recent Ameri-can legal scholarship on the colonial period (see Baker, 220 n3). A further effect, as Baker also notes, is that 'Ontario's contemporary legal culture is more than a little elusive' (221), and its primary discernible quality is its 'advancing presentism or ahistoricism.'

If the processes of cultural cross-effects or translation in Quebec had led to a 'patchwork interface of *ancien régime* French provincial law and English commercial and public law in Canada East' ... 'the inaccessible and uncertain quality of the laws of Canada West was as acute' (227). As Baker insists, nineteenth-century Canadian legal culture is terra incognita (233), in which, citing Richard Risk, cases and doctrine 'seem utterly divorced from any context in space and time ... Apart from discussions about the constitution ... law was virtually not discussed or thought about' (in Baker, 233).

This vacuum, or perhaps more accurately remoteness, and the resulting inability to respond to particular questions dealing with intellectual influences on the development of Canadian jurisprudence, leads Flaherty in his 1981 essay to comment on the striking absence, in comparison with the U.S. of distinguished legal scholars like Joseph Story or James Kent in the early nineteenth century, as well as the absence of anything comparable to the American sociological movement in law of the late nineteenth century. He notes, for example, that in 1920 in Canada there were only six full-time professors of law in a total of five Canadian law schools (15). As Risk hypothesized, the consequences would be a legal culture 'express[ing] attitudes and values within narrow limits,' characterized by highly 'technical reasoning ... that [did not] have a major impact on society,' and little used as instruments 'to focus [on] and make apparent [the] problems ... of relatively powerless groups' (in Flaherty, 18). Focusing upon Upper Canada as a case study, Flaherty observes that the courts were particularly used 'as instruments for elite control' (20), especially before 1860; that judges long remained an arm of the executive; that the social philosophy of the elite was deeply conservative, and yet tolerated a degree of government intervention in public enterprise that would have been unthinkable in, say, Hurst's studies of Wisconsin's legal culture (32). And yet, as Flaherty remarks, there is still 'too much groping in the dark' (33); on one page alone, he lists some thirteenth research questions still to be explored, not the least of which being the influence on law and legal institutions 'of life in the Old Province of Quebec,' and other regional variations throughout the rest of Canada.

And this was the picture, or the outline of it, in the early 1980s. A decade and a half later, as Jim Phillips notes in a 1997 review article on recent publications in Canadian legal history, some thirty volumes of historical research had seen publication, including the first volume of Murray Greenwood and Barry Wright's monumental series of Canadian state trials (1996). Noting the major shift in recent decades from the earlier 'lawyer's legal history' (237) to the socio-legal history that now 'overshadows' the field, Phillips mentions recent work on the social history of crime and punishment, on labour law, on women's legal history, and on race (237). Focusing specifically on nine recent studies, he has high praise for Brian Young's *Politics of Codification* (1994), 'one of the best books yet produced in ... Canadian legal history' (247). He is not, however, as thoroughly pleased with the others, particularly those attempting a general legal history of Canada, such as Wesley Pue and DeLloyd Guth's 'Canada's Legal Inheritances' (1996). If one can conclude anything, according to Phillips, it is that 'Canada has many legal histories' (253), in which the role of law and legal institutions varied in different regions and at different times, and was 'funda-mentally determined' by local conditions (253). On one level, this may not seem like much; on the other hand, given the emphasis in Parker or early Flaherty on the overdetermining role of external influences, this is undoubtedly the reflection of a major shift in the loci of emphasis. Still, for Phillips, one of the major problems is that Canadian legal history is mainly taught only in law schools 'and does not seem to have inserted itself into the list of categories into which we ... divide our history' (257).

So we find ourselves back again with the generalities of Canadian history, or do we? We would argue that we have not come back full circle, but have instead come to a fresh starting point, one that has recognized many of the problems of the general interpretations of Canadian history, and that recognizes too that historiographical issues go hand-in-hand with the continuous processes of the rewriting of history – which is at it should be. But rather than proferring yet another general interpretation, we would argue that the neglect of legal history, until the early 1980s, left out of the study of Canadian history highly significant dimensions for understanding the formation of this country's civil culture, dimensions that if still by and large confined to law schools or departments of law, have now begun to flow back into the larger historical field. This is happening not only in Canada but, as we have suggested above, it is part of the transitions to the globalization of law. A word of caution is nonetheless called for. If some work by some historians has made significant headway in making up for decades of earlier neglect, that work tends to remain confined to certain research centres. One thinks here of the pioneering work of the Montreal History Group on the imbrications of class, gender, and law in eighteenth- and nineteenth-century Quebec (see, for example, Fyson 1993, 1999). On the other hand, among law professors struggling to bring critical cultural-legal studies out of the confines of law schools, Rosemary J. Coombe, for instance, in a recent survey article on the existence of a cultural studies of law, sounds a more pessimistic note (see Coombe 2001). While she recognizes that over the past two decades, there has been a proliferation of legal studies that borrow from the methods and approaches of the humanities and have focused self-consciously on the textualities of the law, she finds that 'no substantial body of work demonstrating the methodological commitments, theoretical premises, and political convictions that characterizes the interdisciplinary field of cultural studies has yet appeared with respect to law' (1).

Yet, even if still largely conducted either in law schools or in the pages of legal journals more than within the historians' profession as a whole, contemporary legal-historical scholarship has nevertheless brought back into the equation elements of understanding of fundamental import as to how social institutions 'communicate' not only between themselves but with citizens, and what this latter term implies in terms of the capacity of citizens not only to talk back, but to grasp the importance of their own place in the communicative process. Further, we must remember, turning back to the Canadian case, how little we still know about the civil culture of this country. Some enthusiasts have found in Canada's weakness as a national state, the always contingent condition of a sense of national identity, and, as a corollary of this, the pliability of Canadian law, evidence in Canadian legal discourse for a postmodern acceptance of plural identities, the protection of emergent social identities, and the promotion of a politics of dialogue across a range of identities; others remind us to be wary of such optimism, in part precisely because of the ambivalance of Canada's legal culture, its profound ambilingualism. As Barry Wright has recently remarked in this vein, based on his ongoing study of Canadian state trials: 'Canada's fragmented national identity ... has never hindered wide resort' to a sustained, historical capacity for repressive actions (1998: 232–4). 'Far from accommodating diverse identities, Canada has a long historical record of repressive measures' against aboriginal populations, the Acadians, and immigrant populations from non-loyalist Americans in the last century to Asian and Caribbean immigrants in this century (233–4). As Wright notes, under the rubric of repression, in addition to recurring reactionary anxieties, an intolerance of dissent and the persistent influence of the executive over government and the administration of justice, these measures have also included 'exploiting the language of British justice, constitutional liberties and the rule of law' – in short, of displaying 'a comparatively vast record of repression' (234). The resulting repressive matrix persisted well into the late twentieth century, in which 'British subject status rooted in pre-modern concepts of allegiance and the social dimensions of citizenship were imperfectly formed ... [by] a dominant political culture with an emphasis on "peace, order and good government and deference to authority"' (234). It thus seems to us that in tabling these issues for historical debate, research, and reconsideration, contemporary legal-historical and critical scholarship has rendered a signal contribution to self-understanding, and in particular (and more so than outrightly repressive acts) to the rather more subtle and complex role that the law has played, not only as an instrument in the above, but in configuring a socio-cultural imaginary of presentism, ahistoricism, invisible discourses, and silent networks of cultural cross-effects that requires to be better understood. This we attempt to do in some detail in the chapter that follows, as we examine the problems posed by the transition and translation to the new British legal regime that followed the cession of Canada to England.

3

The Legitimacy of Conquest:
Issues in the Transition of Legal Regimes,
1760s–1840s

Vous aurez la liberté de porter vous-même le remède à vos maux, mais nous vous interdirons tout moyen de les connoître.

Pierre Bédard, journalist (1808)[1]

Ambilingualism in the Law

In his thoughtful collection of essays, *Justice as Translation*, James Boyd White, one of the leading American scholars of the legal imagination, makes the argument that at the heart of law (and justice) is what he terms 'translation.' This is not the 'transportation' of a certain view of meaning from one place to another 'like an object that can be picked up' (1990: 234), but rather a complex process of the interpretation of texts' meanings from one cultural environment to its interpretive reproduction in another, and the difficulties that this process entails. Very apropos to our concerns is that Boyd White, in his essay 'Translation, Interpretation and Law' (229–56), fastens upon a Canadian illustration of what he is writing about. At the height of the Royal Commission on Bilingualism and Biculturalism's massive effort to spell out the implications for both governance and lifeworld of living in an officially bilingual country, the Commission struck a number of studies, one of which was written by Montreal lawyer Claude-Armand Sheppard entitled *The Law of Languages in Canada* (1971). As Boyd White remarks, it is one thing to proclaim that the languages of the law are theoretically of equal status, 'but how does this work out in practice?' (241). Are they to be drafted in one language and then translated into the other? Are they to be simultaneously drafted in both languages? And how is this supposed to be actually carried out?

He notes that the established practice had been to draft all national legislation in English first, and then translate it into French. The import of Sheppard's study is to show that this practice 'operates on a set of false assumptions not only about translation but also about the process of statutory drafting' (241). The result – in fact but not in practice – is a profound clash of cultures that is completely ignored by the literal process of translation. In Sheppard's words: 'Anyone who has examined the French text of any federal statute, even in the most perfunctory manner, has become painfully aware not so much of grammatical errors as of the totally non-Latin and non-idiomatic use of language. In fact, the French text is frequently almost incomprehensible to a French lawyer' (cited in Boyd White, 242). Sheppard goes on to explain further that the development of ideas in French and in English relies on different mentalities, turns of mind, and methods. 'Unless the two languages have a common genius and the intellectual processes of both ... are identical, any attempt at translation is vain if it is not preceded by a complete dissimilation of the legal idea to be transplanted' (cited, 242). What should emerge – but does not – is 'a new concept of the law' that would take differences into account, and effectuate a new legal synthesis.

In Boyd White's view, the alternatives are 'a mindless literalism' as against an act of translation-interpretation that requires the kind of imagination 'implied in the making of any real text' (243). This represents 'a genuine ethical and intellectual difficulty,' one calling for 'the creation of *a whole new idea of law*, a culture in the space between cultures, resulting less in a "translation" from English to French than in the invention of a new language, a new world' (243–4, emphasis added). The Canadian context, however, concretizes these difficulties in particularly poignant ways, constituting a civil culture at the centre of which are constantly resedimented replays of the spaces *between* cultures, repeating over and over the problems of the contact between European law and aboriginal societies, the problems of the transition from French law to British law, and the problems, in turn, of the adaptation of the local environment in the synthetic emergence of Canadian law – problems which, as we just saw, have led not to the best, but to the worst of both worlds. Replete with grammatical errors, cultural incomprehension, nearly meaningless literalisms, unexamined and ill-understood assumptions, unacknowledged networks of cultural cross-effects, this vast iceberg of the transmission of meaning forms the little-known entity collectively subsumed under the rubric of 'the law,' and has been more or less completely ignored by Canadian historians until only recently. At one end of the resulting scale of possibilities is the 'whole new idea of law' that Boyd White and others, such as de Sousa Santos, see as the horizon of the future of law and legal studies. At the other end is the particular case of Canadian civil culture as a poisonous tangle of mutual recrimination, as

J.R. Saul sees it, or, as one still replete with postmodern possibilities of dialogue across the spaces between Canada's constitutive cultures. In the present chapter, we turn in some detail to the concrete problems posed by the change from one style of administration of justice to another as this was experienced in Canada in the late eighteenth century.

Hermeneutics of 'the Conquest'

To an unusual degree, the historiography – and, indeed, the civil culture – of Quebec still bears the scars, some 240 years after the event, of the military capture of New France in 1759–60 that would be formalized in the Treaty of Paris (1763) and the subsequent handover of the French empire in North America to British administration. The clerico-nationalist perspective associated with the work of *chanoine* Lionel Groulx (1878–1967) represented the apogee of a hegemonic interpretation that predominated for approximately the century between the 1840s and the 1940s – namely, that the founding of New France and the subsequent survival of Quebec's distinctive culture, laws, language, and religion were evidence of providential intervention in human affairs. From a secular perspective, this offers a caricatural illustration of a problem of historical explanation that continues to resonate into the present. How can a series of events that occurred over two centuries ago take on such lasting proportions when they affected at most a total population at the time of some 70,000 people? Indeed whether 'the people' were implicated at all remains a point of historiographical contention (see Hamilton 1988: 28). Furthermore, the events of the period are not known to have been accompanied by the excessive brutality, massive acts of cruelty, deportations, and sanguinary reprisals that can be found in other contexts of military conquest elsewhere, or at later moments in Canadian history.[2] The question raises all the problems that have preoccupied subsequent Quebec and Canadian historians (to maintain our focus on this particular category of analyst). In other words, it focalizes these as cultural problems, that is, as questions, above all, of a constant emphasis on interpretation – but which interpretations and by whom, beginning with the very name given the period itself.

To call these events, as historiography traditionally has, 'the Conquest,' immediately introduces highly resonant connotations of winners, losers, and defeat. To give one recent example, the late sociologist Fernand Dumont in *Genèse de la société québécoise* (1993), in a paragraph heavily loaded with interpretive freight, as well as a strange periodization, writes: 'Depuis les origines de la Confédération, nous avons vécu une espèce de double nationalité, canadienne et québécoise; la dualité est devenue aiguë, au point de départager des citoyens entre ces allégeances' (13). He goes on to add that, behind these constitutional conflicts, 'se creuse une blessure profonde.' In the next sentence, he offers an explanation of the source of this profound wound: 'Depuis la Conquête, il n'y a pas seulement au Québec des Français et des Anglais, mais deux sociétés juxtaposées, avec leurs institutions respectives, deux références collectives qui ne sont pas arrivées à se réconcilier' (13).[3] If we take his analysis seriously, what seems to be, at one level, a problem of a double nationality and differing modes of constitutional interpretation since Confederation (an argument that has some plausibility) is in fact more than that for it is preceded by the existence of a deeper wound occasioned by the Conquest, (also a claim not without plausibility, although calling for further explication). But this wound is of a odder sort still, for it is a hermeneutical wound, a stigmata, as it were, of the interpretive faculties: less perhaps because the Conquest consciously inflicted the violence resulting from a disparity of power but, rather, because the series of events subsumed under the term 'the Conquest' was instead an interpretive misrecognition (and, as a result, a misnomer) of the fact of the sudden bringing together of two separate, already completely formed 'societies,' each with its own institutions, and each with its own respective frames of collective reference.

Now, this is a much more interesting hypothesis, but before examining it further, we should also be clear as to what it entails as a set of claims. Above all, it clarifies that the nature of the Conquest was of a particular kind, namely, the kind that English common law distinguishes between 'settled' and 'conquered' colonies (see Cote 1977). This, however, is a somewhat misleading distinction since the actual meanings are the opposite of what the words seem to suggest. Examples of conquered colonies include the Cape Colony, conquered from the Dutch; Quebec, captured from the French; but also the Indian subcontinent. In Cote's words, 'conquered colonies are territories which had a civilized government and system of laws at the time of British settlement.' Here, 'the rule has been to leave as much of the existing law in force in such areas as possible ... with the exception of constitutional laws or particularly barbaric laws' (Cote, 36). By contrast, a 'settled colony' is 'a largely uninhabited and unorganized territory settled by British subjects ... deem[ed] ... to have brought English law with them on the foundation of the colony,' examples being the Australian colonies and some West Indian colonies (Cote, 35).

In the light of such distinctions, New France was thus 'a territory with a civilized government and a system of laws,' which lends support to Dumont's claim that the colony already constituted a society with its own institutions and collective cultural references. At the same time, however, this also raises the problem of how to understand the latter, and in particular the system of laws of

New France. If the former dimensions of the problem persist into the present (in the ongoing debates concerning the extent of Quebec's 'distinctiveness'), the latter dimensions rapidly became a matter of intense preoccupation, not only for the local British administration but also for the Imperial Parliament, and as well for those representatives of the old regime who elected not to return to France and remained as participants in the colony's transition from the French regime to that of England. In short, the issues would entail the problems of the transition of legal regimes and the resulting instabilities of the next seventy years, and longer. Evelyn Kolish summarizes the complexity and unprecedented aspects of what would be a major social experiment:

The decision of the British government to restore Canadian private law in the Quebec Act in 1774 would launch an unprecedented experiment in the more general experience of the transfer of European legal systems to the new world. A body of law developed within the framework of the continental civil law tradition was to be administred by judges trained in the Common Law within a judicial framework modelled on Westminster. Such an ambitious project would in itself have been difficult enough, since the normal process of feed-back between the colonial legal system and its European 'parent' had been completely disrupted. However, in addition, British legislators had failed to appreciate the need for a precise definition of what constituted 'Canadian law,' leaving the unravelling of this Gordian knot to the colonial judges and legislators. (Kolish 1987: 324–5)

The preceding discussion, then, helps to reduce some of the emotivity carried by the term 'the Conquest,' and explains why contemporary historians have often turned instead to the more accurate use of the term 'the cession' as a name for this period. Rather than emphasizing the connotations of defeat, this also allows us to better situate our object of analysis more specifically within the general experiment of the transfer of European legal institutions to the new world. It further brings into focus a related issue raised by Dumont (as well as other Quebec sociologists of his generation; see for example, Dumont & Martin 1963), namely, to what extent did the society of New France, in fact, constitute a pre-existing 'totality' prior to the cession to British rule?

Issues in the Historiography of New France

Louis Hartz, in his well-known *The Founding of New Societies* (1964), had argued that the loss for former colonies of the umbilical connection to the metropole, whether the Thirteen Colonies vis-à-vis Britain, New France vis-à-vis France, or Australia also vis-à-vis Britain, meant that the developmental trajectory of the colonies would of necessity be vitiated, in substituting a fragmentary developmental basis for what had formerly been a more 'organic' unity. Hartz's thesis, for all its problems and exceptions, remains nonetheless of some pertinence, and particularly so in the context of a change in the framework of legal systems. As of 1663, after the colonization failures of the great mercantile companies, New France was formally incorporated into the system of royal government radiating from Versailles: for roughly the next century, it became an integral part of France, as much as, say, Orléans or Champagne.

At least, in theory. And in theory it was subject to the various and multiple codifications of French law (e.g., the 'Code Marchand,' the 'Coutume de Paris,' etc.) then prevalent in parts of France. But France itself was still an unstable, evolving entity (and would become even more so throughout the eighteenth century). As the work of historical geographer Edward Fox (1971) and Genovese and Hochberg (1989) has shown, there were at least two 'Frances' in contention, a contest that would continue to influence French institutional forms well into the twentieth century: 1) a centralized, land-based, peasant-supported France of heavy taxation and standing armies, and 2) a coastal France, from Normandy to Bordeaux, of maritime trade and parliamentary government. It had been precisely from the latter area that the navigators and sailors who 'discovered' New France had come, and, indeed, variants of these conflicting 'groundings' of settlement in the tension between the mobility of trade favoured by merchants and the fixity of entailment to the land favoured by landlords and rulers repeated themselves throughout the North Atlantic world of the seventeenth century (see, e.g., Davies 1974; Steele 1986).

New France, however much it may have become integrated into the system of royal government, was nonetheless a colony. However much Versailles (or Colbert) wanted to make it just another part of France, between the theory of royal government and established colonial practices there were substantial discrepancies. As Frontenac discovered in 1672, for instance, when he attempted to recreate in the colony an order of estates similar to that of the metropole: 'You ... should very rarely, or to speak correctly, never, give a corporate form to the inhabitants of Canada ... for it is well that each should speak for himself and no one for all.' Colbert rebuked him (cited in Diamond 1967: 86; see also Archives Nationales, Série F, folio 121 [1673]). Not only was the colony not to develop corporate forms, such as the estates of 'ancient usage,' but 'it is the part of prudence to prevent in ... the growing state of Canada all those vexatious revolutions which might render it monarchical, aristocratic, or democratic ... and give rise to such a dismemberment as France suffered by the creation of such sovereignties within the Kingdom as Soissons, Orléans, Champagne, and others' (cited in Diamond, 90). The 'feudalism' that the royal government would attempt to transplant to New France was thus of an experimental sort, stripped of the encumbrances produced on the European mainland by a long history of medieval custom and local sovereignties: a modernized, rationalized version of feudalism, as it were. As Sigmund Diamond has described it, in an often reprinted essay:

What, above all, characterizes the plan [to adapt existing institutions to frontier settlement] is that it bore so clearly the stamp of that passion for rationality ... which is the hallmark of bureaucratic endeavor. It would be anachronistic and yet truthful to describe the objective of the French authorities in Canada after 1663, not as the creation of a society to be governed by political means, but as the creation of an administrative system in which persons would have fixed positions in a table of organization ... and would be manipulated, deployed, and disciplined by measures more compatible with the requirements of a formal organization than of a society. (Diamond, 84)

The irony is that, despite the rigidity of the model of a formal organization of peace, order, and 'good police,' France created instead in New France, in Diamond's words, 'a social basis for disobediance, a society in which deviance became the only means of survival' (96).

The point being raised here – and it is Hamilton's key point (1988: 42–3, 110–11) – is not only that a lack of appropriate comparative attention has framed the historiography of New France, but that, more attention must be paid to the extent to which the writing of history has been implicated with political agendas. Thus, in her view, much of the historiography of New France, particularly that written in English, would be overdetermined by invidious comparison to the experience of either England or the Thirteen Colonies and, in the French language, by 'the particular and distorting shadow' (110) of post-Conquest historiography's various attempts to explain away the taint of the 'defeat' of 1760 (from the workings of Providence to the inadequate basis for 'normal' capitalist development). For Hamilton, as for Dumont above, what is fundamentally at issue was the clash of 'two very different societies.' In fact, the Conquest did not represent just another in a long line of defeats in French state-building; it was instead the takeover, for only the second time in history, of a 'feudal' (or precapitalist) society by a capitalist one. The first such event, and the model for all subsequent English colonizations, was the English conquest of Ireland (see Pawlisch 1985).[4] Given the crucial role that law comes to play in the transition, 'the history of statemaking in Canada,' Hamilton writes, 'from the Conquest to the most recent constitutional crisis has been, in large part, the history of how ... *British liberties have been manipulated* in a way that ensured that the French would never have the required majority to be able to impose their political will on the English' (111, emphasis added). In other words, the clash of these two very different societies came to focus centrally on a clash between conceptions of, and the manipulation of, 'the law.'

Information, Communication, Translation

This brief look at some of the historiographical issues over the social organization of New France thus serves to highlight the fact that we are concerned with the interactions between two 'very different' societies. And specifically how debates over 'the laws' became the transformer or connector between systems and lifeworlds, a central conduit for informational or communicative interaction. In this light, we turn to the model of the social organization of New France first proposed by Gilles Paquet and Jean-Pierre Wallot (1974). Highly influenced by the structuralist analyses of the time, Paquet and Wallot present a grid of analysis of New France in the context of the cession as an intersection of informational networks. As with a number of other analysts, they share the view that the 'culture' of post-Conquest New France, or what became, under British administration, Lower Canada, was (and would continue to be) characterized by what they term a *malaise diffus* (510), an equivalent to what historian Serge Gagnon has called 'the pathological character of its [Quebec's] collective memory' (1978: 27, our translation) – in short, the 'trauma' of the Conquest and the resulting series of subordinations (military, economic, demographic, political, and cultural) to which francophone Lower-Canadians would be subjected with the change of administrations. Largely, although not exclusively, as a result of the major structural changes occasioned by the former New France's insertion into the architecture of the British Empire, Lower Canada by the beginning of the nineteenth century is described by Paquet and Wallot as forming a desynchronized, socio-material system of internal blockages (510), a fundamental structural distortion that, they argue, illuminates the subsequent practices of the various social groups that are the object of their analysis. If their study is consistent with many others (e.g., Creighton, Faucher, Ouellet, Dubuc) in emphasizing the analytical primacy of material (socio-economic) factors, Paquet and Wallot innovate by their insistence on privileging 'the informational aspects' of social phenomena (see 1974: 514–15). For them, social exchange, or in Durkheimian language 'a social fact,' is significantly to be understood in its informational or communicative (515) dimensions. In other words, social exchange is not solely or simply a matter of establishing subordination over others, but also includes a broad range of intangibles such as the bonds of, for instance, friendship. At the heart of social exchange, they insist, is a principle of communicative uncertainty that gives rise to such phenomena as 'false consciousness' or 'ideology' as instruments of the simplification of more complex social transactions, but also and at the same time as 'an instrument of *publicity* for certain social goods' (517 and emphasis added).

To the extent, as we saw with Evelyn Kolish's remarks above about the new administration and in particular its agents in London and in the Imperial Parliament leaving considerable latitude or, if one prefers, communicative uncertainty, to the discretion of local administrators and judges to define what might constitute 'Canadian law,' colonial relations within the new order were characterized by a high degree of ambiguity, and legal documents, such as the Quebec Act (1774) or the Constitutional Act of 1791, offer considerable grey zones of interpretation. The latter, for instance, as Henri Brun (1970) has suggestively argued, contained embryonic elements of a dual conception of sovereignty: the primary sovereignty of the metropole in the person of the governor (or Crown), but also the subordinated sovereignty of the colonial collectivity via its new representative organs (the legislative assembly). To the extent (as Paquet and Wallot, following Brun, remark) that the 1791 Constitutional Act 'only vaguely' defined the functions of the colonial legislature, this left 'to experience alone the development of modes of social interaction and collaboration ... thus abandoning the new rules of the political game to largely customary forms of explanation' (521).[5] Within the constraints of the new imperial structures, which would include not only London's effective deployment of imperial sovereignty but also what Paquet and Wallot nicely term 'the costs of transethnic communication' (521), a subsystem of Lower Canadian politics established itself experimentally in which the language and practices of local politics rapidly became the privileged site for the deliberation, the expression, and the attempted resolution of the principal social antagonisms and conflicts; in short, sites of rhetorical experimentation. This produced, in their words, not 'apriori domination or univocal or simple forms of domination, but rather [domination as] a privileged channel of access' (523) by which political debates served as the surface for the competition between communicational networks of social groups over the terms of their *dominium*. Thus, the debates that would ensue over the control of political power 'reverberate[d] throughout the civil society as a whole' (562). Paquet and Wallot identify a multilevel conjunction of conflicts (constitutional, social, ethnic, and economic – although, curiously, they here leave out communicational) whose articulation through different social networks, they argue, constituted 'la spécificité bas-canadienne.' This, they stress, produced a distorted global system whose 'malaise' is systemic because it is a society where self-expression was blocked horizontally and dephased vertically: a society of discord, social duopoly, equilibria conflicts, blockage, and stalemate (see 564). Paquet and Wallot, then, introduce into the discussion crucial categories (such as those of information, networks, and publicity) that previous analysts had largely left out. At the same time, although their paper does introduce such notions as 'transethnic communication costs,' the model of political power they end up with is, if more complex, ultimately not that different from the (largely socio-economic) analyses they criticize (e.g., Creighton, Dubuc). But they at least opened pathways of analysis that can be fruitfully pursued further.

If we take the view, as a result, that the social organization of New France, however else it might be characterized, up to the period of the cession, formed a complex of informational networks both within the colony and back and forth to France – a central one, of course, being the St Lawrence River on which were carried people and goods, as well as the many communications between government officials, religious orders, and the like – the Conquest and subsequent cession represented, from an informational perspective, not only a massive disruption in the colony's networks of communication, but furthermore the superimposition of an entirely new system of communication, that of the British military and imperial administration – and in a new language as well.

Pierre Legendre in his history of French administration (1968) uses the concept of *projection coloniale* as a framework for the discussion of French colonial administrative theories and practices, particularly in the nineteenth century. He emphasizes that what was at issue was something more than a mode of territorial organization, it was a 'moral' project characterized, on the one hand, by the complete assimilation of the colonies to metropolitan control, in which 'the law' emanated from the metropolis by means of written codifications and, on the other, by a *mise en condition* or programming of the indigenous populations, especially through education (religious or secular), to inculcate in them a taste for the competitive race for social position (158, 186). As well, Legendre makes a fundamental distinction between two types of French colonization: that of the ancien régime, and that of the industrial era of the nineteenth century (195). His study is more concerned with the latter, stressing that the French attempt to colonize North America was a failure, largely for demographic reasons and because of the disinterest of metropolitan public opinion. If, at one level, 'le transfert du Canada à l'Angleterre était dans la logique des choses,' he also observes that 'la colonisation produit des effets de masse et à très long terme' (195–6).[6] These long-term effects not only project forwards in time in the form of institutional continuities; they just as much project backwards. This is why Legendre (and especially so in his many subsequent studies) focuses the study of colonization in a broader perspective that situates it as a specific type of 'juridical and institutional reception' in the history of the education of peoples. This history echoes back to the *imitatio imperii* of the Roman attempt at 'colonizing the world' and its subsequent influence on medieval glossators as the common foundation of the models of acculturation deployed by the Europeans in their contacts with non-Europeans (see 197).

That said, the particularities of French ancien régime colonization attempts, in their general schema, were not only their high degree of 'rationality' (in the form of the would-be destruction of indigenous societies through assimilation), but, more importantly, that colonization was predominantly the attempt to 'rationally' (re)create administrative mechanisms in the colonies, but not institutions (159 and n2). This concurs nicely with Diamond's remarks above about the French attempt in Canada to create an administrative system in which persons held social positions within 'a fixed table of organization.' The rigidity, hierarchy, and fixity of the French ancien régime model of colonial social organization – its profoundly 'apolitical' and personalized culture of subordination, and subjection to inherited, traditional forms of privilege (see e.g., Nicolai's 1992 study of the *mentalité* of Montcalm's officer corps) – raises a number of questions regarding not only its social 'reality' (as we saw above, in Diamond's argument, this may well have been the paradoxical creation of a society of insubordination), but also its transferability to a new regime of British administration. How well would such a rigid system effectuate the transfer?

Nicolai's study of the socio-cultural views of the French officer corps at the time of the cession notes that officers were baffled by certain aspects of the culture of the English colonies, and in particular by the notion of 'British liberties,' 'consider[ing] the representative governments of those provinces not only subversive, fostering parochial political attitudes and disloyalty to the crown, but basically illogical' (1995: 256). One officer attempting to analyse the sources of England's new-found greatness (and the British government's acts of aggression against foreign shipping and colonies) attributed these specifically to the English Constitution and the Navigation Acts of 1660 (see Nicolai 1995: 254). Furthermore, if, as we have also seen, New France, as a conquered colony in the terms of English law, constituted a civilized form of government, characterized by a system of law, what happened to French law in the wake of the cession? The question is doubly central in that, given the French model of an administrative table of social organization, the sources of the law would have been predominantly metropolitan rather than local. It is perhaps putting it mildly to suggest that the sudden severance of the juridical links connecting the colony to its now-former metropole may have been not only radically unsettling, but actually amplified by the appearance of a new legal culture that was above all perceived as illogical (most notably, in the idea of 'juries' as opposed to magistrates versed in codal interpretation).

Modes of Acculturation and the Uncertain Status of Communication

In the coming together of different societies, especially if these are seen as informational networks, a model of how different networks connect is necessary. A term that has emerged from social science literature to describe such a model is 'acculturation,' defined as 'culture change that is initiated by the conjunction of two or more autonomous cultural systems' (cited in Denton 1966: 29). 'Conjunctive' relations refers to the 'intercultural networks that not only establish the framework of contact but also provide the channels through which the content of one cultural system must be communicated and transmitted to the other' (cited in Denton 1966: 29–30). In the Canadian context, then, the importance of the period from 1759 (the military capitulation) to the early 1800s stems from the claim that it is in this period that the structure or pattern of future relations between French and English was ostensibly 'determined.' From the literature, two predominant versions of this determining pattern or structure emerge: 1) 'assimilation' or the view that the newly dominant networks of the British administration would attempt to fully absorb the networks of communication of the former French colony (e.g., language, law, custom [especially land tenure], and demography), and conversely 2) the failure of the assimilation model, to varying degrees. Denton argues for the latter, which he terms 'reactive adaptation.' In other words, in his argument, the conjunctive relations between French and English tended to discourage any assimilation during this period (35). 'While there was no assimilation, there were definite changes which did occur' (35–6): for example, the exclusion of a trading French-Canadian middle class bourgeoisie after 1760, and as a result the increased separation of towns from countryside in a context that saw a rapid doubling of the rural population over the next quarter-century. In Denton's view, French-Canadian society maintained the rigidity of pre-Conquest social organization: the model of political organization under the British fundamentally replicated that of New France, the principal difference being that the cession allowed the Catholic Church to tighten its social position, in integrating religion, local government, and the local unit of social identification (the parish) (1966: 39, also table 1, 49). In Denton's view, then, assimilation was a 'complete failure' (40): 'French and English lived side by side in a stabilized pluralism. The two cultures in contact failed completely to lose their autonomy' (40). This 'stabilized pluralism,' however, changed after 1800 as a growing class of educated French Canadians aspired to a greater say in political control and in economic activity. One of the related problems that Denton identifies is what he terms 'the problem of communications in French Canada' (37): specifically, the limited (or nonexistent) number of newspapers until after the handover, the separation of town and countryside, and the lack of communication among the various members of the French Canadian community (37). This is a point of view that largely replicates late 1930s–1940 sociology of rural French Canada as isolated, homogenous, self-sufficient, but still growing in population – a sociology that would be radically reappraised in the 1950s (see Falardeau 1953). In sum, while Denton, like Paquet and Wallot, insists on the importance of the conjunction of communication networks in structuring acculturation, unlike them, he goes on to argue that these communication networks did not particularly communicate either with each other, or in the context of the former New France, within itself: the British simply overlaid their networks of communication atop those of New France, and things, for a while at least, simply went on as before. We need to examine some of these issues more closely.

The Social Status of French Law and the French Language in the Wake of the Conquest

The authors of a 1993 textbook on Quebec civil law make this comment:

At the close of the French colonial period, New France was ... equipped with a complete legal system in both the public and private spheres, this latter including commercial law and procedure. The legislative, administrative, and judicial branches of this legal order collapsed, for the most part, as a matter of law, with the change of sovereignty in 1763 and, as a matter of fact, had already ceased to function during the military government that preceded it (1760–64), although the parish and seigneurial organization of society did remain in place. (Boodman et al. 1993: ss.10–11)

Several points follow from this observation that are worth emphasizing because they are paradoxical. For one, 'the law' of the French regime did not enjoy the prominence it would gain subsequently under the English common law regime. In part, this is because, in practice, written law had already given greater place to 'droit non écrit' in the form of custom. Second, there remains a lack of comparative historical studies on whether the colonists 'really observed the law as it was unfolding at the same time, in continental France' (Boodman et al., s. 12). Third, the richness and complexity of the doctrinal sources of legal normativity derived from European sources, not local ones. For example, Canadian jurist F.-J. Cugnet's attempts in 1768–9 to summarize for Governor Carleton the sources of French law, while self-described as 'treatises,' were more like pamphlets, brief and partial summaries, than the actual treatises that Cugnet acknowledged his indebtedness to (notably, the works of continental jurists such as Ferrière, Duplessis, Bacquet, Domat, Loiseau, and Jean Mesle) (see Cugnet 1775b: 14[7]; see also Cugnet [1720–89] in *DCB*, IV, 1979:182–6). And fourth, the notion and laws of equity, peculiar to English common law, had no equivalent either in French law or in New France.

That said, in the thirty years following the military capitulation, 'profound uncertainty' (Boodman et al., s. 13) prevailed as to the status of the continuity of the legal order of the ancien régime, largely due to the equivocal attitudes of the English imperial and local authorities. Not until the Quebec Act of 1774 restored 'the laws of Canada' in 'Property and Civil Rights' did some of the ambiguity gain a degree of clarification. Broadly put, until then, three possibilities had been debated and partially experimented with: 1) that the entirety of English law had come into force in 1763, 2) that Canadian law remained in place unless expressly repealed, or 3) that English criminal law replaced French criminal law as part of English public law, whereas French civil law remained in place (see Shortt and Doughty 1918: 437). The Quebec Act, prompted by the rebellious and bellicose conditions in the Thirteen Colonies, however, remained 'silent on [which legal system] would be applicable in matters other than those specified' (Boodman et al., s. 14) – exercise of the Catholic religion; the applicability of the old laws of Canada to property and civil rights; a legislative council, established in 1777, with some latitude in varying the applicability of 'the laws of Canada'; a system whereby the English land tenure of free and common socage would apply to new land grants made by the crown; freedom of willing (as in England); and reaffirmation of the place of English criminal law (on the Quebec Act generally, see Neatby 1937; also Canada, 1839/repr. 1966).

Even in this form, with fundamental ambiguities, and even if strengthened in certain respects by the Constitution of 1791 – by which in Prime Minister William Pitt's words, 'it seemed to His Majesty's servants the most desirable thing ... to divide the province [into Upper and Lower Canada], and to contrive that one division should consist, as much as possible, of those who were well inclined towards the English laws, and that the other part should consist of a decided preponderancy of the ancient inhabitants, who were attached to the French laws' (cited in Tousignant 1973: 231) – the end result would be, as Boodman et al. put it, 'the alteration ... of Quebec Civil Law into the law of a bijural jurisdiction ... [in which] portions of English law coexisted with the body of old French law reinstituted under the [Quebec] Act' (s. 14). Or, this can perhaps be even more clearly stated in William Pitt's hope expressed in 1791: 'Dividing the province [would universally lead the inhabitants of Canada to prefer the English Constitution and the English laws] ... since by doing so the French subjects would be sensible that the British Government had no intention of forcing the English laws upon them, and therefore they would, with more facility, look at the operation and effect of those laws, compare them with the operation and effect of their own, and probably in time adopt them from conviction' (cited in Tousignant 1973: 230) – in other words, it was a plan for progressive assimilation through legal 'superiority.' And indeed until the codification and law reform movements of the 1840s and 1850s, the tendency of legal change was piecemeal, touching only upon specific points of law, repealing some facet of the old law and replacing it with a concept drawn from English law: for example, evidence in relation to commercial matters according to English law introduced in 1777; trial by jury in commercial disputes, 1785; maintenance of French measure in the absence of agreement providing for English measure, 1799; judicial probate of wills, as in English probate, 1801; and so on (examples in Boodman et al., s. 15).

Given the tendency of the new legal order to structurally 'drift' toward increasing incorporation of English legal norms and concepts, a substantive part of the problem stemmed from the uncertainty as to what constituted Quebec civil law, from want of local doctrinal sources. As Boodman et al. put it: 'There was no author comparable to Pothier, Blackstone or Kent who successfully laid the basis for a progressive interpretation of the law' (s. 15) – or, rather, there would not be until Beaubien in the 1830s, Doucet in the 1840s, or Bibaud in the 1860s. The resulting 'conjunctive relations' between the old and the new legal systems were thus characterized by tremendous ambiguity and only partial, unclear autonomy in select defined respects within the emergence of a new legal order containing elements of both legal systems, but now framed in the hegemonic status of English law. This, then, tended to stretch the fabric of the old laws, or what explictly remained of them, in land tenure and social relations (dowries, hypotecs) at the level of local practices. The resulting tears became the means by which English legal concepts, piece by piece, seeped into the texture of a system that tilted increasingly towards bijurality.[8] It is important to stress, however, that the ensuing bijurality was unidirectional – from English to French – and not reciprocal. Complicating the continued uncertainty with respect to the civil law was an equivalent uncertainty concerning the status of the French language.

Maurice Lemire and Denise Saint-Jacques edited a monumental study of Quebec literary life since 1764. It is part of a continuum of responses to Durham's famed and severe assessment of both the 'unchanged civil laws of ancient France' and of a people 'with neither history nor literature' (Durham 1839), a continuum that first gave rise to F.-X. Garneau's celebrated *Histoire du Canada*. Lemire and Saint-Jacques argue that written French, the language of the administration and the clergy under the ancien régime, had ceased by 1760 to possess a public character (Lemire 1991: 108). 'La langue publique est anglaise, exclusivement' (108). The language of the law was therefore exclusively in English, and French henceforth only existed as a language of translation. Even more strongly stated, French was now a 'dead' language, equivalent to Latin, which continued to be the language of instruction. A 1778 letter to Fleury Mesplet's *Gazette littéraire et commerçiale* complained (perhaps with some exaggeration) that college students by the age of eighteen had greater facility in Latin and could barely put together a few written French syllables (cited in Lemire, 108).

Lemire points out that, to some degree, the public status of French, or lack of it, in newspapers, public libraries, or any form of public education, can be traced back to French colonial policies, which had led to what he terms paradoxically 'the overdevelopment' of the tertiary sector of society (especially governmental or administrative communications). Relative to the small population of the colony, the ancien régime had produced an enormous quantity of reports, memoirs, and accounts, but they were largely written for metropolitan audiences by French-born and French-educated writers, for whom a stay in Canada was at best a brief episode in their lives (72–3). In a population that, at the time of the cession, consisted in proportions of 70–80 per cent of rural 'habitants,' the 'literate' classes were divided between the seigneurs, the clergy, and a petty bourgeoisie strongly anchored in rural surveying and the 'notariat.' Among the professions, medicine was monopolized by the English, the legal profession was roughly equal in its linguistic composition, and architects and engineers tended to be English (data in Lemire, 104–5). The cession, then, reinforced the conditions of linguistic rupture between a French-speaking and predominantly rural population and the English-speaking language of powerholders concentrated in the towns and in the new metropole. In order for the latter to 'speak' to (some of) the former, English documents and proclamations had to be translated. Accordingly, the ensuing difficulties initially included relations between the literate, administrators, merchants, and professions, and then spread to encompass social relations as a whole (109). As with the bijurality of the laws, the result saw the spread of an assimilative bilingualism, in order to communicate with the literate population in either English or French, and also to encourage the learning of English by the French-speaking population. For instance, the *Gazette de Québec* (created in 1764), a quasi-official newspaper for the publication and translation of governmental communications, in its first French issue offered a word-by-word translation of the English originals; in subsequent issues the French was of slightly better quality. Freelance translators were contracted on a yearly basis. As Lemire puts it: 'These improvized translators, however, seemed to manage for better or worse, although they at times muddled the two languages to produce a kind of "Frenglish"' (109). Translation, as we shall see shortly, in addition to being the principal channel of communication between the new administration and its new subjects, also became rapidly in certain instances a channel of upward social mobility.

The concept that Lemire uses to describe the resulting cohabitation of the two languages, in a differential relationship of power, is that of 'colingualism' (as opposed to the more commonly used 'bilingualism' which suggests a reciprocity that was not the case). But for Lemire, the case of Lower Canada offers a particular variant of colingualism as the association, either official or grammatical, of 'state languages' (here, that of France and that of England) (108). Rather than a partnership – the nineteenth-century historian Benjamin Sulte would remark with some surprise that, when Vaudreuil and Lévis dictated the terms of capitulation, they omitted to provide for the future protection of the French language (cited in Horguelin 1977: 15) – Lower Canadian colingualism became, as did so many other processes of acculturation, a site of contestation, and one that persists to this day. Above all, the ambivalent status of French, as the receiver-language in an initially unilateral new language of 'translationese,' helped contribute to the establishment and reinforcement of what Lemire terms 'le discours sur l'ignorance des Canadiens' (106–8): a discursive formation rapidly established by the British, and perpetuated subsequently in the civil culture of English Canada (although at times shared by francophone elites), that consisted of invidious comparisons between the superior English culture and mores, and the Canadian population that was ignorant, inert, lazy, apathetic, and so on – in short, the familiar tropes of the racist language of the colonizer vis-à-vis the colonized. And perhaps nowhere was the British sense of their own superiority more pronounced than when it came to the self-evident superiority of their institutions – their laws, in particular, and their profound belief in English liberty. Historian Donald Creighton states it very clearly:

In Lower Canada, the political struggle grew out of a deeper and more passionate social conflict. In the lower as in the upper province, there was, of course, the same division between the merchants and the farmers; but the dispute between the two groups was intensified by the lingering survival of the semi-feudal institutions of New France. Their quarrel was more than a quarrel between two social groups ... it was a struggle between commercialism represented aggressively by the merchants and a decadent semi-feudal society defended by peasants and professional men ... Aloof, dogged and apprehensive, the French Canadians came to cling to the old ways of life ... They wished to save their patrimony for the society of the future; and they soon came to realize that the laws and customs of their forefathers were the best protection against the domination of an acquisitive, speculative and alien race. (Creighton 1956: 126–7)

Law, Translation, and the Emergence of a Public Sphere

The spread of a nascent translationism affected initially, under the military regime (1759–64), official proclamations, and the administration of justice and, after 1763, questions of commerce. The generals in charge of the new administration (Amherst, Murray, etc.) each appointed a bilingual secretary to act as intermediaries in their administrative districts (Quebec, Trois-Rivières, and Montreal) between the military governors and the population. These secretaries were themselves British officers, but of Huguenot descent; while seldom holding a rank higher than captain, they served as privileged intermediaries for the new governors, writing their correspondance, sharing their secrets, and transmitting orders to the ruling circles of the colony. It was through these men (Cramahé in Quebec, Bruyères in Trois-Rivières, and Maturin in Montreal) that the principal proclamations in French were drafted or translated, either with or without the assistance of Canadians – Horguelin argues that in 1760 no *Canadien* knew enough English to translate the text of the proclamations (1977: 16). As Horguelin remarks: 'The French of the proclamations, aside from some interferences [from English], was quite decent. If one can reproach it with possessing a local flavour (but is this a reproach?), it was certainly not a servile copy of the English [text]' (19, our translation).

Ironically, it is with the establishment of a civil government in 1764 that the quality of 'official bilingualism' shows the first signs of degenerating: Cramahé's subsequent translations of proclamations are full of anglicisms and literalisms. The first issue of *The Quebec Gazette / la Gazette de Québec* (1764), the first Canadian newspaper founded by two printers from Philadelphia, achieved, in Horguelin's words, 'the dubious honour ... of creating a new language: Frenglish' (1977: 20, our translation). Until the Quebec Act of 1774 restored specific sections of the civil law, the military governors had rapidly concluded that it was impossible to properly administer justice in the colony with magistrates who did not speak French and were unfamiliar with French law. Further, the establishment of a civil government had reinforced the juridical apparatus and multiplied the points of communicative contact between the administration and the so-called new subjects of the Crown. For Carleton, who replaced Murray as governor in 1767, it was essential to identify, classify, and translate the laws and *ordonnances* of the French regime, a task the English-speaking magistrates had declared themselves incapable of. Carleton's French secretary, appointed in February 1768 as 'French Translator' and 'Secretary to the Governor and

Council' at a salary of five shillings a day, would be the first Canadian-born holder of such a position. François-Joseph Cugnet (1720–89) was born in Quebec into a family of French jurists and his life is profoundly emblematic of the problems of the transition period. Imprisoned in La Rochelle in his youth over a duel, unproven rumours would later circulate that it was he who had shown Wolfe's troops the pathway to l'Anse-au-Foulon that allowed them to reach the Plains of Abraham. He was under investigation by Vaudreuil and Bigot in the final years of the French regime, an inquiry that came to nought with the fall of Montreal to the British. Appointed by Murray judge-administrator of three north shore parishes, he reportedly performed his job with such zeal that he became the object of a petition demanding an investigation of his judicial performance (see Horguelin 1977; Leland 1961; P. and M.D. Tousignant in *DCB*, IV, 1979). These rumours notwithstanding, Murray would appoint him Attorney General of the north shore of the District of Quebec in 1760 and *grand-voyer* (commissioner of roads) of the same district in 1765.

Cugnet's friendship with Carleton would also lead to his encounter with his lifelong opponent, the new Attorney General Francis Masères (1731–1824), also a Huguenot descendent, like the other French secretaries before Cugnet, but unlike them a barrister and author of numerous books, including treatises on mathematics. The two would clash repeatedly over the nature of the colony's juridical regime, a clash in which Cugnet would be preserved in the mythology of subsequent history as 'the champion of French laws' (see Huberdeau 1947). On the other hand, Masères, in spite of his many publications, particularly in the period of the Quebec Act, would be, according to the same mythology, demonized for 'his inveterate Huguenot prejudice against the Roman Catholic Church' (Wallace 1959: 25) and subsequent lack of restraint as a result of which Carleton attempted to replace him as attorney-general. (In the more moderate view of later historians, his influence was, in fact, not great either on Carleton or on the ministers of the Crown in London.)

These two figures, contrasting yet in many ways equal, help us focus on some of the issues surrounding the transition of legal regimes. On the one hand, Cugnet headed the project of the official translation of the views of the new administration into French for twenty years, a job that, in Horguelin's words, he executed 'à un niveau très convenable' (1977: 25). Conversely, the various abstracts of the parts of the Custom of Paris received and practised in the province of Quebec at the time of the French government, the sequels to these, the abstracts of the criminal laws, of royal edicts, and the *loix de police* were, together with the contributions of the Church lawyers Jacreau, Deschesneaux, and Pressard of the Seminary of Quebec, the principal conduit by which the laws of the old regime, or portions of them, were preserved through the transition.[9] As Huberdeau remarks, Cugnet's works represented 'une *espèce* de codification des nos lois et coûtumes' (1947: 90, emphasis added), that served as guides to the codification work of Beaubien that began in the early 1830s; Cugnet's labours, in historian Thomas Chapais's words, were 'dignes précurseurs' of the subsequent work of the 'grands légistes' of the 1830s and 1840s (in Huberdeau, 92). One of those great jurists, Bibaud, would also say of Cugnet that he was nothing less than 'le premier bourreau de la langue française au Canada' (in Huberdeau, 88). And for his part, Pierre Daviault finds specifically in Cugnet's writings 'la naissance de cette *langue de traduction* qui est maintenant notre plaie' (in Hoguelin 1977: 23, emphasis in original).

But there was something even more complex involved here – a clash of fundamentally different legal cultures on the one hand and, on the other, a loss of connectedness to the legal culture of France that one finds first in Cugnet and would often be repeated subsequently. De Montigny in his *Histoire du droit canadien* (1869) would drive at something similar, as he lamented in this work what the loss of French law represented in cultural terms:

Ainsi se trouvaient abolies les lois françaises si précises, si claires, si sages, et y étaient substituées les lois anglaises, amas confus d'actes de Parlement et de décisions judiciaires enveloppées de formes compliquées et barbares ... (cited in Huberdeau 1947: 45)[10]

Maseres, for his part, encountered a similar gap in translatability, but now in the other direction, as he pondered what seemed to him to be the deeply cryptic, and overly concise, French law-language, a language that he was not unfamiliar with, as we have seen:

General Carleton had engaged one Mr Cugnet, a very understanding man here, to draw up a short abstract, or Code, of such parts of the Custom of Paris as were in force, or rather in use, in this Province ... Yet it was very difficult to Mr [Chief Justice Douglas] Hey and me to understand from the great conciseness and technicality or peculiarity of the French law-language ... I remember we were above four hours understanding the first five pages of it, though we had Mr Cugnet at our elbow all the time to explain it to us. In short it was like a lecture upon a chapter of *Justinian's Institutes*. When I did understand it, I thought the several propositions neatly and accurately expressed. (Wallace 1959: 103)

Masères went on, in this 1768 letter to the under-secretary of state of the Earl of Shelburne, to argue that if the general purpose was to provide a short account to the court of England of the main points of 'our law and customs,' then the Cugnet version might do (though Masères himself thought Cugnet's was too complicated). On the other hand, if the design (seemingly Cugnet's and the later codifiers') was to develop a new code that the king might enact and make it the law of the province for the future, then it was to be rejected, not only because this would be tantamount to having the English sovereign legitimate in toto the laws of a rival sovereignty, but also because the Cugnet version, in the view of his local detractors, had left out important aspects of the Custom of Paris. Already in agreeing to tolerate the practice of the 'Romish' religion in the former colony, a religion still proscribed under English law, the British Crown was making an extraordinary and unprecedented concession to the new subjects (see e.g., Milobar in Lawson 1995). The larger problem, as Masères put it, was that 'there is a strong mutual connection between the different parts of this System of laws that makes it very difficult to change or abrogate one part of it, under a notion of it's being useless, without weakening and rendering ineffectual other parts' (Wallace, 107).

The problem was not only the clash between Roman civil law and the English common law, as represented by Cugnet and Masères respectively. It was also a clash of legal logics, between an *esprit de système* in which 'the law' formed an interconnected totality and the pragmatic common-law view that if a law or portion of it was now 'useless,' it could readily be modified. But in addition to this, the external clash was also reproduced internally between differing interests within the colony, now within the same legal culture, with disagreements among other things over the nature of the former property regime. Having lost its connectedness to the continued development of French law as a result of the Conquest, the legal 'fragment' that remained in the colony and the continued uncertainty surrounding its 'codification,' became in turn another object of contention both among internal networks of communication and in those networks' contacts with the legal apparatus of the British regime.

However piecemeal or ill-defined, the Quebec Act (1774), by officially restoring portions of the civil law, broke the deadlock that this situation produced, i.e., contending networks of influence, with too much and yet not enough information, in a linguistic conduit already constrained by the enveloping English-speaking environment. Not surprisingly perhaps, as Boodman et al. would remark, 'no major [i.e., formal] dislocation of the old law occurred' (1993: s. 15) prior to the 1840s, an inactivity that stemmed in part from the legal compromise of the transition post-1774, but also from the fact that control for the legislative assembly now became the main site of contest. Unable to resolve the legal issues, the problem became more directly political.

And yet, despite the appearance of stalemate and deadlock, some things had changed. Not only had the advent of the British regime put the 'legal' question at the centre of the debate, if initially only among the professional *gens de justice* (see Veilleux 1990), it had also paradoxically helped create a public sphere that had not existed under the French regime. The new public sphere came into existence with the establishment of the colony's first newspapers. Or perhaps it might be more exact to say that a public sphere began to take shape in the colony in the form of a communicative network that eventually also became a channel for the dissemination of the ideas of the rebellious Thirteen Colonies. By 1760 Benjamin Franklin had published a brochure about the terms of the Treaty of Paris arguing that British interests were better served by the acquisition of Canada than of Guadeloupe, because Canada would then form part of a strategic, continental system. As deputy postmaster general for the North American colonies, Franklin helped establish the first postal links between New York, Quebec, and Montreal, and would visit the latter towns both before the outbreak of the Revolutionary War and Montreal again during the subsequent, brief American occupation of the colony. The colony's first printers, William Dunlap and William Brown (Brown and Thomas Gilmore becoming the founders of the colony's first newspaper, *La Gazette de Québec/The Quebec Gazette*, in 1764) were relatives of Franklin. With the outbreak of the Revolution, the Continental Congress appealed to the 'habitants' of the British colonies of North America (in Quebec and Nova Scotia respectively) to shake off the tyranny of British despotism and, in Quebec in particular, to renounce the 'perfidiousness' of the Quebec Act, because it was only a pseudo-constitution and by virtue of 'the immutable laws of nature, [and] the principles of the English Constitution ... they are entitled to life, liberty and property, and they have never ceded to any sovereign power whatever, a right to dispose of either without their consent ...' (de Lagrave 1993: 24–5). Charged with publication and dissemination of this appeal into French was the French printer Fleury Mesplet, who had previously worked with Franklin in his print-shop in Philadelphia: he had settled in Montreal in 1765 and would be imprisoned there for his revolutionary activities.

It is important, even in this brief form, to emphasize the extent to which the emergence of a Canadian public sphere is thus implicated with the fundamental debates that racked British America at the time of the American Revolution. Those debates, whatever the subsequent course of military events that brought about the founding of the United States, were concerned with law, natural rights, and their related political theories – in short, with the American extension of the meaning of 'English liberty' or, more generally, the theory and practice of the Enlightenment.

In turn, however short-lived Mesplet's first newspaper (one year), and whatever his own subsequent compromises and legal difficulties with his increasingly conservative surroundings, his initial venture is clear in its conviction that the increased communication of ideas represented the high road of human progress and that the role of the press was to be in the avant-garde of advancement. His prospectus for the *Gazette du commerce et littéraire de Montréal* announced that the paper saw its role as one of raising consciousness, as a result of which 'the citizens will more readily and clearly communicate their ideas. From this will [follow the] progress [of] the arts in general, and an increase in the interconnectedness of individuals' (de Lagrave, 96, our translation). The 'communicative citizen' (as opposed to the subject of the Crown), by the increase of interconnection, would facilitate the increase of commerce, and contribute to an 'always advantageous' social emulation (de Lagrave, 96). Obviously, this communicative utopia came with a price: in seeking permission from Carleton to publish a weekly in Montreal, Mesplet promised only to address 'the healthiest elements of the citizenry,' and to steer clear of anything that might cause umbrage to the government or to religion (de Lagrave, 97). He also promised a discreet silence about 'current affairs,' i.e., the American War of Independence, an ironic concession for the former French-language printer of the Continental Congress. But even at that price, it was worth the venture, as 'until now the greatest portion [of the citizens] have had to confine themselves to a narrow [private] sphere,' not through lack of good intentions in acquiring knowledge, but through lack of opportunity (de Lagrave, 98). The venture, then, opened a window onto a public sphere. In de Lagrave's content-analysis of the *Gazette du commerce et littéraire* and its successor, the *Gazette littéraire* (September 1778–June 1779), showed that roughly 85 per cent of the content was devoted to the public discussion of intersubjectivity (the remainder went to government information or local news): of that 85 per cent, 55 per cent dealt with literary matters (texts and criticism); some 5.6 per cent dealt with the law, fashion (3.5%), education (2.82%), and advertising (4.5%) (data in de Lagrave, 99–100).

The struggle for a public sphere, then, brought new forces into play in the politics of Lower Canada: for one, what Fecteau and Hay would characterize as 'enlightened journalism with a subtext of republicanism' (1996: 151), the precursor of a Quebec political journalism of the early nineteenth century generally described as *un journalisme de combat*; for another, further controversies over the applicability of the laws, a major state trial, and the increased demand that 'English liberty' be actually applied in practice, rather than just paid lip service to; and finally, a democratic political opposition within the Legislative Assembly, brought into being by the Constitution of 1791. It is to aspects of these political developments that we now turn – in particular, the concatenation between an emerging public sphere, a rhetoric of struggle, and the rapid assimilation by allegedly 'aloof and apathetic' French Canadians of the 'game' of British parliamentary practices.

Legislative Practices and the 'Parliamentarization' of the French Language

We have seen above how the ambiguity of the laws left considerable discretion to colonial practices in the elaboration of new customary forms. The development of such new practices, particularly concerning the local adoption of English parliamentary rules and procedures, became the central preoccupation of the Legislative Assembly of Lower Canada, established by the Constitution of 1791; this was one of the key sites for the deliberation of public questions until the Constitution's suspension following the rebellions of 1837–8, and the Act of Union of 1840 that reunited the assemblies of Lower and Upper Canada. The demands for greater application of English liberty to the former French colony led, in part, to the 1791 Constitution. Other factors were also involved – the constitutional crisis provoked by the American rebellion, the early constitutional phase of the revolution in France and, in England itself, the struggle for parliamentary reform of the period 1760–85. There were fiscal imperatives to increase the dependence of the remaining North American colonies, in part to alleviate the loss of income from the Thirteen Colonies, a financial loss that made the risk of granting greater political control to a predominantly French Assembly in Quebec, in historian Vincent Harlow's words, 'almost [a] ... compulsion' (in Tousignant 1973: 227). In addition to the fiscal imperative, there was also an emulative imperative, stemming from the desire to further strengthen 'the old colonial system,' also in the wake of the American revolution, by reinforcing the aristocratic principle in 'our' Constitution and, in the Canadas, through 'a mixed and balanced constitution,' which even at the price of allowing separate legislatures, nonetheless encouraged 'the habit of obedience to the same Government, and by the sense of a common interest' (Grenville to Dorchester, 1789, in Shortt and Doughty 1918: 978–9, 988). After all, as Pitt would tell the House of Lords, were not the French Canadians, by their ancient habits, customs, and usages, already 'peculiarly fitted' for the reception of hereditary honours, and their seigneurs sufficiently possessed with 'with property and respect' to 'make them hold a fair weight in that [new] constitution,' so that they deserved 'that respect and influence that ought to belong to the aristocratical branch of a free Government'? (cited in Tousignant 1973, 233). Thus, in Tousignant's analysis, the 1791 Constitution represented an attempt by the declining landed and aristocratic British holders of political power to maintain, and reinforce in the Canadas, a 'conception féodale de l'ordre politico-social' of the late eighteenth century (1973: 233–4). The irony is that such a conception of political power would itself be overturned in the metropole within fifty years by a rising industrial bourgeoisie, as attested by the Manchester liberalism of Durham's plan to reform the Canadas. Also, of course, the application by French Canadians of the principles of a mixed and a balanced constitution turned out, in practice, to pay more attention to questions of popular sovereignty than to reinforcing the aristocratic branch. Still, there were some doubts – in an illustration of Lemire's discursive formation on the ignorance of French Canadians – as to the capability of Canadians to master an instrument as complex as an English constitution. As one visiting merchant put it: 'The English constitution is too complex a machine to be at once understood, adopted and put into motion, by a simple and uninformed people' (cited in Hare, 1993: 44n5). Others claimed that the key texts on the laws of England and the British parliamentary system (notably Blackstone) were not yet available in French translation; but, as John Hare points out, not only was a French translation of Blackstone available in Quebec in 1784, the other great analysts of British constitutionalism, such as Montesquieu and de Lolme, were themselves French writers (37). Also, as Hare points out, in the wake of the elections of 1792: 'To the astonishment of the English-speaking members, the Canadians displayed considerable skill from the very beginning of the first session in how to take advantage of British parliamentary practices' (89, our translation). The tensions between the two linguistic groups would soon explode over the use of French in the Assembly.

In Hare's account of the origins of Quebec parliamentarianism, a form of institutional bilingualism had been the practice since the military regime. Both languages were used in the legislative council established by the Quebec Act. 'It seemed then that French had acquired a legal status as a result of practices rather than a particular legislative act' (88). But practices, in the absence of a law, need even more constant reinforcement. The debate over language erupted early in 1793 over the rules respecting language-use in the Assembly *Journal of Debates* and in the tabling of bills. The francophone majority of the Assembly rejected the proposals put forward by a majority anglophone committee on rules and regulations, and proposed instead that the Assembly journal be kept in both languages (motions tabled in French to be translated into English and vice versa), and similarly that bills in respect of the criminal law be tabled in English, and those in respect of the civil law be tabled in French, each to be translated prior to debate. The English-speaking minority in the Assembly wanted English to have priority in all legislation – in short, they wanted English to be the legal language. In the view of MLA John Richardson, this stemmed from the self-evident fact that English was the legal language of the Empire, and to be governed by English laws was the birthright of every British subject. If the Quebec Act had allowed for the preservation of the ancient French laws, this was as a favour, not as a right. Not to recognize English as the legal language was to weaken the links binding the colony to the mother country (Hare, 91–3). Richardson's intransigence provoked the opposition of the majority of the Canadian MLAs. Taschereau, a moderate seigneur, avowed that he had initially opposed the establishment of a popular assembly, but his fears had evaporated in the face of positions such as Richardson's. Taschereau likened this to being captured by parliamentary pirates, tabling bills in a language that 'we have the misfortune not to understand or speak,' which had made Canadians 'slaves in this [very] chamber' (Hare, 93).

The debate would continue until autumn 1793, although it would not be brought before the Imperial Parliament. Instead, a ruling by Henry Dundas, secretary of state, on 2 October 1793, seemed to clarify the position of the British government: he saw no objection to a permanent rule that 'bills relative to the laws, customs, usages and civil rights of the province' be introduced in French, 'to preserve the unity of the texts,' as long as the laws proposed were also drafted in English; conversely bills tabled in English could be accompanied by a French translation. French, in other words, was not excluded, although its juridical status was not clarified either. As for the francophone members of the Assembly, they were seemingly satisfied that they had proven to 'the public' that they could act in concert and turn to their advantage whatever issues came up (Hare, 106–7).

The language debate of 1792–3, like that over the laws themselves, was thus not resolved in law, but in practices, by which the use of French became the official practice in the Assembly and in its *Journal of Debates*. But as with the status of the laws themselves, a similar and parallel ambiguity also remained. Not until the 1840 Act of Union would the Imperial Parliament actually unilaterally impose English as the legal language (from 1841–9). But at every preceding crisis point – in 1810 when Governor Craig proposed to suspend the 1791 Constitution in the wake of the electoral successes of the 'Canadian party,' and in 1822 when Richardson and other English-speaking members, exasperated by continued *Canadien* control of the Assembly, again pressed their recurring demand for reuniting the assemblies of Lower and Upper Canada – the English minority in the Assembly consistently revived the clamour for the unilateral imposition of English (107, 115–17; also PRO/CO42/194/195/ 1822–4). (Not until 1867 would the kind of bilingualism first proposed in the 1792–3 debate be officially sanctioned, first by the Assembly of the United Canadas, and then by that of Quebec).

It should also be noted that the functional bilingualism proposed in the

Assembly by the francophone majority was seen by certain deputies as a last-ditch effort to forestall the inevitable cultural assimilation, a pessimism about the future of French that even a Cugnet had shared. On the other hand, the English-speaking members could not get over the sudden ability of these largely conservative francophones, tied to the landed and mercantile aristocracy – and so hardly radicals – to act in concert. This had to be, some argued, because they were tacitly supported by unreliable English elements. As Quebec city merchant and office-holder John Young (1759–1819) remarked: 'Whatever education and knowledge there was came from the English-speaking members; without them, the Canadians could not have managed' (in Hare, 118). Ironically, it would be from the efforts of precisely these conservative electors, initally opposed to the idea of a popular assembly, that later radicals such as Joseph Papineau were led to the appropriate conclusion – i.e., in John Hare's words, that 'the Canadians want[ed] to control the processes of transformation of society: above all, [by] displaying the will to see their interests respected, along with their institutions and their language' (120). As Henri Brun has observed: 'Quebec parliamentarianism formed itself almost exclusively on a customary basis, in parallel to the reforms of British parliamentary institutions, but in a far more greatly concentrated period of time. Its key ingredients, born of concrete conflicts, were the techniques of legislative collaboration, between and among institutional sites' (1970: 19). For Brun, this rapid apprenticeship in parliamentary practices further reinforced the 'double sovereignty' that in his argument was already implicit in the 1791 Constitution Act, that of the metropole and its local representatives, and that of the legislative assembly – in other words, of the 'parliamentarianization of state authority' (Habermas 1991: 58). The problem of sovereignty *in* the state was simultaneously, in Quebec, that of increasing the sovereignty *of* the Quebec state (Brun 1970: 19).

Towards Codification and Recodification

It is, of course, highly pertinent to our understanding of the processes of the transfer of legal systems and cultures that began to form the civil culture of contemporary Canada to stress that the transitional period that is the focus of this chapter occurred in a context of *both* a revolutionary and a post-revolutionary era. We have seen how Lower Canada was part of the communication network of the ideas of the American Revolution. De Lagrave has argued (1993) that the sympathies of the 'habitant' population for the rebellious 'Bostonians' were far greater than the traditional claims about the loyalty of the new subjects to the British; were it not for the fact that the adult population was evenly matched by an equivalent number of troops rushed in to defend the remaining British North American colonies, those sympathies might have taken, he suggests, more active forms than just welcoming or feeding the invading revolutionary forces. For his part, Tousignant (1991) argues less speculatively that the *Canadiens*, in fact, only had two choices following the cession: either to return to France, or to turn toward England in the light of what he terms 'the seduction of the British constitutional model' (231, 229). The latter he attributes largely to Montesquieu's celebrated admiration for the English constitution and the separation of powers in *L'Esprit des Lois*. In Tousignant's view, the influence of the American Revolution only further strengthened the resolution of the Canadians to accede more fully to the conditions of 'English liberty,' through agitation for constitutional reform that would be reinforced in the wake of the Du Calvet affair (1784) and subsequent petitions for a legislative assembly. The 'seductions' of English liberty stemmed from the fact that, in the words of one contemporary tract, 'it is recognized that the English constitution is the most appropriate for securing the felicity of a people ... [and] is envied by all other nations and admired by their very best writers' (in Tousignant 1991: 233). Compounding this belief among Canadian reformers were contemporary events in France, at least until 1792; the French people, like themselves, were engaged in a similar struggle for 'the privileges of a free Constitution.' As Tousignant puts it: 'The course of events in France that should have resulted in the establishment of a constitutional monarchy and occurred in the same year that the British Parliament adopted a new constitution for Lower and Upper Canada, contributed to the belief of the Canadian reformers that there was a perfect convergence between their own liberal aspirations and those of the representatives of the Third Estate in the National Assembly' (234). The year 1792, then, inspired in the Canadian reformers the belief that a new era of political liberty had dawned. What they got instead was counter-revolutionary panic produced successively by the French Terror, the Napoleonic wars, and a second unsuccessful American invasion of Canada.

Murray Greenwood (1993) has argued that revolutionary republicanism, and the French Revolution and its aftermath in particular, had a lasting impact, not only in reinforcing 'the garrison mentality' of local, English-speaking elites after 1792, but also in shaping the counter-revolutionary 'revulsion' that remained strong not only after the events of 1811, but even more so after the defeat of the rebellions of 1837–8, and contributed to the ideological orthodoxy of French-Canadian elites that would last into the middle decades of the twentieth century (247). Among anglophone elites, the garrison mentality was characterized by 'the enactment of security legislation more draconian than British law; its enforcement ... [in] the manipulation of justice [in the sentencing and trials of the 1790s] ...; much of the constitutional warfare of the Craig era [1810–11]; the emergence of strong anglicization sentiment; and the Baconian stances taken by the judiciary' (249). While some of these effects were specific to their immediate times, Greenwood argues that others became lasting features of Canadian civil culture, particularly in the tendency during perceived political crises to drastically curtail civil liberties, to enforce draconian legislation that went even beyond the limits of British law, and to show political partiality in the Bench (260–1). The ease with which the legal system would subsequently be manipulated, especially during security crises, leads Greenwood to call for continued vigilance by members of Canadian civil society.

More specifically, for our purposes, are the ways in which the legal culture of postrevolutionary France influenced the movement to codify the civil laws of Lower Canada that began in the 1830s. Greenwood, for one, 'emphasize[s] that nothing like a cultural divorce developed ... [t]here were, rather, patterns of selective borrowing orchestrated by the francophone elite' (247–8). The liberal lawyer Gonzalve Doutre complained in the 1860s: 'Advocates of French-Canadian nationality are unwilling to accept modern France but rather the France at the time of the Conquest' (cited in Greenwood, 248). The result of this selectivity, as far as it impacted on the codification of the laws of Lower Canada, was that 'the Lower Canadian civil law codified in 1866 was *pre-Revolutionary* and not Napoleonic in inspiration. This would be the case until the 1960s' (249, emphasis added). Greenwood goes on to suggest that, from about 1840 and for a century thereafter, 'French Canada borrowed [legal] "form" from France but tended to eschew substance' (248). On the other hand, Boodman et al. (1993) argue that, in large part, the Quebec Code was derivative of the French Code 'not only in organization and style but also in substance' (s. 25). This interpretive disagreement calls for further discussion.

Kolish (1987) quotes an observation by a Swiss-born Patriote sympathizer of the mid-1830s: 'Il y a encore aujourd'hui la même confusion de lois françaises et anglaises, les mêmes incertitudes dans les décisions, le même caprice dans l'application de la loi qu'il y eut il y a 50 à 60 ans' (319).[11] The stalemate of the post-1774 compromise had, in other words, persisted and would continue to persist through the 1837–8 rebellions, the reactionary aftermath, Durham's denunciation of the confusion of the ancient and the new laws, and the reforms that followed the stabilization of the post-1840 constitutional reorganization. As Brian Young has argued in his fine study of the politics of codification of the Lower Canadian Civil Code (2615 articles in French and English adopted in 1866), pre-rebellion reformers had, as we have seen above, strongly empha-sized the links between codal law and politics in which 'a code ... would serve to block judge-made law emanating from arrogant anglophone judges ... imper-vious to legislative control' (1994: 44). The failure of the Rebellions not only 'broke the common front of law and language' (44), but the period 1840–65 would be one of profound social transformation as well as stabilization of public institutions, particularly the legislature and the judiciary. The old social contract of the ancien régime legal order of the customary privileges of, in particular, married women, artisans, and seigneurs was replaced by a new social contract of capitalist legal social relations – equality before the law, individual freedom, freedom of contract, and the priority of exchange (43–4). Along with these transformations arose a new 'class' of lawyers 'who, between the rebellions and Confederation, acceded to power in politics, on the bench, in the new university law faculties, and elsewhere in the colony' (44). Once in power, these lawyers acted 'to depoliticize the law' (44), imbuing it with 'a rational, scientific, and ostensibly apolitical approach to legal reform and codification' (44). In this scientific and rational conception, 'access to the subtleties of Civil law *uniquely through the French language* was abandoned, to the chagrin of nationalists, and passage of an English version of the code became an important benchmark in the institutionalization of civic bilingualism' (44, emphasis added). In a similar vein, Boodman et al. point out:

The codification of the private law of Lower Canada was, primarily, *a technical reordering* of a complex body of norms that was intended to make this private law more accessible in both its language and substance to legal professionals and to reformulate the relationship of commercial law to other private law relations. It was, moreover ... an *essentially conservative* measure in respect of its substantive content. (1993: s. 23, emphasis added)

As a result, the civil law 'came to be seen as almost exclusively encapsulated in the Code itself,' a feature stemming from its predominantly technical conception. They further observe: 'Although the Code later took on a political colouration as an essential element of French culture in the Canadian context, *codification was not essential* to secure the place of the Civil law ... in the constitutional context of the time' (s. 23n84, emphasis added), a place secured for the civil law by the 1840 Act of Union (3 & 4 Vict., c. 35), although English remained the official language of the legislature.

Several implications arise from these changes. For one, as Roderick Macdonald points out in a perceptive study of the problems of Quebec civil law scholarship, codification did not remove the difficulties of defining the scope of the civil law in Quebec; it only added to them. In a supposedly bilingual and legally bicultural country, the fundamental distinction between public and private law that is central to the modern civil law tradition tends to become confused, in part because it has no bearing in the common law culture but also, as a result, because 'federal law is not really a part of the basic private law of Quebec' (1985: 575). Second, legal scholarship performs different functions in civil law than in common law. In the former, scholarship is to a greater extent, *'constitutive* of law' (577, emphasis in original): 'Because the code purports to announce legal norms, it has a much greater capacity to structure scholarly discourse and to set the agenda for ... legal research' (579). The problem, however, is that 'too often a code is permitted to assume its own legitimacy and ahistoricity ... [but] to the extent it demands primary intellectual allegiance to its own puzzles, codified law can be viewed as an intellectual "why-stopper"' (580). The paradox, Macdonald points out, is that a legal culture of codification requires and authorizes fundamental conceptual analysis, while at the same time facilitating the production of 'inadequate legal scholarship' (581).

In Quebec, then, when factoring in the two additional elements of language and ethnicity, this 'translate[s] into a preoccupation with the survival of the local, vernacular civilian tradition' (585) – in other words, an impoverished form of civil law characterized by orthodoxy and 'purity.' While possessing a formal affinity to French academic legal commentary (or, more strongly, *positivisme étatique*), its written form substantively resembles common law analysis – one thus ends up with 'the *worst of both* worlds' (584, emphasis added). This is, in more forceful language, what Greenwood was alluding to above. In Macdonald's words, 'the point is that Quebec private law scholarship typically has embodied only *a fragment* of the civilian tradition,' preoccupied 'with survival and purity,' and reinforced by a 'custodial mission' by which civil law scholars 'conceive of themselves as guardians of their civilization through their insistence on a particular theory of law, legal science and legal scholarship' (586, emphasis added). Such ideas can be found embodied, for example, in the Quebec Civil Code Revision Office's claim in 1978 that the impetus for codification in the Union period 'was to construct a Code which, embodying the past, would serve as a defence against outside influences which threatened the integrity of the Civil Law,' a patently false claim. Similarly, we see it in jurist Pierre-Basile Mignault's (1854–1945) complacent belief – he was appointed to the chair of Civil Law at McGill in 1914 and went to the Supreme Court in 1918 – that 'une cloison étanche et infranchissable sépare les deux grands systèmes juridiques [civil and common]' and that there was neither 'immixtion ou absorption de l'un au profit ou au détriment de l'autre' (both cited in Howes 1987: 528, 548).[12] Needless to say, positions such as these have been problematized by Quebec legal scholars

Louis Baudoin (1963), following Mignault, returns to the problem of the inadequacy of the traditional explanations articulated before the early 1950s (the Conquest, the severance from France, the ideology of survival, etc.) to tackle specifically the problem of the organization of Quebec's civil culture as 'a closed circuit, subject to latent crises or explosive convulsions resulting from clashes with a majority Protestant [surrounding] population and a foreign language' (1963: 4, our translation). He goes on to argue, like Mignault, that this apparently closed system, despite its appearance of arrested development, not only represented a sort of 'law of silence' but was in reality a silence of the law, that masked instead an unusual instance of what he terms, after Vico, 'the communicability of the law' (6), as a result of which Quebec civil law 'remains little understood in the North-American context, [and] nearly totally unknown abroad' (6). What distinguishes Quebec's legal culture is 'its juridical autonomy that represents by its techniques [of reasoning] an [intellectual] spirit that is totally the opposite as such of the English-Canadian common law provinces' (5). It is this very real difference that creates a trompe l'oeil effect, producing on the surface 'a factitious lethargy' and 'the appearance of a vegetative legal culture' that stems instead from the actual complexity of the Quebec, or more generally Canadian, case as an instance of the comparative reception of legal systems. Citing Mignault, Baudoin notes that 'the most remarkable fact' about Canadian legal culture as a whole is that it offers an ideal typical case for the study of the reception of both the common and the civil law (10–11). Regarding the latter, Baudoin makes the argument that codification in Lower Canada/Quebec was more than an element of legal formalization; it represented, as did the Louisiana Code, beachheads for the reception of French law, in its fundamental concepts, in North America. If French law represented a mid-point between Germany on the one hand and England on the other in a positive- to-negative continuum as to the reception of Roman law, the impact of the Napoleonic code on the codification of European continental law (not to mention in Latin America, Japan, and elsewhere) points beyond purely political factors or the temporal brevity of the Napoleonic empire itself as an explanation for the subsequent spread of civil law codification (1963:13–16). If it were solely a matter of political power, Baudoin notes, England could have until 1866 imposed a common-law regime on Canada as a whole. But it did not, because 'long experience had demonstrated that the infiltration of English legal concepts occurred more surely and more profoundly over time as a result of judicial decisions that, in colonized countries, reproduced the structure and spirit of British law' (16).

As J.A. Prince noted in 1923, it was 'une chose étonnante en ce temps' that the codification of Lower Canadian law, 'cette entreprise éminement sociale et française' was able to succeed during the Union period (Baudoin 18n2). As Baudoin points out, Lower Canadian codification was 'more than the reception of a formal framework; it was also a willed decision to opt for a similar juridical spirit [as that of France]; the affirmation of the identity of a general conception of the role of a code; a shared desire for systemacity, order, precision and clarity' (20). As Mignault remarked, 'the merit of a code is in its clarity and its concision; not its multitude of details' (cited in Baudoin, 20n1). Behind it, and implicit, lay a long history, in France, of the development of a science of jurisprudence going back to canon law, to the royal ordonnances that partially codified customary institutions, and the doctrinal contributions of jurists such as Dumoulin, Loysel, Domat, and Pothier (see, e.g., Legendre 1992). In Quebec, where that legal past was only partially encapsulated in the Coutume de Paris, the lack of historical-jurisprudential density would facilitate the infiltration of English legal concepts (such as the declaration of trust, freedom of willing, and commercial contracts) with the result that 'avec des mots français, on fait des lois anglaises.' But, although Baudoin does come back to the alarming implications of this legal-linguistic inflitration (see 1963: 49 ff), he takes the view that the codifiers of the 1850s were not only more successful than not in acclimatizing to local circumstances French concepts of a common origin – one very notable difference being the maintenance of the pre-Revolutionary matrimonial regime – but also in naturalizing foreign (i.e., English) concepts. In this sense, the codifiers 'firent oeuvre de véritable comparatistes, oeuvre dont la jurisprudence, au lendemain de la codification, devint le symbole' (22). If the work of codification of the civil laws of Lower Canada/Quebec represented, in the best possible light, a synthesis in the communicability of the reception of the civil and common-law legal orders 'in a juridical system that could one day become the model of comparative law' (70), his conclusion is far more pessimistic. Where, for a Mignault, the coexistence of the two systems had not been overly prejudicial to each other, for Baudoin the work of legal-linguistic and conceptual 'minage et érosion du code et de son esprit' (67) had by the early 1960s reached a point where not only was the civil code itself threatened, 'mais bien tout le système juridique québécois' (67).

Jean-Maurice Brisson (1986) begins his thoughtful study of the problem of civil procedure in Lower Canada between 1774 and 1867 with precisely this problem; namely, as a result of the constant seepage and infiltration of common-law notions into 'the Code,' there was a near-immediate and subsequently constant need for its revision. The process began soon after the adoption of the Code in 1866 and would continue until 1965. As jurist Maximilien Bibaud had observed in his 1859 comments on the codification project: 'It was absurd to proceed to the codification of the laws of a country where these are changed every year' (in Brisson 1986: 23n20). Brisson's study, in a nutshell, argues that the codifiers, in attempting to reconcile the diversity of substantive legal sources, the diversity of languages of those sources, the absence of contemporary commentary on those sources, and the incorporation of the subsequent codification experience of Louisiana and the French *Code civil* of 1804, had overlooked the crucial importance of the *Ordonnance* of 1667 as, in effect, the pinnacle of civil procedure in the legal order of the French regime. This so-called Code Louis represented the *summum* of Colbert's attempts to reform and centralize the administration of justice and produce 'a model worthy of serving all ages and nations' (cited in Lemieux 1901: 217, our translation). While various textual problems concerned the extent of the applicability of the *Ordonnance* subsequent to the Quebec Act, not to mention the actual text of the *Ordonnance* itself (which was not determined until after codification), and subsequent recourse to French commentary on it to clarify gaps of interpretation, the problem was that the administration of justice in Quebec under the English regime had proceded anyway in a multiplicity of often conflicting practices, courts, and juridical districts, a confusion of legal sources ranging from local statutary decisions to the laws of the metropole, and assorted fragments of the legal order of the ancien régime (see Brisson, 124–5). From a civil law perspective, in the absence of 'un ensemble *unique* de principes directeurs, destinés à pallier le silence des textes' (79, original emphasis) or, even more so, of a codal culture that could illuminate what the wording of the text alone could not, the result could only be the practice of a juridical chaos that, by the force of circumstance, would be heavily influenced by the penetration of English law (for examples, see Brisson 100–1). From this followed the belief that, for judges and for lawyers, in practice English law and French law were fundamentally in agreement on a given problem and did not offer divergent solutions (109). As a result, Brisson points out, it is hardly surprising that the Code would turn out not only to be a bilingual one (118), but as well it left fundamental problems of legal scholarship unresolved. As a writer in *La Minerve* put it in 1857:

Quelles sont les lois qui nous régissent aujourd'hui? Qui peut le dire? Quel est le citoyen, quel est l'avocat, quel est le juge même qui puisse dire 'voilà la loi.' La loi! Mais nous n'en avons pas, ou du moins nous en avons tant, de si vieilles et de si nouvelles, de si usées et de si contradictoires, que les meilleurs juristes s'y perdent. (in Brisson, 125n266)[13]

Not only, then, would many of these problems be built into the Code, and thus necessitate the constant revisions of it, but the projected Code itself, destined to be, in Brisson's words, 'inaltérable, ou ne pas être' (25), would turn out to be a far more imperfect instrument than a Mignault, say, had imagined. On the other hand, as Baudoin points out, just as it would require a century in

France after the adoption of the Napoleonic Code for there to develop a jurisprudence that could grasp 'que tout le droit civil n'est pas dans les seuls textes du Code' (1963: 9), the maturation of 'juridical doubt' would equally require a century to develop when it came to Quebec's Civil Code. This was, as Baudoin argues, potentially positive, especially if it helped reposition the entire problem of the transfer of legal systems from one context to another as a unique problem in comparative communication. The problem, for Baudoin and for others, was that Canadian circumstances, for all its ideal typicality as a case study in legal reception, turned out to be more unfavourable than not.

As then Chief Justice of the Superior Court of Quebec Jules Deschênes would put it, in an often quoted speech given in 1978 on legal separatism in Canada, the time had come after a century of federalism to inquire 'how efficiently we have seized upon our unique opportunity to use two great legal traditions in order to forge a single federal law ... that could be recognized as original Canadian law' (1979: 31). His answer was blunt: 'Québec has shown the willingness and the ability to contribute to the building of such a national scheme of federal law, but the legal community of the rest of Canada has, by and large, closed itself off ... by simply ignoring the Québec contribution. There now exists an actual separation in legal Canada, but it has been worked upon Québec from without, not by Québec from within' (32). Quebec law, he continued, had always kept up with legal developments in the rest of the country, and so had contributed to the unity of the Canadian legal system. The same, however, could not be said of 'common law Canada' and he went on to detail examples (see 33–40). 'Obviously, there is, and has existed for a long time, a one-way lack of communication between our two legal communities ... rooted in a language difficulty which idealism would overcome through bilingualism, but which realism teaches us can only be cured successfully through a permanent translation process' (40). If Deschênes felt at the time of this speech that time was running out, the situation could still be remedied, although the burden of reciprocity squarely rested upon 'common law Canada.'

While the above discussion may at times appear to be highly technical, or even an attempt to cast blame upon particular parties, it is important at this point to bring forth with greater forcefulness what lies beneath these interactions, or lack of them. We have seen above again and again – whether with Mesplet's notion of the 'communicative citizen,' Paquet's and Wallot's emphasis on the disruption of the communicative infrastructures of New France and their after-effects, the various jurists' attempts to make of the civil law a closed communicative system, and so on – that at issue here are fundamental disagreements over the nature of the processes of communication, focused upon but not limited to the differences between the French and English languages. We shall be discussing at length aspects of the latter in how English law language constitutes constitutional orders; here we turn to a detailed explication of the distinct conception of sociable communication that underpinned the French ancien régime, especially in its final decades.

Communication as Sociability

Daniel Gordon has shown, in his 1994 study of French thought between 1670–1789, that the apolitical public sphere of the French ancien régime provided a model of 'citizenship without sovereignty,' a description that also serves to characterize well the painfully slow evolution of Canadian practices of sovereignty that were not fully reclaimed in law from Westminster until the 1982 Constitution Act. Instead, as Gordon argues, French absolutism drew deeply from the conception of benevolent sociability of the 'well-policed state,' whose outstanding theoretician was the dean of French police officials, Nicolas De La Mare, in his three-volume *Traité de la police* (1705–38). In the sixteenth century, the term 'police' was a translation of the Greek *politeia* – polity or constitution, and denoted the superiority of a mode of collective life over others, usually referring to barbarism, and especially that of the savages of America. In a well-policed state, the monarch was absolute as opposed to constitutional, as 'the traditions limiting his authority never rested in the hands of an authoritative agent of enforcement' (14; also 7ff). Nevertheless, older constitutional arrangements and complex patterns of private law left the institutional order of the absolute monarchy with two important tensions; one was procedural, between a mode of government based on consultation (with corporate representatives of the social status orders), and a mode of government based on command. The second substantive tension was that between justice, in the sense of the preservation of customary distinctions, and public welfare, in the Delamarean 'police' sense of the mobilizing of resources to maximize centralized communications, wealth, and revenue (Gordon, 18). In seeking to ground the roots of 'police' in Roman history and in the early French constitutional tradition, Delamare attempted to 'read' back into history what was in fact an emerging statist and utilitarian mode of performing power in a way which had never existed before: 'more centralization, more regulation, more population, more welfare, more power for the sovereign' (Gordon, 23). As Gordon remarks, the centralization of government in the system of 'police' became 'the primary forces working to break down tradition, including traditional modes of thought' (23). The idea of complete freedom of action as the essential trait of sovereignty was one precondition of the Enlightenment: the freedom of royal sovereignty made possible the idea of progress, the redefinition of political goals to transform rather than preserve the community, and the elevation of the potential of human welfare. 'From absolutism to Enlightenment to the welfare state of today, there is more continuity than one usually imagines' (Gordon, 24).

However, Gordon comments that while the theory of the well-policed state usefully illustrates the presuppositions of absolutism as a political system, it does not provide a basis for understanding the dynamics of the ancien régime as a corruption of sociability that does not completely come to an abrupt terminus in 1789. As numerous contemporary observers, from Bernardin de Saint-Pierre to Diderot to Joseph Addison, had remarked, eighteenth-century France both saw itself, and was seen by foreign observers, as 'the most sociable' of nations (Bernardin); as possessing 'an extreme *sociabilité*' (Diderot); and as having a distinct 'communicative temper' (Addison; all cited in Gordon, 28). Gordon thus proposes a typology of sociability that includes the love of exchange (as convivial interaction), the propagation of absolutism (in the security to merit and advancement provided by the well-policed state), socialization and education and, most importantly for our purposes, 'the recovery of *logos*' (40–1; also 33ff). In the context of the growth of police and the centralization of administration, 'sociability may be defined as a mode of action designed to sustain or recover *logos* in the face of shrinking opportunities to exercise the faculty of deliberation. The redemption of human nature could occur within the absolutist system ... through the depoliticization of *logos* itself and the elaboration of forms of rational discussion and virtue that were not threatening to the state's official monopoly on political judgement' (41). This is Habermas's 'apolitical public sphere' (1992: 29) with a vengeance; namely, one in which the art of conversation of the seventeenth and eighteenth centuries not only thrives, but is an original and creative response to the strictures of absolutism, giving rise to intertextual semantic fields in which authors learn to work within a set of given terms, playing with inflection and neologisms to create novel utterances and new words (40–50).

Gordon goes on to make some provocative critiques of Norbert Elias's considerable influence ([1939] 1994) on subsequent historiography and sociology (Pierre Bourdieu's, notably). According to Elias, in Germany moral ideals were constructed in the process of criticizing courtly elites. French culture on the other hand fell under the complete hegemony of the court, absorbing a rigorous code of deference structured to preserve a sense of hierarchy in all aspects of life. The attributes of courtliness thus become those of the French 'national character,' 'characterized by frivolity and superficiality' (Bourdieu cited in Gordon, 91). Civility, in this perspective, is entirely at the service of hierarchy: the rules of civility function to 'assure an adequate and readable translation of the hierarchy of estates' (cited in Gordon, 92). 'What is remarkable in these accounts,' Gordon writes, 'is the degree of servility that is ascribed to the French character. It is as if the court nobility, having been domesticated by the French monarchs, proceeded to domesticate the entire nation without resistance' (92). The theme of the 'servile' French national character under the old regime was to be repeated not only by nineteenth-century liberal analysts of Canada's political problems, like Durham in his famed *Report*, but would as well be a major theme in the work of twentieth-century Canadian historians, notably D.G. Creighton. On the contrary, Gordon shows, that 'the culture of civility created a space of its own outside the hierarchy of estates' (93). For Gordon, the essence of courtly civility was its asymetrical structure: if in some versions, the rules of polite behaviour were ones in which respect flowed upward but not downward, other models of civility emphasized the basic distinction of reciprocity; specifically, as Elizabeth Goldsmith has shown, the culture of the salons was designed to sustain 'the illusion of a world where hierarchy does not exist' (cited in Gordon, 93).

French civility in Gordon's analysis helped establish a 'philosophical space in which the spirit of distinction merged with the spirit of universalism ... a territory that has been left uncharted by Elias, a territory that contains the roots of what I have called the "Self-Centred Cosmopolitanism' of the Enlightenment' (94). While Gordon does not specifically deal with the French colonies, and New France not at all, one can nonetheless see that his conception of 'self-centred cosmopolitanism' offers a model of selfhood in the context of French absolutism that could be extended to New France, if differently manifested in, say, the greater personal freedom of the *coureurs-de-bois*, or by what historian R.L. Séguin has characterized as the extensive *libertinage* of the cultural mores of New France (1972), and so provides a different communicative expression of self than Jorge Arditi's 'British' model of relational selfhood through etiquette (1998). However, Gordon does show that the ideal of conversational, convivial sociability, manifested in the cultivation of the art of conversation, allowed for the possibility of freedom under absolute monarchy – that is, that the profoundly monarchical and the profoundly liberal were not mutually exclusive. In this sense, the ideals of 'egalitarian politeness' (112) – the non-existence of 'tyranny' in conversation – could develop into 'an intelligible political alternative to absolutism' (112). For this reason, he sees egalitarian politeness as 'a *postdemocratic*' rather than a protodemocratic ideal, and the public sphere in apolitical form as 'repudiating political action by investing the concept of a nonpolitical public with value' (112, emphasis added). It was in this (apolitical) sphere that the 'highest public ideals (equality, rational communication, virtuous action) could be effectively realized' (112). The lessons of this would not be lost on the Canadian experience of civil culture and, indeed, they provide elements for emphasizing traits of civility, politeness, and substantial value-investment in the nonpolitical public sphere that have often been identified with the Canadian experience, but in a far more productive light than has previously been the case.

What is of especial interest to us here is how the emphasis on sociable communication ran afoul of the French Revolution. Note that the idea of sociable communication here is not without a resemblance to the rhetoric of Kenneth Burke and also his student Hugh Duncan in such books as Duncan's *Communication and Social Order* (1962). The previous influence of the Scottish Enlightenment's model of the negotiation of the transition to commercial societies without losing sight of the centrality of a practical rhetoric as part of the process (Hirschman 1977) is obvious and, in turn, its influence upon Upper Canadian theories of education in the nineteenth century (Hubert 1994). In particular Gordon examines how eighteenth-century liberal reformer André Morellet's ideals of communicative sociability (and the influence of print technologies and public opinion in the conduct of administration) clashed so profoundly with the Revolution's transformation of historical temporality and he examines the murderous deployment of language to reveal the ideals of communicative sociability as literally impossible in a revolutionary regime.

For one, in abolishing the feudal system – the ancien régime of the Revolution's own invention – the Revolution sought to abolish the past as a whole, leaving meaningful history with only one dimension – that extending into the future (Gordon, 229). Second, revolutionary culture, to the extent the revolutionaries believed they were regenerating the world from a state of total corruption, sought to dissolve all the relationships that existed between the individual and the state under the old regime. The revolutionary state was thus not bound by any previous laws, privileges, or customs, and so was free to reinvent time, history, and the world. Third, and most relevant for our argument, the revolution developed forms of communication never encountered before. Gordon claims: 'Revolutionary political culture ... was grounded in the substantive ideal of *civisme*, not the formal ideal of *civilité*. Virtuous deeds, not polite manners, were important. Direct action meant more than words, or more precisely, language became a mode of direct action in a way it had not been in the Enlightenment. In the system of denunciations and interrogations of the Revolution, language became a means of imposing a public identity on others so as to justify their annihilation' (233). Violent language, and the more violent the better, became the measure of proving one's patriotism, as Marat's *Ami du peuple* newspaper demonstrated (and, in a somewhat different context, as would *Der Stürmer* in the context of the Nazi revolution). Gordon states: 'Revolutionary violence ruined the myth that politeness was modernity's essence and that France was the most sociable nation in the world' (240). He goes on to observe that the democratic revolution generated 'an attitude toward communication' that was a perversion of the ideals of communicative sociability. 'The purpose of speech was not to create truth but to prove to others that one identified with it, or that others did not. With the truth defined in advance, politeness could be nothing but a superfluous ornament to language, and language itself could only be a tool of didacticism and denunciation' (234). In this sense, 'democratic communication' becomes something of an oxymoron, introducing into the performance of social appearance 'a competitive spirit ... a voracious pursuit of power, and a degeneration of language that render absurd the Enlightenment belief that free communication is enough to constitute and temper authority' (243–4).

On the other hand, and this was crucial for the continuities of Canadian civil culture's maintenance of key aspects of the apolitical public sphere of French absolutism, Canada was never a revolutionary polity. On the contrary, and even more so once New France fell under British colonial administration, British North America (and the survival of its French prerevolutionary civil culture) saw itself at least for a time as an emblematically counterrevolutionary social formation. The next chapter turns to the British contribution to this mode of performing power.

Conclusion

It would be unfair and inaccurate to claim that common-law Canada's legal culture was monolithic in its *in-difference* – the work of Tina Loo (1994) on British Columbia legal culture or Blaine Baker's brilliant reconstruction (1985) of late Victorian legal culture in Ontario strongly suggest otherwise. However, our preoccupation in this chapter with some of the fundamental problems occasioned by the transfer of legal regimes, from French to English and then to what Brisson terms 'compound law' (*le droit mixte*), has brought out, we believe, with sharper focus the complexities of communicative interaction in the translation from one context to another. The persistence, not to say repetitiousness, since the late eighteenth century, of the same problems that continue to preoccupy contemporary, particularly central Canadian civil culture (debates over cultural distinctiveness and constitutional change) illustrate how little has been resolved in this regard, and how much time, energy, and effort has been spent in avoiding coming to grips with the particularities – dare one say the 'uniqueness'? – of Canadian civil culture. To be sure, some progress was realized and stabilization did occur sufficient for the establishment of a working legal system within the framework of a Canadian federalism; but such stabilization was at best of brief duration; sooner or later, as we will see in the chapters below, there was destabilization by the constant recurrence of 'crises' over constitutional issues, questions of language, education, or religion – in short, of the fundamental figurations of social life understood as symbolic interactions.

What took shape in the form of 'Canada,' the law acting here, for the reasons we have seen above, as emblematic, was an unstable framing structure whose dual sovereignty would find itself, at least until the 1980s under contestation, in particular by appeal to British legal instances. Instead, what took shape as 'Canada' was a series of discrete subsystems – of laws, and of political party organization (see Stewart 1986) – that created a technically functional order of governance that did not act as a connector between system and lifeworlds. The following chapters, then, turn in detail to these subsequent problems of connectivity and the struggles by the citizenry to open them up to public deliberation. We begin, naturally enough, with the problem of constituting constitutions, in the absence of agreement on a structuring entity such as 'the law' (as opposed to a technical understanding of the 'rule of law') or a sovereignty-embodying figure such as 'the people' (as opposed to the more technical concept of 'the Crown').

4

Constituting Constitutions under
the British Regime,
1763–1867

In the preceding chapter, we saw how the difficulties involved in developing a workable regime of laws for Quebec provided opportunities for the emergence of politics and a protopublic sphere. This was in part a consequence of the logic of conquest, which included Britain's recognition of prior institutions and practices and a certain willingness to grant them some continued form of standing. For all of that, however, the colony was now British. Regardless of their origins, form, language, spirit, or dispositions, the laws of the colony now stood, in effect, as expressions of a British sovereign will. In other words, they were British laws. Even today, Quebec's Civil Code ultimately receives its authority, even at a great remove, from the acts of Britain's Parliament that constituted Canada. It is those acts that have formally established Canada's very existence as a state with the capacity to enact legitimate laws. Canada was created by and through law, and the Canadian state (including the provinces) forms a complex apparatus for forming and enforcing laws. Law is the medium of statehood.

In this chapter, we will consider the constitution of Canada in and through law. More specifically, our emphasis will be on 'constitution,' as the very process of making Canada, as a legal entitity, *come to appear* through the enactment of a first law. From Great Britain's perspective, the constitution of Canada was, as for France, a technical problem and, as such, a form of police. Nevertheless, Canada's constitution was fundamentally political, a manifestation of the metaphysics of the British model of sovereignty.

The Deep Structures of Constitution

Britain had to develop a system of governance for its newly acquired colony that would be both appropriate to the lifeworld of its colonists and consistent with British interests. To this end, Britain constituted Canada five times: through the Royal Proclamation of 1763, the Quebec Act of 1774, the Constitutional Act of 1791, the Canada Act of 1840, and the British North America Act of 1867. As such, there are five major British Canadas, and each was a prudential response to the technical and political problem of governance. Each of these constitutions established a different Canada, understood as a juridical entity. Each constitution established a regime of law to govern the colony's lifeworld, and each constitutional change can be understood as an attempt to devise a better or more effective regime than its predecessor, particularly in the context of changing political, social, and economic conditions. But each constitution was more than that, even for Britain, since each 'technical' problem was of course also political, and so required a 'British' solution, that is to say, one compatible with British constitutional principles and political culture, which were from the outset tainted by democratic sentiments. Not only was British authority founded in the recognition of some form of popular or collective rights, but even as police, Britain recognized that the governed must at least feel that their interests are taken into account.

We can best understand Canada, its political and civil culture, and the manner in which authority was configured by probing its constitution in law in order to reveal the grammar and forms of the constitutional discourse of authority and power. For this reason our focus is on the discourse of constitution in its 'rhetoricality.' We will proceed by uncovering the metaphysical principles and rhetorical figures and procedures by which constitutions have the binding authority that the status of 'law' entails. Our method consists of a close interpretive analysis of certain discourses understood as situated rhetorical speech acts. We will not be reading them as historians would, seeking to reconstruct the thought of the period, or as legal scholars concerned with interpreting how a law should best be interpreted and applied, but as rhetorical analysts concerned with how language 'does things,' and how it constitutes relations and realities through figurations and appeals. We speak of five Canadas because each constitution as law refigured the polity, not only territorially, but in terms of the nature of lawful authority, the character of its inhabitants as subjects, their occasions for speaking, and their rights, interests, and obligations. These Canadas exist in legal language. It is worth noting that they do not include the Atlantic colonies, which were not 'Canadian' until Confederation, both in their own self-understanding and in terms of the analytic framework of this study. Indeed, our methodological and political conceit is that only a revisionist reading permits speaking of one transhistorical Canada, for doing so requires a problematic anthropomorphization of distinct territories and populations into a collective subject within a historical narrative, problems which we discussed in chapter 2.

In what follows, we will consider British Canada's five constitutions in order
to identify the deep structures of constitution itself. We will focus primarily on
the first and last of the series. The Royal Proclamation of 1763 is by far the most
interesting, for it introduces British authority into what had previously been
France's Royal Province of Canada even as it opens a space for political
resistance to imperial aspirations. In the Royal Proclamation we can clearly see
the very grammar and rhetorical form of British constitution and its rhetorical
and prudential figurations of authority. Furthermore, it sets the stage for all that
will follow. The British North America Act of 1867 also commands our interest
because it 'resolves' Britain's colonial problem, rendering Canada quasi-
independent from the mother country. It marks the beginning of Canada's
sovereignty as a legal entity.

The Royal Proclamation of 1763

Quebec becomes a British territory with the Treaty of Paris, which as a contract
between monarchs established the terms by which 'Sa Majesté très Chrétienne
cède & garantit à Sa dite Majesté Britannique, en toute Propriété Le Canada
avec toutes ses Dépendances' while Britain's king cedes a number of territories
and fishing rights and agrees to grant to his new subjects 'la Liberté de la
Religion Catholique ... en tant que le permettent Les Loix de la Grande
Bretagne' (Shortt and Doughty 1907: 75) as well as the right to sell their
property and emigrate to France.[1] The Treaty of Paris establishes the basic legal
framework for Canada's first British constitution, the Royal Proclamation by
George III in 1763. Without making too much of the treaty itself, it is important
to recognize that at the outset French colonists remain subjects; they do not
become property. Indeed they become British subjects with property and
religious rights. Furthermore, the treaty as law binds the new monarch. His
sovereignty is subordinated to his word as given to his peers before all.

From London's perspective, the Treaty of Paris posed the problem of the
constitution of a 'governable' inhabited territory. From the point of view of
British lawmakers, Canadian constitutionalizing is the technical endeavour of
establishing functional institutions and procedures though a basic law. However, logically prior to forming a system of government, the colony itself
needed to be created – to be made real in law. This occurred through the
Proclamation, which renamed the colony, stated its boundaries, and specified
the basis of legal authority within them. The Proclamation is a public declaration that has the force of law. In establishing the colony, it is an illocutionary
speech act that makes real a set of obligations and institutions. It is also
rhetorical. It is a discourse addressed to the public that offers reasons for what it

has undertaken. As such, the proclamation establishes a complex of discursively structured relations of power. Over and above the particular provisions of the Proclamation, it provides the colony, through its performance, with a grammar of authority which, not surprisingly, is fundamentally British. That is to say, the Proclamation renders the colony 'British,' not at the level of language, religion, or statute, but in terms of the very manner that power was to be tapped into and deployed.

These are the words that transformed France's Canada into the British Province of Quebec:

WHEREAS WE have taken into Our Royal Consideration the extensive and valuable Acquisitions in America, secured to our Crown by the late Definitive Treaty of Peace, concluded at Paris, the 10th day of February last; and being desirous that all Our loving Subjects, as well of our Kingdom as of our Colonies in America, may avail themselves with convenient Speed, of the great Benefits and Advantages which must accrue therefrom to their Commerce, Manufactures, and Navigation, We have thought fit, with the Advice of our Privy Council, to issue this our Royal Proclamation, hereby to publish and declare to all our loving Subjects, that we have, with the Advice of our said Privy Council, granted our Letters Patent, under our Great Seal of Great Britain, to erect, within the Countries and Islands ceded and confirmed to Us by the said Treaty, Four distinct and separate Governments, styled and called by the names of Quebec, East Florida, West Florida, and Grenada ...

And whereas it will greatly contribute to the speedy settling of our said new Governments, that our loving subjects should be informed of our Paternal care, for the security of the Liberties and Properties of those who are and shall become Inhabitants thereof, We have thought fit to publish and declare, by this Our Proclamation, that We have, in the Letters Patent under our Great Seal of Great Britain, by which the said Governments are constituted, given express Power and Direction to our Governors of our Said Colonies respectively, that so soon as the state and circumstances of the said Colonies will admit thereof, they shall, with the Advice and Consent of the Members of our Council, summon and call General Assemblies within the said Governments respectively, in such a Manner and Form as is used and directed in those Colonies and Provinces in America which our under our immediate Government. (Shortt and Doughty 1907: 119 –20)

Savour the language here. Weigh its words and its form, for these incarnate law. They enact Canada's first constitution as they are addressed, in the very gesture of performance.

Consider the Proclamation in all of its 'publicness.' First, it is informative, making known the king's actions to all those with an interest. Second, it places the king's subjects under the law. In being told of the law, they are now subject to it, claimed by it. Indeed, they become legally real. The Proclamation does not only inform, but enacts and constitutes. The colonists have nothing to say in the matter. Their voice is absent. And yet they appear as they are addressed, and figured as the recipients of benefits produced by the king's measures. Third, the Proclamation subordinates the king's sovereignty, because it offers justifications for his actions. After all, a fully sovereign act requires no justification and is tied to no formalities.

To what is the king subject? Why must the king provide reasons for his act of constitution and to whom? The answer can be found within the very principles of the British Constitution subsequent to the Glorious Revolution. Subsequent to the alleged 'abdication' of James II and his execution, the British monarchy was no longer absolute. The king was now constrained by the Whig principles of the British 'Constitutional Settlement,' which understood king and subjects to be bound by a compact, where the former must justify his actions with respect to the interests of the realm and the latter owe him their loyalty for that reason. In other words, the king rules in order to serve his loyal and loving subjects (Lucaites 1984: passim).

The king's proclamation is thus rhetorical, offering 'good reasons' for his actions. However, this rhetoric must be understood as addressed to both his subjects and the law. The king after all does not need to justify himself to the French colonists in any practical sense. They have neither right nor means to contest his authority. The king must, however, justify his actions before the law, for his authority is a legal one. Jurists, parliamentarians, and all those with an interest in the law (dare we say the law itself?) witness the Proclamation, and it is before them that Crown and subject are joined in a relation of obligation. As such, the proclamation stages the king and his authority. The king represents himself in the theatrical sense (Habermas 1991: 7–12). Were his subjects his only audience, he would at most have to appear regal. Here, however, he is at pains to present himself as 'lawful.' His actions proceed with the 'advice and consent' of the Privy Council, and derive their authority from the Great Seal. Furthermore, as the Proclamation proceeds, it ordains constitution of political and legal institutions, and consistent with this, we should recall that this Proclamation stands as a legal act.

In practical terms, the king must maintain the authority necessary to govern. While the colonists at the time of the Proclamation were scarcely in a position to rebel, royal and legal authority must continuously resecure the recognition of the ruled. Concomitant with the practical necessity of legitimation are formal requirements upon the exercise of power. British custom as well as practical necessity requires that the exercise of authority be accompanied by the giving of reasons. The king must appear legitimate before the law. Great Britain is not a republic of course; the people are not sovereign. But neither is the king. Both are bound to each other through history and law. Thus, the king must proclaim his paternal affection for his subjects even as he bears witness to their love for him.

The formality of the language of the Proclamation bears witness precisely to the legal constitution of the monarchy itself. Thus, while the Proclamation uses figures of persuasion it is also 'constitutive,' for it proclaims and renders legally real a relationship between Crown and subject. The Proclamation, as an act of constitution, is an illocutionary speech act which establishes a 'reality,' in this case a regime of right and authority, by its very performance. It also brings or re-calls into being an ethical relation between Crown and subject based on the logic of gift-giving, which as Mauss (1970) observes, reveals and establishes a structure of obligation. The king figures himself as father through a constitutive act, an act of power, itself figured as an act of 'Paternal care.' Originating with the sovereign, the colony is a gift of love to his subjects, figured as his 'loving' children. Even so, they are not minor children but mercantile subjects, capable of benefiting from the 'Advantages' of British commerce. Acting as an enlight-ened parent, the king indicates concern for his subjects' autonomy, for their 'Liberties and Properties,' which are secured by the British Constitution and its 'feminized' model of power, which McGee traces to the reign of Elizabeth I. She secured her authority as queen through a rhetoric that privileged British 'liberty' as 'precisely a *spirit*, a feeling "in the presence of" a peculiarly comfortable form of power' (McGee 1980: 45).

This then, is a remarkable model of 'conquest,' for while the colonists themselves do not speak to the right or wisdom of this constitution, they are represented in the theatrical sense: they are placed 'on stage,' figured both before and within the Law so that they have equal standing with the 'old' subjects who would emigrate to the colony. The Proclamation effects what is almost a transubstantiation, at least with respect to legal essences. The Procla-mation entirely identifies the 'new subjects' with Great Britain and its interests. Their particularity is effaced in the process, even though their difference is acknowledged obliquely through reference to the Treaty of Paris and later clauses in the Proclamation that recognize religious rights. Their difference is, in other words, admitted but incidental to their attributed identity as subjects. This simultaneous recognition and denial of difference will trouble Canada's constitutions from that point on and will receive greater treatment below. For the moment, however, suffice it to say that the subject constituted in an obligation by this act and its gift is 'imaginary,' projected by these discourses themselves onto the real. So imagined, subject, colony, and the realm share a common ethos, which finds its interest in commerce, navigation, and manufacturing, and is cemented by an affective bond. In other words, the Proclamation constitutes the colony's inhabitants as rights-bearing, king-loving mercantile subjects.

Rhetoric and Recalcitrance

In the Proclamation, we find the deep logic of Canada's constitutions. The Crown translates and constitutes an inhabited territory into a colony in its own image through a law referencing rhetoric. But there is, of course, more to the constitutive process. Constitution not only provides an identity to the colony, but also establishes its 'magistracies,' its apparatus of governance. Thus, the Proclamation extends British law to the colony and mandates the calling of an assembly and the establishment of courts. More importantly, the Proclamation constitutes a governor as the king's agent and proxy, with judicial and executive authority and a limited power of constitution as well. The Proclamation thus continues:

We have given Power under our Great Seal to the Governors of our said Colonies respectively to erect and constitute, with the Advice of our said Councils respectively, Courts of Judicature and public Justice within our Said Colonies for hearing and determining all Causes, as well Criminal as Civil, according to Law and Equity, and as near as may be agreeable to the Laws of England, with Liberty to all Persons who may think themselves aggrieved by the Sentences of such Courts, in all Civil Cases, to appeal, under the usual Limitations and Restrictions, to Us in our Privy Council. (Shortt and Doughty 1907: 121)

Logically here, we move from the general to the specific, from broad legitimations to instruments of governance. As in the previous paragraph of the Proclamation, royal authority finds its legitimation in what, as we noted above, McGee terms a 'feminization of power.' The laws are a benefit, compatible with equity, and hence a positive good. We can see more clearly the nature of executive authority by also considering the king's commission of and instructions to Quebec's first British governor, James Murray:

We, reposing especial trust and Confidence in the prudence, Courage and loyalty of you the said James Murray, of our especial grace, Certain Knowledge and meer motion, have thought fit to Constitute and appoint, and by these presents, do Constitute and appoint you, the said James Murray to be Our Captain General and Governor in Chief in and over our Province of Quebec in America ...

And we, do hereby require and Command you to do and execute all things in due manner that shall belong to your said Command and the Trust we have reposed in you. (Shortt and Doughty 1907: 126–7)

Murray, the man, comes to occupy the place and becomes invested with the identity of governor, inhabited by the obligation to enact the Crown's accompanying instructions, which in eighty-two paragraphs stipulate the institutional machinery for enacting and enforcing law. The Proclamation does more, however, for it also recognizes the limits of specification and the need for a governor's discretion:

And whereas it is directed, by Our Commission to You under Our great Seal, that as soon as the Situation and Circumstances of Our said Province will admit thereof, You shall, with the Advice of our Council, summon and call a General Assembly of the Freeholders in Our said Province; You are therefore, as soon as the more pressing Affairs of Government will allow to give all possible attention to the carrying of this important Object into Execution: But, as it may be impracticable for the present to form such an Establishment, You are in the mean time to make such Rules and Regulations, by the Advice of Our said Council, as shall appear to be necessary for the Peace, Order, and good Government of Our said Province, taking Care that nothing be passed or done, that shall any ways tend to affect the Life, Limb or Liberty of the Subject, or to the imposing any Duties or Taxes. (Shortt and Doughty 1907: 135)

The application of laws requires that they and circumstances be interpreted. Thus, we should expect that any governor, prince, or executive will be granted the power to judge. Under the British constitution more is involved, however. Recall that the power of the king is not based in absolute right, but derived from a compact which requires that he act to further the interests of his subjects. The king's authority is, in other words, derivative of his seeking to be prudent. As the king's representative, the new governor similarly must use his judgment and rule with regard to what is best.

Prudence or *phronesis* is an intellectual virtue discussed by Aristotle in *The Nichomachean Ethics*. It consists of acting in such a manner as to favour the realization of the contingent good for a polity. It is based in deliberation and the capacity to act. The contingency and particularity of human affairs renders judgment inevitable and necessary. Prudence is the virtue of judging and acting well. In these instructions, the governor must not only seek to act prudently in administering the laws in a narrow sense, but must also exercise the power of constitution itself prudently. Murray is only to summon an assembly when circumstances permit. Similarly, he is to apply the laws of England only as they are agreeable with Equity, an abstract and vague principle that only the governor's judgment can instantiate. Thus, what is constituted is not simply a delivery system for instructions from the appropriate British secretary or minister. Rather, provision is made in law for its subversion in order that the constitutional compact be maintained.

As soon as Murray executes his authority, the constraints upon prudent governance become apparent. Murray was instructed to establish a system of justice, his authority to judge all cases being an interim one. Murray did so by issuing an ordinance on 17 September 1764 that constituted a system of courts with jurisdictions, powers, and prerogatives:

His Excellency the Governor, by and with the Advice, Consent and Assistance of His Majesty's Council, and by Virtue of the Power and Authority to him given by his Majesty's Letters Patent, under the Great Seal of *Great Britain*, hath thought fit to Ordain and Declare; and his said Excellency, by and with the Advice, Consent and Assistance aforesaid, *Doth hereby Ordain and Declare*,

That a Superior Court of Judicature, or Court of King's Bench, be established in this Province, to sit and hold Terms in the Town of *Quebec*, twice in every Year, *viz.* One to begin on the Twenty-first Day of *January*, called *Hillary* Term, the other on the Twenty-first Day of *June*, called *Trinity* term.

In this Court His Majesty's Chief-Justice presides, with Power and Authority to hear and determine all criminal and civil Causes, agreeable to the Laws of *England*, and the Ordinances of this Province ...

In all Tryals in this Court, all His Majesty's Subjects in this Colony to be admitted on Juries without Distinction. (Shortt and Doughty 1907: 149)

In like manner, the ordinance also constitutes an inferior court, a 'Court of Common-Pleas,' that will sit concurrently with the Superior Court. This lower court is less strictly tied to English law and the authority of French law is recognized even as it is rescinded, since:

The *Judges* in this Court are to determine agreeable to Equity, having Regard nevertheless to the Laws of *England*, as far as the Circumstances and present Situation of Things will admit, until such Time as proper Ordinances for the Information of the People can be established by the Governor and Council, agreeable to the *Laws of England*.

The *French* laws and Customs to be allowed and admitted in all Causes in this Court, between the Natives and this Province, where the Cause of Action arose before the first Day of *October*, One Thousand Seven Hundred and Sixty Four ...

Canadian Advocats, Proctors, &c. may practise in this court. (Shortt and Doughty 1907: 150)

As was bound to happen, Murray's ordinance could not be implemented smoothly and provoked resistance and controversy. In his discussion of power, Michel Foucault observes that all power encounters resistance. By this, Foucault is not speaking of resistance in the heroic political sense, but rather in the manner a physicist observes – for every action there is a reaction. Power and resistance form a pair (Foucault 1980: 147). Resistance can be inertia or noise as much as a refusal and a response. The application of law in all cases encounters a 'resistance' that must be overcome, for law is regulative and disciplinary, and its raison d'être is to shape what might be otherwise. Here, not only is there resistance in that material sense. The colonists and their lifeworlds are more than matter to be absorbed and translated with difficulty by law and power. The colonists represent themselves. They make themselves visible through speech. Within a month of the emission of the ordinance, the Grand Jury of Quebec, or at least its British majority, made presentments that asserted that as the sole representative body in the province, it should be consulted before any ordinance be passed into law, and also objected specifically to the quality of justice rendered by the lower courts and justices of the peace, to the number of cases to be decided by jury, and to the presence of Catholics on juries, especially when both litigants are Protestants (Shortt and Doughty 1907: 153). The French Grand Jurors responded, point by point, objecting in form and substance to most of what the majority had declared, but recommending that French-speaking jurors should be provided with translations in cases with English-speaking litigants, all the while proclaiming their affection to His Majesty and arguing that there was no legal basis for reducing 'new subjects' to slavery by excluding them from juries and the holding of other offices (Shortt and Doughty 1907: 157). Shortly thereafter, a number of French-speaking subjects addressed the king. In that address, they invoked the compact between monarch and subject and protested the unhappiness that had befallen them:

La véritable gloire d'un Roy conquérant est de procurer aux vaincus le même bonheur et la même tranquilité dans leur Religion et dans la Possession de leurs biens, dont ils joüissoient avant leur deffaite: Nous avons joüi de cette Tranquilité pendant la Guerre même, elle a augmentée depuis la Paix faitte. Hé voilà comme elle nous a été procurée. Attachés à notre Religion, nous avons juré au pied du Sanctuaire une fidelité inviolable à Votre Majesté, nous ne nous en sommes jamais écartés, et nous jurons de nouveau de ne nous en jamais écarter, fussions nous par la suitte aussy malheureux que nous avons été heureux; mais comment pourrions nous ne pas l'être, après les Temoiganges de bonté paternelle dont Votre Majesté nous a fait assurer, que nous ne serions jamais troublés dans l'exercice de notre Religion ...
Depuis quatre ans nous jouissons de la plus grande Tranquilité; Quel bouleversement

vient donc nous l'enlever? de la part de quatre ou Cinq Personnes de Loy, dont nous respectons le Caractère, mais qui n'entendent point notre langue, et qui voudroient qu'aussitôt qu'elles ont parlé, nous puissions comprendre des Constitutions qu'elles ne nous ont point expliquées et aux quelles nous serons toujours prêts de nous soumettre, lorsqu'elles nous seront connües; mais comment les Connoître, si elles ne nous sont point rendües en notre Langue?[2] (Shortt and Doughty 1907: 161–2)

They further asserted that the new laws had resulted in citizens being imprisoned without being heard, ruinous legal costs, and the settlement of family affairs being obstructed by individuals 'à qui on ne peut parler qu'avec des Guinées à la Main.' They then concluded, in the same humble tone, by scapegoating the English Grand Jurors:

Pour ne point abuser des Moments précieux de Votre Majesté, nous finissions par l'assurer, que sans avoir connu les Constitutions Angloises, nous avons depuis quatre Ans goûté la douceur du Gouvernement, la gouterions encore, si Messrs les Jurés anglois avoient autant de soumission pour les décisions sages du Gouverneur et de son Conseil, que nous en avons; si par des Constitutions nouvelles, qu'ils veulent introduire pour nous rendre leurs Esclaves, ils ne cherchoient point à changer tout de suite l'ordre de la Justice et son Administration.[3] (Shortt and Doughty 1907: 163)

And they then plead for a set of measures that will insure their access to French law in the French language.

These subjects do not challenge the legitimacy of the British constitution that the Proclamation has bestowed upon them. On the contrary, they precisely adopt the same rhetoric of legitimation of that constitution, and place themselves within its logic of mutual affection and obligation. The Proclamation as such has established the rhetorical figure one must employ in order to appear rhetorically. Through that figure, they protest the improper application of the law, and the efforts by a very small number of British merchants to exclude several thousand new subjects because of their religion and ignorance of English, and hence of British laws and customs. In a most telling argument, they declare their willingness to submit to all laws made for the good of the colony, but ask only that they may understand them, that they be in the French language.

Such exchanges marked the period from 1764 until the Quebec Act, a decade later. Because abstract constitutional principle is instantiated in the application of law to cases through a judicial framework, it is precisely here that tensions in the colony are manifest and play themselves out. Furthermore, these exchanges instantiate the fundamentally agonistic structure of Canadian constitutional history. It is important here to stress that while the Proclamation as constitution and the law itself 'imagine' and 'figure' the colony, the efficacy of the laws requires that such figuration not encounter excessive resistance or recalcitrance. The law therefore must manage or anticipate the 'appearance' of that which it governs. The law in this is rhetorical, for it figures its object, takes counter-arguments into account, and establishes the regime of appearance in which claims and colonists come to presence.

A Brief Excursus on Law, Rationality, and Legitimate Authority

The challenge facing Great Britain was to establish a working British constitution for its colony. For a constitution to function, it must have sufficient internal coherence to operate as technical apparatus. It must, in other words, be technically rational. Second, the law is not a 'closed' discursive machine but is open to the lifeworld. Law must translate and encode the lifeworld, including common-sense notions, established practices, and prior laws and legal objects. In doing so, law reconstitutes the lifeworld. It brings into being legal subjects, legal objects, legal institutions, and legal discourses. In some cases, this process of constitution proceeds from and provides technical meaning for prior extra-legal practices. In other cases law constitutes practices that are fully its own. In all cases, however, law seeks to contain practices, to rationalize them, and to define them in terms of normatively specified procedures.

In order to function, law must offer a codification that is not only hermeneutically adequate but also practicable. It must also be socially rational. Thus, as the Attorney General of the colony, Edward Thurlow, explains in a report to the king, some at the time contended that when formerly French colonists were guaranteed their property through the Treaty of Paris, French property law came with it, since 'property' has no meaning outside of a legal framework (Shortt and Doughty 1907: 305). From this perspective, attempts to regulate the property of new subjects through British law would result in social rationality deficit, because 'property' itself is a different entity in the two legal regimes. Finally, as Habermas observes, law as a technical system requires legitimation (Habermas 1996: 30). The legitimacy of that system is derived from apparent rationality, as outlined above, as well as from broader ideological principles. In the context of contemporary normative democratic theory, such principles include popular sovereignty and human rights. In eighteenth-century Britain, analogous principles were the authority of the Great Seal and Liberty and Justice.

The law's legitimacy and functionality derive from its appearance. Rhetoric's province is appearance and for this reason the law is thoroughly rhetorical. As noted above, law cannot function if it is technically or socially irrational. The risk of such irrationality is contained, however, by the instances of judgment the law itself provides. Judges and governors have the task of rendering the law rational, through rhetorical interpretation. Furthermore, the hermeneutic adequacy and 'social rationality' of the law cannot be the product of a mere correspondence of law and lifeworld for, even under the best circumstances, the lifeworld exceeds its codification. The law cannot name and constitute its own domain without recalcitrance. Governors, legislators, courts, etc. who are concerned with the application of law must interpret it in order to implement it. These interpretations are rhetorical, directed toward securing assent and maintaining the practical and ideological legitimacy of law.

Britain's fundamental rhetorical problem was to set up a constitution that the colonists would agree to be governed under. It was exacerbated because Canada was a previouly settled colony, itself already constituted, albeit incompletely, through the legacy of ancien régime categories. Britain had to attend to prior orders of appearance. To secure legitimacy, Britain had to establish an order that appeared prudent, that is to say, appeared rational and workable. The governor could only govern well if he appeared to, so that he could prove the rightness of his and the Constitution's authority.

The Rhetoric of Constitution and Governance

Effective rhetorical discourse, as a form of 'symbolic action,' includes an appreciation of counterargument, adaptation, and change. We can observe this rhetorical dynamic in the responses of British power to the problems arising from the colony's reconstitution as British. London does not react; it responds. Murray receives additional instructions from the Colonial Office, which interprets the Proclamation, and states that the extension of the benefit of British laws to the colony should not be understood as taking away from the 'native inhabitants' the modes of ownership, descent, and alienation of real property, or of excluding them from participating in the administration of judicature. Murray quickly issues a new ordinance that temporarily reinstates French law with respect to property. Other ordinances reduce the class of cases requiring juries, link jury composition to the origin of the litigants, British for British, Canadian for Canadian, and six of each when the contending parties are from both groups. Murray subsequently interprets his instructions liberally, and in many cases yields to customs of French origin, or does not fully enforce British laws that might restrict the rights of Catholics despite the Treaty of Paris. Such operations reconfigure the law in accordance with those subject to it in their capacity of 'audience,' as interpreters and judges of the law's validity with respect to day-to-day practices. Also, because British law required that assemblymen renounce under oath their faith in certain Catholic doctrines (the consequence of which would have been to exclude Catholics, and hence nearly all 'new subjects' from an assembly), Murray defers establishing that body and governs by order-in-council. The formerly French colonists had no experience with legislatures, and as such, a paternalistic 'Crown colony' appeared more just and legitimate than would have an assembly composed of recent British immigrants legislating their own interests.

Murray's capacity to govern and constitute prudently was limited, however. While the Proclamation figured old and new subjects together, the traders in their self-representations refused that figuration. For them, the new subjects were 'other,' not British, not English-speaking, but loyal to the pope and ignorant of British law and custom. That figuration found its mirror in the petitions of the new subjects, who signified their attachment to the Crown and the disloyalty of their antagonists. Prudent governance requires that the ethos of a colony be stable and that a sense of common good be recognizable. Because the colonists themselves figured the colony as divided, Murray's attempt to decree a procedure for the execution of laws was unsuccessful. While the restoration of the old system of land tenure and other measures offered some relief to the majority, it could only do so by deviating from British norms, hence alienating the vocal British minority.

Prudence in the Aristotelian sense is nearly impossible in the absence of a constitutional settlement that secures authority through law and force, and it provides an ethical horizon against which the 'good' of the polity can be interpreted. Prudence usually depends upon a proper amount of ambiguity. The greater the complexity of a polity, and the less predictable its particularities and contingencies, the greater the need for judgment and prudence over and above law. At a certain point, however, when a polity is divided against itself, and has no substance or 'constitution' in the metaphysical sense, the challenge to prudence might well be insurmountable and order might require a normalizing power.

This is what happened under the Proclamation and Murray's governance. In the colony, neither his executive authority nor his ordinances were sufficient to secure effective government. In his efforts to figure authority in a manner appropriate to the colonials, he was faced with two audiences with radically different lifeworlds, interests, and corresponding expectations. Consequently, Murray's ethos became impeachable. The merchants figured themselves as the true loyal colonists before England as they petitioned the Lords, demanding political and judicial institutions in their image. They became Murray's rhetorical antagonists before London and within the colony:

The Governor instead of acting agreeable to that confidence reposed in him by your majesty, in giving a favorable Reception to those of your Majesty's Subjects, who petition and apply to him on such important Occasions as require it, doth frequently treat them with a Rage and a Rudeness of Language and Demeanor, as dishonourable to the Trust he holds of your Majesty as painful to those who suffer from it. (Shortt and Doughty 1907: 169)

Murray responded by scapegoating them as 'Fanaticks,' figuring them as madmen consubstantial neither with the colony nor with the loving ethos instantiated in the Proclamation. It is in this latter context that we can understand Murray's hyperbolic letter of 29 October 1764 to the Lords, in which he also condemns his antagonists, the British merchants unhappy with his sympathy toward the French-speaking majority:

Little, very little, will content the New Subjects but nothing will satisfy the Licentious Fanaticks Trading here, but the expulsion of the Canadians who are perhaps the bravest and the best race upon the Globe, a Race, who coul'd they be indulged with a few priviledges which the Laws of England deny to Roman Catholicks at home, wou'd soon get the better of every National Antipathy to the Conquerors and become the most faithful and most useful set of Men in this American Empire. (Kennedy 1918: 40)

The governor is the locus of translation between Britain and the colony. One of Murray's responsibilities was to advise the Lords of Trade regarding the colony's administration. Murray as such had the task of rendering the colony and its lifeworld to Britain, in order both to justify his own prudential decisions and to bring Britain to adapt its legislation to the colony, consistent again with 'technical' imperatives of governability and broader issues of 'legitimation.' Over and above whatever sympathy toward new subjects historians attribute to Murray, one can also discern in this gesture of praise an attempt to sway the Lords by comparing in the most disproportionate of terms the meagre costs of overcoming antipathy (only an 'indulgence' is required) against the great benefits that would accrue. That is to say, Murray figures the colony so that the king's secretaries and Parliament will refigure the terms of its constitution in order that it be more secure at all levels.

Reconstitution and Refiguration

The eleven years from the Proclamation to the Quebec Act reveal the life cycle of the process of Canadian constitution under the British regime. British law figures authority and a government apparatus that includes nodal points for the prudent application of laws. Difference within the colony strains given representations and challenges the ethos of its governors and the prospects for prudence. Eventually, the law itself becomes the instrument for the colony's refiguration. As such, the process of constitution never realizes perfection. Each constitution is the result of a moment of stasis in an ongoing but punctuated historical dynamic. In rhetoric, stasis occurs when the elements of a case have crystallized, when all the arguments for and against a proposition have been made, and it is time to judge and act. Similarly, each constitution is a response to a historical conjuncture that has 'come to a head.'

In what follows, we will briefly trace that dynamic by considering Britain's three subsequent attempts to refigure and reconstitute its colony in such a manner as to overcome the difficulties that came to the fore under the Royal Proclamation. Each of these subsequent Constitutions is a response to what preceded it and is thus in some sense an innovation, contributing to the form of what will follow. Also, and more importantly for our purposes, each reveals an additional aspect of the very logic of constitution in British North America. With the Quebec Act (1774) we see the dynamic relationship between law and prudence. We will also see starkly the implications of the logic of gift and counter-gift in a system of mutual obligation. The Constitution Act (1791) reveals the degree to which British authority is founded upon its ownership of the territory. We will also see the implications of constituting a new regime of appearance in law, with the establishment of a legislative assembly. This undermines the constitution's capacity to contain difference. The Union Act (1840), Britain's last constitutional initiative, when read in the context of Lord Durham's report and with Lord Sydenham's governance in mind, offers some insight into the accommodation possible between seemingly incompatible figurations of the basis for authority.

The Quebec Act 1774

From the outset, Canada was a problem for Great Britain. The distinctions between new and old subjects, the *écart* between British laws and the *coutume canadienne*, and indeed the very piety (and silence) of colonial subjects in the Proclamation (and their eventual unruly appearance in the colony) foreclosed any possibility for discursive and rhetorical closure, for a 'noise free' legal apparatus. Rather, each refiguration of the constitutional order is best understood as arising from a stasis point in Canada's ongoing constitutional *agon*.

Britain sought a legislative solution that would be technically and socially rational, but that remedy did not come quickly. The colony was but one concern among many for Britain. It was far away and the true state of affairs there was unclear. Furthermore, as should be evident from the preceding chapter, any blending of British law with pre-Conquest *Canadien* law, which was not quite French law, would be beset with difficulties. And so, during the administration of Murray's successor, Guy Carleton, he and his superiors in London continued to receive petitions, addresses, and other representations from (and of) His Majesty's old and new subjects. These enumerated wrongs and grievances, primarily arising from technical matters, such as the number and duration of court sessions, the quality of lower magistrates, high legal costs, and the severity of debtors' prison. Propertied merchants continued to demand an Assembly, where at least Protestants would sit. Catholic subjects further petitioned the king for equal privileges and rights as a free people. Within the apparatus of state, these issues were analysed with care. Pending a wholesale revision of the colony's constitutional framework, Carleton responded to some of these concerns by issuing an ordinance that rationalized the court system, increased the number of sessions, rendered judicial misconduct a heavily fined offence, and explicitly stipulated legal and judicial procedure. Meanwhile, legal opinions regarding the implications of the Treaty of Paris and the Proclamation were prepared, the status of current laws and regulations in the colony were examined, the implications of enforcing either French or English law in the colony and of calling an Assembly were considered with respect to the interests of both the Canadian colonists and Britain itself, and the extent of toleration of Catholic institutions, including the tithe, was debated. Recommendations for British legislation were formulated and draft bills were prepared.

Britain's considered response was the Quebec Act of 1774. The Act declared that the provisions of the Proclamation respecting civil government had been found socially irrational and imprudent, and hence 'upon Experience, to be inapplicable to the State and Circumstances of the Said Province,' and repealed the Proclamation, its attendant commissions, and every ordinance concerning civil government and the administration of justice. It wiped the slate clean. The right of Catholics to profess their faith was recognized, as were the rights of clergy to dues. Catholic subjects acquired the same rights as Protestants to hold offices, and the loyalty oath they had to take was replaced by one that did not require a renunciation of Catholic faith or doctrine. In civil matters, Canadian custom was reintroduced wholesale. The criminal law of England remained in force, because its 'Certainty,' 'Lenity,' and 'Benefits and Advantages' had been felt by the inhabitants. An assembly was declared inexpedient, and the governor was to appoint a council to legislate, subject to his consent and His Majesty's approval, but with no power of taxation, save for roads and buildings. Funds for the cost of government and the administration of justice were provided for in the accompanying Quebec Revenue Act, which specified duties on the import of wine, spirits, molasses, and syrups. Any other taxation would have required representation, which was, however, withheld.

In a sense, the Quebec Act arbitrated the dispute between new and old subjects when it repealed significant portions of the Proclamation and by implication the merchants' interpretation of it as promising a new English colony for commercial exploitation. Of course, the act did not silence debate. The traders quickly petitioned for its repeal, but the act placed Governor Carleton's ethos beyond reproach, as his prudent measures were constitutionalized and the ethos of the colony as a French part of Britain was affirmed. Furthermore, the Quebec Act did more than close a chapter in the history of the colony. It also opened a new one by redrawing the colony's boundaries. These were extended considerably, especially to south and west, into territories that might be claimed by the rebellious American colonies. This alteration of boundaries should remind us that, for Britain, the colony was not identical with its population. The 'Province of Quebec' was constituted neither as *polis* nor a nation, but as a territory only partially inhabited by both its subjects and an indigenous population whose special status was also recognized. Britain's authority was figured through ownership of territory. Colonists were, as such, subjects of His Majesty rather than 'citizens' of some country in the republican sense. It is precisely because the colonists did not form the 'people' of a country that Britain could without difficulty withhold an assembly, even though Britain as a general rule favoured such institutions. The colony and its colonists were not consubstantial. The former was an administered territory while the latter were tied to something greater, being British subjects, albeit differentiated, in a curious province of the realm.

When one considers the amount of study and debate that preceded the Quebec Act, the fact that it remained in force for only fourteen years should give pause. Considered as a theoretical 'ultimate' solution to the Quebec question, it must be seen as a failure. But such a judgment would be based upon a misrecognition of the nature of constitution and law. These should be understood as responses to historically contingent conditions. The Quebec Act was born in tumultuous times and it is in that context that it must be considered. Much happened between 1774 and 1791. Most importantly, the American colonies fought for and attained independence and the United Empire Loyalists were either chased out of or chose to leave the new republic. That Quebec remained a British colony must be considered a measure of the Quebec Act's success when judged from the perspective of tactics, rhetoric, or prudence. While the act did not inspire many new subjects to take up arms against the Americans, as some had hoped, these subjects did not side with the revolutionaries either. Without major grievances and lacking popular political institutions, the new subjects had neither motivation nor a forum to articulate opposition to colonial authority.

The American victory, as formalized in the peace between Britain and the Americans in 1783, transformed the dynamics of the colony. Of course, much appeared to remain the same. The British merchants in Montreal continued to press for British laws and representative institutions, while the new subjects, or at least their elites, resisted any modification to their constitution as established in the Quebec Act. But the colony's economic development and the potential for trade with the Americans became an increasingly important question. At the same time, the revolutionary new republic became a hostile place for those who had remained loyal to the British Crown. Loyalists were the object of threats, harassment, and violence in America. They were treated as traitors or political criminals to be purged. Their property was seized, many were tarred, and they were driven from their homes. From the British perspective, Loyalists were political refugees. They were also loyal and able-bodied potential colonists. They were to populate the colony with its newly extended boundaries. The fundamental British constitutional principle of mutual obligation inexorably led to Loyalist settlement.

As we have seen, the British merchants were not held in high regard by colonial governors. They were regarded as a self-interested lot, lacking in principles and uncommitted to the interests of the realm. Furthermore, they were impious and disruptive, refusing to accommodate themselves to Britain's desire for order. The Loyalists, on the other hand, owed their miseries to their loyalty to Britain. They were thus entitled as loving subjects to treatment in kind. That is to say, they were more deserving than the merchants in Montreal or Quebec, who recognized this and sought to use it to advantage. In 1784, the merchants and a number of 'progressive' new subjects, either merchants or members of the educated class, again petitioned the king for an assembly and British commercial law. Observe how their case is based less on their own merit than that of the Loyalists:

MAY IT PLEASE YOUR MAJESTY.

AFTER the Conquest of the Province of Canada by the Arms of Great Britain, Your Petitioners in compliance with Your Majesty's gracious and royal Proclamation, bearing date the 7th day of October, 1763, Settled and became established, in the New acquired Colony of Quebec; in the full reliance on the faith of the Crown of Great Britain, as expressed in the Proclamation, for the enjoyment of those Laws, that Freedom and Security in Canada, which the Principles of the English Constitution afforded, in every part of the British Dominions in America. YOUR PETITIONERS and the Inhabitants of the Province, have chearfully on every occasion, obeyed the

Controuling power of the Parliament of Great Britain, and with patience have suffered, during a period of Anarchy and War, rather than wound your Majesty's feelings, or embarrass the Throne with Remonstrances and Petitions, at a time when the safety of the Nation, made sacred every moment of Public deliberation. The Actions and Conduct of Your Petitioners when truly represented, will best express to Your Majesty, the Sincerity of their Loyalty and Attachment to the Crown and Government of Great Britain.

YOUR PETITIONERS look with Concern on the burthen of Great Britain, and with great Pain and Commiseration they see the distresses of Your Majesty's loyal Subjects, who, driven from their Estates, Wealth, and Possessions are daily taking Shelter in this British Colony; though their unsettled and distressed Situation, may for the present hinder them bringing forward their Petitions and their Claims; Your Majesty will readily perceive that a Government similar or Superior, to that under which they were born, had lived, and were happy, must be considered by those Your Majesty's unfortunate Subjects as an Affectionate proof of Your Majesty's Paternal Care and Regard for them; and the first Comfort which Your Majesty in relief to their Distresses can now grant: And the more so, as it will be a Blessing not merely granted to them, but extended to their Children and Posterity. (Kennedy 1930: 172)

This petition again should make clear the degree to which the British constitution is traversed by a rhetorical logic of contingency. This petition renders its claim not in terms of a general right under the law, but in terms of the specific circumstances of both merchants and loyalists. Furthermore, the key topos is worthiness in a logic of mutual obligation.

The petition reveals more than a rhetorical appeal: there is also an 'economy' of obligation at work in the British constitution. The king promised, merchants and Loyalists have suffered. The king is summoned to reciprocate. The petition summons the king to act to provide an 'Affectionate Proof' of his 'Care and Regard.' That is to say, and this is consistent with the logic of gift and counter-gift, it is the social bond that is at stake. The topos of obligation is pervasive. It appears not only in this petition, but also in those by the new subjects (also by now becoming known as Old Canadians) demanding that the status quo be maintained, and in a later petition by the Loyalists themselves. In 1785 the king is petitioned by Loyalists and troops who served during the war. They request that the western portion of the colony become a district distinct from Quebec, with British laws, and their own lieutenant-governor and council (who would nevertheless remain subordinate to the governor and council of Quebec). In this rhetoric, their suffering earns them a right: 'The Petitioners have the more Confidence in the Success of their Application, from reflecting that they do not ask for more than has already been granted to their Fellow Sufferers in Nova

Scotia, for less indeed than is enjoyed by those who are settled in the Province of New Brunswick, and only to be in the same situation with the Settlers in the Island of Cape Breton' (Shortt and Doughty 1907: 526). History is replete with irony. A small one is visited upon the merchants by London. The argument regarding the worthiness of Loyalists is recognized, but their consubstantiality with the merchants is not. They may all be English-speaking Britons, but some have given more and are hence more deserving. The Constitution Act of 1791 grants British institutions to the colony, but also partitions it. Two provinces are created: the territory along the St Lawrence west of the Ottawa river becomes Upper Canada, while the eastern territory becomes Lower Canada. The rule of obligation here remains particular and prudential: the Loyalists deserved British laws, and institutions at least of the quality they had in America. The new subjects, always loving and faithful, deserved to be treated equitably. Thus, both receive an assembly, but to the dismay of the merchants, Lower Canada was constituted with an overwhelmingly French-speaking majority and retained civil law.

The Constitution Act (1791)

The Constitution Act (1791) created two colonies out of one. In Lower Canada, the pre-Conquest civil code was retained, while Upper Canada would be governed by common law. Both colonies were subject to British criminal law and each was to have an elected assembly, an appointed legislative council, and an appointed executive council charged with advising a governor serving at His Majesty's pleasure. As such, this Act did more than partition the colony; it institutionalized the division of 'estates' that already existed. Legislation, including taxation measures, required the assent of the assembly. The assembly's power was checked, however, by the legislative council and by the requirement that legislation receive royal assent through the king's representative, the governor, who was also empowered to prorogue the assembly. As John Hare observes, through this constitution, Britain sought to grant British institutions without recreating the conditions that led the American colonies to break away (Hare 1993: 15). This constitution was a British solution to changing circumstances, but it also institutionalized the constitutive elements of further conflicts.

In considering this new constitution, we should be careful to recognize that it did more than reproduce or formalize previous antagonisms. Rather, old antagonisms would find new expression. The accommodation between the elite *Canadien* aristocracy and the British executive was replaced by a democratic dynamic that, even though much more 'British,' was also much more volatile.

Democracy, even if limited, is productive of new things, even while it has a tendency toward noise and disorder. And so, while this new constitution created new opportunities for conflicts between British and Canadiens, it also ultimately led to divisions between aristocrats and democrats (or reformers).

The new constitution refigured authority within the colony, for it constituted a new mode of appearance for the colonists. Recall that in the Royal Proclamation, the colonists appear but remain silent. An assembly is more than a place where certain members of the colony may speak to each other, adopt resolutions, and send them to a governor. An assembly, like the law itself, is a 'discursive apparatus,' which constitutes occasions to speak in a certain form, for a certain purpose, and assigns a particular ontological and epistemological status to speaker, speech act, and what is spoken. The founding premise of a legislature is that its members 'represent' their constituents, and this in a double sense. They are delegates, sent to speak on behalf of the electors of their district, and their speech itself stands as the collective opinion of those within the district. The implicit performative claim of an assemblyman's speech act is that it does not stand on its own, but is authorized by others, and is spoken in their name. Furthermore, the assembly itself stands to its members as they do to their constituents, and through a synecdochic chain, to the colony as a whole. In other words, in an assembly, members 'stage' the colony: they place it in words before others as an object of knowledge in order to elicit interested judgments.

It is important to recognize that in the assembly, and in the ideological underpinnings of that institution, 'representation' is indeed an effect of figuration, because there is no temporally or logically prior will or truth. The assemblyman speaks for his constituents only by displacing them. His speech can never be theirs, and indeed some of his constituents would disavow his speech if given the chance. He is figured by the institution and underlying political theories and ideologies of representative government. So figured, he has the rhetorical burden of figuring himself, of performing before both the assembly and his constituents as their representative. Now, in claiming that such speech is figurative, we do not mean to assert that it is disconnected or fully autonomous from the colony's lifeworld outside of the assembly's walls and discourse. What we are denying is the existence of an ontologically prior 'true' state of affairs that can be mirrored in assembly speech. The assemblyman might very well relay discourses from outside of the assembly, or present commonly held understandings of colonial affairs, but these themselves are tributaries of prior figurations. And clearly, an assemblyman's speech circulates back into the colony itself. In speaking, the assemblyman must abstract and reify, must attempt to render fixed what is unstable and contingent. In like manner, because the assembly is a legislative body, and in legislating speaks as with one voice, its own bills and declarations also are within an epistemology of representation, laying claim to speak of the colony itself as if it were a totality, identical with itself. The consequence of this figuring, and of the underlying epistemological claim, is that each colony comes to *appear*, in and through speech, as a distinct polity with a distinct collective identity. That is to say, the constitution of a legislature leads to the reification of the majority as a totality and gives rise to a virtual collective subject, the 'people,' with an institutionalized collective voice.

We will not here retell the struggle for responsible government, which is central to most accounts of Canadian political history, nor will we go into the details of the failed rebellions in both colonies. We will only point out that the 1791 Constitution Act set the stage for political paralysis. Because each assembly could be figured as representing 'the people,' and because the governor and appointed councils were in no way responsible to the people's representatives, they came to be figured as tyrants. Furthermore, in Lower Canada, English-speaking members of the assembly came to align themselves with the executive, particularly over issues of property and commercial law, leading to the unhappy conflation of practical and 'racial' differences. The same logic pertains to Upper Canada, as it had previously to the American colonies, with the obvious lack of a 'racial' figuration. At issue was not the accommodation of a non-British legal lifeworld, but the wisdom of local knowledge and the legitimacy of the local administration of local affairs. The distinctiveness of the English-speaking colonies was circumstantial, and not amenable to easy reification. Even so, an assembly, once constituted, establishes a difference between colony and empire that can be figured as fundamental and necessary. The American colonies did so when they proclaimed independence. In the Canadas, lines were drawn somewhat differently, but there was a rebellion in 1837, and independence from Britain was loudly advocated. Particularly in Upper Canada, the autonomy of executive authority (the absence of 'responsible government') was confronted with demands for popular sovereignty inspired by the American Revolution. At the level of constitution, two fundamental issues came to the fore: were the provinces extensions of a sovereign Great Britain, fully subject to its authority and thus without the right to select or direct the governor and his council? And later on, and more starkly, were province and metropole indeed consubstantial, and could the Crown acting under the Great Seal thus bestow a constitution as a binding gift?

While attacking particular governors and their councils, reformers in both colonies also sought constitutional solutions. They demanded that constitutional authority itself in the colonies be refigured, so as to find its roots in 'the people' themselves. What they demanded was not merely a technical reform, to overcome a technical rationality deficit within the constitution that led to gridlock. Their demand for an elected legislative council and for an executive council responsible to the assembly would have changed the very logic of constitution established in the Proclamation, undermined the role of the governor as the agent of British colonial policy, and challenged the sovereignty of the British Parliament. And yet, for all of this, reformers in both colonies did not set out to challenge directly the covenant between themselves and the Crown.

The '92 Resolutions' adopted by the legislature of Lower Canada in 1834 stipulated grievances and attacked the governor, the legislative and executive councils, and the colonial secretary for not modifying provisions of the Constitution Act in accordance with principles of British justice but at the same time loudly they proclaimed the colony's loyalty to the Crown and love for British principles. As such, they follow initially the genre of petition so well known to the British Constitution. A profession of faith is followed by listing of grievances, actions are defended as necessary, and suggestions are made to the Crown regarding the means to alleviate the grievances specified. Consider the first of three resolutions to establish again the loyalty of His Majesty's subjects.

Résolu, Que les loyaux sujets de Sa Majesté, le Peuple de cette province du Bas-Canada, ont montré le plus grand attachement pour l'Empire Brittanique doint ils forment partie; qu'ils l'ont défendu avec courage dans la guerre, à deux diverses fois; qu'à l'époque qui a précédé l'indépendance des ci-devant Colonies Anglaises de ce continent, et ils ont résisté à l'appel qu'elles leur faisaient de se joindre à leur confédération.[4]
(Lower Canada 1834: 1)

As we observed previously, the rhetoric of petition under the British Constitution proceeds out of the logic of obligation. The colonists have shown their love through their gifts and expect a reciprocal gesture. However, the revolutionary rhetoric of the eighteenth century provided new inventional topics permitting figurations of the ethos of the people and their Parliament in a manner unseen during the Glorious Revolution. Gone is the humility of the pious subject. The people will not be meek but will assert their rights. Thus, resolutions 49 and 50 declare:

Que cette chambre et le Peuple qu'elle représente, ne veulent ni ne prétendent menacer; mais qu'appuyés sur les principes des lois et de la justice, ils sont et doivent être politiquement assez forts pour n'être exposés à l'insulte d'aucun homme, quel qu'il soit, et tenus de le souffrit en silence; que dans leur style les dits Extraits de Dépêches du Secrétaire Colonial, tels que communiqués à cette Chambre, sont insultants et inconsidérés, à un degré tel, que nul corps constitué par le loi, même pour des fins

infiniment subordonnées à celle de la legislation, ne pourrait ne devrait les tolérer ...
[C]ette Chambre croirait manquer au Peuple Anglais, si elle hésitait à lui faire remar-
quer que, sous moins de vingt ans, la population des Etats-Unis d'Amérique sera autant
ou plus grande que celle de la Grande Bretagne; que celle de l'Amérique Anglaise sera
autant ou plus grande, que ne le fut celle des ci-devant Colonies Anglaises, lorsqu'elles
jugèrent que le tems était venu de decider, que l'avantage innapréciable de se gouver-
ner, au lieu d'être gouvernées, devait les engager à répudier un regime Colonial, qui fut,
généralement parlant, beaucoup meilleur que ne l'est aujourd'hui celli de l'Amérique
Anglaise.[5] (Lower Canada 1834: 11–12)

The governor's defenders responded to such agitations by casting the majority
as disloyal and ignorant (Kennedy 1930: 291). While the assembly battled the
legislative council and the governor over the raising of funds for the executive
and the administration of the province, other spokesmen for the 'people'
emerged. Speaking outside of the legislature, and no longer addressing the king
as loving subjects, these adopted a more 'American' tone, repudiating the
governor, disavowing his authority, and asserting the illegitimacy of their
constitution for not according them the affection and rights deserved by every
British subject. Indeed, they declared broken the compact of mutual obligation
so fundamental to the British Constitution, and first articulated in the colony by
the Royal Proclamation. Thus, the 1837 declaration of the Patriots at St Ours
could anticipate the coming rebellions and declared: 'Ne nous regardant plus
liés que par la force au gouvernement anglais, nous lui serons soumis comme à
un gouvernement de force, attendant de Dieu, de notre bon droit et des
circonstances un sort meilleur, les bienfaits de la liberté et d'un gouvernement
plus juste'[6] (Latouche 1977: 72). Justice and liberty are no longer the product of
the British Constitution but gifts from God, and while the king is not here
explicitly repudiated, Britain's authority to govern certainly is.

   In Upper Canada, reformers, forming a majority in the legislature, also
opposed the arbitrary power of the governor and pejoratively termed the
colony's governing clique a 'Family Compact.' As in Lower Canada, effective
governance was blocked because of a stalemate between the legislature and the
executive. As in Lower Canada, reformers demanded an elected legislative
council. When rebellions erupted in Lower Canada in 1837, Upper Canadian
radicals followed suit. The rebellions were easily put down by British soldiers,
however. Lower Canada's constitution was suspended. A further rebellion in
Lower Canada in 1838 was also put down and many of its leaders escaped to the
United States, some were jailed or transported to Australia, and a few were tried
and executed. Britain had demonstrated that it was unprepared to see its

interests or its laws violated in what it considered to be by right its territories. It refused a figuration of authority founded in popular sovereignty and did so, not only through words, but also through arms. However, the defeat of the rebellions in both Canadas could not fully resolve the matter. The problem of governance remained, and the rhetorical difficulty of constitution had grown significantly greater as a result. With the collapse of the rebellions of 1837 and 1838 and the repeal of that portion of the Quebec Act that granted Lower Canada a legislature, British authorities were faced once again with the prospect of beginning anew. The challenge for Britain was still to develop a constitution that would render the colony governable, and to install a system of law that would be technically, and more important, socially and ideologically rational. They were still primordial. How could Britain establish such a system once the colonists had not only appeared but had been granted a voice in law? What innovation could Britain devise that would satisfy its interests and secure legitimacy?

The finality of a constitution is good government. Subjects and sovereign, laws and institutions, practices and procedures must all be constituted so as to permit prudential administration, with respect both to the terms and logic of the particular constitution as well as with respect to its remainder, the unincorporated aspects of the lifeworld. An effective constitution must be rhetorical, figuring authority, the people, and the real itself in a manner that elicits agreement or assent. In this regard, the Constitution Act of 1791, as administered by its governors and the Colonial Office, was a failure. It constitutionalized differences without providing effective means for transcending them.

The Act of Union (1840)

Britain commissioned John Durham governor of its North American colonies and commissioned a report on their state of affairs. Subsequently, and following his recommendation, Upper and Lower Canada were reunited and English was established as the official language of record for its government. French Canadians became a minority in this colony, which Durham had hoped would lead to their gradual assimilation into a majority destined to prosper on the North American continent. The Act offered few other changes to the system of government. The power to constitute remained vested in Great Britain, a governor would continue to represent the Crown, legislative authority would be shared by an elected lower and an appointed upper house. Furthermore, the two former colonies retained their own laws. The only other innovations of significance were that taxation measures could only be introduced with the assent of the executive, as was the rule in Great Britain, and that a 'civil list' funding the executive branch of government was placed beyond the reach of the legislature, which otherwise would determine expenditures. Also, and against Durham's recommendation, the two former colonies were granted equal representation in a new assembly.

While the Act of Union was not particularly innovative, the politics from 1840 to 1867 were. Political coalitions between English- and French-speaking colonists emerged and successive governors gradually introduced 'responsible government' by forming executive councils that had the confidence of the assembly. These changes are fundamental to Canadian constitutional history, but can scarcely be attributed to the act of Union. At most, by reconstituting the boundaries of the colony, the act transformed the political dynamic in the Canadas. As Durham had hoped, the act rendered a politics of 'race' unproductive. French Canada did disappear, however, since political advantage could be gained through linguistic accommodation, but politics were realigned on the basis of policy, as indeed had been prefigured in the affinities between reformers in the two Canadas during the rebellions. Also, with the act came a new legislative council, and thus the colony's first governor was provided with the opportunity of starting afresh. Furthermore, because the new governor would not begin as the assembly's antagonist, he would have the opportunity to exercise prudence.

Prudence dictated a course other than the one followed by previous governors, which had led the colonies toward rebellion and ruin. Those governors had not figured themselves or their advisers responsible to the colonists, but at most to British policy and interests. Durham considered the continuation of such a model not only unproductive of good government but likely only to contribute to the colony's eventual disaffection with the mother country. In proposing responsible government, Durham offered a new prudential model as he inserted a new figure for the tie between colony and Crown into the state discourse. He was not the first to propose such a colonial relation, but his stature and the quality of his report, testifying to his ethos and prudence, gave it a particular rhetorical appeal. As Azjenstat's remarks imply, Durham's report must be understood in persuasive terms (Azjenstat 1988: 74–5, 87, passim). It was crafted rhetorically. Thus, Durham presents this innovation as merely the extension of the British principle of cabinet government into a British territory. Furthermore, Durham figures this change as reasonable through a refiguration of the nature of a colony itself. In the rhetoric of his report, the relation of mutual affection fundamental to the British constitution is refigured as an 'attachment,' hardly the same as an obligation; such a tie and colonial autonomy became simultaneously possible:

I believe that neither the interests nor the feelings of the people are incompatible with a Colonial Government, wisely and popularly administered. The proofs, which many who are much dissatisfied with the existing administration of the Government, have given of their loyalty, are not to be denied or overlooked. The attachment constantly exhibited by the people of these Provinces towards the British Crown and Empire, has all the characteristics of a strong national feeling. They value the institutions of their country, not merely from a sense of the practical advantages which they confer, but from sentiments of national pride; and they uphold them the more, because they are accustomed to view them as marks of nationality, which distinguish them from their Republican neighbours. I do not mean to affirm that this is a feeling which no impolicy on the part of the mother country will be unable to impair; but I do most confidently regard it as one which may, if rightly appreciated, be made the link of an enduring and an advantageous connexion. The British people of the North American Colonies are people on whom we may safely rely, and to whom we must not grudge power. (Durham 1970: 284–5)

Furthermore, Britain's gift of government as offered in the Proclamation took on a new cast, one in which the gift is now good government as the capacity for self-government. This marks a remarkable transformation in the colonial system, for colonials are no longer in the subordinate position of petitioners. The executive is now in their service. It becomes possible, without figuring the people as sovereign, to present them as preeminent by right.

The transition to cabinet government and an attendant party system was not an immediate consequence of the 1840 Constitution, but developed gradually, as each new governor figured his own role in government. Only with Lord Elgin, in 1847, did cabinet government fully take form, led by Lafontaine and Baldwin, former rebels in Lower and Upper Canada respectively. At that point Kennedy tells us, the governor came to be held in a much different regard, no longer partisan, but above the fray, as the bearer of the constitutional principle (Kennedy 1938: 242). Shortly thereafter Britain reinstated French as an official language of record at the colony's request.

For all of this, however, the Act of Union remained a failure according to the usual criteria. Not only did it not banish discord – no democratic constitution can do that – but it did not lead to stable government. Parties, factions, and coalitions were not strong enough to form stable majorities, and hence support ministries for more than brief periods. However, unlike the previous constitution, in which disagreement culminated in armed conflict between popular parties and their executive, division remained in the House and culminated in a coalition that would seek to determine the terms of its own reconstitution.

The British North America Act (1867)

In this last section, we will consider the British North America Act of 1867. It constitutes the fifth Canada as an essentially independent nation, a Dominion under the British Crown. The uniqueness of this Act derives from the fact that it is Canadian in inspiration and marks the moment where Canada falls away from Great Britain, not acquiring sovereignty in a grand gesture, nor exactly finding sovereignty at all, but crafting its own constitution nonetheless.

In his essay 'Declarations of Independence,' Jacques Derrida addresses the question of how a people can constitute themselves, looking particularly at the American case. Derrida observes: 'There was no signer, by right, before the text of the Declaration itself which remains the producer and guarantor of its own signature' (Derrida 1986: 10). Thus, Derrida asks of the Declaration: 'Is it that the good people have already freed themselves in fact and are only stating the fact of this emancipation in (*par*) the Declaration? Or is it rather that they free themselves at the instant of and by (*par*) the signature of this Declaration?' He then answers: 'This obscurity, this undecidability between, let's say, a performative structure and a constative structure, is required to produce the sought after effect' (9). What Derrida goes on to describe is the metaphysics of self-constitution. The signers of the Declaration (Jefferson et al.) are indeed only cosigners, acting as representatives of the people, even as it is only in signing that a people for them to represent truly comes to exist. And yet, that signing retroactively permits the people to claim injury by George III, which itself is adduced as necessitating the declaration. Or as Derrida succinctly puts it: 'The signature invents the signer.' We have, in the Declaration, a metaphysical *coup de force*. The 'is' and 'ought to be' are cojoined, and God 'the Supreme Judge of the world' is invoked as validation. God authorizes this constitutive moment. Sovereignty itself emerges in this speech act.

The constitution of Canada as a dominion proceeds quite differently. No equivalent to the declaration exists. There is no signifying moment where a people emerges and constitutes a state in its own image. There is no assertion of right, no appeal to the Supreme Judge, and no metaphysical tautology. There is only a petition. In the Legislative Assembly of the Province of Canada, John A. Macdonald did not move that a constitution be adopted, but only: 'That an humble Address be presented to Her Majesty, praying that She may be graciously pleased to cause a measure to be submitted to the Imperial Parliament' (Canada. Parliament 1865: 5). While the matter was considered of great import in the British North American provinces, Macdonald's motion seems in retrospect rather tame in contrast to the American declaration. His is not a 'sovereign performative.' His constitution will not proclaim itself and in so doing establish a new sovereignty. His constitution begins by submitting to an authority that is other.

Could we then say that Macdonald's constitution is devoid of metaphysical éclat? No, but its metaphysics are quite different from those that Jefferson instantiated. The American declaration's metaphysics puts in place, with God as guarantor, a sovereign subject, the people. The people as sovereign possess the extra-legal authority to constitute themselves politically. Confederation does not have an extra-legal genesis nor does it confer sovereignty upon the people. Indeed, ironically, there was no agent that had in itself the sovereign authority to constitute confederation in one illocutionary act. Clearly, the 'people' could not. Only the British Constitution itself, a dispersed communicative system, had sovereign authority. The metaphysical principle upholding the Canadian Constitution was not an extra-legal sovereign subject but, on the contrary, the principle of legality itself. Thus, instead of an eloquent declaration, we have the manipulation by elites of a specialized language, the law, in response to an exigency.

That constitutions are metaphysical should give us pause. Typically, they are thought of as the fundamental set of principles or rules of procedure that authorize governance and state action, whether written, as in the American model, or unwritten but instantiated in a normative history of practices, as in Great Britain. This understanding leaves little room for metaphysics, which resides both in and outside of any particular 'fundamental law.' Constitution can only be fully apprehended by broadening our conception to include the relation between constitution writ narrowly and the extraconstitutional. As Kenneth Burke observes, the constitutional and extraconstitutional form a dialectical pair. Burke notes that 'constitution' is a word belonging to the 'stance family,' and as such is deeply implicated in the metaphysics of substance. Outside of its political usage, constitution denotes an object's make-up, the principles and components that provide it with an identity or essence. Substance, however, is paradoxical, for the term simultaneously identifies what an object really is, its essence, and what is beneath it and supporting it, its substance (Burke 1969: 21–58).

In other words, constitutions can only be understood as what is properly external to them. A constitution cannot in itself provide all of the elements for its own interpretation and application. Something else is required to give a constitution meaning. Burke uses the term 'constitution-behind-the-constitution,' which consists of the 'social, natural, or supernatural environment in general,' wherein the motives to constitution as act may be found. It thus includes metaphysical principles, rules of interpretation, standard meanings, criteria of reasonableness, existing institutions, forms of social and economic relations, etc. This 'constitution-behind' lacks of course the formality of a political constitution, but serves more as a constitutional resource, whether as hermeneutic context or material determinant. Thus, for Confederation, the metaphysics of legal continuity, the political histories of Lower and Upper Canada and the Maritime Provinces, the category of race and the public significance of religion, and an economic history originating in the fur trade all form part of this constitution-behind-the-constitutional scene from which the BNA Act emerged.

Metaphysics has consequence. The constitution-behind-the constitution structures how authority to constitute is figured. Derrida observes that Jefferson is not the author of the declaration, because he pens it as representative of the people-in-constitution. Authority is thus deferred. Jefferson is but a delegate of the future perfect. And yet, as delegate and representative, he is consubstantial with the people that have God as their warrant. Macdonald, in presenting the Quebec Resolutions also defers, but in a radically different way. He defers his own sovereignty as he marks the *écart* between his own will and what is prudent:

I have again and again stated in the House, that, if practicable, I thought a Legislative Union would be preferable ... But, on looking at the subject in the Conference, and discussing the matter as we did, most unreservedly, and with a desire to arrive at a satisfactory conclusion, we found that such a system was impracticable. In the first place, it would not meet the assent of the people of Lower Canada ... We found too, that though their people speak the same language and enjoy the same system of law as the people of Upper Canada, a system founded on the common law of England, there was as great a disinclination on the part of the various Maritime Provinces to lose their individuality, as separate political organizations, as we observed in the case of Lower Canada herself ... So that those who were, like myself, in favour of a Legislative Union, were obliged to modify their views and accept the project of a Federal Union as the only scheme practicable. (Canada 1865: 29)

In this rationalization, Macdonald defers to circumstance and figures his own deferral as the very substance of the constitution that he is proposing. That is to say, what authorizes this constitution is not a metaphysical declaration of sovereignty, but a deferral to the will of others. Nevertheless, we should not see Macdonald like Jefferson, figured as the synecdoche of a sovereign collective will. Rather, he stands as one element in a network of deferrals. Thus, at the outset, he defers to the will of the people of the provinces, if only for practical reasons, when he consents to modify his own position in accordance with their objection. He further defers to the authority of the Crown, which itself must defer to the Imperial Parliament. Furthermore, he defers to practical reason itself figured in the spirt of compromise – the matter was discussed 'most unreservedly.' Finally, he and his fellow delegates at the Quebec Conference defer to the topos of the contingent good, for the first Resolution submitted to Her Majesty begins: 'The best interests and present and future prosperity of British North America will be promoted by a Federal Union under the Crown.'

The cycle of deferral continues. The Imperial Parliament is not sovereign either: it cannot proclaim a new constitution for British North America. Only the Crown can, and only after Parliament so legislates. And furthermore, Macdonald also figures the Imperial Parliament and Great Britain as deferential to the colonies:

If the people of British North America after full deliberation had stated that they considered it was for their interest, for the advantage of the future of British North America to sever the tie, such is the generosity of the people of England, that, whatever their desire to keep these colonies, they would not seek to compel us to remain unwilling subjects of the British Crown. (Canada 1865: 34)

Thus, while Macdonald figures himself and Confederation as instantiations of *phronesis* (i.e., prudence or practical wisdom), the logic of constitution itself remains a transcendental principle. That is to say, law as sanctioned procedure is held against the 'sovereignty' of unhindered will. Constitution is an affair for prudent representatives who must conform to the pace and form of the law as language game. Thus Macdonald can assert that British institutions are far better suited to the protection of minority rights than those of the American experiment.

The underlying metaphysics of constitution, understood not only as a body of rules that specify and constitute the institutions and procedures of governance, but also as an act that sets these into place, is significant to the manner in which civil society will be figured and political discourse will proceed. Kenneth Burke observes that a constitution must be understood as addressed, as a speech act. 'In propounding a Constitution, "I" or "we" say what "you" may or should and may not or should not do' (Burke 1969: 360). As such, a constitution is normative and wedded to an idea, which is its finality. In discussing constitutions or *politei*, Aristotle observes that to each there is an end and corresponding character or ethos. Ethos, or character, is an attribute of communicative performance, and is based in the attribution by others of prudence, virtue, and goodwill. The latter two of these are 'relational.' Goodwill is clearly so, since it pertains to one's disposition toward others. Similarly, the Aristotelian virtues, which include courage, magnanimity, philanthropy, and so forth are civic, pertaining to the manner in which one acts toward the community and one's fellows. Thus, there is more to a constitution than a set of procedures that authorize governance; there is a corresponding 'civil culture,' consisting of a disposition toward others in one's community or political society. In Confederation, we find a *culture of deferral*. This is not the meekness of the colonized subject, but the playing out of the displacement of sovereignty in the British Constitution.

Two major figures of justification are available for constitution. Justification from *substance to command* and from *command to substance*. The first figure is theological (as are doctrines of natural rights). It begins with an assertion of a given essence, be it 'man,' the 'people,' or 'God's will' and then derives principles or norms that would serve to actualize what exists in the realm of divine ideas. The figure merges the 'what must be' with the 'what is.' Prescriptions acquire the form of doctrine and are ontological. As such, constitution would formalize and render explicit an already present (albeit perhaps only latent) substance. This is what Derrida tells us in his discussion of the Declaration of Independence. Conversely, the movement from command to substance in constitution begins with a wish. Against ontological expression, it promises to constitute an object of a desire: 'We want such-and-such – i.e., all men of good will want such-and-such – and my statement represents them, as it will represent you also ... if you agree with me' (Burke 1969: 362). In this second case, constitution arises from the consubstantiality of desire and imagination rather than being.

Theological constitution, as it occurs in the American declaration, warrants a political order as the expression of the substance of what already is. Thus, the scene of constitution is figured as fundamentally in harmony with the constitution itself. On the contrary, *wishful* constitution, as in the BNA Act, does not express the scene so much as seek its transformation. In this latter form, the constitution-behind-the-constitution provides motives and resource for constitution, but constitution itself emerges quite paradoxically as an act by contingent and hence non-sovereign wills who nevertheless have intent and agency.

Let us return to Macdonald's defence of Confederation. As we already noted, the project instantiates the metaphysics of legal continuity and authority. Law, rather than will, is the first principle. But will does appear. In the first instance it contributes to the exigence of the situation. The project of uniting British North America must compose with the wills of the people of the provinces. In that sense, the federal form is authorized by prudential reasoning. But will appears in another guise, for the project itself is figured as the means to realize an object of desire:

And it seems to me, as to them [the other delegates], and I think it will so appear to the people of this country, that if we wish to be a great people; if we wish to form – using the expression which was sneered at the other evening – a great nationality, commanding the respect of the world, able to hold our own against all opponents, and to defend those institutions we prize: if we wish to have one system of government, and to establish a commercial union, with unrestricted free trade, between people of the five provinces, belonging, as they do, to the same nation ... This can only be obtained by a union of some kind between the scattered and weak boundaries composing the British North American Provinces. The very mention of the scheme is fitted to bring with it its own approbation. (Canada 1865: 27–8)

Considered agonistically, Macdonald here so much as says: 'We are not a great people; we are not a great nationality.' Precisely this lack motivates constitution. Substance exists in a historical future. Unlike the Declaration of Independence, there exists no people that can author itself, for this great people are not latently present only to appear through the 'word magic' of the illocutionary force of constitution, but will be the historical result of a refigured scene. Constitution and people are not consubstantial, but stand in relation as means and end. The constitution of Confederation is traversed by the metaphysics of legislation, in which authorized procedures beget new procedures directed toward desired outcomes. A constitution is an instrument designed to operate upon and transform its scene. Confederation is figured in time, as a becoming, as a bequest, rather than as an unconcealing.

Constitutions establish the authority of one system of governance in lieu of another. In other words a constitution is an address that is an agonistic instrument. It seeks both to deny *and* assert. It serves to counter other possible substances or desires. During the Confederation debates, the Canadian Constitution was explicitly presented as a defence against American expansionism and as an alternative to the colonial status quo. The extra-constitutional is composed therefore not only of unities but also of antagonisms. Note, however, that while the Declaration figures its antagonist as wholly external and posits a common substance to the states, Confederation's primary antagonist lies within the polity itself: stalemate, provincialism, sectarianism, and republicanism, and while their transcendence is wished for, it is in no way guaranteed. Thus, we cannot baldly state that Canadian 'civil culture' per se is deferential and future-oriented, for civil culture itself cannot be understood as coherent. Perhaps we can only recognize that each constitution will imagine a civil culture that it seeks to realize and so concede that 'civil culture' is a reification, and more properly recognize that there is at best a struggling hegemony that seeks to regulate competing metaphysical principles, figures of authority, and codes of decorum.

Taking up again this distinction between the technical and metaphysical aspects of law, we can observe that the Canadian Constitution – and constitutions generally – are interfaces between the two. In the strictest sense, constitutions are metalegal. They set in place a technical language and provide authority for illocutionary speech acts. They also provide technical procedures for their own amendment. But they also require the extra-constitutional (more than the sphere of 'communicative' communication) as *sub-stance*. Without this *sub-stance* they would not have a substance. They would lack a metaphysical legitimation as well as a substantive meaning. They would be irrelevant to the lifeworld. As such, they require figurations of authority that are external to legal procedure. They require a civil culture, logically prior to law and constitution but nevertheless immanent to their phrasing, which organizes the civil relation and the disposition of each toward others in one's community or political society. This culture consists in part of stock figures and communicative styles, as well as a catalogue of virtues. Indeed, the same could be said for the law itself (as an extension of the constitution) as soon as it requires judgments that are synthetic or invokes principles from the constitution-behind-the-constitution, such as 'reasonableness' or 'justice.' Furthermore, because law and constitution seek to organize and speak an always resistant lifeworld, the figures and styles of civil culture cannot achieve a happy perfection or fixity, but carry the strain resulting from the *aporia* (necessary incongruity) within representations of the polity itself.

The five constitutions of Canada, culminating in 1867 with the BNA Act, were constituted neither through terror nor through a harmony of free self-determining wills. Each was the result of conflict, compromise, accommodation, and an imperial authority that, while at times violent, was primarily guided by prudence. Furthermore, and fundamentally, the process remained within the law. The point is not that Canadians are particularly law-abiding, but that authority remained invested in received law. No people emerged as sovereign law-giver, enacting and legislating their own appearance. Rather, these colonists inhabited the legal order that brought them to North America, and it is within that order that they struggled to appear, to establish modes of governance, and to both maintain and overcome difference. As we shall see in the next chapter, however, these constitutions were only possible through the law's displacement, refiguration, or incorporation of a prior lifeworld. Before the law's subjects appeared, there were other regimes of appearance. The land was, after all, not uninhabited.

5

The Limits of Law: The North-West, Riel, and the Expansion of Anglo-Canadian Institutions, 1869–1885

In the preceding chapters, we have considered the fundamental place of law in the formation of Canada's civil culture and the importance of prudence in 'constituting' Canada within a largely English tradition of political liberties and their institutional forms. Law was the medium of European authority and governance, and thus as Robert Williams observes in *The American Indian in Western Legal Thought*:

Europe's conquest of the New World was a legal enterprise. The archives of Western colonialism in the Americas reveal a profusion of laws that were drafted, enacted, obeyed, ignored, or defied in pursuit of Europe's will to empire in the New World ... While the colonizing nations of Europe interpreted and applied their presumed mandates in the New World in radically divergent ways, each assumed that law was an appropriate instrument of empire. (1990: 6–7)

For Williams, law was more than a way of establishing jurisdiction and providing for rational, which is to say procedural, governance, but also a rationalization of evil, for 'law and legal discourse most often served to redeem the West's genocidal imposition of its superior civilization in the New World' (ibid). But the full story is more complex, and for that reason other analysts take a more dialectical view, as have we in our preceding chapters, recognizing the peculiarity of Western law, namely, that it is never completely just a veneer *for* power nor conversely completely autonomous *from* power; it is both and not simultaneously; or as Berman (1983) has argued, it is both revolutionary in its questioning of authority and conservative in its legitimizing of it. Another way to put this, in the words of Green and Dickason, in a study that in many ways parallels the historical ground covered by Williams, is that 'it must be remembered that international law is a vital and progressive rather than a sterile system' (1993: 3).

In this chapter, we will consider some of the complexities involved in the legal constitution of Canada with respect to those populations who were not fully contained within the colonial order, which is to say the Amerindians and the Métis. To varying degrees, while these people became legal subjects, they were not colonial subjects. They were rather incorporated outsiders, figured by the law but not fully consubstantial with it. Their presence was a troubling challenge, which reveals the limits of law in constitutional ordering. In this chapter, we will consider the attempted extension of the 'jurisdiction' of European legal regimes, and subsequently of Canadian law, to the Native societies and 'nations' of North America. In the course of this discussion, we will see how, following the cession of New France to Britain, the discourse on the 'ignorance' of the French Canadians, discussed in chapter 2, was readily transferable to First Peoples in a repetition of the dialectic of the Conquest, with a similar resistance posed by native claims to self-governance. We will also examine how the problem of 'the law' and its relation to a European conception of the legal subject became greater in the context of the events provoking the Northwest Rebellions (1869 and 1885), and the treason trial and subsequent execution of Louis Riel (1885). Because the Northwest Rebellions involved a clash between the westward expansion of the legal regime and authority of the Canadian state and its applicability to indeterminate 'subjects,' that is, those who were simultaneously both Indian and European ('half-breeds'), the Riel case, with its poisonous long-term consequences for French-English relations (both in Quebec and within Manitoba's legal order) illustrates with particular poignancy the difficulties of the dominant legal regime's acceptance of plural-istic legal subjectivities, which its very logic paradoxically keeps bringing to the fore. This problem, as we have seen in the previous chapters, is fundamental to an understanding of Canada's civil culture as pluriconstitutive. In this sense, Louis Riel remains simultaneously the absent Father of Confederation and as such the originator of the multiculturalism that would increasingly come to play a role in the Canadian identity politics of the 1980s, one hundred years later.

Olive Dickason, in her analysis of concepts of sovereignty at the time of the first contacts (1993), stresses the contradictory tensions in the Western legal imagination. In the contact with the Amerindians, a central point of contention became the question of whether or not they fell within the purview of natural law, a lengthy debate harking back in part to Aristotle's conception of natural servitude, but also to related debates over what constituted civility or *civitas* (in the form of kinship networks, social and urban organization, clothing, land tenure, etc.). People searched for explanations as to why the Amerindians did not seem to fit any of these categories and thus had such a 'problematic' relationship to the law. Dickason cites Montesquieu's analysis – that the development of civil laws was closely tied to the forms of landholding; thus the communal landholding of the Amerindians explained the absence of a civil code. As she observes, the importance of European typologies of classification 'is almost impossible to overestimate,' making of the contact a problem of theoretical principle 'rather than ... direct experience' (188).

Dickason's discussion usefully insists on the elements of ambiguity in both the medieval tradition and the subsequent development of secular international law. She stresses that protests against the European wars of conquest were 'surprisingly frequent' (243) and 'usually made under the banner of human rights' (243). Even so, she recognizes that while Amerindians 'lost out on several counts' (246) – their rights under natural law were not translated into positive law, and similarly they were beyond the pale of *jus gentium* – they were often able to retain their own social forms even under colonial rule. She notes as well the difficulties of national states in working out their laws and enforcing these within their 'national' territory, an ambiguity that only multiplied with overseas expansion. Above all, 'for every law or recognized practice claimed on the part of a colonizing nation seeking to legitimate its position, there was a challenge or counterclaim solidly based on legal precedent' (248), and for these reasons she concludes that 'the American colonial conquests [remain] in the highest possible degree a living past.'

This position is powerfully taken up by Michel Morin in his recent *L'Usurpation de la souveraineté autochtone* (1997). Morin claims that a return to the legal literature of the sixteenth and seventeenth centuries reveals a perspective in which 'a majority of authors recognize the independence of Aboriginal peoples; and many affirm that the latter do occupy their hunting grounds which, for this reason, the European powers cannot touch' (12). It is with nineteenth-century jurisprudence, he claims, that the arguments develop that Aboriginal peoples have no claim to their lands and are automatically subject to the authority of the state in which they live. Thus, in the seventeenth century, according to Morin, while New France's existence was 'justified' by evangelization and the development of commercial relations, these claims were not established in the face of indigenous opposition. On the contrary, given its rivalry with England, 'France ha[d] every interest that its military and commercial allies maintain their independence' (100). Even more strongly put, 'treaties and diplomatic memoirs [of the period] recognize in the clearest possible terms the existence of indigenous peoples [and this] on the level of international law. Naturally, each crown pretend[ed] that some of these peoples either submitted voluntarily to royal authority, or were subjected against their will. But the basic premise was always the same: that of their independence' (101).

Morin's reference to France's interests suggests that its recognition was at least strategic rather than principled. France established alliances with Amerindians in an attempt to circumvent some of the ambiguities in the bulls of Pope Alexander VI and develop trade relations that did not require permanent colonies. 'Once the French succeeded in establishing a colony at Quebec in 1608, they were soon making grants of land to colonists without any prior consultation with the aborigines' (Dickason 1993: 223). While the English colonies in North America initially had greater difficulty than the French in recognizing the autonomy of the Natives, this changed in the late seventeenth century, so that the experience of both sets of colonies shared a common view of the Aboriginal peoples: they possessed their own customs; and their members prized equality, liberty, consensus, bravery, and gift-exchanges; they concluded alliances with other peoples, through formal ceremonies and speeches; and these alliances respected their partners' hunting grounds. International law recognized the international personality of Native peoples and the treaties contracted with them. And yet the equality between Native peoples and Europeans was not fully complete, as the former were obligated to peacefully receive those wishing to trade with them. But in the predominant view of the French and English authorities, political and legal, 'these peoples remain independent and occupy territories determined by international law; [and] this position ha[d] the merit of being simple, clear, and coherent' (Morin 1997: 37).

The transfer to British rule did not significantly change things. After a difficult beginning, when General Amherst, for example, attempted to stop the practice of gift-exchanges with Native peoples and the British initially proved powerless to restrain settler seizures of Native lands, the situation was stabilized by the Royal Proclamation of 1763. This document, which was discussed in the previous chapter, reestablished the legal framework for the recognition of Native independence that in Morin's argument had emerged from the contact period. Rather than establishing the sovereignty of the Crown over Native peoples, the Proclamation, Morin argues, 'clearly recognized that the aborigines [continue] to govern themselves and are not subject to British law. Those laws that attempt to regulate crimes committed on native lands do not apply to them, even if they are broad enough to do so. Native peoples thus maintain their independence ...' (155), although he notes that that independence was not guaranteed by specific legislation. The Natives themselves recognized this and sought additional guarantees before declaring themselves 'subjects' of the Crown.

Recognition of Native independence would be clearly upheld until after the War of 1812 and the resulting treaties (notably article nine of the Treaty of Ghent), although with the ending of hostilities and the increasing pressure of the white population, the need to continue to respect Native independence gradually diminished. Nevertheless, the terms of the Royal Proclamation, with its recognition of Native lands and the applicability of English law to the whites only, or to Natives who had formally become subjects, remained in force at least until the early 1860s in Lower Canada. The annexation of Rupert's Land by Canada in late 1869 and 1870 sparked the first Northwest Rebellion. After that, the transfer of territory from the Hudson's Bay Company to the Canadian federal government included provisions that Canada would have to undertake 'effective measures' for the protection of the Indian tribes, 'whose interests and well-being are intimately linked to the cession,' in conformity with the principles of equity that had uniformly guided the British Crown in its relations with the Aboriginals (Morin 1997: 203). Subsequently Canadian law, however problematic, and a Canadian Supreme Court, however reluctant to emerge from beneath the shadow of the executive, even as late as 1956 upheld the distinction between 'the internal Canadian legal order' and treaties entered into with Native peoples. So did the 1982 Constitution Act in which article 35(1) protects indigenous 'existing rights – whether ancestral or arising from treaties with autochthonous peoples' (Morin 1997: 161).

Morin's view appears to be in sharp contrast with the one asserted by L.C. Green, in his summary of international law pertaining to Native peoples in Canada:

Analysis of the practice of the explorers, of the rulers who commissioned them, of the treaties made between those rulers, of the administrations appointed by these rulers ... as well as the decisions of the courts called upon to deal with Indian rights ... all confirm that whatever title the Indians were acknowledged as having in the land, they certainly did not and do not possess anything similar to sovereignty. Their title is solely that which is acknowledged as remaining with them by the Crown; it amounts to no more than a right to live on and enjoy the use of such lands as have not been granted to settlers or taken into the complete exercise of jurisdiction by the Crown ... From the point of view of international law, such inhabitants became the subjects of the ruler exercising sovereignty over the territory. As such, they enjoyed no rights that international law would recognize, nor was international law concerned with the rights which they might enjoy or which they might claim under the national law. (Green 1993: 125–6)

One should note that while Morin is concerned with the practical recognition that Aboriginals received, Green is concerned with sovereignty in terms of the jurisdiction of European law. Green is fundamentally correct in that both the Charter of the Hudson's Bay Company and the Royal Proclamation are fundamentally indifferent to whatever claims Natives might have made on their own terms. Indeed, Amerindian 'law' is invisible to these acts, just as they were to

Canada's original populations until Britain or Canada sought to exercise its sovereignty in a concrete manner. From the perspective of British law, its order constitutes a polis, a region of reason and civilization, while Aboriginals, although recognized, belong to a pagus, a wild place that must be contained with boundaries. The Proclamation and the Charter were contrary to Native sovereignty in that they effectively denied any other European powers the right to treat with Ameridians. While Natives had standing before the Crown and had a limited corporate existence as 'peoples' or 'nations,' the land they trod upon had become British and they were, like its new subjects in Quebec, 'enveloped' by the British regime. However, the Native populations were not fully subjects. They remained other: outsiders within the British Empire, to be contained and accommodated, one could say 'normalized,' or ultimately transformed into subjects, if so 'willing.' In other words, their rights were a matter of British rather than international jurisdiction. And so, even today, Aboriginal land claims are negotiated with Ottawa or argued before the Supreme Court of Canada rather than heard in the Hague.

The Exceptionalism of the Métis

The challenge to British sovereignty posed by the presence of Amerindians was contained with relative ease: They were other, to be dealt with, but on terms that would never be their own. And, while Native land claims remain a pressing issue in Canada, they have largely been 'normalized,' incorporated into the federal bureaucratic machinery, notwithstanding some notable and unusual exceptions, such as the 1990 Oka crisis in which armed Mohawks confronted the Sureté du Québec and the Canadian Armed Forces. Far more troubling to the law and its normalization however, were the Métis, for in contrast to Canada's Indians, the Métis came to presence within the law, not outside it.

While many today would term them 'Aboriginals,' the Métis are not properly speaking 'Indians,' but the product of a hermeneutic (and procreative) encounter between 'whites' and Aboriginals. In the language of the nineteenth century, they were half-breeds. That term may today offend, but it was commonly used then, both by the Métis to speak of themselves, and by whites in their oratory and legislation. Indeed, Métis often only referred to French half-breeds, as opposed to the English half-breeds (sometimes 'English Metis'), descendants of Scottish men and Native women. Clearly, the Métis cannot be considered prior occupants from time immemorial. Furthermore, while Métis may have originally shared Native understandings of the land, theirs was a hybrid culture and they gained political significance as a community organized according to European conceptions of property and law. A large number of Métis settled along the Red River, in what had originally been Lord Selkirk's 1812 settlement. The settlement was based in the private development of property, with land apportioned according to the river-lot system that characterized New France. As such, the settlers presented themselves as private owners of their land, even if title was rarely actually transferred from Selkirk or the Hudson's Bay Company to those occupying it. Furthermore, the settlement was governed by a council with judicial and legislative functions whose authority was derived ultimately from Acts of British Parliament, and while this council was not elected, its members were appointed so as to be representative of the colony, which they administered in the name of the interests of both the population and the Hudson's Bay Company, the ultimate proprietors under the Crown of all of the North-West. When the British North America Act (1867) constituted the Dominion of Canada, the Dominion was granted authority to acquire the North-West from the Hudson's Bay Company for proper compensation. The political 'troubles' in Assiniboia find their roots in the manner in which Canada sought to extend its authority westward through this purchase.

The settlers of the North-West were not consulted regarding the transition to a new order that would both establish a new regime of law and authority and bring massive cultural and ecological changes through new settlement. This arrogance or neglect fostered a climate of uncertainty and anxiety in the territory as well as ill-feeling toward the Canadian Dominion. This ill-feeling was exacerbated when the Macdonald government sent surveyors into the territory in 1869 in anticipation of its transfer. In 'mapping' the territory and so coding it for a legal apparatus, the surveyors were not always mindful of the boundaries of the actually settled lots, and often ignored the river-lot system in favour of the more abstract square system. Given that a large number of the settlers did not, in fact, possess clear title of the lands that they were occupying, the survey created a great deal of unease, particularly since the territory had yet to come under Canadian authority. Canada had become an invader. In that context, Louis Riel led a party that successfully prohibited further surveying of settlement lots. Riel and his fellow settlers claimed that the surveyors had no right to survey the land, for Canada had no jurisdiction. More important, they proclaimed that, as British subjects, the inhabitants or people (*population* and *peuple* in the French version) possessed the fundamental right to determine their government.

The protest was from the outset within the terms of the British Constitution and law. Riel ultimately organized public meetings, and framed resolutions calling for responsible government and provincial status, and the maintenance of certain rights exercised under Hudson Bay Company rule. Word of this resistance reached London, and Lord Granville telegraphed Macdonald:

Her Majesty does not distrust the loyalty of Her subjects in these settlements, and can only ascribe to misunderstanding or misrepresentation their opposition to a change which is plainly for their advantage.

She relies on your Government for using every effort to explain whatever is misunderstood, to ascertain the wants and to conciliate the good will of the Red River settlers ... The Queen expects from Her Representative that as he will always be ready to receive well founded grievances so he will exercise all the power and authority with which She has entrusted him, in the support of order for the suppression of unlawful disturbance. (Stanley 1961: 87)

This letter instantiates the rhetoric and spirit of the British Constitution, which had framed legal and constitutional discourse since Britain had acquired Canada from France. As we have seen previously, legal authority finds its justification in a covenant and loving relation between Crown and subject. The queen, or the British government in her name, supported Macdonald's authority and use of power because he was ready to receive grievances. The language is diplomatic and the rebuke is mild, but the political charge is clear: British power finds its legitimation neither in the positive law in itself, nor in the will of the people, but in an attitude of care that Her Majesty's ministers have the duty to make their own. Informed of the resistance his project had encountered, Macdonald decided to delay the transfer of title and the proclamation of the territory's new government in order to resolve the apparent difficulties. The North-West was not part of Canada, after all, and both the British constitution and expediency demand prudence.

While Macdonald exercised caution, Riel and his followers instituted a provisional government with significant popular support among both half-breeds and whites. On 1 December 1869 at Fort Garry, they adopted a List of Rights in a public meeting. This list was also within a metaphysics of law, but its foundational authority was vested in the people themselves. It stated:

1. That the people have the right to elect their own Legislatures.
2. That the Legislature have the power to pass all laws local to the Territory over the veto of the Executive by a two-thirds vote.
3. That no act of the Dominion Parliament (local to the Territory) be binding on the people until sanctioned by the Legislature of the Territory.
4. That all Sheriffs, Magistrates, Constables, School Commissioners, etc., be elected by the people. (reproduced in Peel 1974: 18)

The sovereignty of the people was also alluded to in further resolutions stating that the military must be composed of the Territory's inhabitants, that public documents and government in the Territory must be in English and French, that the people be adequately represented in Canada's Parliament, and that 'all privileges, customs and usage existing at the time of the transfer be respected' (18).

This List of Rights was located outside of the positive law and emanated only from the people. As such, while not incompatible with its spirit, this list had no legal standing under the British Constitution, but claimed for itself another foundation, the people's rights and will. That is to say, its authority was thoroughly rhetorical, relying on a shared belief that certain rights exist in civil society and supercede the authority of Parliament. This claim was stated more strongly at a public meeting on 8 December 1869, in which a provisional government was declared. The Declaration of the People of Rupert's Land and the North West began by proclaiming two principles as common knowledge: 'It is admitted by all men, as a fundamental principle that the public authority commands the obedience and respect of its subjects. It is also admitted that a people when it has no Government is free to adopt one form of Government in preference to another to give or to refuse alegiance [*sic*] to that which is proposed.' This assertion then offered a narrative about how the Hudson's Bay Company came to govern the territory, and how it received the allegiance of the people in spite of its defects until 'contrary to the law of nations' the Company transferred the territory to Canada, and then declared:

It is also generally admitted that a people is at liberty to establish any form of government it may consider suitable to its wants, as soon as the power to which it was subject abandons it, or attempts to subjugate it without its consent, to a foreign power; and maintain that no right can be transferred to the foreign power.

1st. We, the Representatives of the people in Council assembled at Upper Fort Garry, after having invoked the God of nations, relying on these fundamental moral principles, solemnly declare in the name of our constituents and in our own names, before God and man, that from the day on which the Government we had always respected, abandoned us by transferring to a strange power the sacred authority confided to it, the people at Rupert's Land and the North-West became free and exempt from all allegiance to the said Government.

2nd. That we refuse to recognise the authority of Canada, which pretends to have a right to coerce us and impose upon us a despotic form of government still more contrary to our rights and interests as British subjects than was that Government to which we had subjected ourselves through necessity up to a recent date ...

Be it known, therefore, to the Canadian government, that, before seeing our country coerced into slavery, we shall employ every means of defence that Divine Providence has placed at our disposal. And that it is not to see our country which we have so often defended at the price of our best blood against hordes of barbarians (who have since become our friends and allies) invaded by the stranger.

That meanwhile we hold ourselves in readiness to enter into negotiations with the Canadian government, which may be favorable to its agrandisement [sic] and our good government and prosperity.

In support of this declaration, relying on the protection of Divine Providence, on oath we mutually pledge ourselves, our lives, our fortunes, and our sacred honor to each other. (Reproduced in Peel 1974: 20)[1]

The above Declaration echoes the form and sentiments of the American Declaration of Independence, with its figuring of the people as patient and long-suffering, with its invocation of divine authority over against illegitimate law, and with the figuring of its antagonist as coercive, tyrannical, and enslaving. While the pending transfer of the North-West to the Dominion would have been legal, it had not provided a constitutional medium through which the North-West could call on the law and bind it to an obligation. Against such a law, not itself subordinated to the ideas of British justice or liberty, they sought to constitute themselves in law through their own voice. Their declaration, thoroughly traversed by a legal imagination, figures a modern, multicultural political subject of a territory figured as a country, with a civil society founded upon a constitutional order in which differences of race, language, and religion are subsumed by a common standing under the law that is contractual in nature. Furthermore, the consubstantiality of this collectivity is secured by a common bond forged in the face of otherness. This country, a polis, has been paid for in blood, against the 'barbarians,' the Indians who are of a different kind than the people, itself not figured racially.

Barbarians lack 'civilization,' and thus a respect for law, property, or reason. And yet, at the same time, these 'barbarians' are now friends and allies, sharing a common foe even while remaining outside of the community. While the Indians do walk on the same land, they are not part of its 'people,' just as not all those who lived in Athens were members of the polis. Rather, in this proclamation the people are 'civilized' in contradistinction to these barbarians, who roam the *pagus*. Given that these barbarians are now friends, the people must be a civilizing force. However, this close relationship between Indian and the people of the North-West is paradoxical. While the settlers have asserted a claim over the land with their 'blood,' the majority of them share 'blood' with these barbarians. Indeed, we could say that the language of law has distilled the settlers' 'blood,' rendering it different from those with whom they would otherwise be consangual and hence consubstantial. Indeed, the people have far more in common with the 'stranger,' with whom they share the idiom of law. As such, their relationship to the stranger is not one of 'difference' in a fundamental sense, but of antagonism, or what Lyotard would refer to as a *litige*, a litigation argued in the language of international law before the tribunal of 'all men,' which is to say the 'universal audience,' to which one attributes the faculty of disinterested reason. In this address, reason and the language of law form the medium, through negotiation, for the constitution of a legitimate government that would be part of the Canadian federation. If the people can develop a friendship with barbarians, who lack the language of law and hence remain 'other,' how could they not with men of reason with whom they share a loving monarch?

The First North-West Rebellion, 1869–70, and Its Aftermath

The Declaration of the People of Rupert's Land and the North West offered a successful rhetoric of natural rights and communal solidarity that did not need to be sanctioned by a distant and indifferent legislature. Rather, its ultimate authorization rested in the loyalty and sheer will of those whom it spoke for. The pledge with which it concludes is an illocutionary speech act, a promise, which binds those it speaks for through an obligation. That is to say, it constitutes them within a law that they give themselves. Furthermore, this pledge also functions rhetorically, serving to remind its signatories of their promise, offering a point of identification for others in the colony, and finally standing as proof of the seriousness of their intent to all other parties, notably those in Ottawa. Against this constitutive moment, the Canadian Dominion could do very little.

As a 'stranger,' its rhetorical resources were limited, and the Northwest was far from Ottawa and thus difficult to subjugate by force of arms. Ottawa and indeed Great Britain's law had little force. The provisional government, on the other hand, held elections, an assembly met, civil servants were employed, and a police power was constituted. Some Dominion agents were taken prisoner to serve as hostages, while opponents to the new regime were arrested and held until they swore allegiance to the new government. One of these opponents was Thomas Scott, who in an ad hoc military proceeding was tried for refusing to recognize the authority of this government. Without such basic British rights as legal counsel or the opportunity to speak on his own behalf, he was sentenced to death for his impertinence, and ultimately faced a firing squad. The penalty was undeserved, incommensurate with whatever his crime might have been, which leads Stanley to conclude that it was 'a deliberate act of policy' on Riel's part, designed to clearly demonstrate the authority of his government (Stanley 1961: 106). If we follow Stanley's analysis, Scott's death would be the provisional government's foundational act of violence.

Delegates were sent from the North-West to Ottawa. While the legal status of the provisional government was never explicitly and fully recognized by Ottawa, negotiations nevertheless took place, and led to the Manitoba Act of 1870. Manitoba became a province with representation in the Canadian Parliament. In recognition of the bilingual and multidenominational character of the Territory, article 22 guarantees the right to denominational education while article 23 grants equal status to the English and French languages in the legislature and courts, and requires that all acts be published in both languages. The passing of the Manitoba Act was a victory for Riel and the people of the North-West, in that it confirmed their 'right of resistance,' as understood in the Whig interpretation of the British constitutional settlement of 1688. That right, which Walpole argued is and must always be absent from the positive law (Lucaites 1990: 49), is fundamental to the British Constitution, protecting the people from tyranny and the Crown's violation of the covenant of mutual love and obligation. Canada's Parliament further implicitly recognized that right by ultimately granting an amnesty to all involved in this rebellion. The amnesty was not granted in a grand and generous manner, however. Many in Canada, especially members of the Orange Order in Ontario, thought Scott's execution a murder and held Riel, figured as a French-Catholic, responsible (Stanley 1961: 145). The amnesty was only granted in 1875, after a great deal of ill-feeling and political wrangling, by a new Grit government, and even then required that Riel and other leaders of the rebellion first be banished from Canada for five years (Stanley 1961:174).

Finally, and curiously, as the Manitoba Act sought to normalize at least part of the North-West under Canadian law, it introduced and immediately sought to regulate a troubling difference. The Act included a provision for a Native land claim settlement in Manitoba that was not included in the List of Rights proclaimed by the Provisional Government, which formed the basis for the Acts's negotiation. Article 32 met the settlers' request that they be granted title to the lands they had settled on. Article 31 had gone further, appropriating 1,400,000 acres of ungranted lands to be distributed to the families of 'half-breed residents,' while extinguishing Indian title. In doing so, Ottawa recognized such title even as it asserted its underlying sovereignty over the territory. Also, the Act created a new legal category, the half-breed, who while not an Indian, might very well have the right to a land claim by virtue of Native ancestry. Half-breeds are not treated as Aboriginals, however, for the grant is to individual family members, and not to a 'nation' or tribe. 'Half-breed' is not a constitutive particularity, deserving particular institutions and prudential consideration, as did Britain's new subjects a century earlier. Their land fully became property, and thus a marketable commodity. As such, the Act only identifies a particularity so that it can be abolished.

The political battle in 1870 not only upheld the principle of responsible government in the face of Canadian and Imperial designs, but also affirmed the right of resistance against 'un-British' positive law. The conflict did not, however, settle the problem of the North-West, nor did it bring to a close the story that the name Riel brings to mind. At most, it revealed the rhetorical resources provided by the language of the British Constitution and the tension between the language of rights, justice, and authority. The Manitoba Act was in many respects a hollow victory for the Métis. While it established the legal framework for a province with a Métis majority whose linguistic and religious rights were guaranteed, it could not secure their future there. Furthermore, the half-breed land grant was not administered in a satisfactory manner, but proceeded with 'ministerial incompetence, parliamentary indifference, and administrative delay. Instead of being a measure of conciliation, the grant proved to be a source of constant irritation for the half-breeds' (Stanley 1961: 244). The influx of settlers from the east transformed the culture, economy, and ecology of Manitoba, and reduced the demographic weight of Métis there. Also, many fell prey to speculators who bought their land settlement for a pittance and left them in poverty. For all of these reasons, many Métis moved westward, founding the colony of St Laurent, in what we now know as Saskatchewan. Outside of Manitoba's limited territory, the North-West did not acquire self-government nor linguistic rights, but became a colony of the Dominion. There, the problems of Manitoba would play themselves out again, but with a less happy result.

Riel and the 1885 Uprising

In the absence of adequate local government, the Métis of St Laurent created their own legal order. The Métis were settled on land divided according to the river-lot system which government surveyors sought to map according to square lots. They sought to have their title to occupied land recognized and demanded a half-breed land settlement as was provided for in Manitoba. In addition, Métis, English half-breeds, and white settlers were united in seeking local 'responsible government' and representation in Parliament to protect their rights. They were distrustful of the Dominion government which ruled them as a Crown colony. Furthermore, the changes that would accompany the oncoming Canadian Pacific Railroad and its attendant land grants to colonization companies gave rise to uncertainty and concern. The period from 1875 to 1885 saw many petitions sent from half-breed and European settlers to the Territory's lieutenant-governor and to Ottawa, but with little practical effect. In 1878, Ottawa passed the Dominion Lands Act which 'granted a quasi-recognition of the principle of a métis claim to an aboriginal title' (Stanley 1961: 248) and delegated power to the Governor-General in Council to effect a grant of land or scrip to half-breeds in order to extinguish whatever title they might have. The law was scarcely acted upon, however, and this and other discontents led to meetings and political agitation, particularly in the face of Ottawa's indifference, neglect, or malice. As in Manitoba, the British Constitution was invoked in support of the people of the North-West. On 21 March 1884, for example, the Prince Albert newspaper published an editorial where British liberty took centre stage:

We presume that the descendants of men who wrested from the hands of grasping monarchs the safe-guards of their rights and liberties contained in the Magna Charta, Bill of Rights, Grand Remonstrance, Habeas Corpus, Act of Settlement, must be fully alive to what their constitutional rights consist of; and when they remember that the stroke of the axe which deprived King Charles I of his head, ended the theory of the Divine Right of Kings in our fathers' land, and the attempt to tax without a Parliament, it is not likely that we will long submit to taxation without representation. (Stanley 1961: 266)

The language is plain. The right of resistance that was the basis of the Whig settlement is once again invoked, and Ottawa stands in place of Charles I, as the unloving ruler.

With respect to constitutional argument, the 1885 Rebellion offered little new. The demands of settlers were similar to those of 1870. Furthermore, the settlers sought out Louis Riel, by then an American citizen living in Montana, and called upon him to return to lead them in their search for a redress of grievances. Riel did so, assisting in the drafting of petitions, and as in 1870, he ultimately gained support at a public meeting for a provisional government. From there, however, events did not follow the course of 1870. There was a famine among the Indian population, caused by problems they encountered in adapting to agriculture, including drought, and by the disappearance of the buffalo. Riel himself was a complex and troubled figure. He had expressed the view that he had been betrayed by Ottawa in 1870, never receiving his land grant and being forced into exile because of the delay in obtaining an amnesty (Riel 1874). Before settling in Montana, Riel spent time at asylums in Quebec, where he was considered to be suffering from mental illness. It is commonly argued today that he was insane, although some contest that view, and describe him as a misunderstood self-styled prophet (Flanagan 1998: 224; Mossmann 1988: 235). Certainly, his writings and conversations were marked by strong and unorthodox religious views that at times coloured his political thought. Furthermore, in part because of the Scott affair, and in part because he adopted a stronger line than he had in 1870, Riel's political support among the non-Métis was far more tenuous than it had been fifteen years earlier. Finally, the political phase of the 1885 uprising was extremely short. Instead of political negotiation, the North-West saw military conflict. The circumstances were less propitious than they had been the last time. There was no constitutional vacuum, as the North-West had become a Canadian Territory at the time of Manitoba Act. More importantly, however, the uprising became the opportunity for Ottawa to treat the law as a means of control rather than as an instrument of justice. While the Canadian Pacific Railway had not yet been completed, there existed a sufficient number of rail segments to permit the rapid deployment across Canada of Dominion troops. Technology, rather than British liberty, would secure the Dominion's authority.

The Rhetoric of Tribunals

In his postmodern inquiry into judgment, Jean-François Lyotard reflects upon what he defines as the *différend*, a 'case where the plaintiff is divested of the means to argue and becomes for that reason a victim' and in which 'the "regulation" of the conflict that opposes them is done in the idiom of one of the parties while the wrong suffered by the other is not signified in that idiom' (Lyotard 1988: 9). Lyotard offers a number of illustrations of the *différend*, the most significant of which is the Holocaust. Against the demand for proof of its existence by revisionist historians such as Robert Faurisson, eyewitnesses of the gas chambers cannot speak: they are dead. But the *différend* does not require such extreme violence. Lyotard also gives the example of the Martinican who cannot find a tribunal to hear of the wrong he suffers by virtue of being a French citizen. As a French citizen, he must seek redress through French courts, but these cannot entertain a complaint against the very constitution that gives them and the Martinican a legal voice (Lyotard 1988: 27) . Lyotard's signalling of the *différend* as a phenomenon places the question of judgment under the scrutiny of the categories of language pragmatics. No case can exist unless a plaintiff becomes present in language, a wrong is figured in words, that wrong can be 'witnessed,' i.e., is established through some procedure of verification, and a competent tribunal is constituted to hear and judge the case. When these obtain, we have litigation *(litige)*. A *différend* arises when this particular 'language game' cannot be played. Under such circumstances, the party claiming a wrong might very well appear insane (Lyotard 1988: 7).

  Lyotard's discussion of the pragmatics of forensic judgment offers us a way of reflecting upon the Riel affair, and more generally upon the law's place in the Dominion's developing constitutional order. What justice did the law provide? Did the complexities of the case defy a just phrasing? Does the name 'Riel' still haunt the Canadian imagination because it evokes a feeling of injustice? These questions regarding justice resist an easy answer, however, for we cannot know that which lacks a phrasing. At most, we can consider the figurations that were present and the tribunals that could hear them, and then reflect upon whether one of the parties was 'divested of the means to argue' because an appropriate speaking position and idiom had yet to be imagined, or because no authorized tribunal had been constituted to hear one's claim, to provide it with the backing necessary for its illocutionary force.

Figural Dimensions of the Riel Case

In the Riel case, the 1870 provisional government can be considered a tribunal constituted to hear the wrongs felt by the settlers of the North-West. While the ideographs of 'British liberty,' 'popular sovereignty,' and 'reason' permitted the phrasing of claims, the tribunals the settlers addressed had not been particularly competent: they either could not or did not act effectively. At most, Her Majesty intervened on their behalf before Macdonald's government and, following their act of self-constitution, they became a new collective subject, which could then speak to Ottawa and negotiate terms of entry into Confederation. In 1885, the Riel case was heard before several tribunals, the most infamous being the court of Mr Justice Hugh Richardson, a stipendiary magistrate of the North-West Territories, in Regina on 6 July 1885. The case was also given presence by other tribunals. The first 'tribunal' was the trial by battle that pitted the Métis against Canadian forces. The second was public opinion, as mediated by press reports. The third was the Dominion Parliament, for subsequent to the defeat of the rebels, Parliament debated a motion that charged the government with 'neglect, delay, and mismanagement' and, subsequent to Riel's execution, the matter received a second hearing in the House, which debated an Opposition motion expressing deep regret that the execution was carried out. While there are categorical distinctions between a criminal trial, an armed conflict, newspaper coverage, and parliamentary debate, each dealt in its own way with the Riel case; each was agonistic in character, authorized by the law, and finally, upheld legally constituted authority.

Violence and Necessity. The military conflict between government troops and

Métis rebels can only be considered a tribunal metaphorically. While warfare is a medium for resolving a conflict between parties, its pragmatics are not based on the adjudication of claims concerning rightness or justice. Of course, the warring parties in the Northwest Rebellion claimed that law and justice were on their side, but in doing battle, they did not submit to a judging instance but rather sought to impose their order. Despite the battles, however, what was at stake were appearances. That is why the troubles of the North-West were primarily a legal conflict, a 'case' for which 'Riel' stands as proper name. Its main feature was talk. Arguments and petitions were met with counter-arguments, promises, and silence. At one point, however, words yielded to arms. How can we account for this? At one point, the rhetoric of the conflict deemed battle necessary.

As Walter Benjamin observed, law is not antithetical to violence, nor is violence its negation. On the contrary, violence is immanent to the possibility of law itself. Not only are orders of law founded through violence, but the authority of law is secured by the possibility of violence. By this, Benjamin does not mean only that laws ultimately are enforced through coercion, but that the very idea of law demands its monopolization of violence. Any violence outside the law threatens its very authority and demands a violent response, even to the point of transgressing legality (Benjamin 1978). As such, violence begets violence, especially when orders of law are in conflict. But there is more, for law monopolizes violence in order to subordinate its wildness to procedural reason. On the side of reason, law promises freedom from necessity. Necessity, which is contrary to freedom or reason, is a form of violence upon the will. Paradoxically, law presents itself as necessary in the name of freedom, and only in freedom is justice possible. In other words, the founding of law is a violent act that seeks to hold the violence of necessity at bay. Consequently, arguments from necessity are contrary to the idea of law. They deny the possibility of reason and judgment, but instead raise the spectre of lawlessness, disorder, and ultimately the negation of civilization. Necessity is a form of violence and invites a violent response, whether to defend the current legal order or to establish a new law.

The 'Indian.' Necessity's challenge to the law in the North-West was mediated in the first instance by the figure whose civilization and rationality was the most suspect, namely, the 'Indian.' Native peoples did not enter this dispute figured as belligerents, however, but as victims of necessity, and thus outside of the law but within the realm of violence. The 1885 uprising coincided with widespread famine among the Native tribes. The 'Indians' were thus on the side of nature, with a natural right to survival, but also a nature-driven potential for violence. Significantly, the first of a list of grievances penned by Riel and sent to the Governor General on 12 December 1884, having been approved by a settlers' committee, was 'that the Indians are so reduced that the settlers in many localities are compelled to furnish them with food, partly to prevent them from dying at their door, partly to preserve the peace in the Territory' (Riel 1985 3:41). The settlers are figured as victims of violence. They are compelled to offer food to preserve peace. Of course, their compulsion also is figured in part as a moral one, arising thus not only from expedience but also from a sense of obligation, but in either case they have lost freedom. Furthermore, their plight is pressing. The threat of disruption or indeed of an Indian war is figured as a possibility. The 'Indian' is not free, but the government is and should act.

More fundamentally, the 'Indian,' like the violence of rebellion itself, was figured outside of rational order, as indeed could be the half-breeds, with whom they shared 'blood' in spite of the distance that they placed between themselves and the 'barbarians' in 1870. In reporting on the history of the 1870 rebellion in the context of the 1885 conflict, the *Toronto Globe* observed: 'The rebels – to their credit be it spoken – did not attempt to enlist the FIERCE PASSION OF THE INDIANS' (26 March 1885: 8). As such, the rebels remained on the side of reason, in contrast to the 'Indian,' here figured as dangerous by virtue of untempered passion. But this gesture by the *Globe* implies its negation: The Indians might have been enlisted then, just as they could be now. In all of this, agency is located within the rebels rather than the Indians. To their credit, Riel's followers in 1870 did not unleash a savage force. The unstated premise of this argument is that the attempt to enlist such passions would have been extremely dangerous if not disastrous. That is to say, in the face of seduction, the 'Indian' would have succumbed.

By figuring the Indian as fundamentally reactive, the *Globe*, an opposition newspaper, could lay blame on Macdonald's government for its risking provocation of the Indians of the North-West, which could result in the unleashing of a savagery that under better conditions could be contained. This figuring of the Indian as potentially both peaceful and treacherous is well rendered in the following commentary in the *Globe*, titled 'Treachery of Government Officials to the Indians':

The poor Indian, from all that I can learn, has had a sorry time of it since the treaty. His supplies have been cruelly cribbed in every quarter and there are many, indeed the bulk of the people do not wonder that they should be ready to take up arms under any leader against those who have so persistently and systematically wronged them ...

They [the Government] knew that the Halfbreeds were holding meetings all through the disturbed district; that they were desperate men, who had made their last appeal for the redress of their wrongs; that they meant to enforce their rights behind rifles if that were necessary ... There was still abundance of time to avert the rising if the Government had seen fit to exert themselves. The Halfbreeds' petition sent through Dewdney was cast aside, and no effort made to check the rebellion, which is now likely to cost the Dominion so much in both the precious lives of her loyal citizens and the resources of her treasury ... The intending rebels were at work among the Indians, inciting to massacre a people who revel in the butchery of unprotected settlers, whose whole nature is blood-thirsty and treacherous at best, and rendered infinitely more so by the wrongs and cruelty to which they had been subjected. This is the result in the first place of the wretched cribbing of what had been promised to the Indians by treaty; in the second place of the Government's criminal delay and neglect. (23 April 1885: 3)

This report from a *Globe* correspondent does not offer clear division between Indians and whites, where the former are all necessarily evil while the latter are all innocent. Indians are figured here as victims of exploitation and desperate in their hunger, but also driven by a 'nature' that if roused will be cruel. They are, in a sense, like sinners, capable of overcoming their nature under the proper circumstances, if treated well (and brought into the church; i.e., the law), but they are also prone to fall (it is in their blood), especially if provoked.

The Blood of the Métis. In this affair, the Métis are not quite granted the consubstantiality with white settlers that they claimed for themselves in 1870, but are ambiguously positioned as white and Indian. Even so, they are commonly figured as a mediating and civilizing force, as they were by Lord Dufferin, who observed in 1878 with regard to Manitoba:

There is no doubt that a great deal of the good feeling subsisting between the red man and ourselves is due to the influence and interposition of that invaluable class of men the half-breed settlers and pioneers of Manitoba, who, combining as they do the hardihood, the endurance, and love of enterprise generated by the strain of Indian blood within their veins, with the civilization, the instruction, and the intellectual power derived from their fathers, have preached the gospel of peace and good will and mutual respect, with equally beneficent results, to the Indian chieftain in his lodge, and the British settler in his shanty. They have been the ambassadors between the east and the west, the interpreters of civilisation and its exigencies to the dwellers on the prairie, as well as the exponents to the white man of the consideration justly due to the suscepti-bilities, the sensitive self-respect, the prejudices, the innate craving for justice of the Indian race. (Quoted in Adam 1885: 228)

Of mixed blood, the Métis could communicate Western civilization to the Indians, even as they could represent the nobility of the first settlers to the late-comers. If the half-breed were located between white and Indian, however, he equally could inherit Indian vices, should these be highlighted in a less flattering figuration of the Aboriginal. In such a case, treacherous or fallen Métis, even if moved initially by just grievances, could be particularly prone and able to incite an Indian rising. Indeed, the Métis rebels in 1885 offered some grounds for such an interpretation, as we can see in a letter signed by Riel and addressed to the English half-breeds of St Andrews and Ste Catherine, where the Indians are figured as a strategic ally:

As to the Indians, you know, gentlemen, that the Half-Breeds have great influence over them. If the bad management of indian affairs by the canadian government has been fifteen years without resulting in an Out break, it is due only to the Half-breeds who have up to this time persuaded the Indians to keep quiet.

Now that we ourselves our compelled to resort to arms, how can we tell them to keep quiet? We are sure that if the English and french Halfbreeds unite well in this time of crisis; not only can we control the indians: but we will also have them weigh on our side in the balance. (Riel 1985 3:60)

Necessity compels the Métis to take arms, just as it has driven the Indians to desperation. Furthermore, that necessity is itself a contingency, the product not of the fates but of 'bad management,' of bad law, since law is the medium of government action. The government has brought violence to the North-West in this account, and to save themelves, the Métis must master nature, 'control the Indians,' to establish a law that will protect them from necessity once again.

Religion. The Indians, aligned with nature and compelled by necessity, were figured in the North-West as incarnating lawlessness. They were a threat to the law because both their nature and circumstances would drive them to violence. But constitutional order in the North-West faced another challenge, God's law as relayed by Riel. When addressing British institutions, he spoke the idiom of rights and justice. Thus, as we have already seen, the 1869 Declaration that he co-authored invoked God no more than other political declarations in that genre. In his writings to family, prelates, and other Métis, however, religion figured prominently. In 1884, with the blessing of Bishop Grondin, Riel had founded in Batoche the Union Métisse de St-Joseph and claimed that he was on a mission from God (Stanley 1961, 303–4). When the clergy in the North-West opposed his plan to form a provisional government in March 1885, they proposed a novena (nine days of prayer) during which time the Métis should seek God's guidance. At that point, Riel broke with the Catholic church, forming his own sect. Religion was central to his mobilization of the Métis and the consolidation of the authority of its governing council. Riel also adopted the name David, after the prophet, called those in the provisional government's ruling council *exoved* (out of the flock) and the council itself the *Exovedate*. Against the positive law and indeed the 'Law' of the British Constitution, Riel invoked the law and command of God, a law which, as Abraham knew, is prior to reason and can be ignored only at great peril. Riel had answered that call, and against the current secular and religious order, he called for a new papacy and the partitioning of the North-West to various nationalities in order to constitute a new egalitarian democratic society. Not surprisingly, Riel's sanity was questioned outside the faithful. Riel at the very least claimed to hear a voice that others did not, and the political order he at times envisioned certainly was outside of the rational order of Western constitutionalism and the Whig and republican ideologies of that period. What began as the quest for responsible government and the resolution of grievances arising from land claims and settlement rights became a movement driven by necessity, and hence toward violence, even if also a God-ordained crusade for justice and a new divine order.

Chaos, Violence, Law and Order. According to many historical sources, the precipitating cause of the battle of Duck Lake, which inaugurated the rebellion, was a remark on 18 March 1885 by Lawrence Clarke to the Métis that their petitions would be answered by police bullets and that 500 policemen were coming to capture them (McLean 1985: 97). Whether the comment was actually uttered or only rumoured at the time to have been said, it transformed the rhetorical dynamics of the North-West agitation. Hearing of it, Riel cried *aux armes, aux armes* (cited in McLean 1985: 98). In 1884, the constitutional agitation had begun within the law. It conformed to the principles of the British Constitution and the genre of petition based in the Crown's concern for her subjects. Indeed, the list of grievances submitted in December to her Majesty's Canadian representative, the Governor General had ended: 'In conclusion, your petitioners would respectfully state that they are treated neither according to their privileges as British subjects nor according to the rights of people and that consequently as long as they are retained in those circumstances, they can neither be prosperous nor happy' (Riel 1985 3:45). A police attack would have violated this covenant, and the 1885 declaration of a provisional government in anticipation of such an illegal response was as such an assertion of North-West law in the face of chaos.

In 1885, however, the constitution of a provisional government could not guarantee a regime of law, for the chaos against which it stood was not merely an absence, a juridical vacuum, but violence, the positive violation of law and reason. Against such violence, the law finds its translation and application in force, and proceeds not out of freedom but necessity. Rhetoric hardly serves to mediate between parties and create a common ground, but rather to rally the troops and intimidate the enemy, paradoxically translating the fear of chaos into a call for violence.

On 30 March, after shots were fired, The *Toronto Globe* reported on the mobilization of volunteers in an article headlined: 'READY! / Toronto Men in Marching Order / AND MOST ENTHUSIASTIC.' In the *Globe* account, 'the sentiment common among all was a cheerful alacrity to respond to the call of arms in their country's defence and an earnest wish to be one of the 500 chosen for the service' (30 March 1885: 3). This happy figuring of the formation of a military force and the imposition of positive law under the Canadian constitution complements the *Globe*'s argument on the necessity for battle: 'Law and order must be maintained. The rebellion must be suppressed at any cost. It is better that the Government, which seems now to be alive to what under present circumstances is its duty, should do too much than too little. The more promptly and throughly the rebellion is quelled the better for all parties' (2 April 1885: 4). The rebellion represents untenable disorder. Even an excessive response would be acceptable because the reassertion of law, that is to say Canadian law, would benefit even those who have suffered on its account. This claim becomes possible by distinguishing between the Law and Constitution and their instantiation in a government, even if the latter stands only through the authority of the former. The article continued:

But how deplorable it seems that this must be done when we know that it might all have been prevented! How dreadful it is to think those whom we send our young men to subdue, to shoot down should that prove necessary, are Canadians who, as all admit, have grievances to complain of, and who in their ignorant, criminal impatience, revolted because they had long sought redress in vain; because they thought that SIR JOHN MACDONALD'S [illegible] expressed the intentions of the Canadian people, and that they would be deprived of their property because the Government did not do its duty! (2 April 1885: 4)

In other words, as Canada enters into battle, the first obligation is to law and order, a precondition to civil society and, more importantly, to the current legal order, which imposes duties not only upon Macdonald (to have better governed) but upon its armed forces (to quickly win). The law *avant tout*.

The Scene of the Courtroom

Recognizing the imminent defeat of the Métis, Louis Riel elected to surrender himself to General Middleton rather than flee across the border to the United States. He was delivered to Regina to stand trial for high treason. When he entered Judge Hugh Richardson's courtroom in July of 1885, he did not do so as an aggrieved party. On the contrary, he was accused of 'waging war upon Her Majesty' and so violating a British High Treason statute dating from George IV. The aggrieved party was the Crown, personified in the form of 'Her Majesty,' in her capacity of guarantor of peace, order, and good government in the Dominion. The charge itself was not only framed in terms of the positive law, but it also presented an affront to the British Constitution and its covenant of mutual loyalty and affection. Furthermore, the formal charge identified a cause for his traitorous behaviour: he was 'moved and seduced by the instigation of the devil.' He was not a man of God. As such, Riel had not only violated a law, but was outside of the law itself; he was inhabited by evil, by lawlessness incarnate, for only that could justify spurning Her Majesty's love. The language of the charge was, of course, arcane, even at the time. The prosecution was not going to attempt to demonstrate that Riel was 'possessed' by a devil. They would, however, seek to demonstrate that he was an evil man with dishonourable intentions who brought calamity to the North-West in the pursuit of money and power.

The rhetorical framing of Riel's crime and the case itself continued in initial arguments. In his opening address to the jury, William Bath Osler, the leading prosecutor, framed the case as follows:

No constructive treason is the crime we seek to bring home. No treason such as may be made out from meetings, treasonable acts or letters, but we seek to bring home on those counts treason, involving the shedding of brave men's blood; treason which roused the whole county, treason sounding from the dead bodies lying on the blood-stained snow, and which brought a response from end to end of the land, which would make any man with treasonable ideas in his head tremble at the thought of the power invoked by such crime. (Riel 1974: 71–2)

Osler here seeks to underline the seriousness of Riel's offence. He is before a jury, even if only of six men, and this use of pathos serves to legitimate what could otherwise be seen as an arbitrary, 'political' prosecution. Riel has undermined order, and so attacked the British Constitution, the very basis of law. He stands accused of treason against the idea of British liberty, for while liberty is a feeling of 'comfort in the presence of power,' treason is a power that makes a man tremble, and spills blood onto the white winter landscape.

In the agonistic process of a trial, each claim demands a response. If for Osler, Riel had attacked the British Constitution, for the defence, British liberty became precisely what Riel sought and what his trial threatened. The opening gambit of Riel's counsel was to contest the competence of the court and of Riel's prosecution because they denied his rights as a British subject to a grand jury and a trial before twelve peers, of which half would speak his language:

Why then should the North-West Territories be deprived of the rights and privileges guaranteed to the other Provinces? Is there anything in the [BNA] Act that says that the Magna Carta, the right to trial by jury, shall not extend to these territories, but shall be given to other Provinces? Is it because the North-West Territories have no voice in the legislation, because they have no power to send a representative to defend their rights? I say it is contrary to the British Constitution. (Riel 1974: 16)

The appeal is eloquent, but more so to our ears than to those of the court. While the spirit of the British Constitution can serve in legitimation arguments, the court's standing was secure under the positive law and in precedent. Over against the principles of the 'British Constitution,' the court was explicitly constituted in a Canadian statute whose authority devolved from the BNA Act, an act of the Imperial Parliament. Nevertheless, the principles of the British Constitution were not banished from the trial by the court's pre-trial ruling affirming its jurisdiction, for 'the British Constitution' and the civil culture it stood for remained the raison d'être of the positive law and thus an important resource for the defence. While the British Constitution could not absolve Riel, it could serve to legitimate the rebellion as rational and necessary, even if unfortunate and illegal, and so undercut the prosecution's claim that Riel's ambition was the first cause of the troubles that we signify with his name. The opening portion of Charles Fitzpatrick's closing argument is worth quoting at length:

It is right for me to say, gentlemen, that the Government of Canada had wholly failed in its duty towards these North-West Territories ... and I say, gentlemen, that is it a maxim of political economy that the faults of those whom we have placed in authority necessarily injuriously affect ourselves, and it is thus that we are made the guardians of each other's rights. The fact that the Government and the people placed in authority have committed faults towards the North-West to a large extent do not justify the rebellion; but, gentlemen, if there had been no rebellion, if there had been no resistance, is there any one of you that can say to-day, is there any one of you that can place his hand on his conscience and honestly say that the evil under which this country has complained would have been remedied? I know, gentlemen, that it is not right to preach treason, and it is in no part of my duty to do it. I know that it is probable some of the doctrines may be looked upon as socialistic, but I say that the plant of liberty requires the nourishment of blood occasionally. I say, gentlemen, look at the pages of history of our country, look at the pages of the history of England, and tell me if there are in all those bright annals any that shine brighter than those that were written by Cromwell at the time of the revolution? Tell me, gentlemen, if the liberties which Britons enjoy to-day were bought too dearly, even with the life blood of a king? I say that they were not. (Riel 1974: 287–8)

Fitzpatrick's defence continued in this manner, damning the government for not responding to 'constitutional political agitation.' In doing so, he offered a counterpoint to Osler's image of blood-stained snow. Blood was no longer poured onto barren ground in waste, but onto the fertile ground from which British liberty springs. Riel thus becomes a minor figure in an historical drama. Indeed, he is the spokesman for the wronged Métis, whom he depicts as 'the bond of union between civilization and the Indian ... [which] has been one of the greatest factors in the civilization of the Indian' (Riel 1974: 289).

Fitzpatrick's address could be heard as a justification of the Rebellion, but he was not speaking to the body politic or the tribunal of history. Rather, he was pleading before a jury of six men, residents of the North-West, who would judge whether Riel was guilty of treason. In that tribunal, those words would not be sufficient to exculpate Riel. Under the law, there is no justification for treason. As such, the pragmatics of a criminal trial require that a defence of the Rebellion be displaced even as presented. Observe that the address makes clear that it is 'not right' to preach treason even when circumstances and unresponsive government render rebellion itself necessary. One cannot preach treason even while one might, from a philosophical perspective, excuse an uprising. As such, Fitzpatrick's account can only serve as a preamble to an argument concerning Riel himself. Fitzpatrick places responsibility for the uprising on the government, and responsibility for Riel's actions upon circumstances beyond his control. In Fitzpatrick's account, Riel becomes an insane man caught up in an ongoing and glorious struggle for liberty.

While the opening and closing portions of the trial were sources of heady rhetoric, such appeals were ultimately of secondary importance. Trials are for the most part narrow forensic procedures directed toward determining whether laws have been violated. The trial for the most part consisted of the presentation of evidence in support of the charge that Riel led a rebellion, and furthermore did so in order to advance his own interests. In this forensic procedure, only 'agent-centred' motives were open for interpretation. Broader questions are excluded.

As such, the trial affords Riel little opportunity to articulate the wrong that he feels that he has suffered. Indeed, when he does try to speak, to cross-examine Charles Nolin, a former associate now testifying for the Crown, his own counsel asks that he be quieted. Against the presented evidence, Riel's counsel offer no rebuttal, except to seek to figure Riel as insane. They sought to demonstrate that Riel's actions were not the result of a rational will, but of an internal compulsion. Given that this tribunal was not competent to hear of the wrongs suffered by the Northwest, Riel's counsel sought to render Riel himself not competent. They sought to accentuate the *différend* by rendering Riel's speech meaningless, and so locating a *différend* within Riel himself. Paradoxically, the Crown, which seeks to incarcerate or execute him – and so silence his voice – wishes to grant him the fullness of his voice, and even would have permitted him to question witnesses, in order that they might hold him responsible for his own words.

The challenge for the defence was that to many, Riel seemed quite lucid. They thus sought to demonstrate that his insanity was not always evident, but only appeared when religious or political matters were raised. It was not enough to show that Riel was unorthodox, but that he was bereft of reason, beyond all reasonable doubt. And that, of course, would be a matter of interpretation. Consider this examination of Father Vital Fourmond by one of Riel's counsel:

Q. Have you made up your mind about the prisoner being insane as far as religious matters are concerned? A. We were much embarrassed at first, because sometimes he looked reasonable and sometimes he looked as a man who did not know what he was saying.

Q. Finally? A. We made up our minds there was no way to explain his conduct but that he was insane, otherwise he would have to be too big a criminal. (Riel 1974: 241)

While one could argue that all religious faith is 'irrational,' the thesis offered here by the defence is more specific: Riel could not consider religion in a rational way. There is here no doubt that Riel's expressed calling is outside of reason. What remains problematic, however, is whether Riel's unreason is real or feigned, designed to gull the half-breeds upon whom, as Father Fourmond further admitted, religion had a great influence.

The relationship of a religious belief to that of sanity received additional elaboration from Dr Daniel Clark, the Superintendent of the Toronto Lunatic Asylum, also called by the defence:

Q. You said a moment ago that the conduct of this man might be consistent with the conduct for instance of such a man as [Joseph] Smith or [Brigham] Young, and you were about to make a distinction between the two, and you were stopped?

A. Oh! Smith and Young were religious enthusiasts. They carried out consistently their system. If you read Brigham Young's Bible, or if you read Mahomet's Koran if you like, or if you read any of those books issued by those men, who are religious enthusiasts, you will find that consistently with common sense, they have tact and discretion to carry on successfully till the end of their lives without intermission, a successful crusade of this kind, and their books contain sufficient consistency throughout to show you that these men were sound in mind as much as nature provided them with a sound mind, that is the different [*sic*].

Q. Do you find anything of that kind in the present case? A. Oh, no, I don't think that he would have made a very good Brigham Young, or El Mahdi. A. You say that he is quite capable of distinguishing right from wrong, subject to his delusions? Subject to his particular delusions? A. Yes. (Riel 1974: 261)

The prosecution seeks to rebut this defence claim by presenting Riel's speech as responsible but false. Indeed, their case depends upon demonstrating that Riel's speech was not expressive, but rhetorical, and indeed that his rhetorical competence, his capacity to adapt effectively to a given audience, was a sign of his reasoning powers. For that reason, they call Dr Jukes, the senior surgeon of the NWMP, who while admitting only a limited familiarity with Riel and his case, nevertheless presented Riel as a likely manipulator of ignorant followers.

Q. So you think the conduct of Mr Riel perfectly compatible with the conduct for instance of a man like Mahomet or man like Smith or a man like Young? A. No. I don't regard him so far as I understand them – Mr Riel's views in that light. My opinion is rather, in regard to Mr Riel, if you will allow me to say it, as far as I have been able to judge from my own personal knowledge, that he is a man of great shrewdness and very great depth, and that he might choose, knowing the great influence which he exercised over these people who had a much inferior education to his own, that they regarded him in the light almost of a Saviour, I have thought that he might have assumed for the purpose of maintaining his influence with them, more than he really believed. (Riel 1974: 273)

The burden of proof for the claim of insanity rests with the defence. The law requires rational and responsible subjects. Aware that unreason threatens the very foundation of law, it patrols the border between reason and unreason very carefully, and will only deliver up insane speech to another rational order, medical science, which also will negate its meaning. The law offers no place for divine madness and its idiom. As such, whether a madman or a patriot, Riel can say nothing to the court – his idioms are disqualified from the outset, and only the grounds for its exclusion are open to question.

Under the law, there exists no tribunal in which the law itself can be contested, since the law establishes tribunals. As such, the imposition of the law itself, and its foundational violence, depends upon a *différend*. But as this case reveals, a second order of *différend* must also exist, for the law orders and regulates the appearance of other idioms. In this case, Riel cannot find a court to listen to his idiom. He is not granted the political trial he had expressed a wish for, but a politicized criminal trial, where all that is at stake finally is whether he caused the Crown to suffer, and whether he shall suffer in return. Innocent or guilty, Riel is thus doomed to suffer the loss of his speech, just as the constitution of the Northwest required the absence or abjection, not of difference, but of difference's idioms. The paradox of Riel's trial is that both the prosecution and the defence attempted to organize Riel's speech, and both sought to deny the validity of his idiom, even if for contrary ends. The prosecution presented him as offering false speech, while the defence sought to render him speechless. Riel's defence recognized the irony by which only the negation of his speech and agency could shield him from another suffering. Their plea of insanity sought to disqualify his speech and indeed they would have very much preferred that he not speak at all, lest the prosecution take possession of his words. As such, for both the defence and prosecution, Riel became a 'barbarian.' For the former, he would have been 'irresponsible' since his language would not truly be his own but the effect of some malady. Consequently, Riel would not have been responsible for his irresponsibility. A *différend* would thus obtain between his being and his words and actions. For the latter, Riel was 'reckless' in his use of language, as he 'endeavoured to rouse the Indians,' but unlike them he remained responsible for his irresponsibility. In such a case, there would be no *différend*, since Riel's act could be fully figured in the law's idiom. In either case, however, the place of Riel's speech within the 'true' was denied, and his words were not to be taken as valid statements, but as indices of either a criminal or a psychiatric pathology.

Riel was dispossessed of his speech in Richardson's court, but his voice was heard nevertheless. A peculiarity of treason trials under the law at the time was that a defendant can address the court and jury upon the conclusion of his counsel's case. After being spoken of and for, Riel availed himself of that right and sought to reclaim his voice and its capacity to tell the truth. Riel's defence sought to place Riel outside of the Law of Reason and hence spare him from its force. Riel's rhetoric was directed against that defence, for he refused the dispossession of his speech. On the contrary, Riel rhetorically performed his sanity. That is to say, his address displayed a self-conscious mastery of language, and hence of reflective intelligence, that itself stood as proof of his claim to be sane. Thus, his address began:

Your Honors, gentlemen of the jury: It would be easy for me to-day to play insanity, because the circumstances are such as to excite any man, and under the natural excitement of what is taking place to-day (I cannot speak English very well, but am trying to do so, because most of those here speak English), under the excitement which my trial causes me would justify me not to appear as usual, but with my mind out of its ordinary condition. I hope with the help of God I will maintain calmness and decorum as suits this honorable court, this honorable jury. (Riel 1974: 311)

Later, nearing the end of his address, he again offers his own performance as evidence of the soundness of his mind: 'I wish you to believe that I am not trying to play insanity, there is in the manner, in the standing of a man, the proof that he is sincere, not playing' (Riel 1974: 322). Riel disposed of no material evidence to support his claims both to sanity and sincerity, of course. He had only his rhetorical artistry, and the topical resources of reason and paradox. If, like the prosecution contends, Riel's political and religious convictions were a 'sham,' a stunning performance designed to strengthen his following, why would he now not play insanity? Riel offers his audience no possibility of judging him insane on the basis of his performance, for his arguments are proportionate, and if self-serving, are not more so than one would expect of any advocate.

Riel's first task was to place himself within reason, but also to construct in his address an ethos that would support his claim of innocence under the law. To do so, he called upon the common knowledge his jury would have of the North-West. While respectful, he claimed a place in history, referring to himself as the 'founder of Manitoba' (Riel 1974: 318) and explained his presence in the North-West in terms of his continued sympathy for all the inhabitants of the North-West, with whom he shares blood:

When I came to the North-West in July, the first of July 1884, I found the Indians suffering. I found the half-breeds eating the rotten pork of the Hudson Bay Company and getting sick and weak every day. Although a half-breed, and having no pretension to help the whites, I also paid attention to them. I saw they were deprived of responsible government, I saw that they were deprived of their public liberties. I remembered that half-breed meant white and Indian, and while I paid attention to the suffering Indians and the half-breeds I remembered that the greatest part of my heart and blood was white and I have directed my attention to help the Indians, to help the half-breeds and to help the whites to the best of my ability ... I believe I have done my duty. (312)

To have done one's duty is to have answered a call, to have submitted to a law. It is also a mark of responsibility, for answering the call of duty requires a willful submission to an obligation. This moment of will implies a 'distance' or 'gap' between the call and the act in which a responsible subject emerges, for this gap or moment of linkage renders possible another response, a refusal of obligation or dereliction of duty. In other words, doing one's duty is a form of *action*. Insanity, by contrast, is marked by the yielding to compulsion, and hence by a lack of reflective distance, and as such would be a form of *motion*, for will would not have separated itself from desire.

Riel can produce no material evidence in his defence. Only his ethos, as constructed in his speech, can support his account. And, apparently confident of the authenticity of his voice, he presents a version of the events where he would be the wronged party. The police would be outside the law on the side of violence, an illegitimate force, an instrument of repression not concerned with his life or justice, but only with maintaining an unconstitutional order. And yet, for all of this, Riel figures himself as a man of goodwill, and not the least bit rancourous. Furthermore, against the charge of madness, he contraposes faith. He would be a 'religious enthusiast': 'If it is any satisfaction to the doctors to know what kind of insanity I have, if they are going to call my pretensions insanity, I say humbly, through the grace of God, I believe I am the prophet of the new world' (322). Riel would be answering the call of a voice only he hears. While his jury cannot, of course, hear his call, they can, like he, hear the voice of God, of reason, and of the spirit in the British Constitution. Thus, Riel confidently asserts: 'I simply trust, that through God's help, you will balance everything in a conscientious manner, and that, having heard what I have to say, that you will acquit me.' Then, ironically troping his own defence and punning on the principle of 'responsible' government, he continues: 'British civilization which [sic] rules to-day the world, and the British constitution has defined such government as this is which rules the North-West territories as irresponsible government, which plainly means there is no responsibility, and by all the science which has been shown here yesterday you are compelled to admit that if there is no responsibility, it is insane' (323). Developing this theme, he observes that the government ignored the numerous petitions it received from the North-West and concludes: 'That fact would indicate an absolute lack of responsibility, and therefore insanity complicated with paraly- sis' (324). Riel's counsel had not offered a rebuttal of the material facts of the case. Riel's address, perhaps at times too clever, perhaps at times too manifestly rhetorical, might well have secured his claim upon his voice. The jury sided with Riel against his defence, not judging him insane beyond a reasonable doubt. Riel's address could not, however, refigure the evidence that was presented against him. Neither Riel nor his counsel mounted a clear political defence inciting the jury to exercise its right of 'nullification' and find for Riel in spite of the material evidence in the interests of justice. The jury found Riel guilty, even though a wronged party and a 'decided crank' (cited in Riel 1974: xxx) and thus did 'recommend the prisoner to the mercy of the Crown' (Riel 1974: 350).

In spite of the jury's recommendation of mercy, and of a second address by Riel, prior to sentencing, in which Riel's political thought appeared less coherent and rational, Judge Richardson condemned Riel to death by hanging. Under the statute governing the administration of justice in the North-West, responsibility for carrying the sentence fell upon the Privy Council, and hence John A. Macdonald's government in the name of the Crown, the very plaintiff that Riel was found to have wronged. After appeals had been exhausted and various stays been granted, Macdonald's cabinet ordered that the sentence be carried out. Riel was executed on 16 November 1885.

The Debate in Parliament

The Crown's victory on the battlefield and in the courtroom ultimately silenced Riel, but it did not bring an end to the case of Riel. Indeed, Riel's criminal trial was not the only site under the law to hear that case. Even before Riel's surrender to General Middleton and the Dominion victory in the North-West, the opposition began to grill Macdonald's government in Parliament for its handling of the North-West's affairs. The pragmatics of parliamentary speech are far less regulated than those of a criminal court, and the debate was far-ranging. Central to the discussion, however, was Opposition Leader Edward Blake's charging the Government with 'grave instances of neglect, delay, and mismanagement, prior to the recent outbreak, in matters deeply affecting the peace, welfare, and good government of this country' (Canada 1885: 3075). In his address, Blake used the fundamental principles of the British Constitution to indict the government: The Territories had been denied responsible government, the half-breeds were not outsiders or 'Others' but Canadians, fellow subjects who had been misled and deeply wronged (Canada 1885: 3077). Furthermore, the government should have foreseen the potential consequences of not doing its duty, of not offering the kind of caring governance that the British Constitution demands. Blake, an attorney, for seven hours made a case before the House against the Macdonald government. He offered a narrative of the events leading to the Rebellion, of the government's inaction even days before the outbreak, and the government's speedy action once shots were fired:

'What a change! What a pleasing and cheering spectacle is the action of the Government at this stage! What a pity they did not do this earlier! What a sad commentary on the condition of things they had allowed to exist for so many years! It is true that they show great diligence now; but alas it is too late' (Canada 1885: 3094). This reversal stands as prima facie proof that the government should have acted sooner. Blake developed an overwhelming case that the government was not innocently ignorant of the trouble brewing but either uncaring or malicious in its neglect. How else to account for the fact that the government moved more speedily to deal with the claims of white settlers than that of the half-breeds?

Court and legislature are distinct types of speaking places under the law. In the classical schema, they are directed toward different ends and as such are characterized by different genres of speech. Courts are directed toward justice and hence are the site of forensic rhetoric, concerned with the past; legislatures are directed toward the framing of expedient laws, which emerge from deliberative rhetoric, focusing upon the future. Of course, these two genres will in part interpenetrate, and both will be tributaries of epideictic rhetoric, which affirms values through praise and condemnation. Here, however, Parliament acquires a primarily forensic role. Justice is at stake. Blake moves a motion of censure and indeed remarks that 'in old and sterner times men would have been impeached for conducting in this way the public affairs of the country' (Canada 1885: 3110). Parliament is called upon to act as a court, where the government is charged with inflicting a wrong upon the country.

In a narrow sense, Parliament and Judge Richardson heard distinct cases. Different wrongs were alleged, and different parties were to be judged, but of course both tribunals were concerned with the case called 'Riel.' Indeed, these two tribunals were not one deaf to each other. As Sir John A. Macdonald observed in response to Edward Blake's lengthy speech:

There is one thing I think there can be no doubt about on either side, and that is that the hon. gentleman, in his speech, has furnished gratuitously a most able brief for the counsel of Louis Riel ... You may sneer but you will find, this House will find, that in the speeches of the counsel for Riel, when the trial takes place, as it will, within a few days, the substance, the basis, the apex and the bottom of that defence will be the speech of the hon. gentleman ... I would ask any hon. member in this House if the whole speech of the hon. gentleman is not a justification, an apology, an excuse for the rising in the North-West; a justification, an apology, an excuse for murder. (Canada 1885: 3110–11)

Macdonald refuses the splitting of the case known as Riel into two parts, with two moments of justice and judgment. As such, Macdonald anticipates the case that Riel himself would make before the jury, and places Blake on the side of injustice for speaking in a manner that might assist Riel. In doing so, Macdonald even more than Riel, distorts the immanent pragmatics of justice and forensic judgment that requires each judgment to be attentive to particularity. Macdonald impeaches Blake's ethos in an argument that subordinates a consideration of justice to expediency.

As Macdonald continues, he denies any government responsibility for the conflict, blaming 'agitators.' He then denies not only the validity of half-breed claims, but their very specificity as a subject:

Now, the half-breeds must be considered as either white men or as Indians. A great many of them chose to be considered as Indians, to go to the bands of their brothers to enjoy all the advantages of the treaties, to get their annuities, their supplies, and the presents that were given to them. Others said: No; we are white men; we will be considered as white men; we will have the right of white men; and if so, they had the same rights as other white men living outside the Province of Manitoba. (Canada 1885: 3114)

Then, as he concludes, he plays paradoxically on the difference of the half-breeds, a difference that his entire address is directed toward denying:

We have had a wonderful success [in the North-West]; but still we have had the Indians; and then in these half-breeds, enticed by white men, the savage instinct was awakened; the desire of plunder – aye, and perhaps the desire of scalping – the savage idea of warlike glory, which pervades the breast of most men, civilised or uncivilised, was aroused in them, and forgetting all the kindness that had been bestowed upon them, forgetting all the gifts that had been given to them, forgetting all that the Government, the white people and the Parliament of Canada had been doing for them, in trying to rescue them from barbarity; forgetting that we had given them reserves, the means to cultivate those reserves, and the means of education how to cultivate them – forgetting all these things, they rose against us. Well, Sir, we are not responsible for that; we cannot change the barbarian, the savage, into a civilised man. (Canada 1885: 3119)

Macdonald's address is curious, but plays out the rhetoric of recognition and disavowal of difference that we have seen before. On the one hand, his figuring of the half-breed, consistent with the idea of British liberty, has a progressive moment in spite of itself. 'Race' is placed outside of nature, and indeed can be a product of the will. Half-breeds can choose to be white. This echoes Lord Durham's view, a century earlier, that French Canadians could – and should –

choose to become English. Racial identity is thus not fully nominated by law, as it would continue to be in the United States after the abolition of slavery. And yet, this liberalism does not erase difference or hierarchal 'othering,' or what Kenneth Burke terms 'scapegoating.' The half-breeds must be different, more savage than even white civilized men can be, to be enticed by white men who, we must presume, are less civilized than the Canadians that Macdonald's government represents.

Macdonald's assertions did not go unchallenged. Wilfrid Laurier, sitting across from him in the House, attacked his arguments head-on, as the pragmatics of parliamentary debate, as constituted under the law, require. Laurier specifically rejected Macdonald's disavowal of responsibility because the savage was unchangeable. On the contrary, he located their savagery, refigured as 'wildness,' in the land rather than in their souls, and made its management the criterion for judging prudent administration. Locating the conflict in the events of the events of 1870, he then observed:

It may be conceived that these people, who had been accustomed to the wild liberty of the prairie, who had been accustomed for generations and generations to rove all over the whole continent, who looked upon the country as their own, and regarded as their own every plot of land on which they chose to pitch their tents; I say it may be well conceived that these people, half wild as they were, would regard with something like jealousy the doings of a Government which suddenly came in upon them, and assumed authority over the Territory ... One would have thought that it would have been at least prudent on the part of the Government to take some conciliatory steps towards these people, but instead of that they went into the country and treated the people as people used to be treated in feudal times. (Canada 1885: 3121–2)

In other words, the love of 'liberty' itself, the principle so dear to the British Constitution, would animate these 'half wild' beings. They were, in other words, noble in their savagery. The Macdonald government, in contrast, had been not only imprudent, but ignoble, acting in a manner inconsistent with British principles, denying them not only liberty but also that other fundamental British principle, justice. The government's administration of the North-West became a 'vexatious tyranny' (Canada 1885: 3126) that must be held accountable before the bar of justice:

Sir, if something more than everything else could condemn the action of this Government, it would be this act of sending the police force to Carlton to meet the petitions of the people by an armed force. This is not British justice; this is not British administration; this is not the manner in which a British Government usually meets the demands of its subjects; but, Sir, this is the Russian way of administering law. This is the way Russia meets the demands of Poland. Whenever the Poles rise and claim their rights, the Russians do exactly what has been done by the Canadian Government – they send armed troops to Warsaw. (Canada 1885: 3127)

Laurier's address subordinates expediency to the law, where the latter is constrained 'liberty' and 'justice,' which stand not only as ideographs rhetorically mobilized to support his claim against the government, but also as regulative ideas that will structure the pragmatics of power.

Laurier rebukes Macdonald's attack upon Blake because it seeks to undermine justice in the name of expediency. In Judge Richardson's court, the question of justice for the North-West cannot receive a full hearing. Before that tribunal, the case of 'Riel' can only appear as the case of the Queen vs. Louis Riel. The only tribunal authorized under the law that could hear that case in all of its complexity is Parliament, but it is poorly constituted to address forensic questions. Riel was unable to speak of the wrong that he suffered before a competent court. His idiom was a political one, and Richardson's court could only hear arguments based upon the positive law. As such, Riel suffered the violence of having his idiom denied and indeed having to chose between his life and the dispossesion of his voice. The case of 'Riel' can find an idiom in Parliament, but there, Riel will not speak. He and the half-breeds will be spoken for by members who do not represent them, who will figure the wrong that has been suffered in terms of the British Constitution, and who seek advantage from their suffering. Neither the quest for advantage nor the mixing of genres is necessarily contrary to the interests of justice – pure genres only exist among the philosophers – but the House is devoid of an instance of judgment that can proceed with justice as its only horizon. Indeed, the Macdonald government held a majority in the House, and the outcome of the vote on Blake's motion of censure was a foregone conclusion. At most, the debate challenged the ethos of the government and called for a political sanction by the electorate.

Political Speech and the Loss of Voice

When Riel addressed the jury prior to their deliberation, he did so as an orator. That is to say, his speech was self-consciously directed toward them. It was crafted for them. In that, Riel was not addressing them in *his* idiom, if the term suggests an 'expressive' language consonant with some inner speech or voice. Indeed, we could go further and argue that rhetoric itself imposes a *différend*, precisely because its task is to speak a language that can sway its addressee. Rhetoric subordinates the expressive function of language to the agonistic function. It demands that the 'phrasing' of a wrong open a space for forensic judgment. That burden yokes rhetoric to the intelligible and thus to reason. Thus, we can understand that Riel could appear 'sane' – and so possibly guilty – in his first address to the court. Subsequent to the reading of the verdict, and prior to sentencing, Riel had the opportunity to speak again. This speech lacked the rhetorical unity of the first. Whether it more accurately reflected his 'own' idiom, or the exhaustion of his rhetorical resources, or indeed was intended as a rhetorical performance of the mental condition he had previously sought to disavow, Riel's final speech bore witness to the presence of a *différend*, and to an unintelligibility that neither the court nor Parliament could address as they figured the case.

When Riel was told by the judge that the jury had been discharged, and that he was not addressing them as well, Riel quipped: 'Well they have passed away before me' (Riel 1974: 350). Riel then presented the verdict as a victory, for at least he would be known as a sane man, and then offered a rationale for not being executed:

I think the verdict that has been given against me is a proof that I am more than ordinary myself, but that the circumstances and the help which is given to me is more than ordinary, are more than ordinary, and although I consider myself only as others, yet by the will of God, by his Providence, by the circumstances which have surrounded me for fifteen years, I think that I have been called on to do something which, at least in the North-West, nobody has done yet. And in some way I think, that, to a certain number of people, the verdict against me to-day is a proof that maybe I am a prophet, maybe Riel is a prophet, he suffered enough for it. Now, I have been hunted as an elk for fifteen years. David has been for seventeen, I think I will have to be about two years still. (Riel 1974: 351–2)

Here, Riel was still marked by a rhetorical consciousness. He figured the verdict as not only proof of his sanity but also of his divine mission. His argument drifts, however, for his reference to David, whose name he had taken during the troubles of 1885, does not contribute to a case he would make for clemency. He then retold the events of 1870, and spoke of the legitimacy of that rebellion as recognized by its outcome, in order to claim the justness of his mission in 1885. Furthermore, he sought to explain the significance of 'sevenths.' The Manitoba Act had ceded 1,400,000 acres of Manitoba to the half-breeds, a seventh of its total territory of 9,500,000 acres (Canada 1885: 353). The half-breeds demanded a seventh of the North-West, and if the government would not grant this demand, they would reclaim all of it, and grant sevenths to the parties that would help them: the Italians in the United

States, the Bavarians in the United States, and so on. Riel elaborated on who would receive sevenths under his plan and then observed:

The idea of the seventh, I have two hands, and I have two sides to my head, and I have two countries. I am an American citizen and I have two countries, and I am taken here as a British subject. I don't abandon my idea of the seventh. I say because the other is an extreme and extremity, I don't wish for it until extremities have come, and I have, coming to extremities just now, but there are some hopes yet for me, my heart is full of hope; but my friends, I suppose that many of them think that I am gone. (Riel 1974: 357)

His address continues without any clear rhetorical structure. It revisits his plan to divide the territory, reasserts his sanity and ascribes his apparent insanity to his role as a prophet, and concludes, calling for a commission of doctors to determine whether he is an 'imposter' (and hence guilty) or acting according to his conscience.

Riel was sentenced to hang. After a number of delays, the execution was carried out. The effect of the silencing of Riel's voice was to a spark new and violent debate in the country. In Parliament, the Opposition called his execution a 'judicial murder.' The matter was tried again in Parliament and in public opinion. Each party sought to refigure the events leading to Riel's death in rational, 'ideological' terms. For some it was justice, and the tension between the positive law and 'British' principles. Precedents were cited from British history and jurisprudence. This was supplemented by a discussion of the meaning of insanity under the law. For others, and the government in particular, what was at stake was the preservation of 'law and order,' particularly since Riel – in that account – had already been pardoned once, in 1870. Against this view, a parallel was drawn between the amnesty given to the leaders and army of the American Confederacy at the end of their civil war, and a claimed international precedent of not executing men for 'political crimes.' As such, justice itself, justice toward Riel and the preservation of the country as a just and lawful order, were dominant topics in that debate. Furthermore, throughout the debate the topics of race and religion became key and lasting new figures of public speech. Riel became a French-speaking Catholic, and his treatment was attributed to that status by many of his Quebec supporters, who themselves claimed only to be asking for justice. In Ontario, the inverse argument was heard, and his support was ascribed to racial and religious sympathy, against the idea of blind justice that would treat all equally.

The divisions were irreconcilable. The case of 'Riel' was and remains troubled, traversed with anxieties and excesses that could not be contained by the institutions that the law provided. On the contrary, 'Riel' became the occasion and site for all that the law could not code without recalcitrance to reappear. Riel's trial and execution opened up a space for an unhappy civil society to be heard. This was particularly so since no rational idiom could fully contain the case. Riel's religiosity and the insanity defence worked to undermine the ethos of the rebellion. No heroic narrative, either of victim or victory, can be told that links the North-West, Riel, and Canadian justice through a happy process of identification. Rather, a revisiting of the case requires an identification with some kind of failure: of meaning, of law, of reason, of justice.

The historical consequences of this 'uncontainability' and unhappy consciousness are well known, if not well understood. The idea of a common nationality advanced by Cartier in the Confederation debates was undermined for the foreseeable future by *ressentiment*. Macdonald's Conservative party lost its Quebec base, and nationalism became an important source of political energy in Quebec provincial politics. Simultaneously, Quebec became a stronghold for the federal Liberal party, and its Quebec lieutenant, Wilfrid Laurier, who had proved his oratorical genius in the Riel debates, became its leader and ultimately Canada's longest ruling prime minister. More than that, however, the case undermined the legitimacy of the founding principles of the Canadian Constitution. The law was set against liberty – or perhaps more properly, political authority no longer needed the moral authority of British liberty and justice. These would stand external to a law that would no longer be the expression of a sovereign's love, but rather a medium for administration. Perhaps we could say that the case known as Riel instantiates, more clearly than other crises in Canada's early history, the displacement of Her Majesty by a disembodied Crown. It is to some of the ramifications of this disembodiement of both law and voice that the next two chapters turn.

6

'Impious Civility': Woman's Suffrage and the Refiguration of Civil Culture, 1885–1929

In our preceding chapters, we explored the struggles over Canada's legal and constitutional order with respect to its limited capacity to 'presence' difference, to recognize new and different subjects. As we have seen, the problem of difference is constitutive of Canada itself. Of course, difference and a coming to terms with otherness are not unique to Canada, but we would assert the particularity of the Canadian rhetoric attendant to the inscription of difference in law. The very act that established Canada as a British colony under British law also recognized otherness and ambiguously acknowledged other legal orders. Canada's emergence as a modern polity occurred through an ongoing negotiation of the tensions between competing models of law and authority as well as through their translation into new and changing circumstances. While the Canadian experience has not been fully happy, neither has it been marked by the triumphal advance of one grand imperial narrative and legal *nomos*. Canada emerged in ambiguity and ambivalence and its inability to silence its constitutive differences in the name of a will to greatness has contributed both to its unhappiness and to its relative success as a place to call home.

The conflicts and tensions that we have considered up to now have been fundamentally 'Canadian' in their substance, arising from the particularities of its colonial circumstances. However, Canada's particularity cannot be reduced to the identity of its historical actors nor to the subject matter of its disputes. Rather, these have given rise to a particular civil culture, manifested in the very forms of rhetoric in which the right of subjects to appear has been claimed. This culture imparts a distinct set of manners for treating questions or issues that are not uniquely Canadian, but part of that much larger formation often called modernity or the West. Here, we will consider some aspects of this particularity by focusing on what is arguably one of the most significant international 'modern' political phenomena of the twentieth century, the quest for woman's political rights.[1] In what follows, we will examine aspects of this emergence of 'woman' as a modern political subject in Canada. Our claim is at one level quite modest. We aim only to assert that the process of woman's enfranchisement, and her emergence as a political subject, was different in some respects in Canada than elsewhere. More ambitiously, however, we also want to suggest that the discourses attendant to woman's emergence are particularly telling of the way that Canada's civil culture figures authority, power, and indeed, Canada itself.

The Conservative Rhetoric of Woman's Suffrage in Canada

The Canadian campaign for woman's suffrage is noteworthy because it was remarkably less militant than its counterparts in both Britain and the United States. In these two countries, the quest for suffrage was marked by demonstrations and confrontation. In Canada, the debate was singularly civil and remained within spheres of discourse dominated by elites. Oddly enough, this difference did not seem to matter, for Canadian women gained the vote at roughly the same time as their American and British sisters. This highlights the international character of the movement, and suggests that its success had less to do with the particularities of each national campaign than with transnational forces of modernization and modernity, themselves linked to the Great War. The difference is important, however, because it reveals something of Canada's political culture, both with respect to woman's place in the polity and the distinct lines of argument through which Canada mediates between tradition and the changing circumstances of the modern world. In order to grasp these, we will review the cultural, legal, and constitutional constraints placed upon woman as a political subject, and then consider moments of her rhetorical refiguration.

In her history of the struggle for woman's suffrage in Canada, Catherine Cleverdon observes that 'persuasion, not force, was the lever which gradually caused the gates of political freedom to swing open for Canadian women' (Cleverdon 1974: 4). The quest for suffrage was rhetorical, for women could not give themselves the vote. They had to persuade men to grant it to them. However, persuasion can take many forms. It can seek to convince opponents through good reasons, or it can mobilize others against them and so oppose power with power. In Cleverdon's usage, persuasion means a mannered and civil form of public speech. She opposes persuasion to force and thus tempers the former, since the latter implies a battle of wills rather than discovery of a common ground. Cleverdon contrasts the Canadian campaign to its British counterpart, which was marked by 'flamboyance, bitterness, and even violence'

(4). The woman's suffrage 'movement' in Canada proceeded without solemn declarations and without public demonstrations. It was not a 'mass' movement. On the contrary, it proceeded through only the most conservative means of 'constitutional agitation.'

For Cleverdon, this rhetorical campaign testified to the political skill of suffrage advocates and the reasonableness of their cause. Hers is not the only interpretation, however. Carol Lee Bacchi states that the absence of militancy testifies to the compromised nature of the movement (1983). Between Cleverdon's rhetorical flourish, which tropes suffrage as 'freedom,'[2] and Bacchi's view that the movement was dominated by anti-feminist social reformers, we can identify a 'progressive conservative' element in Canada's rhetorical political culture. In Cleverdon's account, women in Canada obtained the vote through a number of rhetorical practices. The first was rational argumentation. As Cleverdon puts it, 'opponents of the suffrage movement faced the women with a formidable array of arguments,' many of which carried 'great weight at the time' (Cleverdon 1974: 5). In Cleverdon's history, suffragettes and their male supporters countered each argument, point by point, persuading legislators, electors, and women that granting the vote to women was reasonable, just, and expedient. Second, supporters of suffrage engaged in a campaign to mobilize women to express their support for suffrage. They were not asked to march or to try to vote illegally. Rather, they were called upon to sign petitions to counter the claim that women did not want the vote. Third, they enlisted the public support of sympathetic spokespersons and institutions, including editorialists, Protestant clergy, labour unions, and farmers' organizations. Finally, they participated in the 'political process,' lobbying ministers and actively supporting political candidates favourable to their cause. This civil campaign was undeniably successful. Canadian women gained the same federal voting rights as men, subject to property, racial, and other restrictions, in 1919, shortly before American women in 1920. By 1925, Newfoundland and every Canadian province except Quebec gave women and men equal access to the provincial franchise.

Cleverdon offers a lucid and well-researched account. Nevertheless, in offering an historical narrative rather than a philosophical or rhetorical study, she does not reflect upon the very nature of 'woman' as a category in relationship to the political sphere, and she understates the radicalism of the suffrage movement. In stressing the importance of reasoned argument to the suffrage campaign, Cleverdon presumes what in fact the existence of that campaign had to achieve, the constitution in civil culture of woman as a political subject. Because she does not recognize the problematic status of woman as a subject, Cleverdon can present a heroic narrative charting the progress of human rights and the extension of equality. Implicit in Cleverdon, the meaning of 'woman' is not problematic because, in a sense, woman had already 'arrived.' Carol Lee Bacchi contests this historical interpretation. Bacchi does not presume that suffrage either testified to or brought about a new subject, but rather argues that the success of this very civil campaign depended precisely on this subject's subordination and the abnegation of feminist principles. A new woman did not show up. As Bacchi puts it:

The relatively easy victory was due to several factors, chiefly the moderate character of the movement, the nature of its leadership, and political opportunism. Most Canadian suffragists were social reformers and members of a social elite. They asked that women be allowed to vote in order to impress certain values upon society, Protestant morality, sobriety, and the family order. 'Women's Rights' in their view of things meant the right to serve. (Bacchi 1983: 3)

As such, in Bacchi's view, suffrage was hardly about rights at all and did not radically challenge Canada's political culture or ruling elites. On the contrary, advocates of suffrage adapted to their situation by adopting a rhetoric of accommodation: 'Even the feminists when set on the defensive or perhaps for tactical reasons modified their stance on sex roles. Floral Macdonald Denison in one of her weaker moments actually conceded that 'the primal mission of woman is to get married and have children.' This, of course, may have been rhetoric' (Bacchi 1983: 33). The articulation of suffrage with social reform garnered the vote, but 'the feminist cry for women's equal educational and occupational rights became muted and died' (Bacchi 1983: 134). Suffrage as such was disarticulated from rights, and no longer an end in itself but a means. In making this observation, Bacchi highlights that suffrage could have been more than merely granting women rights that they deserved, but also a trans-formation of the very nature of 'woman' and the political sphere. While for Cleverdon, suffrage 'opened gates' and freed women from a limited domain, for Bacchi, their domain was simply expanded. In some respects, Bacchi is noting little more than the principal of audience adaptation necessary to any successful rhetoric. Suffrage overcame opposition because it was figured in conservative terms. Feminism required, as Carlson observed in her discussion of nineteenth-century American feminist rhetoric, a process of 'casuistic stretch-ing' whereby received categories are gradually extended to new situations (Carlson 1992: 21). For Bacchi, such rhetorical adaptation is incompatible with ideological transformation.

In what follows, we will explore the tension between these two interpreta-tions, focusing upon how the Canadian suffrage campaign could be 'conservative' and yet contain a radical moment. In other words, we will identify how suffrage, as a means to moral reform, refigured woman into a public subject, addressing the public sphere, even if on what were traditionally considered woman's concerns. That is to say, even when suffrage was not advanced as a principle, it nevertheless advanced new principles, and this at times with patriarchy's unwitting approval.

Woman as Political Subject

The key to understanding the civility of the Canadian suffrage campaign has less to do with its complicity with social reform than with the relative insignificance of 'rights' in Canada's political lexicon. Bacchi seeks a rights discourse, but the Canadian political subject is not primarily constituted as a bearer of rights, and this despite the importance of 'British liberty' to the British Constitution. 'Rights talk,' to use Mary-Ann Glendon's phrase (1991), is incompatible with prudential politics. For Glendon, 'rights talk' subordinates politics to the judicial process. When carried to the American extreme, 'rights talk' impoverishes politics, not only because courts are called on to resolve disputes that would otherwise acquire a political character, but because the figuring of conflicts in terms of rights is incompatible with negotiation and accommodation. As Ronald Dworkin observes, rights are trumps (discussed in Habermas 1996: 203–4). By definition, 'rights' take precedence over non-rights, and hence over considerations of the 'good,' except in extreme and exceptional circumstances where rights are in conflict, and even then 'rights talk' seeks a judicial resolution. Political rhetoric based in 'rights talk' is divisive, because it invokes categorical principles and asserts rules rather than seeks consensus.

For Canadian supporters of suffrage, rights arguments would have been very difficult to develop effectively. Not only was prudence more important than rights, but suffrage was not considered a citizenship right. Property qualifications restricted the franchise to those who ostensibly would have an interest in and hence knowledge of government. It was a legislated entitlement. Furthermore, even if voting were considered a citizenship right for men, there existed no legal or constitutional basis for equality of the sexes. Indeed, legally and constitutionally, women were not only ignored or invisible, but were positively excluded. Under common law and the British Constitution women were marked by a 'legal incapacity' to hold any public office save that of monarch, unless legislation extended that entitlement to them. Thus, women in England, and arguably in Canada, were barred from voting even in the absence of an explicit statute. Finally, each of Canada's constituent colonies had explicitly excluded women from the franchise prior to Confederation, in order to rule out the possibility that women might vote, as a few had in Lower Canada in the 1830s and in Canada West in 1844, in what became partisan disputes (Garner 1969: 158–9). Finally, there were no extra-legal principles, such as 'natural law,' to which one could appeal in formulating a rights claim, since the British Constitution is identified with and displaces natural law. Common law is figured as originating in a time lost to memory, and indeed outside of history, and as such rhetorically stands not as the product of contingency, but as the expression of the people themselves and their reason: 'Reason and nature join in the origin of a common law conceived to be "connaturall" with the people of England ... The immemorial and unwritten character of common law allowed its origin to be placed, beyond memory, in the realm of nature and not of man. The last defense of law was thus to a natural law conceived as the order of things' (Goodrich 1994: 75). Common law is analogous to 'natural law,' but as perfected in British customs and institutions.

An effective tradition of rights rhetoric existed in the United States that could be enlisted against the absence of woman's political rights in law. Suffrage activists could mobilize the language and ethos of the abolitionist movement as well as commitments to a rhetoric of 'liberty' and 'equality.' They could appeal to the very same tradition of 'natural rights' that justified the American Founding. While England did not share that rights tradition, the electoral reform movements of the nineteenth century provided British suffragettes with a powerful language and set of tactics to press their demands (Rover 1967: 51). No analogous rhetorical resources were available in Canada. Constitutional change in Canada was usually granted as a consequence of petition and prudence. For the most part, the authority of law, and its violence, had trumped any militancy and civil disobedience fuelled by a rhetoric of rights or equality. Consequently, while ultimately no more effective, American and British suffrage tactics were at times more 'feminist,' more categorical, and more disruptive than those in Canada. Indeed, even though American and British militants would occasionally speak in Canada and energize Canadian activists, they and their campaigns remained marked as excessive 'other,' counterpoised in public discourse to a Canadian sense of propriety.

The absence of a rights tradition can account for both the relative disinterest of women in suffrage and for the civility of the suffrage debate, but it does not account for the form of the movement's ultimate success. More was involved than the absence of ideological polarization. Suffrage advanced and a new woman subject was constituted through a rhetoric that mobilized elite complicity, an ethos of moral obligation, and a conception of Canada as an ethical project, dedicated to progress rather than to a return to some lost moment of harmony. While the legitimacy of the Canadian state is based on the historical authority of British law, the rhetoric of progress offers Canada as the translation of that order in the New World. Change was possible because suffrage became a prudential rather than an ideological question, where Canadian prudence was guided by the idea of progress and accommodation. As Eugene Garver observes, prudential politics are rhetorical, structured by contingency, and they subordinate purity of principle to practical possibility. In contrast, ideological politics, including 'rights talk,' are driven by principle and not directed toward the contingent good. They are categorical. They are, as such, anti-rhetorical (in the persuasive sense) because they are unwilling to proceed from their opponents' premises. Indeed, Garver for these reasons concludes that ideological politics are no politics at all (Garver 1987: 12–20).

The Canadian suffrage campaign could be prudential because, first, woman's abject status in the British Constitution was itself rhetorical rather than structural. Her absence was not necessary to the law's operation, but an historically contingent element in the rhetoric that secured its authority. By the end of the nineteenth century, the legitimacy of the British Constitution and common law were sufficiently secure to withstand the potential challenge posed by woman's symbolic public presence. In other words, her exclusion was not a categorical imperative. Second, calls for woman's suffrage and the transformation of her status did not proceed from one widely held counter-narrative that placed woman's identity in opposition to Canada's constitution, but rather came through a Canadian narrative of progress. Third, and here echoing Bacchi, suffrage was a means for reform rather than an end linked to woman's 'being,' and so was not reducible to a component of 'identity politics.' As such, the political field in this matter was 'unprincipled,' which is to say, for the most part unencumbered by necessary constitutive categories placed beyond prudential consideration and rhetorical amendment. Under such circumstances, change figured as conservative progress (or progressive conservatism) was possible. Thus, woman could emerge as a political subject pragmatically, through the enactment of a speaking position. Suffrage was 'revolutionary,' in challenging the misogyny of the British Constitution, and possible because championed by civil persuasion, ambiguously or ironically figured and decorously restrained.

Macdonald's Suffrage Initiative

The constitution of Canada as a progressive nation is evident in the Confederation debates, but appears again starkly in the 1885 debate in Parliament over extending the federal franchise to unmarried and widowed women. Indeed, even as Canadian troops confronted Métis rebels in 1885, Sir John A. Macdonald introduced a franchise bill in Parliament that included a provision to grant the vote to unmarried and widowed women who met the general property qualification. Sir John addressed the matter only briefly in the House:

I have always and am now strongly in favor of that franchise. I believe that is coming as certainly as came the gradual enfranchisement of women [*sic*] from being the slaves of men until she attained her present position, almost the equal of man. I believe that time is coming, though perhaps we are not any more than the United States or England quite educated up to it, I believe the time will come, and I shall be very proud and glad to see it, when the final step towards giving women full enfranchisement is carried in Canada. (Canada 1885: 1134)

In so addressing the House, Macdonald figured suffrage, not in the language of rights, but in terms of progress. He did not make their suffrage a constitutional principle at all. Macdonald's suffrage provision was, not surprisingly, defeated in Committee of the Whole. Nevertheless, so presented, the case for woman's suffrage started off already half-made in Canada. Or perhaps, more properly speaking, one might say that the case for woman's rights was initiated elsewhere but here found its Canadian inflection. Britain and the United States had seen vocal suffrage movements whose claims could be heard in Canada. Rights rhetoric is echoed in Macdonald's metaphor of slavery,[3] a strong term given that the American Civil War was within living memory. But Macdonald muted any radical implication, for in any case 'the time is coming':

We know that Mr. Gladstone, the head of the present Administration in England, is strongly in favor of women franchise, although he would not hazard and peril his late Franchise Bill by introducing that question ... We also know that the leaders of the Opposition in England in both Houses, the Marquis of Salisbury and Sir Stafford Northcote, are strongly in favor of extending the franchise to women, to the extent set forth in my Bill. (Canada 1885: 1134)

At most, as he admitted when his measure went down to defeat, Macdonald had hoped that Canada could lead the way in a movement in any case inevitable. Canada could thus be a great if modest country:

In every position in which they have made an advance toward equality with men, they have proved themselves so efficient that there has not been the slightest attempt to retroactive legislation to deprive them of any privileges or advantages that, after centuries of denial, they have at last obtained. I had hoped that we in Canada would have had the great honor of leading in the cause of securing the complete emancipation of women, of completely establishing her equality of a human being and a member of society with man. I say it is a mere matter of time ... I need not enlarge upon the subject, because I am fighting *contra spem*. I believe a majority of this House is opposed to female suffrage. (Canada 1885: 1388)

Macdonald was right. The House opposed suffrage, but even so the debate held open its eventual possibility, for the topic of progress took precedence over one of faithfulness to unchanging constitutional principle. Consider, for example, the curious manner in which Laurier, across the floor from Macdonald, objected to the proposed measure: 'If this Bill becomes law, it will go forth to the world that we in Canada are more advanced than most of the States of the American union; more advanced than republican France; more advanced than Italy; and all this will be due to a Conservative Government' (Canada 1885: 1170). Laurier is a Liberal, and in using the term 'advanced,' albeit wryly, he invoked the idea of progress; of a direction to reform. Inevitability is structured into his very objection. Canada, like the countries cited, would well be expected to move toward suffrage, even if at its own pace. Furthermore, Laurier counters Macdonald's proposal with one of his own:

I claim that I am in favor of the emancipation of woman as much as he can be; but I do not believe that the emancipation of woman can be promoted so much by political as by social reform. I believe that the action of women must be most influential in politics as in everything else, but I believe that action is more effective if exercised in the circle of home, by persuasion and advice, than if woman is brought to the poll to vote. If the right hon. gentleman is really anxious to do something for the emancipation of woman, let him give her the opportunity for more extensive education, let him open for her more fields of employment, and he will do more for her emancipation than by giving her the right to vote. (Canada 1885: 1171)

In Canada, woman's emancipation was not figured as the demand of a radical fringe. Suffrage was already advocated by respectable and influential men in the community. It stood as a matter worthy of reasoned deliberation. As such, while the measure did not command the support of a majority of Canadians or of their representatives in 1885, and would not for decades, the debate had been framed within the very terms of civility that Cleverdon observed. The debate is thus of particular interest, as it mapped the rhetorical field on which the subsequent civil movement for suffrage took place.

Macdonald's Franchise Bill was a government measure, and so guaranteed passage owing to the significant Conservative majority in Parliament. Nevertheless, Macdonald did not demand that his party support his woman's suffrage provision. Indeed, even as he spoke to the measure, he indicated that he would submit it to a free vote in the House. The Opposition denounced the idea of a federal franchise as contrary to the federal principle and provincial rights. No member denied that the federal government had the authority to establish its own franchise, but the Opposition considered it best for the provinces to set voter qualifications, citing the American federal model. They were more generous with respect to woman's suffrage, however, and offered Macdonald more support than members of his own party. While none of his Conservative colleagues spoke in favour of the measure, members of the Opposition were split on the question. Some expressed vigorous support for suffrage, and called upon Macdonald to extend the vote to married women as well. Others held that the measure was unnecessary, for women had not demanded the vote.

Macdonald offered a progressive view of history marked by the gradual emergence of women as propertied subjects, but gender distinctions marked the cultural and legal field in which he made his proposal. Most advocates of woman's suffrage maintained a fundamental difference between women and men. We find the view, still held today by certain contemporary feminists, that for reasons of either culture or nature, women and men differ in communicative styles and affective relationships. Thus, William McCraney argued for woman's public place: 'I do not, for my own part, see any reason why many of the positions in life should not be occupied by women. I say, if my wife is more intelligent than I am, let her take the position, or if yours is, let her have the position. Let intelligence be the rule in our country, and we shall have our affairs much better administered than they are at present.' He considered, however, the moral domain her proper sphere: 'If the women of this country had the settlement of the moral questions that come before us from time to time, the moral sentiment of our country would stand much higher than it does today' (Canada 1885: 1411).

The debate in Parliament reveals that men, at least, presumed a clear distinction between a masculine sphere of public affairs, animated by an agonistic spirit, and a feminine sphere of household and family held together by affection, nurturing, and care. Women, as such, were considered the virtuous sex, animated by a selflessness best expressed in the figure of wife and mother. In the words of Joseph Royal: 'Woman has been created for another kingdom' (Canada 1885: 1390). As such, women were subjects in their own sphere. The two spheres were not categorically distinct, however, and for that reason women were not entirely denied a public presence. As Cecilia Morgan demonstrates, the rhetoric attendant to the war of 1812 constructed Upper Canadian masculinity as different from its American and Indian counterparts. These were 'brutish' and savage, lacking manly self-control (Morgan 1996: 34–5). The patriotic man of Upper Canada, in contrast, was a virtuous 'Christian soldier,' as figured in a sermon by John Strachan, the Anglican bishop of York [Toronto], fighting not for glory but out of humble duty (Morgan 1996: 36). This Christian soldier was a virtuous man, defending women and children, home, and family. Thus, masculine virtue here is itself 'feminized,' not having the warrior as ideal. Women were figured as vulnerable, and masculinity was constructed through an ethos that included both sacrifice and care. As such, masculine virtue could be mobilized to advance woman's condition. Furthermore, given that woman's place was figured as a consequence rather than as a cause of her essential virtues, it remained possible that these virtues might well qualify her for a new and as yet unarticulated public role in a refigured public sphere.

By 1885, women were not restricted to the household. Otherwise, Macdonald's measure would have been inconceivable. Nevertheless, a woman in public remained a troubling and anxiety-provoking figure. Women, especially outside of marriage, were not necessarily virtuous. Macdonald had only proposed giving the vote to unmarried women, and recognized in the debate that this was only a partial measure, in deference to those who feared that the entry of women into the political sphere would disrupt the family. The dangerous flip side of this concession was that only women whose sexuality was not contained within marriage would be given the vote. The concern was then raised that the wrong kind of women would appear in public, that the polling station itself would be corrupted by the presence of 'public women.' François Langelier, opposition member for Mégantic, put the matter plainly. He asked:

Who are the unmarried women who will take advantage of it? There is a respectable class of unmarried women, it is those who abstain from marriage by religious profession; but as to those who abstain from it in order to shun the burdens of it, I think they should not be rewarded. Who are the unmarried women who will take advantage of it? It is a class of women who are occupying in society a position such as to deter the respectable women from exercising their right, because they will not consent to exercise it at the same time as the women mentioned in the first place. Thus in Quebec, Montreal and other great cities of the Dominion, if the right of suffrage was given to all respectable women who form the great majority, then they might exercise it without having to blush for it. But, in the large cities, will we see the respectable unmarried women exercising that right? No, they will be ashamed to do it, because they would be obliged to exercise it side by side with women of loose character. (Canada 1885: 1371, as translated in original)

The anxiety over impropriety that marks Langelier's speech should be understood in the context of Victorian mores, which highly regulated the appearance of 'proper' women, of ladies, in order to deny their fleshliness. This anxiety was also figured through humour, as in these remarks by James McMullen, opposition member for Wellington North, who ultimately spoke in favour of woman's suffrage:

From my little experience in the matter of canvassing, I should very much dread to go through a constituency trying to secure the votes of perhaps forty or fifty old maids who got beyond the age when they may expect to enter the marriage state. I must say that it will be a difficult duty for any man to perform. I was struck with the remark of the hon. member for Algoma (Mr. Dawson), who did not appear to dread any engagement of that kind. Well, he is a bachelor, and he is reaching that age in a bachelor's life when it becomes doubtful whether if he will continue in that state of single blessedness very much longer he will ever get married. He will shortly find himself in as bad a position as the old maids. But if this bill becomes law, and if, in the course of his canvassing through Algoma during the next election, he is not able to get a wife, with the coaxing he will no doubt have to do in order to get votes, I am afraid he will never succeed afterwards. I have no doubt that if this Bill becomes law we will have more actions in our courts for breach of promise than has ever yet been known in the history of this country. It is well known that a great many of these old maids will be only too willing to promise to vote if they are promised a husband; and a single man, in that case, will undoubtedly have the advantage of a married man. I do not know whether a promise of marriage, under such circumstances, would be an act of bribery or not, but if it is, I have no doubt it will be perpetrated. (Canada 1885: 1204)

McMullen's humour, regardless of his stand in the debate, bespeaks an anxiety over a disruption of 'gendered' character of public and private spheres, where the latter includes relations of intimacy. This categorical distinction between spheres is not simply a projection of a stereotype of male and female capacities, but is rooted in the very pragmatics of political intercourse at the time. Parliament and politics generally were figured as an *agon*, a battle understood then (and to a degree now as well) as a masculine domain. Thus, the member for Huron West, Malcolm Cameron, could observe: '[Women] are not anxious to engage in active scenes of political contests. They are not anxious to go to the hustings, to be cuffed and knocked about' (Canada 1885: 1142). Also, parliamentarians in debate would question their opponents' 'manliness.' Indeed, in the debate over suffrage, such charges were levelled at Macdonald for lacking the courage to present woman's suffrage as a government measure and for absenting himself from the House to rest as the debate droned on in the wee hours of the morning.

The pragmatics of political campaigning is, in this model, figured as a contest between candidates who will be judged by the electorate. The relationship between candidates and voters should be one of *philia* uncoloured by *eros*. This is not to say that voters should be disinterested, but that they should find their interests served by the candidate's measures and party. The electoral process would be corrupted by too much friendship, sympathy, or desire. The figure of woman brings these to presence. Furthermore, codes of propriety restricted how gentlemen – and thus members of Parliament – should communicate with women, and this courtly code would clearly be incompatible with the manly pragmatics of parliamentary debate.

Macdonald had not proposed that women be eligible for Parliament, but such a further innovation certainly followed his avowed commitment to equality between the sexes. Wary of such slippery slopes, members of Parliament debated the matter, weighing the implications of granting full political rights to women, including the right to sit in the House. James Edgar (Ontario West), sitting in opposition, observed:

Now, just fancy the confusion which would be occasioned by ladies occupying seats in this Chamber. No doubt it would have a soothing, calming, and beneficent influence in some direction, but what an undue influence might be exercised by them. Just imagine, Mr. Chairman, yourself, with your well known delicacy, having to call a lady to order; how painful it would be to gentlemen of your instincts to call a lady to order, and insist on her sitting down instead of standing up yourself, in her presence.

An hon. MEMBER. The Chairman might be a lady.

Mr. EDGAR. She might, but that would be still more embarrassing to those who would have to address the Chair. Imagine a bashful member trying to catch the lady Speaker's eye! (Canada 1885: 1400)

The admission of women to Parliament, to a place of political debate founded upon the idea of formal equality, would have required a revolution in manners, in the pragmatics of civil intercourse. What was required, in other words, was a new civil culture in which woman, still marked by difference, could appear and speak publicly on an equal footing with man.

We should hardly be surprised that many members termed Macdonald's proposal revolutionary. More telling is that those opposed to suffrage were concerned that this innovation would devalue women. In confessing his anxiety, Edgar further observed: 'Some people say that if we were to give women the franchise and bring them into the turmoil of election contests – which are bad enough, goodness knows, for the men engaged in them – it would unsex the women; it would take away their charms, and modesty and purity – that it would, in fact, make them Amazons' (Ibid). Women would become as brutish as the Americans of 1812, not restrained by the responsibility of protecting a dependent other. One can well imagine how, under such circumstances, a gentleman would be at their mercy.

Most speaking for suffrage did not enlist the topic of equality central to Macdonald's vision of progress. Rather, advocates of suffrage asserted woman's competence and then proceeded from the same topics and gendered typology as their opponents to advance the proposition that women would elevate the refigured political sphere. Theirs was a rhetoric of moral reform, not only asserting woman's competence as a political subject, but as bearers of (feminine) virtues that, while attendant to the private sphere, were unfortunately lacking from the political domain. As such, the entry of women into the political sphere would not unsex them, nor weaken the political relation through *eros*, but would civilize both the House and Canadian society. Even McMullen, unnerved by the prospect of addressing a woman speaker and concerned with whether the vote would be in woman's interest, recognized in Queen Victoria proof that women were fit for political life: 'No man who ever sat on the throne of England exercised so intelligent a sway, so constitutional and beneficent a sway, as does the lady who now occupies the throne of England; and, therefore, no loyal subject of the Queen can, for one moment, logically say that a woman is not capable of being an excellent politician' (Canada 1885: 1399). What remained at issue was the benefit of such an innovation, itself eloquently argued by George Casey, opposition member for Elgin West, as he spoke of those qualities particular to woman:

I do not say that woman has an abstract right to the franchise, because I do not admit that it is a question of abstract right at all; it is a question of expediency, and political and public convenience. If we come to look at it in that light, we see many reasons why it would be expedient, why it would be a political convenience, why it would add to the public interest, to give the franchise to woman. We know that she has a great many qualities which qualify her more than most men, more perhaps than any man, to judge of the character, of the moral character, and the mental ability even, of mankind. (Canada 1885: 1403)

Of course, not all members agreed. Of interest, however, are the containment strategies put forward in jest, that sought to accommodate 'progress' while preserving manly parliamentary culture. Simon Dawson, member for Algoma, proposed that women have a Parliament of their own, where they could debate 'in their own way,' and so follow the Indian practice at the time of the 'old French occupation of Canada' (Canada 1885: 1408)! Of course, Dawson did not make this suggestion in earnest. As he continued, his position was clear: 'Woman should keep her own sphere and leave to men the work that belongs to men.' Fellow member John Curran of Montreal Centre, echoing Dawson, proposed that women be appointed or elected appointed to the Senate, 'particularly if they were ladies who had attained a certain age ... [which would] bring credit to the other branch of the Legislature, and perhaps fasten it still more strongly in the affections of the people than it has been for some time past' (Canada 1885: 1410). In ironically proposing such measures, opponents to woman's public presence as a political subject identified another locus and style for woman's refiguration.

As Macdonald had anticipated, the woman's suffrage measure was defeated. Furthermore, subsequent to becoming prime minister in 1896, Wilfrid Laurier reinstated the system whereby provincial voters lists determined who could vote federally. Suffrage thus became primarily a provincial question. Furthermore, Laurier's franchise legislation explicitly excluded the women of the North-West Territory from voting federally. The question of woman's suffrage only became a serious federal issue again after Manitoba, Saskatchewan, and Alberta, formed out of the North-West Territory, enfranchised women in 1916. This raised questions of justice: Did the federal legislation that enfranchised persons voting in provincial elections apply to women? Furthermore, if it did, was the law extending the federal franchise just to male persons voting in Alberta and Saskatchewan, since women voting in those provinces would be denied a privilege granted their counterparts in other provinces? Some argued that the federal government should extend the franchise to women from all provinces who otherwise met provincial qualifications. These questions, however, were subordinated at least in part to expedience, since the debate ultimately was coloured by the war policy of Robert Borden's government. Borden advocated conscription. Seeking to insure continued support, his government in 1917 modified the franchise for the duration of the war, granting the vote to those who had served in the armed forces, including women and those under twenty-one, and then to the adult wives, sisters, mothers, and daughters of those who had served during the current war. With that precedent set, the franchise at the war's end was extended to all women otherwise meeting provincial criteria (Cleverdon 1974: 118–38). In a sense, ideological questions yielded to expedience. More precisely, expediency provided an opportunity for what Macdonald had considered inevitable.

The granting of woman's suffrage required the prior figuration within Canada's political culture of woman as a political subject. Macdonald's initiative had anticipated rather than followed such a change. Subsequent to the defeat of his measure, support for suffrage developed gradually and unevenly, developing political force in the second decade of the twentieth century. In what follows, we will examine woman's figuration in Canadian political discourse in that interim period, and consider how she gained a place and manner from which to speak. We will not offer an account of suffrage campaigns in each province. Cleverdon, Bacchi, and others have told that story. Rather, we will highlight the interplay between two necessary and complementary shifts in how woman and politics were understood. The first shift refigured woman as a 'public subject' or citizen. The second refigured civil society itself as an extended household, and so transformed the public realm into a domesticated social sphere. These transformations managed the anxiety over woman as sexed subject in the public sphere. As we saw above, nineteenth-century gender categories had, at least in Upper Canada, 'feminized' gentlemen as 'Christian soldiers,' providing them with responsibilities toward both family and woman, even as women were responsible for the moral character of the domestic sphere. The period from 1885 to 1919 saw the politicization of these responsibilities, as reform movements emerged that sought to implant as public norms the maternal values that the parliamentary debate of 1885 had attributed to proper 'ladies.'

Social Reform and Its Subjects

Two great movements of reform marked the turn of the century and contributed to the cause of woman's rights. The first was temperance. The second was what Mariana Valverde refers to as 'social purity' (1991). Temperance advocates, and most notably the Woman's Christian Temperance Union (WCTU), attacked alcohol for corrupting men, leading them to waste their wages on drink, shirk their family responsibilities, and commit domestic violence. 'Social purity' advocates married the scientific discourse of the emerging helping professions with those of bourgeois Protestant domesticity and campaigned to 'clean up' society, in both the literal and metaphoric sense. Both movements were the result of transformations in Canada's social fabric. Immigration, westward migration, industrialization, and urbanization challenged the hegemony of Protestant, middle-class values. As Paul Voisy observes, the arrival of young single men seeking their future in western Canada was followed by a rise in public drinking, prostitution, and gambling. These were a matter of concern both to clergy and 'proper' women who campaigned for relief from this social evil (Voisy 1975:10). In cities, these same social forces also placed even the bourgeois family at the mercy of the social environment and of the market. Tomorrow's citizens were threatened by moral corruption and by polluted air, diseased food, and unclean water. Social purity advocates produced a rhetoric of 'soap, light, and water' to inculcate the values of cleanliness, sexual responsibility, and hard work in Canadian society, and also called for government regulation of food and the environment. Their project was to produce a pure Canadian nation (Valverde 1991: 34–43).

These movements became the motor of English Canada's suffrage movement as they sought to extend the domestic sphere outward and so offered women a gendered civic role. The virtues of ladies outlined in the parliamentary debate of 1885 were figured as necessary to ensure the development of a wholesome and healthy nation. Social purity thus sought a refiguring of both the male and female subject: 'This gender reform meant that some women were given the possibility of acquiring a relatively powerful identity as rescuers, reformers, and even experts ... [Some men similarly] were provided with a potential new identity as reformed, moralized, and domesticated males' (Valverde 1991: 29–30). In addition to providing 'ladies' with the opportunity to serve their community and 'nation,' these movements sought to influence government policies through the enfranchisement of the virtuous sex. This meant, in other words, constituting women at least partly as political equals. Needless to say, these social reformers did not propose the vote only for unmarried women. On the contrary, they considered the woman's vote to be a vote for the family and it was precisely as maternal citizens that they sought woman's political empowerment.

The politicization of maternal virtue is usually referred to as 'maternal feminism,' in that it was based on the claim that women were fundamentally moral and caring beings. Wayne Roberts argues that conservative elites favoured maternal feminism as a way of containing the subversive potential of women gaining access to education. They did so by encouraging educated women to become nation builders and 'guardians of the race' (Roberts 1979: 40). In their view, if women were provided with a moral vocation, they would be less likely to demand true equality. Nevertheless, maternal feminism was feminist for its time. Temperance and social purity were seen as a means of protecting women from male exploitation and violence. Furthermore, the maternal subject figured by social reform would be a citizen, if only to advance reformist policies. Social reform provided suffrage with a conservative raison d'être; however, it also required a public feminine pragmatics of citizenship. To put it more plainly, these reform movements required that women address the public sphere as citizens, that they be 'manly' in advocating and defending public domestic virtues. They required, in other words, a pragmatics at least partially founded in the equality that citizenship confers, an equality that also warranted suffrage as an end in itself, an end consonant with progress, justice, and reason.

In considering the civil emergence of woman as a public subject, two things are worthy of note. First, it depended upon man's complicity. Second, it was a radical development, even when contained by ideologies of reform or of the 'maternal.' We will consider the pragmatic and rhetorical dynamics of that speaking position. For the sake of economy, we will do so by discussing two cases, each a 'representative anecdote' of the dynamics of performing as a female political subject. These are representative anecdotes, in Burke's sense, in that they are '*summational* in character, [they are] anecdote[s] *wherein human relations grandly converge*' (Burke 1969: 323, emphasis in original). In claiming for woman the right to vote, both are dangerous, not only for what they demand, but in the sheer impertinence of being said. Both also are decorous, in that they are aesthetic adaptations to their situation. Finally, one is pious, while the other is not. We would argue that the possibility of woman speaking with authority as a public subject is secured through the intersection of these genres of performance and the corresponding figure of woman that each offers.

Pious Performance

Our first case is Sonia Leathes and her essay published in *University Magazine* in 1914, which argues for woman's enfranchisement in the name of both justice to women and social reform. In doing so, Leathes offers an insight into the difficult and paradoxical nature of suffrage rhetoric, for she makes claims on the basis of both emancipatory reason and conservative responsibility, enacting both the masculine role of citizen and the feminine role of mother. Her rhetoric both asserts and defers. Furthermore, she proceeds through the ambiguity of the topic of progress. Progress, in the sense of the advancement of democracy and enlightenment, justifies woman's emancipation. Also, however, progress in the sense of the social consequences of industrialization and capitalism, imposes an obligation upon women. Furthermore, while advancing suffrage as innovation, she, like Macdonald, places it within a *tradition* of progress. Historical movement is opposed to things staying as they are. Thus, arguing against the authority of antiquity, she asserts:

Antiquity is not a proof of finality ... [Suffrage] is indeed but a further, perhaps the last, chapter in the great history of the individual, black or white, rich or poor, male or female, from social and political disability imposed upon him or her on account of birth alone. This is the true meaning of democracy ... The essence of democracy is the removal of all artificial restrictions which bar the way to the progress, development, and advancement, be it economic, social, or political, of any individual or any class on account of birth, colour, religious creed, or sex alone. (Leathes 1914: 69)

Standing on the side of the future, she invokes the past. This negotiation continues, as she seeks divine authority for her claim, suggesting that God's will now can be better understood. Her address here is civil, even manly, as she invokes the deity and hence 'natural law' against the authority of time immemorial and the received exclusions of common law. Against the authority of an earlier time, she cites the case of slavery: 'a right which the strong exercised over the weak ever since the remotest days of which historical records have reached us, which the Bible even seems to accept without comment, this immemorial right was challenged and abolished less than fifty years ago' (69). The Bible, and hence God one must imagine, once had no objection to slavery, and yet she continues, invoking his will against his word:

As one of the most eloquent preachers asked a half a century ago: 'Has God made woman capable, morally, physically, intellectually, of taking part in all human affairs? Then what God made her able to do, there is a strong argument that He intended her to do. Our divine sense of justice tells us that the being who is to be governed by laws should first assent to them, that the being who is taxed shall have a voice in fixing the character and amount of the financial burden which it is to bear. Then, if woman is made responsible before the law, if she is admitted to the gallows, to the gaol, and to the tax lists, we have no right to debar her from the ballot box.' (69–70)

Leathes's assertion of equality could appear radical even in 1914. She does speak of rights. Her radicalism is muted in two ways, however. First, her argument for equality defers to traditional authority. She presents a tradition of progress that was also espoused by Canada's first prime minister and invokes God's will as given voice by the clergy. Second, she reverts to the rhetoric of maternal feminism in the latter part of her text. Indeed, she argues that man has invaded the domestic sphere.

A hundred years ago the home was not only a family but also an industrial unit. Woman was the spinner, the weaver, the provider of the food and of the clothing for the household; and the impelling motive behind these home industries was love and service ... The milk was pure and the butter sweet, for this was most profitable to the health of the household. There were no other profits to be considered. (73)

With industry, however, 'Food, from being a thing to eat, became a thing to sell. It became more profitable to sell dirty and watered milk, cleanliness being a costly matter' (74). Leathes here offers a trenchant social critique. Her narrative can indeed be described as 'socialistic,' for not only man, but also capitalism is the invader. Even so, its radical edge is limited. She is claiming for woman the right to her traditionally proper sphere. Furthermore, her account is consistent with a strain in Canadian culture that opposed virtuous to rapacious masculinity. In portraying woman as victim, Leathes attenuates the liberal strain in her progressivism, advocating reform as a means of restoring the values of a prior domestic scene.

Leathes offers an instance of 'casuistic stretching,' which Cheree Carlson observed in nineteenth-century American feminist reform rhetoric. 'Casuistic stretching' is Kenneth Burke's term for describing the rhetorical extension of meanings to new cases: '"One introduces new principles while theoretically remaining faithful to old principles." The method consists of removing terms from an accepted context and moving them into new territory' (Carlson 1992: 21). Carlson observes that this rhetoric is ironic because a gap exists between what is said and what is claimed. Leathes's irony is not particularly sharp, however. On the contrary, it is pious. In this rhetoric of reform, the 'very traditions used to keep women docile became impetus to her revolution' (Carlson 1992: 27). In Leathes's essay, woman's domestic responsibilities and virtues demand that she take on a public role. Woman in this rhetoric remains burdened by her maternal nature:

With the average man property interests come first. Man is the restless explorer, inventor, and conqueror ... But there is just one industry from which he is forever excluded: it is the women who hold the monopoly of producing the people who are to benefit by all these great achievements, and without which the world within one generation would become a desert.

To be able to adequately protect human life from the onslaught of property interests, women must today have the ballot ... It is you who decide whether cannons and torpedoes are to blow to pieces the bodies of the sons which we bore. And since all these matters strike at the very heart-strings of the mothers of all nations, we shall not rest until we have secured the power vested in the ballot: to give or to withhold our consent, to encourage or to forbid any policy or course of action which concerns the people – our children every one. (Leathes 1914: 77–8)

Leathes's address, as an instance of maternal feminism, effectively contains rather than exploits the sexual threat that caused such anxiety in the 1885 parliamentary debate. As mothers, and indeed as carriers of the most wholesome values, woman's passion is transformed into motherly care. Thus spoken for, woman (as enacted by Leathes herself in the essay) is no longer an object of desire. The effectiveness of her rhetoric is hindered, however, because it does not synthesize fully the masculine and the feminine, the domain of public rights and the domain of maternal duty. Consequently, while Leathes refigures the political sphere to include woman's concerns and justifies her presence there, she does not offer or perform an integrated and so rhetorically effective pragmatics for women to engage men in public debate. She is pious and moralistic. Her passion remains feminine and thus troubling.

The weakness of Leathes's rhetoric is highlighted in the dismissive response that immediately follows in the pages of *University Magazine*. Andrew Macphail, its editor, does not fear 'Amazons,' but feminist mothers lacking the prudent manners of the political sphere: 'Men are nervous about the incursion of women into the affairs of the world because they know how complicated those affairs really are, and they dread the result of inexperience, coupled with emotions which are uncontrolled by reality ... It is the untempered enthusiasm of women which alarms them. They are afraid, too, of the reformers' zeal' (Macphail 1914: 82). Note here how the maternal duty that Leathes invokes to justify the demand for suffrage is counterpoised to prudence and reflective judgment. Macphail holds up the hunger strikes of British suffragettes as an example of how women approach politics, thus presenting what for men could be courage as shrillness and emotional excess. With a dismissive tone, he portrays social reformers as naive idealists, and then describes feminists as neither sufficiently feminine to share the company of other women nor sufficiently masculine to be man's peer. In his view, feminists lack an effective ethos. They certainly could not be truly 'manly,' nor could they be truly 'feminine.' Leathes had not offered a way of being both and neither simultaneously.

A contemporary feminist perspective would also find moral reform rhetoric flawed. As we have seen, the subordination of rights to duty led Bacchi to consider Canadian suffrage as fundamentally nonfeminist. With a greater appreciation for rhetorical tensions, Carlson observes the limits of 'casuistic stretching' in maternal feminism. In Carlson's account, because reform rhetoric does not contest but indeed exploits woman's traditional role, it risks reinscribing her in that role. Thus Carlson observes: 'As long as the rhetoric stressed "masculine" actions in the defence of "feminine" values, it could weigh the balance in favor of the public arena versus the home ... But, one slip and those traditional values could overcome the balance, thus making irony a tool for further repression – one that sent women back to the home' (Carlson 1992: 28–9). Leathes attempts to negotiate the ironic tension that Carlson describes and that Macphail's misogyny calls to attention. The negotiation and irony are incomplete, however, because the strand of maternal rhetoric Leathes offers does not on its own provide women with either a secure place and manner from which to speak, nor does it offer a means of simultaneously embodying the masculine and the feminine. In other words, the very values and roles that maternal feminism and social reform required could serve to undermine the constitution of woman as a political subject.

We observed earlier that the quest for woman's rights in Canada had been remarkably civil, in part because of the absence of a strong rights tradition to which suffrage advocates could appeal, and also because of a 'progressive conservative' strain with which suffrage and social reform could be aligned. Even so, civility and an openness to reform were not sufficient to transform woman into a political subject that embodies both the feminine and the masculine, the caring and the agonistic, with neither one undermining the other. The emergence of woman as a political subject rather than her reinscription only as a servant of reform, required what Linda Hutcheon terms an 'edge' (1994). In Britain and America, impiety was often uncivil. Mass politics and social disobedience offered an 'edge,' which although not persuasive in itself could nevertheless undermine given hierarchies. In Canada, the piety of social reform found its 'edge' in our second case, the civil and ironic impious folly of mock parliaments.

Mock Parliament as Civil Impiety

Mock parliaments were an instance of civil but impious irony. A recurring feature of the Canadian campaign for woman's suffrage, they were staged and scripted events in which women, in the role of parliamentarians, would debate suffrage and other issues of social reform. They were theatrical performances for which admission was charged to raise funds for suffrage organizations. Precisely because women could not be parliamentarians, mock parliaments were a spectacle, providing audiences with the possibility of exploring the transgression of woman as political subject. Indeed, in the context of turn-of-the-century feminism and sponsorship by pro-suffrage organizations, the very term 'mock parliament' signals an ironic disavowal. But what exactly is the nature of that disavowal? Does 'mock' signal an inauthentic imitation, or is Parliament itself the subject of scornful mockery? Does the seriousness of parliamentary matters overshadow the playful connotations of a mock exercise, or on the contrary, are suffrage advocates engaging in a ludic form of self-mockery, ironically parodying their own political objectives. There is no clear answer because, as staged, an oscillation between all of these interpretations is possible.

Some mock parliaments, such as the one held in Winnipeg in February 1893, resisted the comic frame upon which they were predicated. There, women parliamentarians performed the typical serious arguments both for and against woman's enfranchisement. Such staging promoted civility by recognizing its opponents. Even so, as Kym Bird observes in her excellent discussion of mock parliaments as a form of women's political theatre, the voicing by women of anti-suffrage arguments in such a context is necessarily ironic (Bird 1996: 134). The civility is 'edgy,' because the very frame of the mock parliament as pro-suffrage exercise signals a disavowal of even a 'straight' delivery of an anti-suffrage case. That is to say, civility is constituted in the recognition and legitimation of what is both challenged and disavowed. Other parliaments, such as one staged in Toronto in 1896 and another in Winnipeg in 1914, were more explicitly partisan, and more brutally ironic. They exploited the comic frame by offering stinging satire and a vicious parody of the anti-suffrage stand. In all cases, however, mock parliaments were fundamentally ludic, standing as a form of play, to be appreciated as witty, and hence decorous, even as they politely violated the *nomos*, the dominant normative order. That is to say, the meaning of the performance qua performance is produced ironically, in the interplay of the sense that women can and cannot really be parliamentarians. Mock parliaments, as spectacles, provided a civil means for women to violate the norm that excluded them from the political sphere in part because, as Bird observes, the form accepted the legitimacy of parliamentary institutions even as they excluded women. Furthermore, and this is fundamental, even opponents of woman's suffrage could enjoy the irony, not for its political message, but as sophistic entertainment, an oratorical drag show of sorts.

The ironic valences of these events can be seen in the press coverage that they received. The *Manitoba Free Press* headed a sympathetic article on the 1893 mock parliament 'The Ladies Innings.' The baseball metaphor signals a playful *agon*, and casts the battle of the sexes as entertainment, describing the event as 'rousing.' Entertainment and politics are conjoined, as is evident in the headline describing one staged in 1914: 'WOMEN SCORE IN DRAMA AND DEBATE.' Furthermore, mock parliaments were successful, at least as spectacles. The two cited here were performed to sold-out crowds. That success also provided a rhetorical audience to listen to suffrage oratory and imagine women as parliamentarians. Thus, in its coverage of the 1893 mock parliament, the *Free Press* figured the event as mediation between past and future, providing women the opportunity to rehearse a political role: 'That women have rights is admitted by all men and a good many women, but the trouble seems to be that there is a lack of precedent for the exercise of what belongs to them ... They must not only be told that they are free, some one must go ahead and show them how to use their freedom; but let them get a good start and it is easy to predict that they will need no further coaching' (*Manitoba Free Press,* 10 February 1893: 5). And yet the anxiety that prompted one member of Parliament (Dawson) to ironically propose in 1885 that women have a parliament of their own returns, as the *Free Press* continues: 'It is quite a safe and pleasing thing to behold a mock parliament in our midst. It makes the citizens feel that if necessary something could be done in the way of legislation that would astonish the promoters of political jobbery and at the same time everyone knows that no harm could possibly ensue if the mock parliament declared war or framed a new school bill' (ibid). This same ludic frame reappeared in the somewhat less sympathetic coverage by the *Manitoba Free Press* of the 1914 affair, when it observed that the packed house 'testified to the keen interest taken in the activities of the Political Equality league. More than that, however – it testified to the general opinion that the talented women who are its members were due to provide a splendid evening's entertainment' (29 January 1914: 20).

The irony of mock parliaments does not bifurcate its audience between those who 'get it' and those who do not. No reasonable reader of the *Free Press* would infer that mock parliaments were *only* entertainments and not an element in the pro-suffrage campaign. What this irony opens to, however, is a variety of interpretive valences, themselves modulated by the 'political' dynamic between ironists and audience. To put it baldly, male anti-suffrage elites could regard mock parliaments with ironic bemusement while the feminists of the time could see them as ironically belying an unjust hierarchy. Mock parliaments are civil in their edginess because they maintain a playful ethos. Even opponents on the question of suffrage can share a certain appreciation of the mock parliamentarians for their artfulness or arête at ironic reversal, for the quality of their political performance.

Irony plays in both the performance and reception of mock parliaments. The irony performed is edgy and agonistic, playfully problematizing received categories. The reception of these performances, at least as relayed in the press, is also ironic in the philosophical sense described by Kenneth Burke. He does not focus on irony's edginess, but rather upon its epistemological attitude. In his understanding, irony is dialectical because it permits the holding together of incompatible terms. Furthermore, true irony leads to the humbling recognition of the necessity of antitheses and thus to an appreciation of one's fundamental kinship with one's opponent. It is worth noting that Canada has often been described as marked by an ironic sensibility, because it is aware that it lacks a grand narrative to provide a strong and unambiguous sense of its identity, purpose, or destiny (Doob 1988: 9–14). Such a sensibility approaches what Burke means by irony, whereby the lack of a strong investment in a glorious vision leads to a civil self-ironizing stance that permits an acknowledgment of others. This is the sensibility, not of rights, but of prudence.

The irony of mock parliaments is 'provisional,' where Hutcheon describes provisional irony as 'always containing a kind of built-in conditional stipulation that undermines any firm and fixed stand' (Hutcheon 1994: 51). While such irony can be in the service of equivocation, it provides licence for transgression. More importantly, it can serve also the cause of what might be termed productive ambivalence, holding together but not resolving irreducible tensions. In the maternal feminism of the period, masculine (political) and feminine (domestic) pragmatics were ultimately distinct even as reformers sought to temper each with the other. The irony of mock parliaments, as entertainment and serious business permitted women to simultaneously embody both. As the *Manitoba Free Press* reported in 1893: 'The faces of the "hon. members" were in appearance hard, stern or determined, as one some time meets with in the parliaments of the sterner sex, but all had that kind, motherly look which seems to win the affections and sympathy of everyone' (10 February 1893: 5). Moreover, the proceedings, including the opening of debate with a prayer, were not without effect: 'A look at the face of the twenty M. P. Ps. in the audience might have revealed surprise in every one. That was the first awakening; many more followed in rapid succession, the nearer the night drew to a close, the more rapid did the surprises appear on the scene and there is little doubt that wiser and better men left the house than entered it during the early part of the evening' (ibid). At least when at play, women could be simultaneously maternal and parliamentary, caring and agonistic. They could not only score points in the battle of the sexes, but prompt sympathetic members of Parliament to request that they hold 'similar entertainments' in other cities.

Ironists use language for effect. As such, the irony of mock parliaments is 'performative,' but it is so in a more fundamental sense as well. The meaning or status of the performance as a performance is caught in a deconstructive 'loop,' since it is precisely as an entertainment that it is a serious business. Ambivalence and laughter fuse whatever anxiety woman as political subject might provoke, but her performed self stands even as a resolution of the question of woman's 'true' nature is deferred. Standing both as orators and thespians, the women on stage could speak in manly ways and remain eloquent rather than shrill. It is precisely as adept ironists that they enacted a pragmatics for the feminine political subject, whose difference paradoxically enabled these women to participate effectively in the male political *agon* that usually served to justify her exclusion.

As satire, mock parliaments were occasions for impious rhetoric. As entertainments, they nevertheless remained civil, troubling the gendered categories of Canadian society without themselves being categorical. Through irony, mock parliaments offered their antagonists a way of saving face, by feigning that these were just entertainments. As Hutcheon observes: 'The irony and distance implied by parody allow for *separation* at the same time that the doubled structure of both (the superimposition of two meanings or texts) demands recognition of *complicity*. Parody both asserts and undercuts what it contests' (Hutcheon 1988: 7). Cutting the other way, however, mock parliaments exploited that tension by making it the basis of a political pragmatics. Mock parliamentarians, and by extension women as political subjects, were simultaneously female and agonistic, maternal and masculine, through an 'edgy' performance of indeterminacy. Indeed, their irony could be described as postmodern, because it 'cultivate[s] rather than transcend[s] paradox.' (Shugart 1999: 436) Admittedly, the term 'postmodern' might seem odd with reference to a turn-of-the-century feminist rhetorical strategy. Certainly, mock parliaments did not seek to destabilize all received categories. Also, while suffrage was in some respects a progressive movement, it also had remarkably conservative, classist, ethnocentric, and racist tendencies. Nevertheless, given that the Canadian sensibility is often described as ironic and postmodern, it is noteworthy that the mock parliament was primarily a Canadian form. While feminist theatrical parody of legislative debate was not an exclusively Canadian phenomenon, it was in Canada that it became a standard rhetorical genre, adapted and co-authored by its participants in response to local exigencies (Bird 1996: 90–1). Progressive, conservative, and unstable, the mock parliaments formed an appropriate, decorous, and effective strategy in a political culture based on deference and elite accommodation. While they cannot be given full credit for the adoption of suffrage, they provided the civil edginess necessary for that campaign to succeed.

Of 'Persons' and Progress

The quest for women's formal political equality under law did not end with their being granted suffrage and becoming eligible to sit in the House of Commons and provincial legislatures. Women still could not sit in Canada's Senate. Of course, no one has the 'right' to a Senate seat, since senators are appointed. Nevertheless, once the federal franchise was granted to women, women's rights activists lobbied the federal government to appoint a woman to the Senate. Ottawa would invariably respond that such an appointment would be contrary to the BNA Act and common law (Mander 1985: 95–6). While Ottawa could establish its own franchise and set membership criteria for the House of Commons, the terms of appointment for senators were established in the BNA Act. The Act did not address the question of sex, specifying only age, property, residency, and citizenship requirements in section 23. Nevertheless, the exclusion of women could be inferred by the language of section 24: 'The Governor General shall, from time to time, in the Queen's name, by instrument under the Great Seal of Canada, summon qualified Persons to the Senate.' As we saw at the beginning of this chapter, woman's exclusion from public life, except as monarch, was a fundamental principle of common law.

Ottawa admitted that the exclusion was unfortunate, but did not act forcefully to resolve the matter. Faced with government inaction, five woman's rights activists, led by Emily Murphy of Alberta, decided to pursue the matter before the courts. Ultimately, the 'Persons Case' was heard by the Judicial Committee of the Privy Council in London, which ruled in 1929 that women could sit in the Canadian Senate. The five women who pressed the case before the courts, Emily Murphy, Nellie McClung, Louise McKinney, Henrietta Muir Edwards, and Irene Parlby are today figured as heroes.[4] In 1997, Parliament voted to create a memorial in their honour on Parliament Hill. The statue, unveiled in October 2000, depicts in bronze the five women receiving the news of their victory, holding a newspaper that proclaims 'Women are Persons.' Speaking at the unveiling of an identical monument in Calgary's Confederation Plaza on 18 October 1999, Governor General Adrienne Clarkson praised these women as 'nation builders' who 'rattled the Canadian male establishment' (Lisa Dempester and Dave Pommer, 'Statues Salute Trail-Blazing Women: Famous Five Cast in Bronze,' *Calgary Herald*, 19 October 1999, A4).

Despite such oratory of praise, the Person's Case should not be viewed as part of a pitched battle between conservative and progressive forces. As Clarkson's own address admitted, the 'Famous Five' had 'flaws of vision ... flaws of social opinion ... flaws of not understanding ... where society was going' (*ibid*). As a *Calgary Herald* column by Naomi Lakritz reports, Murphy 'was a racist and anti-Semite' who advocated eugenics. Indeed, Clarkson's observation that Murphy 'would have been thrilled to see a Chinese woman senator [referring to her sister, Vivienne Poy, in attendance] and a Chinese Governor General' ('Everyday Heroines Forged own Successes,' 19 October 1999, A27) is tragically ironic given that Murphy had written disapprovingly of the 'black and yellow races.' Lakritz gives the Famous Five their due as 'every day heroines' but rejects the heroic ideological drama that Clarkson offers: 'The fuss over the Famous Five perpetuates the myth that Canadian women were suffering in a sulphurous cloud of male oppression until [the Five] came along and tidied things up ... One need only look at the stories of ordinary women to find the truth – the Canadian male establishment, quite used to being rattled, had accepted women into its realms for years' (ibid). Lakritz's characterization of a 'myth of suffocation' is of course polemical, but nevertheless underscores the ironic civility of the period and the Persons Case that Clarkson does not render.

The Persons Case was not over whether women were persons, as was commonly reported at the time and is figured today, both in Clarkson's address and in a recent 'Heritage Minute' in which an actress playing Murphy looks back on the case. The case did not, in any simple sense, pit women against the Ottawa male establishment, even if it was a feminist initiative. Rather, the case concerned the meaning of the BNA Act and whether women were 'qualified Persons.' In other words, the case concerned the place in Canada of British common law.

Even though the Supreme Court of Alberta had struck down the common law exclusion with respect to women magistrates in 1916, Ottawa continued to assert its view on the unconstitutionality of woman senators. Of course, the scope of the Alberta precedent was limited, being from a provincial court and not addressing sections of the BNA Act relevant to Senate appointment. Even so, Ottawa could have chosen to act boldly. Instead, the matter was left to Murphy and her associates. In 1927, they petitioned the Supreme Court of Canada to rule on the question. This was not a typical appeal, but a reference to the court which was simply asked to interpret the BNA Act. This procedure can be a very civil way of dealing with controversy because it is hypothetical, and free of the exigencies, constraints, and crisis dynamics of substantive constitutional cases. The Persons Case was civil in a second sense as well. An order-in-council is required to refer a question to the Court. References are sponsored by the government and the Department of Justice assumes legal costs. Here, Borden's government authorized and funded the case against its constitutional position. The humble irony of Canadian political civility is apparent in the Privy Council's request that the reference proceed:

In the opinion of the Minister [of Justice] the question whether the word 'Persons' in said section 24 includes female persons is one of great public importance.

The Minister states that the law officers of the Crown who have considered this question on more than one occasion have expressed the view that male persons only may be summoned to the Senate under the provisions of the British North America Act in that behalf.

The Minister, however, while not disposed to question that view, considers that it would be an act of justice to the women of Canada to obtain the opinion of the Supreme Court of Canada upon the point. (Canada. Privy Council 2034. October 1927)

We see here another instance of the progressive conservatism that we noted earlier, based on elite complicity and deferral. There is humble irony in the recognition of the possibility of error. As such, the case does not begin with a 'rattling' of the male order, but with a set of deferrals, the most important of which is to the law. Furthermore, even though there is an appeal to a court, this is not an instance of 'rights talk,' for no concrete case and interest is at stake. At issue is the government's right to call whom it pleases to the Senate, and its attorneys will argue against that right. Paradoxically, the petitioners are seeking to expand government prerogatives against its wishes.

While the case was and remains about woman's status as a political subject under the law, it was more fundamentally about the place of British common law in Canada. The case did not turn on the common sense meaning of the term 'person,' nor on principles derived from natural rights or fundamental justice, but on the rules of interpretation applicable to the BNA Act as a British statute. The petitioners argued before the Supreme Court of Canada that nothing supported interpreting the expression 'qualified Persons' in section 24 to exclude 'female persons.' In support of their position, they pointed to the accepted broader meaning in other sections of the Act. Arguments against the petitioners' view were legion. The factums submitted on behalf of the Attorneys General of Canada and Quebec argued that the Act should be interpreted in terms of the accepted meanings at the time of enactment, the intent of the legislator, the recognized common law exclusion in Great Britain, and the general principle that a departure from common law principles must be signalled though explicit language.

The Supreme Court ruled unanimously against the petitioners. It ruled that women were not 'qualified persons' in section 24. The justices did not all concur in their reasoning, however. No one disputed that in certain sections of the Act, 'persons' included 'female persons.' All were in agreement that, under section 41, Parliament had the right to enfranchise female persons. But other sections could support a narrow interpretation. Justices Anglin, Mignault, Lamont, and Smith shared the opinion that the common law principle applied to a number of sections, such as section 11 concerning the composition of the Privy Council. Writing for the Court, Chief Justice Anglin argued:

But, in s. 11, which provides for the constitution of the new Privy Council for Canada, the word 'persons,' though unqualified, is probably used in the more restricted sense of 'male persons.' For the public offices thereby created women were, by the common law, ineligible and it would be dangerous to assume that by the use of the ambiguous term 'persons' the Imperial Parliament meant in 1867 to bring about so vast a constitutional change affecting Canadian women, as would be involved in making them eligible for selection as Privy Councillors. (*SCR* 1928: 287)

Using this and similar sections of the Act, Anglin held that a restricted meaning should be applied to section 24 as well. This interpretation was contentious, however. Justice Duff, concurring with the other justices' answer to the referred question, rejected their reasoning and the relevance of the common law exclusion. Specifically, he challenged Anglin's interpretation of section 11:

It might be suggested, I cannot help thinking, with some plausibility, that there would be something incongruous in a parliamentary system professedly conceived and fashioned on this principle [of responsible government], if persons fully qualified to be members of the House of Commons were by an iron rule of the constitution, a rule beyond the reach of Parliament, excluded from the Cabinet or the Government. (*SCR* 1928: 297)

Of course, the Privy Council is not the Senate, but Duff's reasoning directly challenges Anglin's interpretive logic. Ultimately, however, Duff's own interpretation also excluded women. Duff developed an historical argument, and maintained that the Senate was modelled on the legislative councils of the pre-Confederation Canadas, to which women were clearly ineligible. Consequently, despite their difference of interpretation, the Court unanimously held that tradition, accepted practice, and the absence of clear language to the contrary excluded women from entering the Senate.

The Supreme Court's ruling settled little. In Parliament, Minister of Justice Ernest Lapointe indicated that given this interpretation, 'means would be taken to secure an amendment' to grant women 'the equal right to sit in the other Chamber' (Canada 1928: 2311). The legal case was not exhausted, however, since the Supreme Court was not the final court of appeal. The Famous Five were granted leave by Ottawa to appeal the Supreme Court's finding to the Judicial Committee of the Privy Council, and the Department of Justice again covered the costs. There, the matter was treated quite differently.

On 18 October 1929, the Judicial Committee issued a landmark ruling upholding the appeal against the Supreme Court. In interpreting the Act, the Lords looked to both 'external evidence,' including 'previous legislation and decided cases,' and 'internal evidence,' the Act itself (UK *House of Lords and Privy Council AC* 1930, 127). While women were historically excluded from public office, Lord Sankey, writing for the Judicial Committee, limited history's claim upon the present. In their view, laws must be understood as a response to the exigencies of their times:

The exclusion of women from all public offices is a relic of days more barbarous than ours, but it must be remembered that the necessity of the times often forced on man customs which in later years were not necessary. Such exclusion is probably due to the fact that the deliberative assemblies of the early tribes were attended by men under arms, and women did not bear arms ... Yet the tribes did not despise the advice of women. (Ibid., 128)

As such, woman's continued exclusion from certain offices was archaic, a consequence of the weight of law and received custom. For the Lords, however, Canada should not be governed by British traditions or hindered by the legacy of its legal constraints: 'Their Lordships do not think it right to apply rigidly to Canada of to-day the decisions and the reasons therefor which commended themselves, probably rightly, to those who had to apply the law in different circumstances, in different centuries, to countries in different stages of development' (Ibid., 134–5). Furthermore, referring to Duff's opinion, they agreed that the BNA Act was not an 'independent enactment,' a simple law of Parliament, but a step in Canada's independence from Britain. In Sankey's words:

The British North America Act planted in Canada a living tree capable of growth and expansion within its natural limits. The object of the Act was to Grant a constitution to Canada ...

Their Lordships do not conceive it to be the duty of this Board – it is certainly not their desire – to cut down the provisions of the Act by a narrow and technical construction, but rather to give it a large and liberal interpretation so that the Dominion to a great extent, but within certain fixed limits, may be mistress in her own house, as the Provinces to a great extent, but within certain fixed limits, are mistresses in theirs. (Ibid., 136)

Sankey continued, citing Clement's *Canadian Constitution*: 'But there are statutes and statutes; and the strict construction deemed proper in the case, for example, of a penal or taxing statute or one passed to regulate the affairs of an English parish, would be often subversive of Parliament's real intent if applied to an Act passed to ensure the peace, order and good government of a British colony' (ibid., 136–7). In so figuring Canada, Sankey reversed the usual presumption. Against the argument that a broadening of the legal meaning of the term 'persons' required an explicit gesture, Sankey offered: 'The word "person," as above mentioned, may include members of both sexes, and to those who ask why the word should include females the obvious answer is why should it not? In those circumstances the burden is upon those who deny that the word includes women to make their case' (ibid., 138). The Lords then considered the Act itself and rejected constructions that limited the meaning of 'persons' to 'male persons.' Sankey noted that Chief Justice Anglin's interpretation of section 11 excluding women from the Privy Council gave rise to an anomaly, since the Act did not prohibit women from sitting in Parliament. Sankey cited other sections in support of the Lords' position that 'persons' could not be understood in the narrow sense. Also, Sankey pointed out that, by the time of Confederation, women had been 'excluded by express enactment' from voting. Ironically, as Canadian legislatures had acted explicitly to exclude women, they implicitly recognized that women otherwise could hold public office or vote. Thus, even in the constitutional and legal language of the time, 'persons' did not exclude women. Furthermore, while the Lords concurred with

Duff regarding how the Act should be interpreted, they did not accept his version of the place of the Senate in Canada's constitutional development. They dismissed as speculation his interpretation that the Senate was modelled on the legislative councils of 1791 and 1840. As such, they concluded that the only criteria pertinent to Senate membership were those in section 23. Women were thus eligible for appointment.

As a 'living tree,' the BNA Act signalled a break with tradition, and with the authority of British (as opposed to Canadian) custom and common law. Thus, while the Persons Case advanced the cause of woman's rights, its significance is far more reaching: Canada was indeed a new country, still tied to Great Britain by the law's continuity, but free to develop a political and legal culture of its own. Indeed, the Persons Case can be understood as another gesture in the logic of gift and counter-gift characteristic of the early colonial period. Here, while the Canadian government and the Supreme Court expressed devotion to the authority of British precedent, the Lords gave Canada what it would not give itself, autonomy and the right to a political culture of its own. Sankey's ruling was governed by prudence, just as the Crown's intervention on the North-West's behalf had been in 1870. Here the BNA Act itself, intended to secure 'Peace, Order, and good Government,' becomes more that an act of positive law, but confers on Canada the responsibility to prudently govern itself.

The ruling of the Judicial Committee closed another chapter in the quest for women's formal political equality in Canada. While woman's suffrage had been a political question, which incidentally would not be settled in Quebec until 1940, the Persons Case addressed the nature of woman as a political subject in legal and constitutional terms. While legal and political discourse differ fundamentally in many aspects, both the Persons Case and the politics of suffrage had in common an attenuated *agon*. While Glendon argues in *Rights Talk* (1991) that law can be a divisive instrument, it was not in the Persons Case, perhaps because it was only a reference and not a case, or perhaps because the case did not involve any rights except those of the Governor General and Privy Council. Prudence, the antithesis of both ideological politics and 'rights talk,' seems to have guided woman's transformation.

Canadian political culture is ambivalent with regard to 'new' subjects. Their emergence is tolerated as long as they do not demand too much or claim rights arising from natural law or their being. As women of the turn of the century teach us, however, demands can still be made successfully. Despite Canada's conservative reputation, radicalism and impiety are possible, at least if advanced through deferral and irony.

7

The Dialectic of Language, Law, and Translation: Manitoba and Quebec Revisited, 1969–1999

The Forked Tongue

As the previous chapter has shown and as the work of Linda Hutcheon has demonstrated, 'Canadian' rhetoric is a strange and fragmented form of language use. As E.D. Blodgett put it, 'Canadian' is 'a mixed language, *by law ambiguous*, and always offering possible escape routes ... without ever leaving home' (cited in Hutcheon 1991: 1, emphasis added). As had earlier been remarked by Frye, Hutcheon also notes that 'Canad[ians] often speak ... with a doubled voice, with the forked tongue of irony' (1). Seen either as a defensive or offensive rhetorical 'weapon,' for Hutcheon, 'irony – even in the simple sense of saying one thing and meaning another – is ... a mode of "speech" ... that allows speakers to address and at the same time slyly confront an "official" discourse' (1991: 1). While Hutcheon goes on to distinguish various types of Canadian irony (e.g., irony self-deprecating, irony self-protective, irony corrective, irony demystifying, etc.), she observes that what she terms 'postmodern irony' is the recognition 'that, in practice, all communicational codes, especially language, are ambiguous, doubled, even duplicitous' (10). And Canada, she notes, because of its historical communicative doubleness, 'is structurally ripe for ironizing' (15), given all of its historical, political, and other dualisms ('native/colonial, federal/provincial, not to mention English/French,' as well as 'bilingual yet multicultural' [15–16]). These are all spaces between cultures and language in which the duplicities of communication can slip in, saying one thing and meaning another, and producing the interruptions between official discourses and possible ironic responses to them from the lifeworld.

Not surprisingly, then, has the question of language and in particular its imbrication with the apparatus of law been especially contentious in the Canadian context. This chapter follows up on some of the implications stemming from the first Riel rebellion, which saw the establishment of the bilingual province of Manitoba, but we look particularly now at the legalo-linguistic 're-invasion' of Manitoba by the Supreme Court of Canada in the 1980s because of the province's retroactive nonconformity to federal bilingualism policies. We then examine further the continuing contamination of the Quebec civil law by 'translationese,' and the implications for a rejection of federal bilingualism (and multiculturalism) policies, but from a different, indeed opposite, ethos than in the Manitoba language battles. This ethos leads paradoxically to the subsequent displacement of the legal order created by the Quiet Revolution of the 1960s, in a redefinition of sociality less through the French language per se than through its postmodern reformulation as differential language-games. This chapter, like chapter 6, also looks at strategies of the recovery of 'voice' in the public sphere, initially as it is displaced and redistributed by the force of law, and latterly how voice can then be turned against the law as a means of entry into the public sphere.

Official Bilingualism and the Ambiguity of Law:
Linguistic Equality from Sea to Shining Sea

As political scientist Kenneth McRoberts writes in *Misconceiving Canada* (1997): 'The centre-piece of Pierre Trudeau's strategy [as of the late 1960s] for integrating Quebec francophones into a new Canadian identity was official bilingualism ... reflecting his determination that language reform should serve to integrate the Québécois with the whole of Canada' (78). The strategy represented, as McRoberts puts it, 'a very tall order' (79). Historically, the ideal of linguistic equality in Ottawa had never had more than symbolic status: both languages were used in the deliberations of Parliament, in Supreme Court laws, in records of parliamentary debates, and in important public documents. But the federal bureaucracy itself 'was essentially an English-language institution controlled by anglophones' (79), in which the francophone presence had fallen from about 22 per cent in 1918 to 13 per cent in 1946. The public face of the federal civil service changed considerably in subsequent decades, as the proportion of francophones grew from 21.5 per cent in 1961 to 28.0 per cent in 1995 (data in McRoberts, 84). But despite a greatly increased number of francophones and enormous public investment in language training, the federal civil service remained an English-language institution that has yet to become effectively bilingual.

Trudeau's ambitions, however, were grander still: to constitutionally en-trench French-language rights until, as he put it in 1968, French Canada itself would stretch from British Columbia to the Atlantic coast and 'once you have done that, Quebec cannot say it alone speaks for French Canadians' (cited in McRoberts, 85). Demographically, as McRoberts notes, not only had French Canada never stretched from coast to coast under the British form of governance, nor could it be made to do so, as new immigrants tended to join the larger anglophone populations, and francophone minorities in most provinces slowly succumbed to assimilation. If in certain ways Canadian federalism had protected francophones in Quebec by making them the electoral majority, in other ways it doomed francophones elsewhere to political marginality. Furthermore, all provincial governments except Quebec acted 'as if territorial unilingualism and the provision of public services in a single language were operative principles of Confederation' (86), and the terms of Confederation itself did not provide offsetting measures.

Beginning with the Official Languages Act (1969), Trudeau's policies attempted nothing less than to roll back a century of the linguistic divisions of Canadian history. In the end, and despite the deployment of massive resources, only one province, New Brunswick, actually constitutionalized official bilingualism in which French and English 'are the official languages of New Brunswick and have equality of status and equal rights and privileges as to their use in all institutions of the legislature and government of New Brunswick,' and its courts (s. 16.2, *Constitution Act*, 1982). And if New Brunswick has gone the furthest, the government of Ontario has come closer than any other provincial government (other than Quebec, of course), although still avoiding a formal declaration that French and English are official languages. In the late 1970s, under the pressure of Supreme Court judgments, official bilingualism came to the Prairie provinces, and took a particularly acrimonious turn in Manitoba, which we now look at in some detail.

'The Colour of Authority': Manitoba's Bilingual Battles, 1870–1985

As we saw in chapter 5, the settlement of Manitoba, particularly along the Red River, had created a form of social order that was not significantly riven by linguistic or ethnic divisions, but nonetheless had had to struggle, often bitterly, to harmonize the local conception of law (as always, in the form of a representation of 'English liberty') with the legal mechanisms of Canadian confederation, of which it became a part by the Manitoba Act (1870). By the 1890s, however, the formerly equal English-speaking and French-speaking populations had, under the pressure of settlement demographics, lost their equality, with the latter shrinking to some 10 per cent of the population. The resulting turn to English unilingualism in the provincial legislature, compounded by the hanging of Riel in 1885, fuelled growing fears, especially in Quebec, that English-

Canada was determined to commit linguicide upon French-speaking populations across the country, with the tacit agreement of the (largely anglophone) federal government, and that for francophones only the Quebec government could protect them from inevitable linguistic and cultural assimilation.

In Manitoba itself, the legislature in 1890 made English the official language of the province (*Man.* 1890, c. 14). The so-called Official Language Act was ruled *ultra vires* in 1892 by the County Court judge of St Boniface, although neither the legislature nor the government of the province enacted Judge Prud'homme's ruling. Challenged again and ruled unconstitutional in 1909, the Official Language Act remained unchanged in successive revisions of the statutes of Manitoba, the publication of legislative records, journals, or acts. Not until 1976 would a third legal challenge be mounted, again finding the 1890 Act unconstitutional; once again, the Act remained on the statute books, unchanged. In 1979, the constitutionality of the 1890 Act was tested before the Supreme Court of Canada and was unanimously found to be unconstitutional and in conflict with s. 23 of the Manitoba Act, 1870, which had made it mandatory to 'enact, print and publish' all acts of the Manitoba legislature in both French and English. Section 23 of the 1870 Act was deemed virtually identical to s. 133 of the Constitution Act of 1867, specifically outlining the Quebec legislature's official bilingualism. In 1982, the Manitoba legislature finally budged somewhat, enacting, printing, and publishing as of that year the Acts of the legislature in both English and French, but this concession did not apply to 'Acts that only amend Acts,' or to private bills that would remain enacted in English only. The legality of the latter was upheld by the Manitoba Court of Appeal in 1981; and in 1983, the Attorney General of Manitoba tabled a resolution to amend the language provisions of the 1870 Manitoba Act, a resolution that did not pass because of the prorogation of the legislative session. In the spring of the following year, the federal government referred the entire situation to the Supreme Court (background drawn from 1985: 1 *SCR*, 721–83).

In June 1985, the Court issued a 60-page 'reference' on the Manitoba Language Rights question. A reference is an unusual kind of legal exercise, more a strictly limited legal interpretation from the highest court in the land than actual law-making. The late Supreme Court Chief Justice Bora Laskin (whose tenure was from 1973 to 1984) in his 1960 textbook, *Canadian Constitutional Law*, discusses constitutional references in chapter 4 in the subsection entitled 'Avoidance and Confinement of Decisions Turning on Constitutional Grounds' (1960: 144 ff). On the one hand, it is the duty of the Court to 'hear and consider' the questions referred to it, and these shall be 'conclusively deemed' (145) to be important questions; but as for the binding power of such references, 'it has invariably been declared that they are not judgements either binding on the Government, on Parliament, on individuals, or even on the Court itself, although ... this should be qualified by saying that, in a contested case where the same questions would arise, they would no doubt be followed' (180). In Laskin's view, a Supreme Court reference is not a particularly good instrument by which to rule upon the 'colourability' of legislation, a question which he considers would better be dealt with 'in an ordinary case' (181). We will see why this is significant shortly.

Briefly, the Manitoba reference answered four questions. First, were the requirements of s. 133 of the Constitution Act, 1867, and s. 23 of the Manitoba Act, 1870, mandatory for the Houses of Parliament of Canada and the legislatures of Manitoba and Quebec? Second, are the statutes and regulations of the province of Manitoba that are not printed and published in both English and French invalid, based on s. 23 of the Manitoba Act? Third, if so, did those enactments have legal force? Fourth, are the provisions of the Act attempting to modify s. 23 inconsistent with the 1870 Manitoba Act and, given that inconsistency, what legal force and effect do they have? In the case of the first question, the answer was an unqualified 'yes.' The answers to the second and third questions were that the Acts, past and current, of the Manitoba legislature not enacted, printed, and published in English and French were invalid and so had no legal force, but that current Acts were deemed to have 'temporary force and effect' for a minimum period of time allowing for 'their translation, re-enactment, printing and publication' in both English and French. Finally, and ironically, if the act attempting to modify s. 23 of the Manitoba Act had not been enacted in both languages, then it was invalid and of no force and effect in its entirety (see 1985 *SCR*, 721–3).

In effect, the reference, if enforced, invalidated all Manitoba laws passed in English-only since 1890, estimated to number about 4000, creating a curious situation in which the province's legislature would be granted 'temporary' legality. During that time they had to translate into French and re-enact almost a century of legislation, otherwise now invalid, at an estimated cost of at least $20 million, in order to regain an appropriate legality in conformity with the bilingual character of the federal constitution and of the two bilingually legislative assemblies of Quebec and Manitoba. This was a situation which raised such questions as 'what is the rule of law?' 'when is a law not a law?' and similar issues that seemed to strike deeply at the concept of the rule of law itself. We will see shortly how the reference dealt with these problems.

In Manitoba, the reference came at the end of a prolonged period of public, parliamentary, and extra-parliamentary agitation that had gone on since 1976 when Georges Forest, an insurance salesman from St Boniface, now a suburb of Winnipeg, undertook the legal challenge of a English-language parking ticket on the grounds that it fell under the 1890 English-only Act and denied him his constitutional rights as a francophone. The subsequent agitation and supposed near-total citizen opposition to enforced bilingualism is recounted by one of the key opposition leaders, MLA Russell Doern, in *The Battle over Bilingualism* (1985). Doern argues that since Manitobans had lived on the basis of 'laws passed by democratically elected legislatures' creating a coherent social fabric ('our organizations, business transactions, mortgages, marriages, college and university degrees, courts ... and governments are based upon this legitimate law-making' [211]), if Ottawa was so intent 'to force official bilingualism down the throats of the people of Manitoba,' then it should pay for the costs of translating 'obsolete' legislation which would 'only benefit a dozen or more French-speaking lawyers and accountants' (211). As Doern notes, the 1985 Supreme Court reference, after all the preceding agitation and fears of reverse assimilation, was rather an anticlimax: 'There was no legal chaos. No official bilingualism imposed by the courts. No bilingual civil service. No expensive reprinting of all government ... publications in the French language. And no major rift in the province's social fabric' (199).

So, in the end, if nothing resulted that was overwhelming, or even immediately binding, what was all the fuss about? This is difficult to assess with any precision from Doern's blow-by-blow account of radio talk-shows, letters from various opposition groups, and speeches given here and there, but one can strongly suggest that the episode replays the original process of Manitoba's entry into Canada, but now with the key roles reversed. As will be recalled, the original process of entry included fears of being taken over by a 'foreign' and distant power, manifested in the disjunct between a local conception of law (in both instances in the form of a democractically elected local legislature or equivalent) colliding with the abstract principles of the meaning of the rule of law as interpreted by the Supreme Court in the 1890s and then in the 1980s. Just as in the period preceding Manitoba's becoming a Canadian province, 'agitators' from Ontario had pushed for more settlement from central Canada and also the extension of the railroad across traditional hunting lands, so too now the Franco-Manitoban Society was being given 'citizens' grants' of $200,000 by the federal Secretary of State, and the feds were also picking up Forest's and other challengers' legal bills (see Doern 1985: 17–18). Fiery speeches like one widely quoted by Serge Joyal, federal Secretary of State at the time, echoed the Trudeau government's ambitious and hard-line bilingualism policies. Joyal urged English-speaking Manitobans 'to accept the fact that *Canada is a French state*' and, furthermore, 'that if there is one group that has built this country ... that has built this province, here in Manitoba, it is Francophones' (cited in Doern, 153, all in italics in the original). Underlying all this was a clash of differing conceptions of legality, as well as fear of the power of the law to enforce unpopular policies, and indeed to overturn common-sense ideas of what 'the law' itself entails. We turn to the Supreme Court reference to see how it dealt with these fundamental questions.

In addition to the obvious references to the appropriate Canadian case-law and constitutional decisions, the Court's reference, in the Bibliography (727), draws upon two sources of jurisprudence: the first consists of classics such as Dicey's *The Law of the Constitution* and Raz's more recent *The Authority of Law* (Oxford, 1979); but the second consists of two articles from law journals, one entitled 'Reflections on Revolutions,' and the other is a study of the 'doctrine of state necessity' in Pakistan. These last two would seem to be highly unusual sources within the literature of constitutional jurisprudence upon which to base an argument; let's see why.

As the reference recognized, in its discussion of the principles of the rule of law (747 ff.), to invalidate the unconstitutional laws of Manitoba post-1890 risked that 'a legal vacuum will be created with consequent legal chaos on the Province of Manitoba.' If post-1890 legislation was declared invalid and without force or effect, then only laws enacted before 1890 would still have validity, all subsequent laws no longer being valid, unless a rule could be provided by pre-confederation law or the common law. A legal vacuum would result in which not only would post-1890 statutes 'now be unregulated by law,' but also the entire provincial apparatus of governance ('the courts, administrative tribunals, public officials, municipal corporations, school boards, professional governing bodies,' etc.) would now be 'without legal authority,' and all legal rights and other effects established by a regime of unconstitutional unilingual laws would be open to challenge. In short, at first glimpse, the Court's reference would amount to suspending the rule of law in Manitoba. What, then, is the meaning of the rule of law?

In the Court's view, this must mean at least two things. First, the recognition that the law is supreme over both officials of government and private individuals – 'and thereby preclusive of the influence of arbitrary power' (748). The supremacy of law over government is, then, by definition not only an a priori given, it has been established in law by s. 23 of the 1870 Manitoba Act and by the various versions of the Canadian Constitution since 1867, most recently s. 52 of the 1982 Constitution Act. It was this transcendental conceptual enframing within the rule of law that allowed the Court to declare Manitoba's post-1890 laws invalid and unconstitutional, without in fact overturning the principle of the rule of law as that principle remains a pre-eminent one, both in law and in the general principle of normative order. Citing Locke, Jennings, and other authorities to the effect that 'the rule of law ... implies ... simply the existence of public order' and 'the rule of law expresses a preference for law and order within a community rather than anarchy' (both cited on 749), the Court argued that 'the rule of law is a philosophical view of society ... in the Western tradition ...' (749).

The Court thus appealed philosophically to the normativity of the rule of law in the Western tradition as well as to a broad interpretation of the 'supreme law' of the Canadian constitutional order, harking back to English constitutional principles since the Norman Conquest, 'as *a purposive ordering* of social relations providing a basis upon which an actual order of positive laws can be brought into existence' (750–1, emphasis added). To the extent that Canada is 'founded upon ... the supremacy of God and the rule of law' (750), the Court was not, in fact, subverting the principle of the rule of law when it took upon itself the task of having to recognize that Manitoba's post-1890 unilingual laws were invalid, unconstitutional, and without effect! But, because of this, it also followed that it was, in turn, the Manitoba legislature's '*duty* to comply with the "supreme law" of this country, while avoiding a legal vacuum and ensuring the continuity of the rule of law' (753, emphasis added). That established, the reference then addressed 'the vexing question' of clarifying the legal situation of the province during the interim period in which it would have an 'ineffectual legal system' until such time as it had reconstitutionalized its past and current Acts.

To the extent that some interveners had argued that the so-called de facto doctrine might be invoked to uphold the legality of the rights, obligations, and effects that had arisen under Manitoba's unilingual regime, the reference now turned to the problems posed by the authority of governments that were established by force of arms, and that had usurped the sovereign authority of the state, asserting themselves by force against the lawful government. This line of argument is itself worth commenting upon. Note that the constitutionality of official bilingualism very rapidly opens onto, not to say challenges, and calls for a reaffirmation of the sovereign authority of the (central) state, and its powers to inform the authority of subordinate states (on the obvious level, here the Manitoba legislature, but also, beyond it, the ever-present question of the limits of the Quebec legislature's powers in similar regards, which we will turn to below). The issues raised are those of the fundamental authority of the state in the face of potential anarchy or violent or even quasi-legal attempts at usurping that authority.

To the extent that the de facto doctrine is a rule or principle of law that justifies the recognition of the authority of governments established by persons who have usurped the sovereign authority of the state, as in a revolution, or a unilateral declaration of independence, the Court here argued that the de facto doctrine could apply in order to 'maintain the supremacy of the law and to preserve peace and order in the community at large, since any other rule would lead to such uncertainty and confusion, as to break up the order and quiet of all civil administration' (755). Citing an 1896 Supreme Court decision ([1896] 26 *SCR*, 122), the reference quoted then Chief Justice Strong's view that 'the rule of law is that the acts of a person assuming to exercise the functions of an office to which he has no legal title are, as regards third persons ... legal and binding' (cited on 756). In the view of the Court, however, there was 'only one true condition' (756) in which the de facto doctrine might be applicable, and this was that 'the de facto officer must occupy his or her office under *colour of authority*' (756, emphasis added). In the Court's view, the de facto doctrine was 'limited to validating acts which are taken under invalid authority; it does not validate the authority under which the acts took place. In other words, the doctrine does not give effect to unconstitutional laws' (756–7). Thus, in the Court's view, the de facto doctrine, while it saves the legality of the administration of invalid laws and the existence and efficacy of public and private bodies corporate arising out of actions persuant to invalid laws, it does not and cannot validate invalid laws. At best, it only temporarily confers de facto authority on officials and entities in order to uphold the constitutional guarantee of the rule of law and to prevent the province of Manitoba, for example, from being without a valid legal system, leaving it authority sufficient to fulfil its constitutional duty, even if its previous unilingual acts were constitutionally defective and invalid.

This is a tricky bit of legal reasoning, worth commenting on further. In a sense, the Court here wants to be able to have it both ways: to be able to invalidate the English-only laws of Manitoba as unconstitutional, without at the same time bringing about the collapse of the administration of the law and the collateral institutions of civil society. The way it does this is to invoke the problematic notion of 'the colour of authority': in other words, the administration of the state in Manitoba, while in constitutional fact invalidated, does not appear as such to third parties, since the officers of the state retain 'the colour' of their office, and so the appearance of the rule of law can be maintained. As J.E.S. Simon explains it, drawing upon a 1637 text interpreting English legal notions derived from Norman law: 'Sometimes a party put in a plea designed to make what was really a point of fact appear to be a point of law, so as to transfer the decision from the jury to the judge: this was called *colour*' (Simon 1960: 440). In Blackstone's somewhat different view, the manoeuvre of 'colour' is shifted by a plaintiff from the judge to the jury so as to create 'an appearance or colour of title, bad indeed in point of law, but of which the jury are not competent judges' (in *Commentaries* III, 309, cited in Simon, 440).

The Court goes on to seek support for its rationale in other legal doctrines, such as *res judicata* (which prevents reopening of cases decided by the courts even on the basis of invalid laws), and the doctrine of mistake of law. But as both of these apply only in limited circumstances, it turns instead to the 'doctrine of state necessity,' which provides a justification for the otherwise illegal conduct of a government during a public emergency. But state necessity, if narrowly and carefully applied, can still be claimed to 'constitute ... an affirmation of the rule of law' (758–9). The concept of 'state necessity' is drawn here from a legal journal article examining its application in Pakistan. The historical illustration the Court also turned to concerned the validity of the laws passed by the Confederate States of America in the context of the American Civil War. The pertinent principle here is that 'during a period of insurrection, when territory is under the control and dominance of an unlawful, hostile government and it is therefore impossible for the lawful authorities to legislate for the peace and good government of the area, the laws passed by the usurping government which are necessary to the maintenance of organized society and which are not in themselves unconstitutional will be given force and effect' (759). The American example recurs in subsequent discussion of the status of the rule of law under the Ian Smith regime's unilateral declaration of independence in Rhodesia in 1965, and the literature surrounding the invocation of state necessity in the Turkish insurgency in Cyprus in 1963, and a constitutional emergency in Pakistan in 1954. The general conclusion the Court comes to is that the doctrine of state necessity allows avoiding 'the *absurd corollary* ... that a State, and the people, should be allowed to perish for the sake of the constitution; on the contrary, a constitution should exist for the preservation of the State and the welfare of the people' (766–7, all in italics in the original). The doctrine invoked here, the Court remarks, is not one used to support some law which is above the constitution; 'it is, instead used to ensure the unwritten but inherent principle of rule of law which must provide the foundation of any constitution' (766).

After this strange and tortuous discussion of the foundations of the rule of law, the Court returns to the case of Manitoba to conclude that, because of the legislature's 'persistent violations' of the Manitoba Act, the province was 'in a state of emergency.' As a result, all of its laws, with the exception of those passed in both languages, were repealed and without force or effect. But as 'the Constitution will not suffer a province without laws,' temporary validity was granted to the current acts of the legislature, and the rights, obligations, and other effects arising from those 'repealed and spent laws' not saved by the de facto or some other doctrine, were deemed temporarily to continue to be effective and beyond challenge. 'It is only in this way that legal chaos can be avoided and the rule of law preserved' (767). All this talk of insurrectionary governments and the foundations of legitimate state authority, however abstract on some levels, or precisely because of this, must surely give us pause. Were the actions of the Manitoba legislature post-1890 remotely equivalent to those of an insurrectionary government? Had the 'invalid' laws of the legislature in fact produced a state of emergency, however legalistically understood? Why did the Supreme Court here turn to historical examples (the American Civil War, the Rhodesian UDI, etc.) of actual insurrectionary violence and civil strife as a point of comparison for the Manitoba situation? Why in its defence of the rule of law by means of the notion of state necessity, did the Court seek support in the jurisprudence of countries such as Pakistan, Turkey, or Cyprus, none of which are states that immediately come to mind as exemplary illustrations of the rule of law 'in the Western tradition'? The Supreme Court reference, in other words, seems to have searched far and wide for some heavy and obscure legal artillery to bring to bear upon a situation which, at first blush at least, might not appear to call for it. There seems to be a strange discrepancy here, difficult to account for except perhaps in metaphysical terms, attributable to a profound uncertainty regarding the rule of law itself, as indicated by the sleight of hand of invoking the visual metaphor and legally problematic notion of the 'colour of authority.' Some of the discrepancy is particularly striking in the passage above regarding the 'absurd corollary' that 'a State ... should be allowed to perish for the sake of the constitution.' Since for the Court, a constitution exists 'for the *preservation* of the State and the welfare of the people' (emphasis added), the state is by definition the embodiment of the rule of law; that being the case, insurrectionary governments and the like are also by definition incapable of constitutionally valid actions. As we saw in chapter 5 with the Northwest Rebellion and the aftermath, this is historically consistent with a normalizing conception of the *law as force* materialized in the (constitutional) state, against which there is no legitimate recourse, in the name of either the people or a democratically-conceived constitutional counter-order, since the state is itself the incarnation of both, explicitly in the first case and implicitly in the second, given that the state sees itself as charged with the 'welfare' of the people. Such a narrow conception of the rule of law as the normative and purposive ordering by the state of the social order risks becoming all too readily, as we have seen, both a destabilizing influence on society and a source of the delegitimization of the law itself, exacerbating regional, alternative conceptions of what the rule of law entails. The repercussions of the Northwest Rebellion cast greater legitimacy upon the claims of Quebec as *the* state that represented francophone interests in Canada; the policies of official bilingualism of the 1960s were a conscious attempt to, in turn, delegitimize that very claim by attempting to make all of Canada 'a French State' in Serge Joyal's telling phrase. Now we shall look at the counter-example of Quebec and its highly controversial legislative acts in the realm of the public language.

Words versus Language: Law, Language, and Legislation in Quebec since the Quiet Revolution, 1960–

One need only the slightest familiarity with contemporary Quebec civil culture to be aware that the question of language is never far from the surface of daily life. After all, Quebec, in recent years, has become the province of the so-called language police and the official measurement of the size of public lettering; it is the only jurisdiction in the world of the Romance languages to have changed the quasi-universal command of Stop on road signs to that of Arrêt, to take perhaps the best-known, or most ridiculous, examples. It is not, however, the sensational level of the relationships between law and language in Quebec that need concern us here (although the various ironic journalistic writings of Montreal novelist Mordecai Richler are of interest). Rather, as we have seen both above and in earlier chapters, our concern has been more with the asymmetrical relationships of linguistic power that resulted from the transition of legal regimes from French hegemony up to the mid-eighteenth century to British governance subsequently, and the ensuing corruptions of the former at the levels of legal conceptualization, leading to de la Durantaye's lament in the mid-1930s that law in the French language in Quebec had become a deformed shell of mere facticity, without a juridical logic of its own, a near-useless vessel stuffed with (badly) translated notions and concepts derived from English public law (see Gémar 1995, cited viii). In Gémar's more recent and, on some levels, more positive view of the relations between language, law, and society, the 'function' of translation has been historically dialectical: on the one hand, translation, even if mainly from English to French, did contribute inter-linguistically to the preservation and maintenance of French as well as to the development of linguistic activity and its related disciplines of scientific study; on the other hand, intralinguistically, it laid the basis for the development of the emergence of a specialized juridical language in the Quebec context (Gémar 1995: 2–3).

Since the early 1930s, with the creation of a Commission de refrançisation, the struggle for 'taking back' the French language has continued unabated, assuming legislative formulation in the late 1960s with Bill 63, in 1974 with Bill 22, and in 1977 with Bill 101, and succeeding in making French the official language of Quebec (Gémar, 18, and n39). In one analyst's enthusiastic view, expressed in 1986, the struggle for refrancization has been so successful that

Quebec 'for the first time perhaps in linguistic history, has successfully transformed social realities and harmoniously achieved the near-complete francization
of the Belle Province' (de Broglie, cited in Gémar 1995, 18 and n48). According
to a recent study by the Conseil de la langue française, the Quebec government
agency that both studies and enforces norms of francization, it was found that
87 per cent of public discourse in Quebec is carried out in French (*Globe and
Mail*, 2 September 1999, A13).

In Gémar's view, the intervention of the Quebec state in linguistic matters
thus 'constitute[s] the principal political event of the past 30 years' (38). This
has been nothing less than a reversal of the social status of communication from
the vertical and unilateral actions of the dominant vis-à-vis the dominated to a
horizontal and interactive sociality. Historically, and indeed until the changes
brought about by the Quiet Revolution of the 1960s, to cohabitate in order to
survive under the English linguistic regime, 'it was [still] necessary to be able
to communicate; thus to speak the other language, to learn it, and as well to
translate it, most often in the unilateral direction ... of English to French. It was
necessary to communicate in this way for the purposes of commerce, in order to
do business with the other group, to be able to work and earn a living; and all of
this, in the great majority of cases, in English' (32). If such was the case
concerning the primary needs of the individual (food, housing, clothing, employment), how much more complicated did this become at the 'higher' levels
of civil society, religious traditions, and British legal and parliamentary traditions, themselves founded upon respect of 'the law' and 'public order.' That this
was accomplished without utterly sacrificing the 'essence' of French-Canadian
or Québécois cultural identity that is the French language, while at the same
time preserving other key elements of the civil culture (the civil law, the
Catholic religion), was, in Gémar's view, 'a miracle' of cultural survival (33).
That French-speaking Lower Canadian parliamentarians rapidly learned successfully to manipulate the institutions of British governance, as we saw in
chapter 3, helps explain the importance of the recourse to legislative measures
as the principal means for the protection of linguistic rights. Particularly since
the early 1960s, this has produced the inversion of the relationship between
Quebec's two principal linguistic groups, with the socio-economically dominant anglophones becoming a minority, along with the English language; this
has been accompanied by ensuing difficulties resulting from a diminution in
social and linguistic status (39). Gémar is relatively sanguine as to the legitimacy of these changes, whether in terms of the constancy of the mobilizing
powers of the language question among francophones, or the legitimacy of state
intervention in the three pillars of Quebec linguistic policy (in education, in the
workplace, and in general economic activity). He views these as signs of 'the

new order' of a modern state's ability to reorganize the juridical system in ever more hierarchical structures of legal authority, and of the greater systematization of juridical materials (39–40). In short, there has been an undeniable quantitative success as attested by the 1977 Charter of the French Language.

But a few *brillants coups d'éclats*, however impressive, do not necessarily compensate for the inertia of the past. It is the qualitative aspects that are more troubling, and constitute the greater focus of his contribution to jurilinguistics: 'More than just the words, it is ... the "*mentalités*" that must be reformed ... the word of the law can be easily reformed. The language of the law, however, is a much more difficult matter' (44–5). What, then, is to be understood by 'the language' (*le langage*) of the law, keeping in mind that linguistically productive distinction in French between 'langue' (speech) and 'langage' (a language system)? In Gémar's view, juridical discourse (*le langage du droit*) is a particular form of specialized discourse, since one of the social functions of law is to provide a key organizational system of a society (1995: 90–5). That said, specifying exactly what kind of specialized discourse is the onus of Gémar's analysis, along with the question of its relations with language in general. As one example illustrating the difficulties of defining legal language, he cites legal theoretician H.L.A. Hart: 'The great anomaly of legal language is our inability to define its crucial words in terms of ordinary factual counterparts' (*Definition and Theory in Jurisprudence* [1953], cited in Gémar, 91 n30). If one of the crucial traits of legal language is that it articulates forms of responsibility or obligation – in other words, it is a prescriptive and constraining form of language (characteristics which by themselves might be sufficient to distinguish a legal text from another kind of text) – the nature of constraint is further heightened in bilingual or multilingual contexts. In a context such as Canada's, where official languages coexist with two juridical systems that are profoundly antithetical to one another, the constraints become maximized in their contending systems of interpretation, and in their manner of elucidating the intent of the legislator in terms of the legal text, its context, its *telos*, and its history (143–4). In such a context, the tasks of legal translation become exceedingly complex.

Some of the implications, particularly as these impact upon the drafting of legislation, are drawn out by Michel Sparer and Wallace Schwab, both researchers at the Conseil de la langue française, in an article entitled 'Loi et héritage culturel' (1979). They begin by noting the great disparity until the 1970s between the considerable attention paid to questions of legal drafting within English-language jurisprudence and the near complete absence of an equivalent concern in French-language jurisprudence. 'It would seem that in France the secular tradition of written law and of codification has had, on the one hand, a beneficial effect upon the organization of juridical thought, giving to the law the attributes of an organized system of thought, but, on the other hand, has fatally diminished [the attention paid to] the conceptualization and especially the formulation of the rules of law' (403). And in Quebec, they argue, the situation has not been dissimilar to that of France, although doubly confined to complaints by jurists often confusing problems of legal drafting with ones of interpretation and this within a self-enclosed profession seen from the outside as one whose texts were for the most part technical, arid, and otherwise of limited general, dramatic, or literary interest. Sparer and Schwab want to argue differently.

For one, to the extent that the law is applicable to all, it should be expressed in language understandable by all, and not limited to those who have had legal training. Even in the latter case, they note the concerns – indeed, outright dismay (*désarroi*, 407) – often expressed by lawyers, notaries, and judges over legal texts that appear literally meaningless. For Sparer and Schwab, then, a legal text must above all be clear as to its meaning. But this imperative is not as straightforward as it might seem, since if it is difficult to demonstrate that a text is clear, it is far easier to show that a text is obscure or ambiguous. Standing in the way of the objective of clarity that they advocate, are the juridical, stylistic, structural, and lexical elements that obscure the meaning of a legal text. These can be reduced, however. As a means of minimizing these elements internal to a text, they also argue for the equal, if not greater, importance of paying attention to what they term 'the cultural dimension' (408) as the principal filter for the comprehension of a legal text. One sees this, for example, in the disjunction between juridical and societal norms, in which the first, say, can either lag behind the second or conversely surpass them. Related to this, given that the law regulates entire sectors of human activity, is the question: are its aims adequately met by the enunciation of general principles or conversely by the elaboration of detailed rules and regulations?

This latter problem, for instance, arises particularly in a situation such as Quebec's, with the coexistence of civil law and common law. Here, they argue that the law should restrict itself to general principles and the elaboration of the political aspects of a rule, providing 'an ambiant logic' (408) to be worked out by litigants and the magistrature. Second, Sparer and Schwab raise the research question of whether the organization of parliamentary systems lends itself to, or impedes, the drafting of clear legislation. There follows a detailed discussion of the compositional structure of a bill, which they distinguish as optimally consisting of a preamble, title, subtitles, definition of terms, scope of powers, duties, identification of the entity responsible for the law's execution, habilitating and transitory dispositions, scope of applicability, and documentary references. Without going into the details of their discussion, suffice it to say that, in their view, the preamble of a law is less concerned with the enunciation of a legal rule that carries obligatory and direct force, and more concerned 'with the general principles of political order that subtend the legislation. The drafting of preambles is thus more an exercise in *political rhetoric* than an exercise in drafting a juridical norm' (409, emphasis added). In their discussion of the definitions applicable to a bill, they remark that this is 'a habit' drawn from British legislative practice that has begun to spread to other legal systems. Accordingly, in the context of a legal regime whose majority language is French yet whose institutions are of British origin, they observe that the formulation of definitions serves too often as the portal for the seepage of 'a strong English flavour despite careful drafting in French' (413). But, they add, 'since we are living in a time where we are attempting to revalorize the French language, this is not the moment in which to freeze jurisprudence by means of definitions whose purpose escapes us' (413). In other words, for Sparer and Schwab, the specificity of a law in its compositional elements lies primarily, from the perspective of their proposals for clarity of meaning, in the care given to the details of its title and the spelling-out of the objectives of the law (410–11, 413–15).

As regards what they term 'the economy' of legislative texts, they subdivide this into ordinary laws, codes, and rules, a logical categorization for them given their general taxonomic view of laws as articulated from general principles downwards. Thus the importance of codification as a 'documentary methodology' (416) is that it allows for 'the elaboration of an orderly code, according to a logical structure, that better permits the presentation of a rule of law in its generality, but within the pertinent context.' Codification, furthermore, represents a step toward a guarantee of democracy. This is because the code, as a thematically organized ensemble of the laws in given domains, allows for a clearer perception of the general principles and tendencies of particular legislation, thus indirectly providing the citizenry with accurate and up-to-date information regarding their rights and obligations. The code as well makes it possible to identify more easily 'dead' or outdated legislation that otherwise threatens both the coherence of the legal system and, by the related risk of reviving the circulation of *dépassé* opinions, the stability of juridical relations. Not only does the code further serve as a guarantee for practitioners that their knowledge of the law will be up-to-date, it also serves as a 'hard copy' guide to the proliferation of legal materials generated by computerization. Finally, for Sparer and Schwab, codification represents a step toward a common juridical language, allowing for a triage in the pertinence of legislation so as to better foreground the legal measures that are key (416).

Theirs is, one could say, a structuralist view of the law, not only as a form of discourse constituted by its elements, but more important, by its very form or structure, in which meanings derive not only from words and phrases, but equally 'from the structure of the text, how it articulates the positioning of its elements, and in particular by its use of the categories by which the ideas of the law are ordered within the text. This is why it seems indispensable to us that a law as well as a regulation be perceived as a *signifying structure*' (417, emphasis added). Such a signifying structure's guiding logic is a deductive one, from the general to the particular in descending order of importance, an approach which, if already widely practised, still calls for greater systematization on the one hand, and greater concision as regards the drafting of specific articles on the other. The driving imperative is always from the perspective of greater clarity 'in order that the meaning of an article be accessible to the great majority of the "*justiciables*"' (421; literally, those for whom justice is to be enacted; i.e., as subjects of the law), particularly given that the latter are not encumbered 'with the twisted spirit of articulated arguments or the subtleties of grammar.'

And yet it is in the final portions of their article, in their discussion of legal stylistics, that the centrality of the subtleties of grammar becomes especially manifest. The language of legislation can tend toward ready comprehension or toward increasing obscurity. In a context such as that of Canada and Quebec, in which the French language in the juridical domain has long been a language of translation, it is hardly surprising that legal drafting in French has been highly influenced by the forms of English. In particular, in their view, English legal language is particularly characterized by long sentences, with a different phrase structure than French: where the latter in its written form uses a coordinating conjunction to bridge two complete thoughts, English deploys coordinating conjunctions repeatedly and in succession, without the apparent need of recurring to full stops to distinguish one idea from another. The resulting use of long sentences heightens ambiguity, and with it increases 'juridical insecurity' (422). Further stylistic traits that they identify in English include the predominance of the past form of verb tenses, greater use of the passive voice, greater use of negatives, repeated recourse to doublets and triplets (e.g., 'obey, observe, and comply with,' [425]), greater use of synonyms that increase the polysemy of words, impoverishment of the use of personal pronoun complements, too many Latinisms, linguistic interferences in the use of indefinite rather than demonstrative articles, and finally ambiguous recourse to references to earlier articles of a law that are in turn themselves references to earlier articles, leading to referential circularity, and readerly confusion (see 422–9). While the overall thrust of their argument is the pretty blunt equation of French with clarity and

English with ambiguity and thus a corresponding loss of meaning that is compounded by translation from English to French, French itself is not utterly exempt from archaisms or ambiguities of its own. But if hewing to the apparent simplicity of French syntax is not always possible to actualize in practice, 'Well, no matter! ... it is [more] important to respect the basic structure of the French sentence' (426).

Ultimately, what Sparer and Schwab are arguing for is the fundamental incompatibility of the respective schemas of thought of each language; namely, the supposed distinction according to which English linguistic representations attempt to model themselves on the basis of an exterior, empirical, concrete reality, whereas French operates first from a model of the understanding from whence it views 'realities' from the perspective of the general (429). These differences, they argue, constitute 'distinctive ensembles of cultural automatisms' (430), with the principal corollary being that 'the existence of the civil law in North America depends *entirely* upon the ability of its practitioners to understand these differences and to be able to take them into account in their juridical reasoning' (430, emphasis added). This becomes all the more important given the increasing reliance of societies upon the laws in order to regulate their internal social relations. The law thus becomes one of the principal tools of the actualization of a societal project, based upon a culture whose norms it manipulates and interprets on the basis of cultural reflexes proper to it. This is why legal drafting and interpretation partake of these fundamental cultural reflexes and are not 'import products' situated outside of culture. 'If it is true, as we believe, that "importing" the law is equivalent to importing a mode of social organization, the same applies to principles of legal interpretation, particularly as these directly impact upon legal subjects (*le justiciable*) as they concern their capacity to understand the rules that apply to them' (431).

Now all this is very well, so far as it goes. The principal problem, however, is that it does not go all that far, for theirs is, in the end, a perspective on the law not that different from the figurations that we have encountered above, particularly at the level of the federal government or what in Quebec is too often perceived monolithically as 'English Canada' or 'the Rest of Canada' (ROC). In both cases, the law is first and foremost a manifestation of state power for 'the purposive ordering of social relations,' in the Supreme Court of Canada's phrase – that is, as an instrument for social engineering and the implementation of a social project. This could be the imposition of bilingualism in the one instance, or the imposition of a conception of 'French' law or law-in-French that derives much of its form from the Hexagonal, or post-Napoleonic, example, in the other instance. Both impositions, to be sure, can claim to have some basis in 'justice' in the sense of attempts to correct past wrongs and redress past iniquities deriving from asymmetries in legalo-linguistic power. The Quebec examples we have looked at, furthermore, are particularly enlightening in illustrating some of the difficulties involved in the attempt to disentangle a mode of social organization as influential as 'the law,' from habits of thought and linguistic practices heavily imprinted by the long predominance of 'translationese' and legal coexistence. If, for instance, the Quebec bar has been widely viewed as the most thoroughly bilingual of Canada's legal institutions, at least until the 1960s, and as having made far greater efforts to incorporate, draw from, and learn from the law of 'the Other' than has been the reverse case (see, e.g., Deschênes, 1979), the struggle to take back French, and law-in-French, can also be seen in another light: as a conscious attempt to shed a perhaps unique, if complex, legal heritage through processes of 'purification' or, more negatively put, of 'juridical cleansing.' The attempt to 'clean up' Quebec law from the 'corruptions' of translationese is a fascinating study in a historical process of juridical self-consciousness. But it also partakes fully of the driving impetus of 'modern' law's thrust toward increased ever-greater autonomy, systematization, codification – in other words, of its tendency toward becoming an increasingly formalized and technical subsystem of the overall rationalization of modern society. This leads to the resulting problems posed by 'modern' law as these have been analysed and critiqued by sociologists and philosophers of jurisprudence, from Max Weber at the turn of the century to Roberto M. Unger in the mid-1970s (to mention just two outstanding critics of modern legal rationality). But without going further into these questions, let us illustrate a manifestation of precisely such tendencies in Sparer and Schwab's problematic attempt to ground their conception of law within 'ensembles of cultural autonomisms' (1979: 430). If such ensembles were in fact the case (and these authors' attempt to draw greater attention to the role of 'fundamental cultural reflexes' in law is by no means without value), the problem they are trying to deal with – namely, that of rejecting English law as a foreign invasion of the body juridical – is a false one. For either an automatism or a reflex is just that, or it is not. In either case, one is faced with the problem of accounting for the *failure* of the reflex to defend the body politic, and they do not manage to do that. Since they do not, the problem their study tackles still stands in need of further explanation. This we attempt in what follows.

Canadian Law / Quebec Law: Modern or Postmodern?

The respective 'spirit' of the laws of Canada, as well as those of Quebec, particularly in matters of the legislation of language use, is best understood *not* from the perspective of either the English or French language (although this is not insignificant), but from the fact that both legal systems operate on the basis of a shared conception of the *social* role of the law. That shared conception of the social basis of language is above all characterized by the desire to appear resolutely modern.[1] The law here thus provides the armature for the modern state's self-actualization as the incarnation of rationality. We see this in the rationality of 'a just society' (in Trudeau's principal electoral slogan of the 1968 federal election) or its equivalent in the war-cry of the Quiet Revolution of 1960 and beyond: *Maîtres chez nous!* These expressions elaborate the principles of (social and self) control requisite for the stable pursuit of the objectives of progressive social development within the framework and telos of national independence. Problems thus do not begin with clashes over jurisdictions of control that ensue from the competitive struggles between two states or within the arrangements of a baggy federalism (the central state and 'its' sub-states). These are conflicts that are virtually built into the distribution of powers and, as such, are part of the modern political game, and its language-games. Rather, the real difficulties emerge if and when the shared conception of the role of the law itself changes. This occurred with the 1982 adoption of the Canadian Charter of Rights and Freedoms. In many accounts of this event, the law underwent a tilting away from collective rights enacted by the state to a greater emphasis upon individual rights; this involved the withdrawal of *dirigiste* political authority, by the displacement of the locus of social action onto individual actors endowed with greater 'freedom' of interraction, broadly understood as ranging from increased freedom of economic association to increased freedom of individual expression – that is to say, of voice. This change in the role of the law has sometimes been decried as the 'Americanization' of Canadian law – in other words, the abandonment of one of the pillars of the social project of modern law, the pursuit of national political independence, and its replacement by so-called 'free trade' economic development strategies to be carried out by private-sector forces. This change is also seen as one where Canadian law betrayed the modernist pact by making possible a multicultural onslaught upon the idea of *the* modern legal order by adopting a *postmodern* conception of law, thus abandoning Quebec to a solo and frustrating attempt to still make good on the modern compact. Such at least is the argument made by legal scholar Pierre Blache (1994). We will contrast his argument with economist Gilles Paquet's contrary set of claims that it is Quebec society itself that has become postmodern, thus leading to a crisis in governance (1999).

Restated, the disjunct can be posed as the following paradox: either 1) Canadian law has taken a postmodern turn and abandoned the modern project of ever greater institutional autonomy, including the autonomy of the modern legal order, leaving Quebec alone to still make the attempt, or 2) Quebec society itself, in keeping with the generalized changes in the understanding of the social throughout the (still largely Western) world, an understanding often collapsed under the rubric of 'postmodernism,' is also postmodern in the sense that a new conception of sociality from below has emerged that is, in many ways, in conflict with an apparatus of governance that remains resolutely modern in its centralizing and autonomizing steering aspirations. It is perhaps unnecessary to point out that these positions are also variants of familiar ones: the first is another version of the Conquest, in which the agent of legal change is an external imposition on Quebec, or as we saw above, on Manitoba, attributable to the constraints of the federation; the second is a version where the principal agent of social change is internal, but constrained by a self-imposed myth of discontinuity represented by the legal modernity of the Quiet Revolution. Let us look a bit more closely at these positions via their respective authors.

Blache (1994) begins his argument with a premise shared by a number of constitutionalists that Canadian federalism is a fatally flawed system because it does not provide a locus of political arbitration that could adequately demarcate the respective domains and divisions of political powers. With the 'political' thus excluded from the Constitution (which becomes accordingly merely a technical document), Canadian federalism was condemned to be but a theatre for the incessant struggle between centrifugal and centripetal forces. While a political agreement granting Quebec a special constitutional status might have served to reconcile Canadian centralization outside of Quebec with Quebec's demands for greater autonomy, in the absence of such a reconciliation, the worst case scenario could conceivably be the collapse of the federation as a result of the demands made of 'their' respective states by each of the two founding peoples (335). With premises such as these, it is hardly surprising that matters have gone from bad to worse, especially with the legalization of continental free trade and the constitutionalization of the Charter in 1982. For Blache, the importance of the latter document is that it represents the continued liberalization of the Canadian constitutional framework, the diminution of the federal Parliament's 'traditional' role as protector of Canadian unity, and correspondingly the codification in the Charter of the (new) principles of a Canadian political order, in the context of a 'Canadian' interpretation of rights and freedoms that especially reflect the national aspirations of the Supreme Court's view of its place in that political order. More specifically, what preoccupies Blache, in a line of argumentation not that dissimilar from Sparer and Schwab's above, is that the Charter, by explicitly increasing the number of freedoms and cultural rights within a cultural interpretation of what these comprise, exercises a dissolving influence upon Quebec's powers of self-definition and cultural integration (337). In short, this is a clash between a 'Canadian' pluralization of rights-to-culture versus Quebec's power to centralize culture – especially as regards language, particularly as the latter has constituted the mobilizing core of Québécois self-identity for the past decades (340). Fortunately, Blache's argument leaves greater room for ambiguity than the above summary might first suggest. For one, he is aware that over time Quebec's desire to protect its 'ethno-culture' through control of language, civil law, and education has become less culturally homogenous than it once was historically. For Blache, Quebec is today very North American in its modernity and the resulting contradictions of modernity; in a word, it is a pluralist society (340). Quebecers' view of 'their' state has shifted from the enthusiasms of the Quiet Revolution to greater acerbity and scepticism. The fracturing of a once hard-core ethno-culture, however, gives the advantage to the central Canadian state.

These sources of fragmentation are real, although they vie with the constants that 1) the French language is perceived as the central medium of communication,[2] and that 2) the long-standing historical desire to constitute a political majority within a substantial territorial space still thrives. However, other proposals have arisen as a replacement for the earlier, declining ethno-culture. Notably these have taken the form of the idea of a common social project which, while vague in many respects, still represents 'a clear option for a society in which the public powers, trade unions and employers work together in a relatively decentralized framework in order to build a society in which free enterprise, full employment and social justice are harmonized' (342, our translation). In this vision of a societal project, Blache sees a crucial role for the law in helping to bring such a society about, by contributing to the coordination of the social and economic domains so as to 'impose' either the growth of greater autonomy 'or the transition to political sovereignty' (343). Here, Blache sees some elements of convergence between Canada and Quebec, although not with respect to the demand for 'a modern French-speaking society,' over which many tensions and profound anxieties still exist; he sees less divergence as regards the commonalities of a shared social project (forgetting, apparently, the anxieties latent in his phrase on the transition to political sovereignty). For Blache, as for numerous Quebec commentators on Canada, the ROC is 'a chimera' (346) in terms of its cultural unity: English Canadians, in an ethnic sense, today make up less than half of the English-speakers outside of Quebec; the other demographic components comprise widely divergent groups in both ethnic and religious terms. The former majority as a result has developed the culturally protective reflexes of a minority, which manifests itself in two ways: one is a concern with equality in the sense of non-discrimination rights; the other, paradoxically, is an increased demand for collective rights.

These defensive reflexes have shifted the axis of constitutional tensions away from a positive view of the role of the state to one in which one increasingly attempts to protect oneself *from* the state, through granting greater priority to an idea of fundamental rights and freedoms. 'In other words, unable to enforce [majority] values, one is reduced to protecting oneself against the values into others' (346). The consequence for a conception of law, as an ensemble of behavioural norms applicable to all, is its retreat from the realm of cultural values into the more neutral territory of economic and social orderings. On the one hand, as the ROC became a minority, Blache argues, the threat of majoritarian Canadian law vis-à-vis the identitarian concerns of the French-Canadian minority diminished; on the other hand, the increased heterogeneity of the ROC has led to diminished expectations as regards the state's positive role in cultural matters. The central state is thus the 'principal victim' (347) of the resulting economic and legal liberalization since it was historically conceived as the unifying force that protected the Canadian domestic market from the United States, and so has lost one of the key objectives that justified its historical existence. For Blache, whatever functions are left to the central state, and these are nonetheless not insignificant in the current national and international contexts, state powers are now firmly constrained by the Charter.

Some of the resulting implications of his argument are equally paradoxical. The rise of multiculturalism, or a differentialist legal order, has considerable public support in the ROC, among the Canadian intelligentsia and within elements of the state itself, and this has produced contradictory tendencies: increased demands for a more lucid antidiscriminatory legal order, but also for greater ethno-cultural politicization of key sectors of public institutions and in the private sector. Where Quebec, in its entry into modernity, has increasingly stripped itself of ethno-cultural self-definitions, Canada is manifesting contrary tendencies in the rising demands that ethno-cultural factors be taken into greater account by the law. Quebec, in other words, has now surpassed Canada in the modernity game. If the adoption of the Charter has taken place in a 'democratist' (349) context, in which the 'Third Canada' (*le tiers-Canada*) has gained greater integration into the mainstream through increased respect accorded to difference, with the resulting inflections of the legal order, Quebec for its part has resisted this turn toward 'postmodernity,' and has continued to pursue 'a model of modernization that is closer to the traditionally republican models of France and the United States' (350). This last suggestion adds a new wrinkle to the discussion, in particular as it concerns the differing cultures of rights within liberal, republican, and postmodern states and their respective legal cultures. In the traditional liberal conception, it is the individual alone who is entitled to rights against the state. This is the trade-off with the Leviathan: the individual retains certain inalienable rights (in particular, the right to own property). In the republican version of the social contract, fundamental individual rights subsist for the citizen in relation to the state, beyond which, unless otherwise established in law (as in, for example, the Amendments to the U.S. Constitution or U.S. Supreme Courts decisions), there is no further protection. At the same time, however, the foundational revolutionary emergence of republican polity also includes the right of 'peoples' to dispose of their own liberty, a right which will become, under certain conditions, the basis for the modern interstate system of collective rights (based loosely on Blache, 353). To the extent that liberalism and republicanism both emerged in the struggle against absolutist states and the tyranny of the established church, the resulting thrust of bourgeois law was the liberation of the individual legal subject from the restraints of external organized collectivities, and also from emerging internal collective cultural movements that threatened the newly established legal order. If the liberal legal order's response was a grudging, minimal recognition of some collective rights, the threat of internal collectivist disruptions proved far more destabilizing to republican polities, as the French and American examples have repeatedly shown.

As Blache points out (353), the individualistic conception of fundamental intrastate rights, along with the right of self-determination of peoples, favoured the centralizing ambitions of existing states; at the same time, the emergence of collective intrastate rights, however circumscribed (i.e., not just limited to the right to secession), produced powerful countertensions for states, as in the large-scale movements of migratory or refugee populations. There has resulted from this a two-pronged critique of the liberal legal order's individualism focusing on 1) its neglect of collective rights, and 2) its inference that the communitarian rootedness of the subject itself calls for a broader conceptualization of collective rights. Such critiques, together with the increased continentalization (and, beyond, globalization) of economic relations, have contributed powerfully to the perceived loss of sovereignty of the state and a weakening of its juridical prestige. In the resulting vacuum, it is not surprising that there has been a corresponding growth of regionalist tendencies and a rise of differentialist conceptions of culture, leading to heightened contemporary pressures for intrastate multiculturalism. If the translation of these pressures into the constitutional order through the increased recognition of collective rights contributes to the further weakening of the integrative authority of the nation-state, it is Blache's fear that the Charter precisely reflects such pressures, and accordingly diminishes Quebec's powers of integration (355). And, indeed, for Blache, the Charter has produced precisely 'a veritable mutation of the constitutional order' (358).

The fate of cultures within a state, he argues, depends upon the place that constitutional rights, as opposed to freedoms, occupy. If only the latter are constitutionalized, then cultures lose accordingly, unless the constitutionalization of rights also includes the recognition of a cultural dimension. Traditionally, liberal constitutionalism granted considerable priority to the idea of freedoms, in which the state represented a major obstacle against which the bourgeoisie arose to effectuate the passage, either by revolutionary or by incremental means, to the state of law, in which private powers were not seen as threatening: as long as the legal subject had the right of contract and the right to property, 'freedom' would be the inevitable result. With the rise of the clamour for social rights in the course of the industrial revolution, supported in part by the rise of the social sciences and also by the Marxist critique of the 'formalism' of liberal freedoms, the latter 'freedoms,' in particular, were revealed to be the ideological illusions of an inegalitarian society, as a result of which 'bourgeois freedoms' had to be subordinated to material readjustment. Something similar is repeating itself in the contemporary critique of culture, in which critics are demanding additional rights to cultural difference. As Blache states it: 'The traditional insensitivity of the State of Law of liberal origins, as regards cultural belonging, expressed itself in three ways: individualism, the primacy of freedoms, and the restriction of the exigencies of equality within the sole framework of state action ... On all these levels, the heritage of Canadian constitutionalism is being subjected to change under the influence of powerful intellectual currents which have considerable support among numerous Canadians' (360).

Against this background, one is tempted to ask: so what's the problem? Here Blache is less clear, although his objection seems to stem from the restrictions the application of the Charter places on the state and, by implication, on the Quebec state. For Blache, the application of the Charter reveals a conflict around the relationship between rights *and* freedoms, a debate that revives the earlier Marxist distinction between 'formal' and 'real' rights. In the first case, obligations are imposed upon the state, including the power to impose obligations upon the private sector. The implication here is that the state's interventionary egalitarian obligations (of nondiscrimination on grounds of race, gender, and sexuality, etc.) produce such a degree of social control that the aimed-for freedom itself would be extinguished. In the second case, the Charter serves as an instrument for the preservation of freedoms *from* the state, in which eventuality there is no need to constitutionalize positive freedoms or protect these against private-sector forces. In this perspective, one loses sight of the argument that the state itself provides the conditions for the exercise of freedoms by specifying rights *against* the state that could include the imposition of cultural sensitivity and cultural difference as inherent to interdicts against discrimination. Needless to say, this represents, but does not resolve, long-standing philosophical arguments within liberalism concerning the state.

Blache believes that, since the Charter, Canadian constitutionalism has distanced itself from the liberal constitutional model that provided a framework highly conducive to firmly integrationist policies. That model, while not entirely abandoned, has come under serious attack, particularly as regards the priority of individual rights and freedoms, the primacy of freedoms in general, and the universal applicability of the law. To the extent, furthermore, that multiculturalist pressures upon the liberal state not only derive from internal Canadian forces but also reflect phenomena sweeping through international jurisprudence in general, similar sets of constraints impact upon the Quebec state. One might say, then, that Blache's is a conservative defence of the modern liberal state and its legal order, particularly as this pertains to Quebec. Despite certain suggestions that he does not follow up on, such as Quebec's supposed affinity to republican regimes, for instance, there is little doubt that Blache favours the primacy of the modern liberal state and its juridical regime, precisely because of its integrationist capacities. His argument, in this sense, is fully consistent with that of the other modernist observers of the Quebec legal order we have already encountered. Now, what happens if we take a different line of argument? Instead of arguing from the state down, let us shift the terrain from changing conceptions of sociality and their implications upwards to governance and law. This is what economic historian Gilles Paquet proposes in his injunction to 'forget the Quiet Revolution.'

For Paquet (1999), the Manichean tendencies that have underlain certain tendencies in Quebec historiography (see chapters 2 and 3 above) have only perpetuated themselves in the advent of the full-blown modernity project of the Quiet Revolution of the 1960s. The Quiet Revolution remains 'the fundamental break' (11, our translation) around which all discussions of contemporary Quebec pivot, as an ensemble of profound modifications to the socio-governmental steering system that supposedly transformed a conservative, relatively backward, clergy-dominated society into a modern, resolutely entrepreneurial one, principally through the means of a vastly increased field of social action by the state. In its caricatural representation, before 1960 all was the *Grande Noirceur*; since then modernity has triumphed; in other words, this is another version of the thesis of radical discontinuity.

Paquet has long held a contrary view that situates the advent of Quebec modernity in the transformations of the late eighteenth to early nineteenth centuries, in which the economic differences between Upper (Ontario) and Lower (Quebec) Canada were, in fact, smaller rather than greater than now. Here, he is arguing against English-Canadian historians such as D.G. Creighton and A.R.M. Lower who, he claims, have propagated the continuation of a Durham-like view of the radical difference between the two societies, and against the further continuation of this view in late Chicago School sociology's fascination in the 1930s and 1940s with the quasi-feudal, village-based, traditional inwardness of rural Quebec society (Paquet, 14–15). Instead, for Paquet, the Quebec political economy (or 'socio-economy,' to use his preferred term) has demonstrated a remarkable ability to negotiate the numerous transitions since the French regime. These he organizes into five 'institutional epochs' (the economy of the *comptoir*, a dual socio-economy, commercial capitalism, industrial capitalism, and the socio-economy of information), framed at either end by the two major discontinuities represented by nineteenth-century industrialization and the twentieth-century emergence of the information economy (23–4).

Given this fundamentally adaptive background, he argues that the vaunted Quiet Revolution has turned out to be a source of the depletion of social capital and, rather than facilitating the transition to an information economy, thwarts it by having erected the barriers resulting from a now-aging socio-economy, in which social rights are difficult to negotiate. This is a socio-economy characterized by 'the right to immobility' (37), a disguised and growing protectionism, and a smug over-optimism as regards the changes threatened by North American free trade in particular and economic globalization in general, changes that evoke the spectre of a society of freelance labour and generalized precariousness in which subcontracting represents a way of life and rapid socio-economic adaptability has become obligatory – in short, a society embarked upon transitions for which the Quiet Revolution had ill-prepared it (36–7). For Paquet, the fragmentation of the *identitaire*, which (as we have just seen in Blache's argument) would lead to calls for reinforcing the modernity of the Quiet Revolution, has been on the contrary far more extreme, leading to the emergence of a social formation that is profoundly at odds with the apparatus of governance, a social formation of ever increasing fragmentation, in which conflicts are less and less likely to derive from the traditional ones pitting capital and labour and more from the demands of countless, mobile groups deriving temporary cohesion from the diversity of their self-definitions of belongingness and, accordingly, from the variety of their social projects; in a word, of having become a postmodern society.

For Paquet, then, 'Quebec has shortcircuited its modernity' (39), in part as a result of a telescoping of its socio-economic development. In his view, a postmodern economy is one that has liberated itself from the burdens of modernity: its individualism, its excessive deployment of instrumental rationality, and the constraints of techno-industrial planning. Instead, postmodernity is marked by the reassessing of the 'grand narratives' of modernity (liberalism, rationalism, Marxism, nationalism, etc.) and by an acute awareness of the dangers of the unitary rationalization of society; it turns to multiplicities instead (in the ways of processing information, for instance, and in the emergence of new values, new social movements, etc.). 'It is,' he writes, 'nothing less than a rejection of the social contract latent to the socio-economy and the renegotiation of the rights and obligations of each and all that has to be undertaken. But this entails giving absolute priority to the rights each claims to have ... the "right to rights," as it were. There is no ground here for a new moral contract' (45). In this light, Quebec society is an unravelling tissue of fragmenting solidarities, as many diverse groups have emerged from civil society to vigourously defend their particular interests. 'These ... contestations have undermined the legitimacy of the Canadian state and are doing the same to the Quebec state' (46–7), leading to the understandable reaction by the provincial government (or what he calls, in opposition to the nation-state, *l'État-région*) to cling that much more desperately to its powers, both real and symbolic. Contested from above as well as from below, the *État-région*, for Paquet, still has a modest role to play, one which it balks at, seeing in it a loss of status, but one which must eventually bow to the pressures from below and adjust itself to the postmodern reality. Even then, this would still call for 'a revolution in our ways of thinking' (49) that would include rethinking the notion of economy, rejecting the centralizing *habitus*, and adopting new processes of continuous consultation, organizational readaptation, and perhaps accepting 'that even the *État-région* is still too homogenizing and centralizing to meet the needs of a postmodern society (49).

Paquet's emphasis on the emerging pressures from below, the dynamism of Quebec civil society, is most interesting, since it locates the forces of change and the implications for governance and the law so differently, far from centralizing and statist perspectives we have encountered so far. These preoccupations emerge with particular force in his fourth chapter, on rethinking sociality in Quebec.

For Paquet, one of the more unfortunate consequences of the Quiet Revolution has been the tendency in Quebec itself, as well as in English-Canada, to conceptualize sociality in Quebec through the perspective of a radical discontinuity: 'before' and 'after,' in which, in the first case, sociality was seen to be anchored in 'tradition,' and in the second in 'modernity.' Admittedly the concept of 'sociality' is difficult to define and operates in different registers: for example, from the perspective of organizations or institutions, one could define sociality as the decisional grid of interactions resulting from 'rational-choice' actors; alternatively, at the affective level, one can understand it as patterns of 'bonding' (59) of varying degrees of intensity. Paquet accordingly develops a model on three axes (domains, substance, and forms of coordination) that permits a grid for the analysis of sociality, ranging from the coordination-effects of organizational mechanisms to the more complex (and neglected, he argues) terrain of symbolic representations coordinated by the authority of 'theory' and incarnated in notions such as 'moral contracts' or 'intercultural relations' (59–60). This allows him to introduce the notion of 'canonical representations' (61), and so return to his main point; namely, that both 'traditional' and 'modern' representations of Quebec sociality are based on a common culturalist conception that is erroneous. In this conception, in which Quebec sociality is held together by traditional ligatures that in turn gave way to modern ones, one can either celebrate triumphally the passage from the one to the other, or complain that it has been obstructed by exogenous blockages.

Alternatively, one can complain that the completeness of the transition has been slowed down by residual traits of the traditional sociality, so that there is always the constant risk of relapse. This culturalist conception of a permanent crisis of identity, Paquet goes on to argue, stems from the irony that many Quebec intellectuals (and economic historians in particular, as this is Paquet's own field of expertise) have based both their self-image and their strategies of emancipation on the English-Canadian view of Quebec sociality as traditional, antimodern, and antidemocratic; thus they are caught in a permanent logic of belatedness and *rattrapage*. Trapped in the resulting problematic of exogeny, one is faced with either the increased assimilation of mental 'anglo-saxonization' (65) and the exclusive celebration of individual rights, or the pursuit of a sovereignist project that would rebuild an ethnicist society on the basis of a narrow collectivism. But these strategies of assimilation on the one hand or defensive regression on the other are mirror images of a dominant and circular logic that, above all, occludes the fact that it has never been a case of *either* 'tradition' *or* 'modernity'; instead it is a long-standing bridging of both. Rather than discontinuity, it is a question of the recognition of 'the continuity that has allowed Quebecers to maintain their sociality (*lien social*) and a relationship to the collective all the while absorbing a democratic, modern and entrepreneurial *ethos* in the definition of a pluralist identity that is open, integrating and syncretic, and closes the door to the exit strategies of an identity crisis that can never offer more than the simplistic choice between the sovereignist project and the federalist bind' (66).

Rather than being a sociality of the tribe, by opposition to the sociality of the marketplace of English-Canada, Paquet proposes instead that Quebec sociality has for a considerable time articulated itself in terms of three very modern 'mechanisms.' The first – and it is, he says, the principal hypothesis advanced by his study (70) – is that the Quebec socio-economy, in its struggles with many challenges of adaptation, has over time become what Paquet terms 'a spectral socio-economy' (70–1). Second, from such a spectral socio-economy has emerged a new form of 'phantomatic' sociality based on the far more anonymous social relations that replace the traditional rituals of identification, communitarian social control and its rules of civility. 'To be spectral,' he writes, citing Guillaume (1993), 'means to have several faces [or roles], whereas in interpersonal communication one represents only one role' (71). Third, the spectral mode of being, he continues, is one especially well adapted to the emerging information society in which relations with others operate like systems of commutation. In such a context of constant adaptation, which for Paquet and Wallot (1987) has been that of Quebec since the colonial period, 'culture' is less the definition of certain homogenous traits than 'a system of shared differences recognized by its members' (see 72).

This system still presupposes the existence of shared norms. Here he argues that, rather than resting on a version of the 'organic community' that subtends pre-Quiet Revolution analyses, sociality in the Quebec context has always been 'an essentially contested conception' (73), subject to debate, and open to redefinition. To this end he cites the sociologist Raymond Breton in a 1992 observation worth repeating: 'Which philosophy of rights will prevail [in Canada and Quebec]? That of the "without regard to" or that of "the taking into account of," the latter of which [has the advantage of] integrat[ing] within the very structures of institutions, ethnic, religious, regional, linguistic diversities etc.? We have *both* philosophies in this country, and that could be [precisely] one of our strengths' (cited in Paquet, 73, emphasis added). This coexistence entails, Paquet points out, something more than a pact between relations of power, but rather implicit affective relations and an idea of a common good, the kinds of emotional 'connivances' (74) that make communities possible. It is, Paquet implies, a matter of recognizing what one might term the shared 'language' games that make sociality even possible; the problem is that the first principles of these have become so problematized as to obscure possible resolutions.

He goes on to make the case for three fundamental 'moves' that have emerged to correct these blurred first principles: 1) contemporary Quebec sociality has dissolved itself into 'a great variety of open, polycentric and proteiform virtual communities, based on networks of communication, among which citizens have dispersed their belongingness' (74); 2) Quebec did not wait until the recent past to define itself as 'modern,' but as early as the end of the eighteenth century had already displayed sufficient modern political maturity to be able to navigate the transition to the new British parliamentary regime (he goes on to argue that from the 1837 Rebellions had emerged a strategy of decentralized development *à l'américaine* that profoundly clashed with English Canada's centralizing model); and 3) Quebec has accordingly become 'one of the most postmodern societies in the world' (75). As a result, sociality today has returned to the kind of role it played for a moral philosopher like Adam Smith: it becomes a substitute for calculating reason, opening instead onto the notion of 'substantive rationalities' that are the fundamental compasses of social action (see also Wallerstein 1999).

Not surprisingly, perhaps, given the reference to Smith and the Scottish Enlightenment, the latter parts of Paquet's argument constitute a plea for 'the idea of an *empathetic social order* built on tact and civility ...' (79, emphasis added), and an empassioned defence of the idea of civil society as the only firm basis for the new sociality. In this light, he envisages the possibilities of civil society's reintegration in the understanding of the socio-cultural habitus, the reinvention of governance, and an economy (the emerging information economy) that conceives of itself above all on the model of a conversation (see 79–122). His conclusion is 'a wager on *philia*' (147ff), the ties of friendship that in Aristotle designate the links between the inhabitants of the polis.

Utopian all this? No doubt, but we would argue for a very different kind of utopianism than that of the 'modernist' versions encountered above. Paquet's is, we might say, a 'proper' utopianism in the sense that it is not a utopianism of the past, but rather of the present and the future – what Wallerstein terms 'utopistics' (1999: 217), the analysis of possible utopias, their limitations, and the constraints in achieving them. Nostalgic utopianism, on the other hand, suggests that at some point in the past the course of things went terribly wrong, making present and future projects essentially 'corrective' ones, in which the state leads civil society to an orderly future. Paquet's utopistics are still corrective (it is civil society that must give the lead to the state), but is not anchored in nostalgia; rather, it is a plea for the recognition of the fundamental 'healthiness' of social connectedness (based on civility) and of the complicities of social language games, multiple social identities, and so on, that are of themselves 'integrative' because they are shared by social actors. As we have seen in this chapter, 'Canadian' is a strange kind of language-use: as literary critics in particular have pointed out, it is ambiguous by law, and duplicitous in its strategies of ironizing omnipresent official discourses, but nonetheless it manages to express itself, if deviously. Paquet, economic historian and social theorist, argues for the recognition that it is precisely these 'games' of linguistic connivance that make up the domain of the social as a whole (and in Quebec, in particular), and that they are not inherently vitiated. It is high time that this *intellectual* fact be more squarely faced for its positive values, and the appropriate conclusions be drawn for re-understanding governance and law; people shoud not continue to flail about within the vicious cycles of the pursuit of exit, or top-down, strategies that are themselves only 'effects' of a particular language game.

Civil Society and the Paradoxes of Multiculturalism

If the bilingualism policies adopted by the Trudeau government were those that generated the most controversy, they were, in fact, only one flank of a two-pronged strategy to centralize the definition of culture(s) in a vision of Canada in which the principal integrative power was that of the central government. As McRoberts points out in *Misconceiving Canada* (1997), official bilingualism is best understood as a means of regulating *individual* linguistic relations with the state (117). It did not follow from this, as was widely assumed by francophones, that equality of *collective* linguistic or cultural relations were also recognized, especially those concerning the 'two founding nations' (the French and the English). Collective cultural relations were the object of a separate policy, the new multiculturalism policy announced in October 1971. And this, more than official bilingualism, McRoberts argues, 'constituted the heart of the new vision of Canada' (117). From the very outset, multiculturalism was vigorously and unanimously denounced in Quebec as a direct threat to its ability to regulate cultural development as increased francization. McRoberts gives a 'rather negative' (135) assessment of the contradictions of multiculturalism. He sees it first attempting to preserve other cultures, then attempting to reduce racial and cultural barriers to individual mobility, and in so doing undermining French as an official language, etc. (see 126, 135). Hence, the attempt to regulate cultures separately from languages was seriously flawed. In his view, multiculturalism might have been more successful if subsumed under bilin-gualism and biculturalism, more in line with the recommendations of the Royal Commission on Bilingualism and Biculturalism (which clashed with Trudeau's liberal individualism). We saw above with Blache some of the objections to the constitutionalization of multiculturalism, an even more negative assessment than that of McRoberts. We also saw with Paquet some of the intractable dilemmas that result from culturalist self-definitions.

For a different perspective, we turn here briefly to a 1998 paper by one of Canada's leading philosophers of multiculturalism, Will Kymlicka of Queen's University. This paper, entitled 'The Theory and Practice of Canadian Multiculturalism,' was presented as part of a series of talks in Ottawa organized for parliamentarians by the Humanities and Social Sciences Federation of Canada. Kymlicka's argument, to begin with, takes issues with recent critiques of Canadian multiculturalism, such as Neil Bissoondath's 1994 *Selling Illusions: The Cult of Multiculturalism in Canada* and Richard Gwyn's 1995 *Nationalism without Walls: The Unbearable Lightness of Being Canadian*. Both of these authors argue that multiculturalism in Canada is equivalent to the institutionalization of cultural ghettoes – in Gwyn's more inflammatory language, it 'encourages apartheid ...' (cited in Kymlicka, 2). These charges Kymlicka readily refutes empirically by looking at a number of indicators (rates of naturalization, political participation, official language acquisition, and intermarriage) that show quite emphatically that rather than creating cultural or racial 'ghettoes,' the integration of immigrants into mainstream Canadian life, politics, and culture is on the contrary a fait accompli. This is further reinforced by looking at comparative data, especially from the United States, which does not have a multiculturalism policy: 'on every indicator of integration, Canada fares better than the United States ... We would find the same story if we compared Canada with other immigration countries which have rejected multiculturalism in favour of an exclusive emphasis on common identities – e.g., France' (5). 'Canada does better than virtually any other country in the world in the integration of immigrants' (5), the only other comparable country being Australia, whose official multiculturalism policy was inspired by Canada's.

So the empirical data shows high degrees of integration. The second kind of criticism addressed to Canadian multiculturalism is, he admits, more complicated. This line of attack argues that while multiculturalism may have been benign initially, its 'logic' is inconsistent with liberal-democratic norms, and lacks a coherent justification. Here Kymlicka's argument gets more interesting, although as regards the first point, his political participation indicators (i.e., subscription to liberal democratic values) would already appear to have taken care of the matter. As a philosopher, it is the point about the lack of logic of multiculturalism policies that particularly appeals to Kymlicka. And this he is willing to concede as regards the logical *explicitness* of the policies, as there are none. *Implicitly*, however, he argues, the logic is there, although its lack of definition points to a more profound theoretical problem; namely, that of the overall lack of definition of Canadian civil culture (although these are not the terms he uses). The problem, as Kymlicka puts it, is 'that most Canadians have no clear sense of the *limits* of multiculturalism. They have no confidence that there are certain 'non-negotiable' principles or institutions which will be protected and upheld, even if they conflict with the desires or traditions of some immigrant groups. Canadians are not averse to multiculturalism within limits, but they want to know that there are indeed limits' (6, emphasis in original). 'So long as Canadians have this sense of insecurity' about the limits of what constitutes civil culture (Kymlicka's focus is, of course, specific to multiculturalism), then public debate will continue to generate insecurities. The only way out of this dilemma, he writes, is to make the implicit logic explicit by *naming* these principles, and the name he proposes for placing limits on multiculturalism policies is 'fair terms of integration' (7). As well, he goes on to contextualize multiculturalism policies as 'just one modest component' in a

larger public policy package that includes naturalization, education, job training and professional accreditation, human rights and anti-discrimination law,
civil service employment, health and safety – 'the major engines of integration'
(7), or in Paquet's language, the affective connectors that constitute civil
society.

Most interesting of all, the example Kymlicka turns to as illustrative of what
constitutes making explicit the terms of integration – 'the model of multiculturalism' (11) – is Quebec's policy toward ethnocultural groups or what used
to be called 'interculturalism' (11). And in this model, the 'moral contract'
between Quebec and immigrants that makes explicit the terms of integration is
informed by three principles: 1) recognition of French as the language of public
life, 2) respect for liberal democratic values, including civil and political rights
and equality of opportunity, and 3) respect for pluralism, including openness to
and tolerance of others' difference (11). He is aware that 'it may seem paradoxical' to English Canadians to cite Quebec as a model of multiculturalism (11),
although not from the perspective of Paquet's view of Quebec's advanced
postmodernity. Ultimately for Kymlicka, the problem has nothing to do with
immigrants, but instead with the long-standing 'inability to make much headway in dealing with our *non-immigrant* groups – the Québécois and First
Nations' (14, emphasis in original). As he puts it: 'Frustrated at our inability to
resolve these age-old conflicts between our founding nations, we have lost our
confidence in our ability to cope with ethnocultural relations generally, and so
project our fears and frustrations onto immigration and multiculturalism policy'
(14). He thus concludes pessimistically that as long as those 'age-old' conflicts
remain ongoing, it will 'be awhile' before Canadians can recognize immigrant
claims for what they are: reasonable claims for fair terms of integration.

Kymlicka's contribution to this discussion is important for a number of
reasons. First, he resituates the problem squarely outside the immigration
debate and back into the inexplicitness of the terms of belonging in Canadian
civil culture. Second, by singling out Quebec as a model of multiculturalism, he
turns the tables on the perception of Quebec's supposed ethnocultural defen-
siveness, aligning himself more closely with the kind of argument Paquet
offers. Third, although Kymlicka himself does not say so in these precise terms,
he relocates the debate within what Paquet understands by 'civil society.' These
are questions that we will take up further in the next chapters.

Conclusion: Resurgence of the 'culture oratoire'[3]

We hope to have shown above both the pervasiveness and the complexity of the
various language-games that have bedevilled Canadian public life, and the

ambivalences caused by the separation between official discourses that are (or pretend to be) unconscious of the fact that they do constitute a language-game, and the unofficial discourses emerging from the lifeworld that also help perpetuate further language-games through strategies of ironizing, duplicity, or spectral commutative manoeuvres of multiple belongingness. We have seen as well the extent to which the law, reinforced by being itself the complex coexistence of two philosophies, rather than a source of possible strength, only adds to the ambivalence, by conceiving itself, or being conceived, as one of the principal means available to state-power for the re-ordering of modern social relations. We have also envisaged, principally through Paquet's contribution to utopistics, alternative views of what constitutes sociality. In the transition to possible postmodern reunderstandings of the vicious cycles of mainly culturalist attempts at defining belongingness, we looked at some of the paradoxes and challenges for rethinking governance. From within a framework of changing conceptions of contemporary law's role, this would entail enhancing greater individual rights while at the same time, and not without irony, making possible the development of a larger 'culture of rights.' Third, we have also foregrounded, through the example of Quebec, that Quebec is *equally* implicated in the ambivalences of Canadian language-games, either in the form of the supposed radical discontinuity of the Quiet Revolution or, to reverse the perspective profoundly, in Kymlicka's upholding of it as a model multicultural (or postmodern, in Paquet's terms) society. Fourth, and still following Paquet's lead here in reversing the locus of the language-games that have created a predominant public culture of exaggeration or *sentencia*, we have seen that if we shift our perspectives on sociality from a view of it as fundamentally vitiated to one that is, on the contrary, fundamentally healthy in its repeated, demonstrated capacity for extreme adaptability, fresh alternatives become possible. This suggests an understanding of sociality as made up of the connivances of friendship, the wink of the eye that gives away the game qua game. This is attested to, in the end, by the social fact that a public culture of exaggeration not only seldom erupts in outright acts of violence, it equally has the capacity of effectuating reversals within the terms of its own exaggerations. Paquet's plea for a wager on *philia*, on a civil culture that emerges from civil society and so is based on civility and tact is thus a topic well worth further discussion, and for these reasons will preoccupy us over the next chapters.

8

Civility, Its Discontents, and the Performance of Social Appearance

Obviously, then, Canada has not always been a peaceable kingdom. It has seen rebellions and other forms of strife, but it has remained nevertheless a counterrevolutionary country, predicated upon accommodation, respect for the law, and the strained *philia* of parliamentary manners. One could repeat the cliché that Canadians are therefore deferential,[1] yet social peace has often been unhappy, and if the deferral of conflict has often been enforced as a norm, resentment and antagonism have always been close at hand. Thus the previous two chapters have focused with increasing centrality upon the question of civility and the management of antagonism in Canada, as a growing number of contemporary commentators have in recent years found the notion of civility germinal in dealing with current problems of social theory. The previous chapters examined the problem of language in a context broadly understood as a rhetorical culture of exaggeration, in which language accordingly either veered towards ironizing strategies as a way of giving the slip to official civil discourses, or conversely found itself fully implicated within discourses of power and state-led measures to officialize (selected) language use. We saw that one proposed way out of the dilemmas that result when language becomes coerced into the constitutional games of Canadian federalism and harnessed to modernizing strategies for the modelling of the linguistic (and so political) subject was to appeal instead for a culture of civility based on the affective ties of civil friendship. Or, more pessimistically that, in the absence of a better defined understanding of what constitutes civility, Canadian society would remain wracked by underlying insecurities that continue to be both unspoken and, across linguistic barriers, unspeakable among interlocutors, but nonetheless highly influential in configuring the civil culture.

Chapter 6 analysed the struggle for political rights by women who, because of their gender, had previously been denied a voice in civil culture. We saw

there the importance of irony to Canadian civil culture in our discussion of the
constitution of a female political subject. In offering a 'domestic' understanding
of the nation, they 'democratized' and domesticated what had previously been
the monarch's 'parental' duties. As such, they broadened the notion of civil
culture by introducing into it the principle of caring for others, even as they
politicized the role of motherhood. Public and private spheres came to interpenetrate, as Canada was figured as a project directed toward the constitution of an
ethical nation, where personal virtue became political. In the present chapter,
we take up further aspects of a widening conception of civility, in particular
paying close attention to what the notions of civility and civil culture more
precisely entail, and to some of the difficulties attending to the appeal for
greater civility; for instance, that it too easily glosses over the fundamentally
agonistic aspects of civility itself.

Civility as a Dimension of National Security

In keeping with the methodology we have used in the chapters above – that is,
of attending to texts that self-consciously offer themselves as rhetorical alternatives to the diagnosis of a problem of public, and specialized, speech (especially, among the latter, historians, jurists, etc.) – we begin this section with a
discussion of a short book by University of Toronto political scientist, Franklyn
Griffiths. In *Strong and Free: Canada and the New Sovereignty* (1996), Griffiths
seeks to identify the implications that follow from the emergence of a different
kind of sovereignty ('Type Two'), as opposed to the more classic ('Type One')
legal conceptions of idealized political and economic autonomy ('unquestioned
authority') best defined in the 'purified' modern legal order of the nation-state.
Type Two sovereignty, he argues, arises in a context of intensified economic
globalization in which the complexity of interstate economic linkages, in
effect, undermines the former autonomies of Type One legal sovereignty,
plunging the nation-state into a policy crisis of legitimation. Further, Type Two
conceptions of sovereignty also arise when the key problems of military threats
to the security of the nation-state have, to all extents and purposes, been
resolved through interstate alliances, supranational organization, or the
overwhelming military and technological dominance of a single superpower
no longer facing one opposing centre of rivalry. The end of military threats is
replaced by the rise of 'civil security threats' (15), such as pollution, mass
migrations, currency fluctuations, and the like, that are global and multilateral.
The problem, then, is how to coordinate 'defences' against the new civil
security threats without totally eroding what remains of the ideals of Type One
sovereignties, such as the capacity of the state to enforce the laws of the land,

maintain the quality of civil life, and to keep choices open in an increasingly interdependent world (15).

In this transitional era, in which solutions are sought for establishing new possibilities of association (political, economic, social, and cultural), largely through experiments based upon the re-evaluation upwards of information, communications, technology, and culture (using Griffiths's categories, 23), it is the latter category in particular that moves to the forefront as the principal means for a nation-state to cling to a capacity for autonomy. By 'culture,' however, Griffiths means primarily a *culture of civility*: 'If there is one word that captures the essence of what Canada is about, and of what we would encourage elsewhere, it is civility. I mean by civility an attitude of respect and consideration in dealings among private citizens, in relations between state and society, and in the relations of individuals and the state to the natural environment and to other peoples' (37). This is, in many ways, quite a fantastic claim. After all, why *Canada* in particular, especially when he provides next to no evidence that would support the particularism of a claim that any number of other countries could also quite conceivably make or aspire to claim just as much? Second, and in apparent contradiction to the claim just advanced, Griffiths expresses concern that in the years since the Massey Commission *Report* (1951) on the state of the arts and sciences in postwar Canada – a period in which he says 'we were securing our capacity to make a contribution to civilization' (76) – civility in Canada has declined, battered by increasing regionalism and the rise of separatism, to mention just two primary internal factors. His answer, and he does note that it is one that 'others will no doubt find ... strange,' is what he terms 'a security perspective on Canadian cultural affairs ... the fact that Canadian culture and Canadian security have ... become closely interconnected' (76–7).

If, in other words, what Griffiths is really saying is that Canada's culture of civility is, in fact, a security perspective on civility, then his line of argument does align itself with a critical theme in cultural criticism opened up by Northrop Frye (1971), and subsequently developed by others (see Atwood 1972; McGregor 1985; Dorland 1988, 1997) – namely, the view looking out from embattled, defensive, fortresses of 'civility' surrounded by forests of savagery – Frye termed this 'the garrison mentality' – and for which evidence can be adduced going back to generalizations from the contact period between Europeans and First Peoples. Furthermore, such a security perspective, as one of us has argued elsewhere (Dorland 1997), also finds support in ancien régime theories of governance, both French and German, that fall under the rubric of the governmentalization of communication, in an historical continuum going back to the seventeenth century, and whose modern incarnations can be traced to such archetypal nineteenth-century Canadian preoccupations with canal-building, railroads, and, in the twentieth century, broadcasting and mass communication policies. Whether in its colonial context, or in loosely post-colonial projects of 'nation-building,' the securing of the means of transportation and communication against real and imagined external military and cultural threats draws upon a long historical tradition of national insecurity (see also Charland 1986; Wark 1992; Radforth and Greer 1992; Greenwood and Wright 1996; Dowler 1996). In this perspective, Griffiths's claim is hardly a novel one at all, but on the contrary harmonizes with, and reiterates, a historical reading of the project of governance some four centuries old in the Canadian context, and codified constitutionally in the 'Peace, Order, and good Government' clause of the BNA Act (1867). Or certainly with an at times contentious tradition of its interpretation (for differing views, see Laskin 1947; and Eggleston 1996–7).

On the other hand, Griffiths's point can be read more narrowly as the claim that Canada does – or rather once did – possess a certain type of culture of civility, in many respects equivalent to premodern conceptions of 'deference to authority' (see Pocock 1976; also Friedenberg 1980), which we discussed in chapter 4 with respect to the logic of gift and countergift that structured the embodied Crown's relation to his or her subjects. And if such intimations of civility *might* still provide guidelines for the problems of Type Two sovereignty, Griffiths is at the same time willing to admit that 'we do have a [current] problem' (77). A society that is civil and caring is also one that has some self-understanding of its 'indigenous culture and communications processes' (77–8). But is this, in fact, what we have uncovered above, or is it not, on the contrary, one of the difficulties? 'A political culture of civility is embedded in and depends upon the shared experience of participation in a national culture. Take the latter away or dilute it with global culture, and the practice of civility gives way ... under the stress of social change' (40). One could quibble with the wording or the use of terms such as 'national culture'; the issue, rather, is one of the extent of the embeddedness of a political culture of civility or, more precisely here, the lack of it. Finally, when Griffiths writes that 'we have no choice *but to begin* the work of designing alternative forms of association that meet the diverse needs for community and civility in the common space ... called Canada' (60, emphasis added), he seems to be reversing his earlier claim, and aligning himself with similar appeals *for* a culture of civility – one that, it should be added, remains still to be designed, as it lacks adequate embeddedness and only potentially offers glimpses of new forms of association that have yet to be spelled out.[2] Thus, what was initially presented as a flat assertion – 'If one word ... captures ... what Canada is about ... it is civility' (37) – turns out upon examination to be a call for a future-oriented project. Civility-as-national-security may be a ringing slogan for the insecure, but there would appear to be more to civility than security. However, as we shall see below, Griffiths's contribution remains significant to the extent that it posits a model of civility that is state- or security-based; in other words, one in which civil society – and civil culture – is a creature of the state, or more precisely, structured by rather than prior to its constitution and law.

Civility as Civil Society

Political and social theorists on several continents, as well as politicians, have in recent years rediscovered a venerable concept that, depending upon the analyst, has its roots in classical Greek thought (Colas 1997) or in its early modern articulation in the Scottish Enlightenment of the eighteenth century (Seligman 1992), and this is the concept of 'civil society.' Inspired particularly by the antistate democratic revolutions of the 1980s in Eastern Europe and the former Soviet Union, Margaret Somers remarks that 'the notion of civil society holds immense conceptual promise' (1999: 122). For one, it seems to provide a unique political vocabulary freed from the constraints of Cold War dichotomies. As well, it is congruent with recent efforts to theorize the interconnection of democratic values and civic practices in the attempt to institutionalize democratic, participatory, political cultures in a reconfigured global landscape (Somers, 122). This places an enormous burden upon the concept of civil society. 'Civil society has thus come to represent the flourishing of a seemingly novel political and social terrain, a space of popular movements and collective mobilization, of informal networks, civic associations, and community solidarities all oriented toward sustaining a participatory democratic life' (122). Not only, then, does 'civil society' represent an attempt to conceptualize a formidably complex series of organizational phenomena, it also attempts to overturn some three centuries of liberal thought that formed, in Norbert Bobbio's phrase, the 'great dichotomy' of modern political thought; namely that there were only two truly significant actors in the modern world, the administrative state on the one hand and the property-based market on the other (cited in Somers, 122). The concept of civil society was thus called upon to break apart the great dichotomy of the mutually exclusive public and private spheres, and 'liberate a new social and political space, one *in between* and *independent of* both private markets and administrative state authority ... where citizens can participate in the practices of citizenship free of both coercion and competition' (123, emphasis in original). Despite its promise, she continues, the concept of civil society has failed to overcome the burdens it inherited, in particular those burdens represented by what Somers terms 'Anglo-American citizenship theory' and especially the

Lockean account of the formation of civil society. She argues that this was nothing less than a 'revolutionary' invention of 'a new locus of social organization – a prepolitical, prestate and nonpublic *private* entity separate and distinct from the state, a new place for the people alone ... a permanent place of individual freedom and property that would establish the grounds for an enduring collective entity [and] ... serve as a normative reference point for how to achieve freedom from the state' (139, emphasis in original). Locke's political vision, she goes on, in making a separate and prepolitical social space the sole realm of true freedom, 'forever imprinted on our political imaginations [as] a binary spatial divide between public and private' and in so doing 'recast forever our vision of politics' (139). This notion of an 'autonomous prepolitical society' would by the eighteenth century explicitly be termed 'civil society' (140).

One of Somers's stated motivations is 'to make sense of an intriguing but worrisome puzzle about contemporary politics and political argument: namely, *the privatization of citizenship* and the *fear and loathing of the public sphere* – the demonstrable antistatism of our times' (1999: 121, emphasis in original). She uses similar phrasing further on, referring repeatedly to 'the fear and loathing of the state' (see 140, 149, 151). The deep-rootedness of this fear in political thought and argument, however, is, far more than Somers allows, one of the salient, if not outstanding, characteristics of especially *American* political thought on the state and the public sphere – or what Garry Wills recently described as 'a necessary evil' (1999; repeating the characterization of government first penned by Tom Paine). These are derivations to be sure that owe much to eighteenth-century British political theory, but derivations nonetheless in their translation to the Thirteen Colonies.

Of course, this is not to minimize what Somers terms the general antistatism of our times, although one could turn to differing, and in many ways more profound, explanations for the prevalent antistatism, as Habermas, for instance, has argued compellingly in *The New Conservatism* (1989, esp. chapter 2) as regards the exhaustion of the utopian project of the welfare state. And Werner Sombart classically proposed that the United States was an anomalous polity in not having ever been able to generate a significant autochthonous socialist politics and with it an underlying theorization of society based on the idea of social labour (see Sombart 1976; also Habermas, 1989: 52–3). On the other hand, the British state (and so the 'Anglo' component of Somers's Anglo-American doublet), as recent historical and political theoretical studies have shown, represents a far more overarching and pervasive conceptual entity than Somers's account would allow for (see Corrigan and Sayer 1985; Abrams 1982; and MacGregor 1992 as examples from a potentially much longer list). Also, her attempt to identity 'Anglo-American citizenship theory' as the nub of the particular problem regarding the Manichean separation of the realms of the public and the private becomes decidedly puzzling when she invokes Karl Marx's view of civil society as being 'in perfect harmony with Anglo-American citizenship's metanarrative' (see 1999: 154). But within the terms of classic English political theory, she notes that Hobbes's *Leviathan* had proposed an earlier form of solution to the problem of limiting absolutist (or state) authority, but one that did not provide a separate terrain for 'the people' outside of the political body of the sovereign (138–9). It is Locke's narrative that, once and for all, 'cement[s] the association of the public with the coercive administrative state ... setting the stage for the privatization of citizenship' (138). It is this account, more exactly Somers's version of it, that we must look at further.

According to Somers, the radical element of Locke's new narrative of the emergence of civil society consisted in the naturalization of an antipolitical private sphere: 'the private sphere of contractual interaction taken by free agents in the epistemologically, historically, politically and morally *anterior* realm of civil society' (149, emphasis in original). 'Civil society is not only separate and autonomous from the state, but existed *before* it and thus, quite literally, *caused* government's very existence by its voluntary consent ... This is not chronological time but epistemological time' (141, emphases in original). The presupposition 'of a nonpolitical domain of life that could exist sui generis, free from political authority and control ... was the realm of popular freedom *because* it was a collective society with the robustness to exist independently from the state' (140, emphasis in original). Never mind that all this is slightly tautological; it provides a depiction of 'government that exists as nothing more than an *outcome* of the prior activities of the prepolitical community ... But because literally created by the temporally *anterior* sphere of civil society, this consent to government can be revoked at any time: sovereignty resides resolutely in the hands of the people on civil society' (140, emphasis in original). 'Even after the sovereign people create a tamed representative government, strictly under their control, the state as Leviathan hovers as a permanently potential threat always ready to rear its collective head in popular tyranny. Fear and loathing of the state is the wellspring of the story of freedom; it is this that gives civil society its continuous reason for existence' (140). The evil, however, is 'never absolutely eliminated but remains in the shadowy background motivating a constant vigilance' (139).

Several insightful implications follow, but also problems. A first crucial implication concerns what Somers terms the privatization of citizenship: namely, that Locke, she argues, locates the origins and practices of citizenship in the prepolitical sphere of civil society. 'In this paradoxical sense, what is "political," "public," even "civil" about citizenship in Anglo-American citizenship theory [is] ... that government [is] entirely accountable to the private interests from whence it came and from which its authority derives' (150). Despite this account of the paradoxical privacy of the civil realm, Somers spends many pages circling around the problem of the 'collective glue independent of the political cohesion supplied by the state' (143) that would cohere the prepolitical civil community. The best she can come up with is a Lockean vision of a civil society held together less by *logos* than by the murkier workings of 'public opinion' (that seem to operate rather more like communication among insects) and by the ever-present threat of the return of the tyranny of the state. If what coheres 'the people' is the paradox of a prepolitical 'civil community held together through a political culture of public opinion and social trust' (Somers, 142, emphasis added), what indeed of the problem raised by Dolan (1991) concerning the evaluation of sincerity? Might not what Somers is trying to get at work better if the instability of meaning and the possibility of insincerity were admitted, and a civil community was imagined as held together by what Thomas Farrell (1993) has termed a 'rhetorical culture'? The concept of rhetorical culture is complex, however, because it is, as Farrell observes, both descriptive and normative. Furthermore, the term 'rhetoric' itself encompasses not only a wide variety of discursive practices, but competing and often contradictory ethical, political, and ontological commitments. For these reasons, before moving to a discussion of what rhetorical culture can mean or what the prospects of its realization are, we will consider the 'degree zero' of civility, the basic element of *savoir vivre*, manners.

Manners and Civility

This discussion provides one example of what a review of recent literature has called the contemporary 'civic revival' (Burchell 1995: 540) – the 'rehabilitation of elements ... of "the classical civic tradition" ... [namely], the conception of citizenship stemming from Aristotle which sees the citizen first and foremost as an active participant in the public affairs of the *polis*' (540). For Burchell the 'active' or public classical conception of citizenship has shrivelled in the modern world to a far more 'minimal ... style of citizenship' (541), reducing it to a 'passive' or liberal preoccupation with the formal rights of legally defined citizens in liberal-democratic states. In this view, the two resulting principal tensions in terms of thinking about citizenship alternate between views of a 'privatized citizenry' (542), as Somers presents it, contrasted with 'nostalgic ... laments for worlds lost' deriving from a thinly disguised Romantic or Rousseauian cast that 'recognizes the civic impulse only in a purely transcendental form' (542). This broad division, between a neo-Aristotelian and neo-

Rousseauian focus on the citizen as an a priori moral subject, and a 'modern' conception of the citizen merely as a creation of techniques of social discipline, and especially the activities of government, overlooks, Burchell argues, two crucial features of early-modern citizen formation, namely, the relationship between citizenship and urban environments, and second, 'the ethical techniques by which citizens acquired the attributes of the good citizen, and the secularization of those techniques ... through the rubric of "manners"' (549).

We can thus for now trace two paths towards democratic citizenship – one, the neo-Romantic, which draws upon the classical and is centred upon conceptions of virtue (especially political virtue) and regaining it ultimately by means of the political terrorism of the Jacobins and their epigones in what Talmon famously described as 'totalitarian democracy' (1961); and the other, 'the inculcation of techniques of self-cultivation and self-discipline' (Burchell 1995: 555), in which citizens, while they may have lost their 'antique virtue,' gained instead 'an indefinite and perhaps infinite enrichment' of their social personality through new processes of social diversification. As John Pocock puts it: 'Since these new relationships were social and not political ... the capacities which they led the individual to develop were called not "virtues" but "manners"' (cited in Burchell, 555).

Burchell notes:

'Manners' became the characteristic mode of possessing and displaying citizenly attributes in the age of commercial societies. And, in principle at least, while 'antique virtue' required the possession of the material prerequisites for classical civic life – land, property, leisure and a stake in political life – the acquisition of manners was a practical, piecemeal process of enlargening one's capacities across the burgeoning departments of social life. (555)

Burchell goes on to observe that it is no surprise that the Romantic reaction stigmatized 'manners' as superficial, just as the German Romantics would oppose 'culture' (the means of reuniting the sundered human self) to 'civilization' (the outward display of material attributes) in yet another version of the rejection of 'manners' for an abstract and disembodied regaining of virtue (555).

Burchell's account of the early modern paradigm of manners, however, 'provides a crucial impulse behind the practical social construction of citizens in contemporary Western societies' (556), one which he follows through to T.H. Marshall's 'great contribution' to the modern understanding of citizenship and his generalizing of it into a conceptualization of social policy in the modern representative-democratic state. The point here, of course, is not to revert, in turn, to nostalgia for what Habermas terms the 'exhausted utopian energies' of the welfare state, but rather to reiterate, as Burchell does, that the question of manners has not lost its centrality to understanding citizenship in commercial societies – indeed, much of what Yale law professor Stephen Carter understands by civility itself is precisely a preoccupation with manners and what he calls 'the etiquette of democracy' (1998). On a broader historical scale, Norbert Elias's magisterial *The Civilizing Process* (1939/1994) emphasized the role played by *civilité* (in its strongest French, as opposed to weaker Italian, English, or German, meanings) in easing the transition from feudalism. Nor did he cease to stress the crucial and constant relationship of civility to state-formation and the resulting pacification of social spaces that lead to 'more dispassionate' (451) forms of self-control, and the continuing search ever since for balance between controlling agencies and the libidinal impules. Recall too Elias's conclusion that the civilizing process is, as was suggested by Pocock, not only infinite and indefinite, but also 'if the coexistence of men [*sic*] with each other, which is after all the condition of the individual existence of each ... functions in such a way ... [as] to attain ... [that] balance, then and only then can humans say of themselves with some justice that they *are* civilized' (524, emphasis in original). Surely, civility in this sense might be said to constitute the human aspiration for an affective commonality.

Civility as Democratic Political Manners

Stephen L. Carter, as part of a recent, wide-ranging debate on civility and its place in the current conjuncture in American public life (see, e.g., Smith 1997; Schudson 1998; Janeway 1999), argues: 'Civility ... is a precondition of democratic dialogue' (1998: 25). For Carter, drawing upon an observation of de Tocqueville through the prism of the British historian Andrew St George, democracy itself 'can be seen not only as a type of government but as a system of manners, a form of social life' (cited 279). In his 'Guide to Reconstructing our Civility,' Carter proposes fifteen rules that could constitute 'the etiquette' of democracy (see 279–85). In Carter's perspective, civility is principally 'an ethic for strangers' (279), since in a modern, large democracy, we are for the most part strangers to one another, and the protection of democratic freedoms should extend not only to those we know well, but to those we do not know at all. 'Our views on every issue – crime, free speech, taxes, whatever – should not turn on the accident of how we and our immediate friends happen to be affected by the policy in question. Civility supposes an obligation to a larger if anonymous group of fellow citizens' (279–80). Democratic civility for Carter is thus a duty – to trust when there is risk; to be generous even when it is costly; to honour our 'duty to do good' (280); to come into the presence of our fellow human beings with awe and gratitude. But it is also a duty to disagree respectfully; and to listen to others, and value disagreement, diversity, and the possibility of resistance. The two major threats to the possibility of civility Carter identifies are, first, that the values of the marketplace have come to overly dominate the rest of social life and, second, that there is a rush to regulation and legislation instead of reserving it as a last resort after the possibilities of debate have been exhausted. Related to this reining in of the rush to the state is restricting the state's use of education to instil moral principles in children, a 'sacred sphere' that must instead fall to the family since it precedes the state. Carter's view, in short, is one of civility that closely resembles the concept of civil religion; not for nothing was one of his earlier, bestselling books a critique of *The Culture of Disbelief* (1993), nor is it surprising that he sees 'the nation's churches, synagogues and mosques' as the places where alternative social meanings (to the marketplace, primarily) can best take root (see 1998: 283). But as Andrew Shanks notes in his 1995 theology of the relationship between civil society and civil religion, the notion of civil religion of the kind that Carter espouses – namely, as 'the spiritual dimension to civil society' (1995: 68) – is the 'frailest' of three possible modes of civil religion (an example of the first mode being American 'Manifest Destiny' and of the second where religion constitutes a form of social glue) (Shanks 1995: 68). Thus while Carter's attempt to propose an etiquette for democracy is certainly a noble one, one might well inquire how specifically *democratic* is, in fact, the etiquette he advocates, beyond his view of democracy as a system of manners?

A thoughtful response to these problems is provided by Jorge Arditi in *A Genealogy of Manners* (1998), which takes up a task left incomplete by Elias; namely, of adding a third term to the analysis of the civilizing process. If Elias's work focused primarily on the transition from *courtoisie* to civility, Arditi argues that Elias paid insufficient attention to the emergence of the term 'etiquette' in the eighteenth century, and the importance of this term in further understanding the process of the coming of a new order of social relations and the transformation of the person (see 1998: 3–4).

Elias, in stressing the significance of civility at the beginning of the sixteenth century, had marked the growing separation of 'bodies and psyches out of which emerged, two hundred years later, the modern, "civilized" individual.' The latter, operating in an ever-widening matrix of social practices, had begun to be conceptualized in the eighteenth century in approving terms as the valorization of detachment both in social relations and in individual thought (Arditi, 3–5).

Etymologically, 'etiquette,' Arditi reminds us (183), means 'a little ethics' in the dual sense of lesser as well as selectivity. As Arditi points out, one of the characteristics of manners before 1700, not analysed by Elias, was their full embodiment in ethics: the ethics of *ecclesia* in the case of *courtoisie*, and the ethics of the *res civile* in the case of civility. With 'etiquette' – classically given expression in the letters of Lord Chesterfield (published in 1774) – comes a heightened awareness of the separation between manners and ethics now recentred upon 'an entirely new way of being in the world,' 'a different way of sensing and interpreting the self ... a different method of defining oneself in relation to ... others and to the social structures shaping one's practices' (4, 6).

If Elias's path-breaking study can be seen as the examination of a transition in social connectedness, from a connectedness formed by religion to a new connectedness based on the non-religious (the civil), Arditi focuses Foucault-like upon the discontinuties, the disconnectedness or relationalities that arise under the rubric of etiquette. By anchoring his analysis in changing social practices, Arditi shows as well the connections between *courtoisie* and the social institution of the church, civility, and the absolutism of royal power, and etiquette and the self- or group-, not to say class-, consciousness of the eighteenth-century English aristocracy in particular (the French remained much more dominated by the weight of the *res civile*). But what gives the English case its particular import, namely, its emphasis upon pragmatic relationality, is that the model of the English gentleman was not, in the end, restricted to the aristocracy, but becomes instead definitional of what Arditi terms 'the social absolute' as a model of the multicentredness of the 'self': 'the hegemonic mechanisms that the concept of etiquette helped constitute were not necessarily nor uniquely aristocratic; they were akin to class relations and class politics in general ... In this sense, the "rise of the bourgeoisie" did not involve a discontinuous transformation of the plane of practice but the introduction and circulation of a different substance within the existing plane ... Our own reality at the dawn of the twenty-first century is neither the beginning nor the end of anything beyond itself' (220).

Arditi's contribution to the debate, then, returns us to the problems raised by Carter: is 'etiquette' the appropriate concept for specifically understanding the manners of democracy, or is there a further term that would be more appropriate? Carter is concerned with re-establishing the kind of connectedness that in Arditi's view precisely breaks down with the rise of etiquette in commercial societies and the relational, multicentred model of the 'self' and others it provides a 'little ethic' for. An 'etiquette for democracy' may be an impossibly paradoxical concept, although an etiquette for capitalist democracy might not be. Or rather if the notion of etiquette is to retain some validity, it would not be Carter's version that remains in fact a proposal for a full-blown ethics; instead, it would be, as the term suggests, a minimalist ethics, an ethics of pragmatism more congruent with an increased plurality of selves in fleeting belongingness to a variety of social contexts, and networks of multifaceted forms of being. Such an etiquette would, as such, not be linked to a fully centred and earnest subject, but one capable of both concern and distance and so it would enact what Ronald Beiner, in his discussion of political judgment, describes as 'sympathy and detachment' (1983: 102–28).

Given its performative and strategic dimensions, it is worth exploring the degree to which rhetoric, either as human *dunamis* (potential or capacity) or as art (Aristotle defines rhetoric as both) might not provide the elements of such an etiquette. Harold Barrett implies as much when he argues that rhetoric is constitutive of all social relations and civil culture: '*All communicative states* are rhetorical, i.e., functional and instrumental, presented to affect an audience and dependent for success on their potential in bringing about identification ... Found in all exchanges of people are thoughts to be expressed, influence exerted, choices made, purposes and goals decided and pursued, language used ...' (1991: 7–8, emphasis added). Rhetoric, he continues, 'is a civil and dialectical process of social interaction ... Though ... violence and economic power can be used to accomplish certain ends, it is through *rhetoric* that culture is sustained' (11, emphasis added). This is all well and good, but calls for further analysis.

Domesticating Rhetoric

For the Greeks, with the concept of *arete*, the exercise of civility as a social virtue involved adherence to the other cardinal virtues (courage, temperance, justice, and wisdom). Opposed to civility was hubris. Drawing upon writers from Freud, for whom civility was an expedient accommodation between individuality and group claims, to political scientist Heinz Eulau, for whom civility rests upon an ability to distinguish between demands of the self and situations outside the self, Barrett defines civil behaviour as acts of 'persuading, soliciting, consulting, advising, bargaining, compromising, coalition-building' (Eulau), as opposed to coercing, deceiving, manipulating etc. Civility is a social good, effected rhetorically. From this literature, Barrett goes on to argue that civility comprises eight elements (knowledge, will, respect, courage, ability, independence, freedom, and responsibility) (146–50).

Rhetoric's capacity to produce civil behaviour and hence a set of manners for public life rests with its awareness of the contingency and artifice of performance as well as with its audience-centred theory of power and action. Rhetoric does not guarantee a happy or earnest civil society, but can offer a guide to their simulation for the sake of advancing interests. Thus, Barrett's identification of rhetoric with 'civility' might well be too strong, unless rhetoric itself is domesticated or tempered for the polis, as Aristotle sought to do in his *Rhetoric* (the major inspiration of Farrell's project). But when rhetoric is understood as 'symbolic action' and the means for inducing cooperation in what Kenneth Burke calls the 'human barnyard,' courtesy and consideration are not necessary.

This is evident in Burke's discussion of Machiavelli's *The Prince* as a rhetorical handbook 'insofar as it deals with the *producing of effects upon an audience*' (emphasis in original). Burke identifies in Machiavelli's work such rhetorical principles as 'either treat well or crush' and 'do necessary evils at one stroke, pay out benefits little by little' (Burke, 158). While the proper application of these principles will procure advantage to the Prince and might well yield peace, order, and good government, they certainly will not promote social trust. On the contrary, they capitalize on its opposite. Burke's insight that rhetoric's underlying principle is identification (and hence also division) signals that rhetoric cannot be reduced to conversation or rational deliberation. It might, as Machiavelli sought for Italy, produce the well-ordered state. It certainly can lead to civilization through the erection of symbolic structures that permit the coordination of human action. But civilizations are not necessarily civil, even if they are often pious. On the contrary, they can be quite meanspirited in their imposition of hierarchies and their disposal of difference and dissent.

The identification of rhetoric with civility and civic mindedness is, in part, a consequence of the canonical narrative of its origin. As the story is told, rhetoric emerged as an art following the routing of tyranny in Sicily in 467 BC and the return of what at the time was considered democracy. Sophists, as they came to be known, offered rhetorical instruction to litigants going to court to recover seized property. In such situations, rhetoric proceeded through the subordination of claims to the judgment of others. Rhetoric was of course a means for forensic battle, but the outcome was determined by judges rather than by the destruction of one's opponent. Manners as such were important, for judges should not be ill-disposed. Rhetorical victory depended upon a sensibility to what was appropriate (*prepon*). Furthermore, in a 'democratic,' or more properly, a 'republican' polis, judges were fellow citizens, and thus proper manners would have a 'civil' or egalitarian cast. In other words, rhetoric becomes civil when speakers are, unlike Machiavelli's Prince, at the mercy of a judging audience whose divisions cannot be exploited.

This story only begins to elucidate the relationship of rhetoric to civility, however, at least within republican communities. To fully understand the nature of rhetorical civility, we need to look more closely at rhetoric's various guises.

Even in antiquity, rhetoric could be understood in a number of ways. Two are particularly worthy of note: the first, usually associated with the sophists, is constitutive, while the second, Aristotelian, is persuasive. Sophistic rhetoric has a constitutive power. It posits possible ways of being (Poulakos [1984]). Furthermore, sophists taught rhetoric as a means for personal advancement. Rhetoric not only arms the citizen for victory in the courts and in the assembly, but also permits him to impress his fellows through his eloquence. It is as such fundamentally competitive, not only because it marshals argument and counter-argument, but because it is a medium in which citizens can strive to best each other. Rhetoric is in the realm of action so well described by Hannah Arendt. It is marked by the 'agonal spirit, the passionate drive to show one's self in measuring up against others' (Arendt 1958: 194) Indeed, in Greek, *agon* refers both to athletic contest and argument or debate. Rhetoric so understood can at first glance appear antagonistic to civility, particularly since sophistic rhetoric is often seen to be impious and to revel in paradox. Rhetoric is an expression of the will to power, and is a medium through which one can attain excellence, where one can indeed transform values or make worlds. It certainly is not modelled upon deferral. Nevertheless, the full articulation of sophistic rhetoric requires a civic spirit, and hence cooperation in conflict. As Nietzsche, a champion of the sophists, observed, 'rhetoric belongs to republics' (cited in Gilman and Blai 1989). Republics are talkative societies, and Nietzsche locates (sophistic) rhetoric within a culture of speech and performance. In his rendering, the Greeks 'enjoyed speech above all else.' They were not shocked by sophistic inversions of logic, as when Gorgias demonstrated that 'nothing exists' or penned a defence of the treasonous Helen of Troy. On the contrary, they looked upon such artful performances with delight. For both the sophists and Aristotle after them, rhetoric is fundamentally constitutive of ethos, an attribute itself that can only be understood relationally, as an attribution made by others before whom one could distinguish oneself. Even though agonistic, sophistic rhetoric blooms in a community that itself is constituted in the love of speech and in respect for one who speaks well.

While rhetoric so conceived is civic because it is located in the polis and requires a certain civility – a respect for those others who will be its audience – its end is not the polis. That is to say, it is not in the first instance directed toward the production of civic goods. It is furthermore not inherently guided by sympathy for the other, but only by a desire to seduce the other. As Eugene Garver (1994) puts it, sophistic rhetoric is not subordinated to politics. As Garver argues, that subordination is described by Aristotle. Aristotle first restricts rhetoric's domain. He asserts the existence of three rhetorical genres, forensic, deliberative, and epideictic, corresponding to three institutionalized settings and civic offices, the court, the assembly, and the commemorative ceremony. While the sophists gave rhetoric no finality except victory and the gaining of esteem, Aristotle places rhetoric in the service of justice, expedient legislation, and the praising of civic values. The second element of this subordination is shown through Aristotle's insistence that the enthemyme, the deductive argument based upon probability, is the strongest of rhetorical proofs, but that character, ethos, is the most persuasive (Garver 1994: 173). That is to say, Aristotle figures rhetoric as primarily consisting of argumentation, but he locates the force of argument in the character of the speaker rather than in disembodied reason itself. This paradox is a consequence of the ontological domain in which rhetoric operates. Rhetoric is a necessary art because of contingency. Rhetoric is concerned with matters for which there can be no true knowledge, but only opinion. (Garver 1994: 207) As such, rhetoric can prove opposites, and rhetorical education, like legal education today, demanded of its students that they develop proofs for both sides of given cases (the *dissoi logoi*). As a consequence, good reasons in the form of examples and enthemymes cannot on their own produce assent, for they lack the force of apodeictic demonstration. They gain agreement through persuasion, which means that they require the complicity of their audience. Rhetoric's audience must desire to agree, for there is always a possible counter-argument. Thus, as Garver observes, citing Aristotle:

Where reason points in a single direction, there is no need for either character or emotion, no need for rhetoric. Where reason alone is not sufficient, practical argument requires consideration of the source and target of arguments, the character of the speaker and the emotions of the hearers, generating the trio canonized in the history of rhetoric as *ēthos*, *pathos*, and *logos*: 'Since rhetoric is concerned with making a judgment ... it is necessary not only to look to the argument, that it may be demonstrative and persuasive, but also (for the speaker) to construct a view of himself as a certain kind of person and to prepare the judge.' Passion enters the *Rhetoric*, then, at the same place as rhetoric enters practical reason. Any place where argument alone is incomplete, and needs the supplements of *ēthos* and *pathos*, there the emotions will have a constitutive role. (Garver 1994: 109)

As supplementary proofs, ethos and pathos are, like logos, specific to case and audience. Pathetic proofs mobilize the emotions to place the audience in a favourable state of mind, but to do so they must relate particular emotions to the case at hand. In the *Rhetoric*, Aristotle not only offers an inventory of emotions appropriate to ancient Athens, but also outlines their grammar. Emotions are based in specific feelings toward some person, object, or state of affairs, and directed toward specific actions. There is a logos to pathos and ethos, but these two exceed the case at hand as they relate speaker to audience and case. Furthermore, because ethos depends upon trust, it necessarily subordinates the figure of the speaker to the perceptions of the audience. Trustworthiness will necessarily be an attribution made by an audience as they assess the speaker's performance. The constitutive elements of ethos, as Aristotle observes are prudence, virtue, and goodwill. This is, in part, an effect of the style of reasoning that is employed. One cannot move quickly and with confidence to the right rule. As Garver states it:

Aristotle again begins making his case about how rhetorical argument works from the institutional setting of persuasion, but the value of comparative arguments about greater good and greater utility extend beyond the situations in which there are competing hypotheses about what to do. Even the speaker who does not have an opponent, even a speaker who maintains that his recommended course of action is the only one a reasonable person could ever pursue, must, to make a complete and concrete case, show awareness of possible rejected alternatives, as serious alternative – as serious as called for by the case. Awareness of alternatives is evidence of *ēthos* and *phronesis*. (89)

Indeed, excessive confidence in a line of reasoning can undermine persuasiveness. As Garver puts it: 'It is not true that the more logical an argument is, the more believable it is. Sometimes cogency seems to backfire: judged by persuasion, it seems that arguments can fail by being too strong!' (148).

Ethical proof depends upon an audience trusting that a speaker has good judgment with regard to contingent questions, will act in a manner consistent with what is right, and desires what is best, especially for the audience. Ethical proof as such demands a certain manner of civility. As with sophistic rhetoric, a speaker must acknowledge the one being addressed and regulate one's comportment in anticipation of appraisal. Thus, rhetoric-as-persuasion depends upon at least the simulation of a social relation. That relation in itself is not necessarily civic, however, as Garver is at pains to point out.

Consider a stockbroker's advice. The future performance of markets cannot be guaranteed. While arguments will be made concerning the probable direction of the market, a stockbroker will also rely on pathos, invoking our desire for a happy retirement, a good education for our children, and our fear of appearing foolish or becoming poor, and on ethos, as she presents herself as having good investment judgment, as being worthy of trust in money matters, and as caring about us, our investments, and her own professional reputation. While ethos will be central to her appeals, the rhetorical relation so established need not be public or demand any commitment to the community. While some will bring ethical or political desires to their investment decisions, as when favouring 'green' stocks or a stockbroker with a social conscience, such considerations do not flow necessarily from the practical question of investment. When the matter at hand is a civic one, however, and concerned with the finalities of justice, expedient legislation and action, and the celebration of noble acts, this relationship takes on another hue, a hue animated by a sense of consubstantiality and of a *commonweal* as envisaged by Aristotle.

Civic rhetoric is productive of a civic ethos precisely because, in dealing with indeterminate questions, a speaker must proffer proofs in accordance with the values and principles of the audience now figured as a community. This means more than acting is such a manner as to appear agreeable or admirable to an audience. It means that arguments and examples must employ topics in accordance with community values and understandings. It is important to remember that these values are not exhibited in the position initially advocated in a controversy so much as in the means by which that position is held and the ultimate ends to which it is put. As Aristotle makes clear in the *Rhetoric*, particular measures are advocated ultimately in terms of whether they will be productive of happiness, as that is understood in a community and expressed in its constitution. Measures are figured as such through topics, argumentative themes, perspectives from which what is advocated can be judged. An effective speaker, and hence participant in civic debate, must figure himself in accordance with the community's 'social knowledge' (Farrell 1976), its publicly held values concerning what is right and good. Aristotelian rhetoric is based in 'good reasons' (Wallace 1971), but it is not the reasons which are determinative of judgment. Rather, it is the manner in which reasons are offered; it is performance that constructs the ethos of the speaker, and through an identificatory pathos, the collective audience as well. It is civic ethos that compels civic judgment. Through civic performance, the speaker brings the community to presence.

Aristotelian rhetoric is civic because the *agon* is sublimated. The self one is driven to show must appear consubstantial with the community's idea of itself. Consequently, the civic community is one of fundamental affective commonality. Garver describes it as a 'community of pleasure and pain' which is, even so,

a practical community, a community of deliberation. These emotions are predicated directly of a collective deliberative body; they all feel *eunoia* [good will] toward the speaker because they feel *homonoia* [commonality] to each other. The audience thinks that it has feelings and interests in common ... because they not only feel the same emotions, but together agree on the appropriateness of those emotions to the events and themselves ... It is a *community* of pleasure and pain because members of the audience recognize each other as having the same emotions, and that mutual recognition is necessary for *philia*. (132)

Garver does not claim that rhetoric necessarily leads to community or *philia*, meaning 'civic friendship' based in a desire for the other's good. While rhetoric, or persuasion, depends upon emotions, these will not necessarily instantiate a community of pleasure and pain. Certainly, speakers need to figure themselves and their measures in accordance with the desires of their audience, but those desires need not be for community, the common good, or a shared sense of the just and honourable. Somers's privatized citizen can also employ rhetoric, but it would be reduced to a mere instrumentality, if not indeed a goad to cynicism. As Garver, reflecting on contemporary American democracy, also observes: 'A political community might be destroyed when its members start to conceive of its functioning in terms of pure utility as a contract, exchanging taxes for services, or of pleasures of patriotism dissociated from any purposes or actions. Rhetoric based on such appeals destroys *eunoia*' (Garver 1994: 133). As such, rhetoric in itself cannot guarantee civil society. Neither, in Garver's account, did Aristotle conceive it that way. As such, against the common interpretation, he does not consider Aristotle's *Rhetoric* to be an instruction manual for teaching persuasion, nor does he share the commonly held view that rhetorical instruction will give rise to an ethical political community. Rather, he argues that Aristotle's *Rhetoric* is a guide for the legislator, which shows how a domesticate rhetoric could function as a civic art in a polis in the original Greek sense of an ethical community In such a community, Aristotelian rhetoric will serve as a much stronger 'social glue' than its sophistic counterpart, which ultimately has no moral purpose.

Thomas Farrell's *Norms of Rhetorical Culture* (1993) seeks to offer Aristotelian rhetoric as an alternative to the formal etiquette of Habermas's ideal speech situation, which itself forms the basis for normative theories of the 'democratic conversation' and deliberative democracy. Like Barrett, Farrell asserts the inevitability of rhetoric, not because of its place in language, however, but because of its necessary role in democratic governance. In Farrell's view, 'rhetoric is the primary practical instrumentality for generating and sustaining the critical publicity which keeps the promise of a public sphere alive' (1993: 199). In her account, Somers had claimed that the concept of civil society (the idea of a third sphere of citizenship that would source what Habermas calls the public sphere or Locke the normative discourse of public opinion and political culture [Somers, 153]) – characterized by participation, solidarities, and a robust public discourse of rights – was untenable because citizenship in the

Anglo-American understanding is 'a derivative form of social activity whose significance emanates from the morally superior private sphere of the natural free market' (156). Such a privatization of citizenship is so deeply paradoxical, she concludes, that 'the concept of civil society cannot meet the theoretical demands of the ... historical events that precipitated its revival' (156). Participation, solidarities, and a public discourse of rights are accordingly not possible precisely *because* of their publicness; in her view, only the law and a tamed form of representative government, as the emanation of private market interests, count as 'the legitimate institutionalization of public opinion' (153); the rest of 'public' life, one might say, consists then either of silence or merely meaningless private chatter. Farrell's study in part belies Somers's account, for he proceeds, as have we, through a discussion of cases marked by critical publicity that have furthermore been directed toward realizing the promise of a public sphere. Farrell does not assert that such a public sphere is fully realized, but only that it can be glimpsed during certain rhetorical episodes. For Farrell, this possibility is fundamental to the nature of (Aristotelian) rhetoric as a normative practice. That is to say, rhetoric contains within itself norms and standards against which actual practice can be critiqued and perfected. In Farrell's Aristotelian reading, rhetoric is more than persuasion; it is an art of public thought based in part on practical reasoning and the collaboration of audiences implicit in the *enthemyme*, the rhetorical syllogism based in the audience's sense of the probable. Thus, rhetoric depends upon, even as its practice prefigures and calls forth, a community marked by 'reciprocity, civic friendship, affiliative agency, regard, [and] even hope' (50). The existence of such a community, and its public sphere, is not assured, but forever fragile, sustained by ongoing rhetorical practice. The only difficulty with Farrell's formulation, however, is that it presumes what it seeks to realize. That is to say, the civic norms Farrell identifies, constitutive of *philia*, are not within rhetoric *tout court*, but Aristotelian rhetoric, which Garver argues (as we noted above), presumes rather than produces the good polis.

As such, neither rhetorical skill nor its instruction guarantees the 'social glue.' At most, an understanding of rhetoric leads to a recognition of its practical necessity. Alternately, rhetorical training had traditionally been a component of civic education. Indeed, such training was widely offered in eighteenth- and nineteenth-century Canada, although that instruction in a *culture oratoire* was often reserved for elites who already shared social, and hence pre-political commonalities and by the late nineteenth century, had been collapsed into the teaching of literature on the one hand and on the other had been reified in the formulaic prose of the mass newspaper. In the process, what was lost was a preoccupation with the link of performance and civility, leaving journalist David MacFarlane to remark recently in the *Globe and Mail* upon the startling degree to which Canadians politicians are so utterly devoid of rhetorical skills (3 July 2000).

It would be quixotic, of course, to seek to reinstate a rhetorical culture of classical education in a world now marked in part by the antistatism and preoccupation with rights that Somers describes, even though we agree with Farrell that rhetoric is a social good and that it can provide the insights necessary for the development of civic manners. Against a full-blown ethical rhetoric, however, we consider more useful a 'superficial' rhetoric; that is to say, an aesthetic rhetoric concerned with the management of appearances, or what Robert Hariman understands as a rhetoric of style.

Rhetoric and Political Style

Hariman defines a political style as 'a coherent repertoire of rhetorical conventions depending on aesthetic reactions for political effect' (1995: 4). Style is, of course, one of the rhetorical 'canons,' one of the five elements taught in classical rhetoric (along with invention, disposition, memory, and delivery). As described by Aristotle, style is primarily ornamental, not contributing to proof, and concerns both formal attributes of discourse (rhyme, rhythm, etc.) and the appropriateness of particular redactional choices to the subject matter, occasion, and audience. This classical understanding is limited, however, for while it recognizes that effective style is an important aspect of successful rhetorical performance, its place is secondary to invention and disposition, which are considered the heart of the rhetorical art. Hariman, however, considers style as more than an afterthought, but as a fundamental component of the political relation.

In Hariman's analysis, style is more than a property of political rhetoric. That is to say, it pertains not only to the form of persuasive speech, but to the very structure of political authority. 'Style becomes an analytical category for understanding a social reality; in order to understand the social reality of politics, we can consider how a political action involves acting according to a particular political style' (Hariman 1995: 9). The key insight here is that politics is composed in action. That is to say, it is performed, and as such marries meaning with aesthetic qualities. Hariman uses the term 'style' to think through the nature of political aesthetics. Hariman is not concerned with the relationship of art to politics, nor does he consider useful a discussion of politics according to modern aesthetic categories, organized around such principles as form, disinterestedness, and the autonomy of the artwork; rather he recurs to premodern categories that figure practical matters in aesthetic terms, most notably rhetoric and the related art of *decorum*, which offered an awareness not only of stylistic conventions, but also of when they should be violated. As such, in Hariman's rendering, style is an attribute of the pragmatics of performance, a sensibility that pertains to the matters as well as the manners of governance. It is in this sense, then, that style is a constitutional category. As Hariman puts it, a successful style 'articulates specific rules of usage and the composition of self and others in relations of equity and subordination' (Hariman 1995: 7). Style structures the political relation, but itself is prepolitical. It organizes selves and others in aesthetic relations of power. Style governs how one should appear, and thus is the basis for ethos that can support a political culture. Furthermore, and this is fundamental for our purposes, while style is a constitutive element of rhetoric and political action, it cannot be reduced to the relations of authority formally established by law, including constitutional law. Indeed, one cannot even speak of 'legal style' in the singular, although in any given legal culture one style can come to dominate. Style is a mode of enacting appearance. In an extended definition, Hariman describes political style as

(1) a set of rules for speech and conduct guiding the alignment of signs and situations, or texts and acts, or behavior and place; (2) informing practices of communication and display; (3) operating through a repertoire of rhetorical conventions depending on aesthetic reactions; and (4) determining individual identity, providing social cohesion, and distributing power. (Hariman 1995: 187)

Key to Hariman's conception of style is that it is not a state-bound concept, but describes a *cultural* disposition, an element of what we referred to in chapter 4, citing Burke, as the 'constitution behind the constitution.'

Hariman identifies four political styles, while admitting that there are surely others. He examines the realist, the courtly, the republican, and the bureaucratic style. His analysis illustrates that styles need not belong to distinct political societies, but can coexist within the same polity. Thus, Hariman remarks that the Reagan presidency was characterized by the courtly style, while Clinton redacted his public persona in accordance with the republican style. The realist style dominates in international relations, while the bureaucratic style structures the encounters that most of us usually have with the agencies of modern power. This coexistence is not a harmonious one, however. Every political style, and indeed politics itself, is agonistic. In each style that Hariman describes, one finds political actors seeking to bring others to realize their will. Each style structures a social relation, but we do not find here eros consummated. There are hierarchies and conflicts, strategies of attack and defence, of identification and division. Furthermore, and more fundamentally, Hariman places these styles in competition with each other. Like all discourse genres, they find their status in a hierarchical ranking of discourses, where each seeks to claim its place by marginalizing others, seeking to reduce them to incoherence (see also Hariman 1986).

In the following chapter, we will discuss Hariman's concept of style in more detail, and with particular reference to the cases we have treated in this study. For the moment, it will suffice to note that while some form of courtly style dominated in Canada until Confederation, the post-Confederation period can be understood as exhibiting a tension between a republican and a bureaucratic style, where the former inheres in parliamentary institutions and popular movements, and the latter in the judicial and administrative apparatus, and most specifically in the law. Of greater interest for the purposes of this chapter is that, in Hariman's analysis, the reigning style is not overdetermined, but open to performative amendment through the art of decorum. Michael Leff notes that decorum or propriety enables a balancing between 'the mode of expression against the occasion, the subject, and the interests of those who render judgment' (1999: 61). As such, decorum cannot be reduced to etiquette, or to manners understood as an apolitical set of rules that smooth over interaction. Rather, the principle (and art) of decorum 'allows us to comprehend a situation as a whole, to locate its meaning within a context, and to translate this understanding into a discursive form that becomes an incentive for action' (62). Decorum, as such, is an element of rhetoric. However, unlike invention, which leads to the development of proofs, decorum concerns performance itself, leading to propriety, to a style not only appropriate to a situation but to given goals. Decorum 'works to align the stylistic and argumentative features of the discourse within a unified structure while adjusting the whole structure to the context from which the discourse arises and to which it responds' (62). Decorum is as such central to the performance of style as understood by Hariman, and furthermore, while it serves to regulate performance, it does not sublimate all conflict or interest in order to maintain a bland civility. As such, without requiring the republican commitments to community, and hence the potential for the terror of a dominant narrative or sensibility, decorum enables the performance of style, and the redaction of one's public ethos, to adapt to others without simply erasing the self.

The glue that Somers seeks can thus be seen to reside, not in a rhetorical culture per se, but in a culture animated by the art of decorum and its sensibilities to situations. Decorum, unlike deliberative democracy's social reason, is not based in procedure nor is it rule-governed, and it is thus a matter of culture, not law. Furthermore, and more significantly, it does not demand too much of social actors accustomed to imagining themselves as rights-bearing individuals. Finally, decorum, unlike etiquette, accommodates invention and innovation, and so can encompass such ambivalent practices and sensibilities as irony. Thus, for example, while the women holding mock parliaments may have been impious and in some respects ill-mannered, their performances remained decorous as they enacted an ironically-inflected republican style.

Civility as the Demise of the Unhappy Consciousness

Rhetoric alone is no guarantee of civility and there is no certainty that rhetorical instruction will give rise to an ethical political community. Furthermore, while civility can be effected through decorous performance, it requires propitious circumstances. The ideal of a civil culture requires opportunities to enact at least the appearance of some form of affective commonality. Occasions and cultural resources for the emergence and development of such performances have been largely repressed by the predominance of a legal-administrative style that, through juridicalization, elite accommodation, and administrative compromise, has attempted to banish the *agon* of enacting appearance, even that which might stem from *philia*. Instead, what has been maintained is the continuation of a culture of institutionalized civil antagonism on the pretence that it at least can be 'managed' by constitutional conferences, first ministers' meetings, and the like, a pretence which, since the failures of the Meech Lake and Charlottetown Accords (1987–92, 1992–3 respectively), has seemingly reached a near-total impasse. (Recent moves, however, suggest that, as with the Charter, which gave rise to the beginnings of a new culture of rights, one possible solution might be to juridicalize the terms and conditions of a future Quebec referendum on independence, turning matters from the constitutional to more narrowly 'legal' problems). Thus the Canadian political and civil vacuum, in many ways, continues to represent a variant of the problem of the radical break in the mode of performing power introduced by the emergence of democratic discourses.

With the withdrawal of the loving monarch, painfully apparent in the Riel case, the locus of power becomes forever an empty place. As Slavoj Žižek perceptively remarks: 'With the advent of democratic discourse, the locus of Power changes into a purely symbolic construction that cannot be occupied by any real political agency' (1991: 268). Some of the resulting implications, as he points out, are far-reaching: 1) gone is the instantiation of political 'happiness' by means of revolutionary virtue; the best we can hope for, and it is no small matter, is 'enjoyment' ('happiness' in its nonhysterical and ethical form); 2) gone too is the temptation of republican heroics that all too readily revolves itself into accusations of treason; 3) gone as well are 'the People,' 'the iron Laws of historical Progress,' etc.; 4) but what remains is 'the fact that "the

Throne is empty" is now the only "normal" state' (1991: 267; also 260, 268, 272). Thus, we are left at best with weakly institutionalized vestiges of the courtly and republican styles.

In this sense, the withdrawal of the 'loving' monarch, in Žižek's rereading of Hegel's *Philosophy of Right* (269–70, 277n54), in fact changes nothing, even with the advent of the symbolic and temporary character of the 'democratic invention' (Claude Lefort). It need not thus precipitate a return of the unhappy consciousness seeking, in misplaced narcissism, a new object-to-fetishize; rather Žižek argues, with Hegel, that the modern monarch functions 'as an effective protector of the empty locus of Power' (269). Such a view also accords nicely with David E. Smith's 1995 book on the little-understood, because symbolically complex, role of the 'invisible Crown' as the first principle of Canadian governance. For Smith, 'the Crown is [not only] Canada's oldest continuing political institution, it is perhaps the least understood' (1995: viii), in large part because it remains, as Locke described it three centuries ago, 'the power to act according to discretion, for the publick good, without the prescription of the law, and sometimes even against it' (cited in Smith, 32). As a theoretical principle, 'the Crown ... integrates the Canadian polity both vertically, within individual jurisdictions, and horizontally, across jurisdictions' (25). It is, in other words, the source of authority for governance in the broadest possible sense, 'the organizing force behind the executive, legislature, and judiciary in both the federal and provincial spheres of government ... The result ... is a distinctive form of federalism best described as a system of compound monarchies' (x). That is to say it is above all a *civil disposition*, Smith argues, that not only permeates daily government but manifests 'a habitual attitude to government that depends upon access to discretion' (xi). It has, as such, its own style. Paradoxically, however, it is also a very difficult concept to 'see,' in part because of the extent of its ubiquity as transinstitutional, but more important because its meaning has been papered over by a political history that has been primarily focused on the executive, by a juridical history that has 'federalized' the Crown and made it the basis for the intergovernmental rivalries that have plagued Canadian federalism (see 29), and by a constitutional history written largely by lawyers who did not understand the concept of the Crown or, if not lawyers, then by the likes of Bagehot who grossly overstressed its dignity (15). Above all, the Crown is not the state because it is more than the state. This leads Smith to draw intriguingly upon Kenneth Dyson's observations that Britain and its principal former colonies, like Canada or Australia (although the latter presents particular differences), are 'stateless societies' when compared with those of the Western European and civil law tradition (26–7). In Smith's view, Canada represents a little-known and seriously understudied instance of 'compound monarchies,' 'a governing structure ... not cast in a British mould, neither is it of United States design in the way it operates' (7). Rather, it is an instance of what we are going to term 'monarchical republicanism,' in the paradoxical sense that David Bercuson and Barry Cooper have used to describe the evolution of liberal democracy in Canada into that of a 'quasi-republic' (see Smith 191n31). On the other hand, one of the consequences of the ubiquity of the invisible crown 'explains the weakness of the concept of the people as a constituent power' (17). Under the weight of the Crown, decorous performance becomes so difficult because, as Hariman observes of the bureaucratic style, depersonalized writing is privileged over presence and speech. Civil society and an audience for decorous performance must be invented despite and indeed against the Crown.

In our next chapter, we will explore in more detail the possibilities for such invention, which indeed are imminent in the rhetorical episodes that we have considered in this volume, and which can be understood, somewhat contradictorily, as making up a 'monarchical-republican' style. For the moment, to return to the concept of civil society that inaugurated this chapter, there does appear to be a widely shared consensus among a number of scholars that public life in liberal democracies has withered, leading to a renewed search for models of active participatory democracy that would help revitalize the civic (or civil) realm. And it has certainly been a major line of argument of this book that Canada's historical civil culture bears profound scars stemming from a weak civil society, constrained experiments with democratic politics, and the recurring search for a political style of citizen expression rooted in at least decorous adaptation, and perhaps even affective commonality, more than in a mere enactment of the roles assigned by the agendas of the administrative state.

Dialectics of Civility

From what we have seen above, despite the recent return to issues of civility, civic revival, concepts such as civil society, and the place of rhetoric therein, there is no easy solution to the perceived waning of democratic participation in contemporary complex societies. Even the most modest of prescriptions entails not only a fundamental refiguring of the idea of the political and the place of subjects within it, but a corresponding change in the communicative practices of civil society and the organizational culture of political institutions. Consequently, proposed solutions to the problems of an ethic, or the lack of one, and of democratic participation mostly reproblematize matters, raising the question as to why one should continue to insist upon flogging possibly dead horses. The best that these various discussions can offer, it might seem, is a plea for hanging onto a minimum of awareness that social life involves interaction with count-less unknown others with whom we share the obligations stemming from our common humanity, and that part of our common humanity is still to be found in such political institutions as the state – indeed, one cannot dispense entirely with the political altogether in our individual pursuit of happiness, to the extent that politics itself is, as Aristotle pointed out long ago though in different language, part of the pursuit of human happiness (even though that very pursuit is also the source of much human misery and discontent). So we are seemingly left with varieties of minimalism: a minimal art of rhetoric guided by a sense of appropriateness; a 'minimal ethics' in the recognition of our obligation to others; the minimal state and democracy as an 'acceptable level' of risk in civic participation; and the belief that, as Michael Schudson puts it, even democra-cy's discontents still 'automatically impl[y] respect for the rights of others and the willingness to engage in public dispute according to public norms and a public language' (1998: 309), a formulation that leaves unexplained as much as it claims to answer. In short, a rhetorical etiquette – a *little* ethics – as a decorous art of democracy without guarantees; or in Jean-Paul Sartre's supposed death-bed words: 'Contingency! More contingency!' And perhaps, in our time, at the end of the former grand narratives, of multicentred beings that manifest selfhood conjuncturally in more fleeting but also ever more complex forms of associa-tion (virtual identities, etc.), this is perhaps as good as we can hope for. Perhaps.

On the other hand, we might also argue, as has already been suggested above, that all of these problems stem from the radical break in, and resulting uncer-tainties of, the mode of *performing* power introduced by the emergence of democratic discourses; as in any live performance, there is a suspension of disbelief regarding the final outcome of governance, citizenship, public dis-course, the civic or civil culture, etc. Such a performance can offer no guaran-tees because a lack of fundamental certainty is precisely what democracy 'is': an ongoing, experimental form of political life in conjunction with unknown others, always having to be hashed out by the means of public dispute accord-ing to public norms and a public language, with what constitutes 'public norms' and a 'public language' comprising much of the content of the dispute. In a word, the *agon* of the democratic aspiration, from its modern revolutionary upsurges since the English attempt of the seventeenth century, to the collapse of actually realized socialism in the 1980s and the late-twentieth-century ravages of the unregulated capitalist market in the form of dragons and similar mon-sters, has become more than ever before globalized.

That said, however, and so as not to be accused of seeking refuge in a revision of the Enlightenment promise of an open-ended History resignified by the qualifier Democratic, we might defend ourselves with a reminder of the

'Yes, but nevertheless ...' introduced by Žižek's long preoccupation with the contemporary political issue of the importance of 'enjoyment.' To be sure, he has particularly focused his dissection on enjoyment's pathological and totalitarian terroristic forms as the 'injunction to enjoyment' – the diremption of enjoyment in the revolutionary striving for the realization of political happiness (see 1991: 231–7, 253). So let us recall, therefore, his celebration, noted above, of the enjoyments made possible by constitutional monarchy and constitutional authority which, however faulty in its content, is still, in his view, better as 'the spirit of the law' than 'the rottenness' of a momentary form of authority 'which is fortuitously "fair," yet without support in an Institution' (249–50). Recall too his definition of democracy as the *awareness* of the distance separating the locus of power from those exerting power at a given moment, as 'this untresspassable limit preventing any political subject from becoming consubstantial with the locus of power' (267–8). For Žižek, one of the not inconsequential results is that the Left today thus finds itself in the ironic position of having to pledge all its forces to the victory of democracy, after having devoted such enormous efforts in the past to unmasking the illusions of the liberal-democratic project.

But we can further contextualize the Slovene psychoanalyst's discussion of the performativity of democratic discourse by carefully drawing the lessons foregrounded by John M. Cuddihy's 1974 study of the 'passage' of a modernizing Jewish intelligentsia into 'civility,' namely, that learning the 'game' of civility has been, and continues to be, a particularly modern type of ordeal, one with enormous repercussions whose stakes we have inherited.[3]

For Cuddihy, civility is the prototypical case of social interaction; when it occurs between strangers in the complex, highly differentiated societies that fall under the rubric of 'the West,' 'it ... takes the form of a ritual interchange of gifts ...' (4). One of the key points of his argument, focusing specifically on the encounter of Jew with Gentile in the wake of Jewish emancipation in the nineteenth century, is that this form of legal emancipation was not conjoined with social emancipation: 'no "ritually ratified face-to-face contact" took place, no social rites of public behaviour were reciprocally performed, nor were they performed for their own sakes' (3).

Such a drastic 'failure of civility' spread shockwaves throughout the nineteenth century, giving rise on the one hand to the diagnostic explanations of the social sciences (or what a number of contemporary observers called the 'Jewish' sciences, from sociology to psychoanalysis [Cuddihy, 8]) concerning 'anomie,' 'alienation,' etc., – the vacuum of connectedness at the heart of modernity – and on the other hand to the exterminatory catastrophes of the twentieth century, of which the Holocaust remains certainly one of the most horrifying manifestations. The failure of civility that concretized itself in the form of 'the Jewish question' was at the same time the realization for secularizing Jewish intellectuals of the trauma, the culture shock, the guilt of shame stemming from the gap between the normative Gentile culture from which they felt alienated, particularly when looking back at the public and visible vulgarity of their culture of origin. Compounding this double alienation, and this would be the case particularly for intellectuals on the Left, was the realization that the 'rights and duties of the *citoyen*' – emblematized in the Declaration of the Rights of Man and the Citizen – meant in practice more than the exercise of 'bourgeois rights' and the political, legal, and economic entitlements involved, but additionally 'the *performance* of bourgeois rites governing the exchange ... with strangers ... of those gifts known in the West as civilities' (emphasis added, Cuddihy, 36). This was not, as Cuddihy puts it, a 'situated solidarity,' especially not for 'a "pariah people" closed out from social solidarity with respectable society because it was deemed wanting in respectability in the first place'; it was instead a 'mediated' solidarity that as such involved no direct, face-to-face, social interaction with one's fellow citizens. And the social skills for negotiating such solidarity had to be learned, not only at the cost of *appearing* to become bourgeois or 'passing' for such, but also at the price of abandoning or dissimulating one's ties to one's own culture (through assimilation) (36–7). Never mind the difficulties – the ordeal and the shame – of the latter; what was also especially shocking to those intellectuals analysing 'bourgeois' society was that what *it* termed civility was too often indistinguishable from the worst forms of hypocrisy – not to argue that 'bourgeois' society's rituals of exchange were outrightly pathological (on this, see MacDonald 1998). 'Lured by the promise of civil rights, Jews in the nineteenth century were disillusioned to find themselves not in the *pays légal* of a political society but in the *pays réel* of a civil society. Lured by the promise of becoming *citoyens*, they found that they had first to become *bourgeois*. The ticket of admission to European society was not civil rights but bourgeois rights' (Cuddihy, 38). Cuddihy's conceptual diagnosis of the resulting crisis is to situate the problem through the perspective of what he terms the rise of 'social appearance' (98ff.).

For Cuddihy, drawing broadly upon Parsons's sociology of modernity, society (the famed *Gesellschaft* of modernity) is the place where social appearances emerge (e.g., 'respectability') and become autonomous (i.e., 'subjectively opaque'). Like Aristotle's citizen, we are thus constrained to take appearances into account in our behaviour. Not only does behavioural mutation develop, it is also ethical: 'we own up to our accountability for our intentions, our actions, *and* the appearance of our intentions and actions. A whole new dimension – the appearance of the ethical – is born. It is a dimension trivialized by the rules of etiquette, but nonetheless real for all that' (99, emphasis in original). As Cuddihy puts it:

To become modern, then, is to become civil ... caretakers of our social appearance ... We [can] no longer shrug off these visual echoes of ourselves. This is the new 'social reality principle' ... these are the rituals of appearance ... the *rites de passage* that carry us from traditionary into bourgeois-Christian modernizing consciousness. With this circumspection of appearance, this practice of the presence of the generalized other as an inner-worldly ascetic, modernity is born. We intrude, we trespass by our nonintentional appearances into the lives of others in the *Gesellschaft*, as they intrude into ours. 'Forgive us our appearances,' Freud might as well have written, 'as we forgive those who have appeared against us.' (99–100)

His account is not only a profound dissection of what he terms specifically 'the Protestant Etiquette' (4) and the dramatic failure of its encounter with secularizing Judaism, as well as the fierce resistance of modernizing intellectuals who are clinging to the unity of society and culture, and in so doing pitting themselves against the 'inward assent to the disciplines of differentiation, and the practices of its rites, [that] may be viewed as the *paideia* of the West' (10). To us, crucially, this account offers an explanation of the unavoidably tragic character of the modern recourse to civility that other accounts we have discussed do not. If the problematic of social appearance is an unavoidable but difficult dimension of social modernity, due to the ambivalence it accords difference, this is because we appear to unknown others, intentionally or not, and in ways we cannot always control (e.g., as 'the Jew,' the 'long-haired hippie,' or 'the person of colour'). As such, the failure of the obligation of the reciprocity (the 'gift') of civility can only have disastrous consequences. In this sense, we are bound to one another, and so we interact *as* generalized others – we always cast a social shadow that is more than one's singular self – and unless those ties are regulated reciprocally by the rites of civility, we disregard our mutual bondedness literally at our peril.

At the same time, Cuddihy's analysis, while focusing specifically on the failed encounter of Gentile and Jew, makes a second signal, if more indirect, contribution to the dialectic of civility, particularly as it pertains to the intellectuals of late-modernizing, decolonizing nations' belated entry into modernity. As examples, one need only mention the Irish (like the Jewish one, also taking the form, since Swift, say, of a social question to be 'resolved' through extermination at worst, and forced mass emigration at best), the omnipresent 'race question' in the United States, and the modernization crises of traditional societies as exemplified in the telling title of Daniel Lerner's influential 1959 classic, 'The *Passing* of Traditional Societies' (our emphasis). In short, although he does not put it in quite these terms, Cuddihy offers a model for understanding how the once specifically Jewish Diaspora (the *Galut*) has since become a paradigmatic global diasporization in the struggle for belongingness-in-modernity. We will not go into the details of each subsequent 'passage,' and the associated traumas for both intellectuals and societies belatedly negotiating the transition from 'tradition' to 'modernity,' but Cuddihy insists that the 'function' of modernizing intellectuals is predominantly that of developing the ideologies of resistance *to* modernity. One could respond on the contrary that what modernizing intellectuals actually do is to offer a *critique of the civility deficits* of the transitional society. If one can take the 'Jewish' intellectual response to modernity as a critique of the pathologies of Gentile culture or civility, then similarly the responses of African-American intellectuals to the dominant civilities of white America is as much a formidable reproach to it as a redefinition of civility itself (see Robinson, 1999). So too with the intellectuals of colour of the former British colonies' rethinking nationalism and subalternity; or modernizing Islamic intellectuals' struggle to bring concepts such as civil society in line with a liberal tradition of interpretation of the *shari'a* (see Gellner 1994). In short, what has been described as 'talking back to the empire' is part of the dialectic of civility as a process of reciprocity. It is not just rolling over before the juggernaut of the dominant civility of the Protestant Etiquette which, as Cuddihy's study shows, was a failure of staggering proportions.

Finally, as Jeffrey Goldfarb (1998) has argued in a recent study of intellectuals in democratic society: 'Intellectuals are key democratic agents as they stimulate informed discussion about pressing social problems, fulfilling this role by cultivating *civility* in public life and promoting the *subversion* of restrictive common sense' (1). This too is part of the dialectic of civility, and it is not a role restricted to intellectuals in the dominant democracies only, nor is it a sociological claim for a special class- or status-privilege that should be accorded to intellectuals; rather, it is a claim about what intellectuals do 'when they are supportive of democratic life' (3). They provoke hopefully useful, 'serious talk about the problems we face ... Without such talk, democratic polities function undeliberately' (3), and, we might add, undeliberatively.

For all these reasons, then, we argue that there is too much at stake surrounding the complex of ideas, norms, and behaviours that civility encapsulates to be able to dismiss it. We have shown above many of the problems that the appeal to civility entails; we have also shown why, for all these problems, the question of civility, the performance of social appearance, and the resulting dialectic of recognition remains central to our contemporary 'societies of the spectacle,' which are ever more preoccupied with the implications of appearance, from image-politics to advertising, from the fragmentation of the mass media to the reappearance of knowledge as information and the seemingly infinite proliferation of shadows, terministic screens, discourses, and rhetoric that have come to occupy the explosion of appearance. Against this background, we move once more to the Canadian case in the next and final chapter as a particular illustration of the complexities of the analysis of a civil culture caught between tradition and modernity, and the ways in which many of the themes encountered in the present chapter have literally figured themselves out.

9

The Figures of Authority in
Canadian Civil Culture

In this concluding chapter of our study, we return to the specifics of the Canadian case, and attempt to weave together the various topics analysed in the chapters above in a coherent account of the figuration of the civil culture of Canada. Our preoccupations centre upon the various modes of 'performing power,' as these have manifested themselves since the European encounter with the First Peoples of the northern parts of the continent, and particularly as of the French regime in its post-*comptoire* manifestations in the seventeenth and eighteenth centuries. By performing power, we draw upon Robert Hariman's conception of political style as the artistry of power in a correspondence of classical rhetorical analysis and modern social theory. In Hariman's definition of political style – or, more broadly, what we term civil culture – the following elements are key: '(1) a set of rules for speech and conduct guiding the alignment of signs and situations, or texts and acts, or behavior and place; (2) informing practices of communication and display; (3) operating through a repertoire of rhetorical conventions depending on aesthetic reactions; and (4) determining individual identity, providing social cohesion, and distributing power' (1995: 187). Hariman goes on to add that 'the particular rules and the degree to which these rules are determinative of political outcomes will vary across and within particular cultures and events' (187). We might qualify this by noting that 'political outcomes' are only one part of the performance of power which, to the extent that it entails modes and styles of appearance, is to be understood as 'the recognition of the interpenetration of aesthetic and social codes' (187). One of the implications of this, in other words, is that the conventional, modernist account of power, with its emphasis on efficient deployment of force or control of coercive apparatuses is, at best, a partial explanation of the broader issue of the dynamics of the cultivation of appearances (Hariman 1995: 187–90).

With this background in mind, our study has identified five principal modes of the performance of appearance that have historically configured Canada's civil culture. We use these terms: 1) the 'apolitical public sphere' of French absolutism (seventeenth and eighteenth centuries); 2) 'the King's Two Bodies,' or the constitutional transformations of colonial British liberty (eighteenth and nineteenth centuries); 3) 'monarchical republicanism' as an attenuated form of popular sovereignty characteristic of democratic Canada (nineteenth and twentieth centuries), itself in conflict with 4) 'a large infusion of authority,' the legal-administrative style of post-Confederation linguistic dualism (nineteenth and twentieth centuries); and 5) and, finally, various ironic responses to the ongoing conflict between law and rhetoric in the struggle for alternatives modes of social appearance (eighteenth- to late twentieth-centuries). While each of these styles or modes corresponds predominantly to a given historical time-frame, each is also highly sedimented, layering atop one another chronologically and seeping into one another mutually. One does not fully replace the next but draws it into itself and so transforms elements of the previous style, producing a civil culture of profound continuities on the one hand, yet with gaps and disjuncts on the other. This should become clearer as the discussion of each style proceeds, aided in part by our return to the five paintings we first described in the 'Envoi,' paintings that can now be revealed as illustrative of the traits of each mode of appearance we examine respectively.

The 'Apolitical Public Sphere' of French Absolutism

De Tocqueville wrote in *The Old Regime and the French Revolution* ([1856] 1955): 'The physiognomy of a government can best be judged in its colonies, for there its characteristic traits usually appear larger and more distinct. When I wish to judge of the spirit and faults of the administration of Louis XIV, I must go to Canada. Its deformities are seen there as through a microscope' (57n24). This profound observation brings us back to the distinguishing traits of French absolutism and the ancien régime, and how these characteristics were modified in the colonial context of New France. In Habermas' account, what he terms 'the publicity of representation' of the ancien régime, which reached its highest point of refinement in the court of Louis XIV, was entirely *staged*, a performance that 'was not constituted as a social realm, that is, as a public sphere; rather it was something like a status attribute' (1991: 7). Citing Carl Schmitt, Habermas points out that this form of representation was characterized by 'an exalted sort of being ... Words like excellence, highness, majesty, fame, dignity, and honor seek to characterize this peculiarity of a being that is capable of representation' (cited on 7). This is a form of representation very different from the sense more familiar to us 'in which the members of a national assembly represent the nation or a lawyer represents his clients' (7); rather, it is thoroughly auratic and heraldic and so surrounds and endows the authority of the lord. It is a form of representation, Habermas goes on, 'wedded to personal attributes, such as insignia (badges and arms), dress (clothing and coiffure), demeanour (form of greeting and poise), and rhetoric (form of address and formal discourse in general) – in a word, a strict code of "noble" conduct' (8). Or, if one prefers, it is a political style, in Hariman's sense of a mode of enacting being, thoroughly saturated by the courtly. Two examples from New France, one from the late seventeenth century and the other from early twentieth century Quebec art, serve to illustrate this.

Frontenac who, unlike previous governors, insisted upon being addressed as 'High and Mighty Lord' (Eccles 1959: 33), attempted soon after his arrival at Quebec to introduce some of the pomp of the Court of Louis XIV to the colony. His commission had charged him to have 'the three orders of the country – clergy, nobles, and commons – as well as the local governors and officers of the Sovereign Council, swear a new oath of fealty' (Eccles 1969: 32). The ceremony took place on 23 October 1672, and was attended in Frontenac's estimate by over 1000 people. As Eccles puts it in his biography of 'the courtier governor': 'This [assembly] represented a feat of no small proportions, deserving to rank almost with the miracle of the loaves and the fishes, for the outside dimensions of the Jesuit church were only one hundred feet by thirty. Frontenac opened the proceedings with a speech from the throne which was obviously calculated to an audience on the other side of the Atlantic, for he larded it heavily with flattering references to Colbert and the undying glories of the king' (32). Eccles goes on to record that a party of Hurons who happened to be present were so impressed by the proceedings that they 'asked the governor the following day to go through the ceremony again for their benefit, and ... Frontenac informed the minister [Colbert] that he had been pleased to do so' (32).

The gathering together of the status orders of the colony, in appropriate dress and insignia (albeit in a rather cramped setting), the language of the courtier flattering the majesty of the king, and in particular the fact that this display of nobility was especially impressive to the Hurons present shows the performative effectiveness of what Hariman calls 'the courtly style' (Hariman 1995); that is, it was not only performance of the representation of power but, more important, a rhetorical mode of communication *across* cultures: the 'noble savages' were seemingly thoroughly impressed by the nobility of the performance. Contrast the difficulties of communication within the *same* culture stretching its rituals across the Atlantic, in the fact that the account of the performance did not impress Colbert who feared it came close to bringing ridicule upon the Crown (Eccles 1969: 32).

For a second example of the 'the courtly style' as a performance of appearance, we turn to Napoléon Bourrassa's *Apothéose de Christophe Colomb* (1906–12), the unfinished fresco that we first encountered in the Envoi. As we noted then, one of the striking traits of this painting, given the time of its composition, is its temporal schizophrenia – its attempt to bring together the courtly and the legal-administrative styles of performing power despite the visible differences in the physical posture and dress of the representatives of each. In Bourassa's baroque genealogy of 'the law' that culminates in the British North America Act, there is a clear spatial and stylistic break between the classical, almost heavenly figures hovering about the lintel at the top of the painting (the Muses, Genuises, Poets, and some 'historical' figures such as Cicero and Demosthenes) represented in neoclassical and neo-Renaissance styles, and the 'historical' moderns, beginning with Jacques Cartier, who form an S-shaped line of descent that ends at the bottom middle of the painting with Sir John A. Macdonald. The courtly, almost angelic figures in the top half of the painting literally float on clouds of glory, and represent the majesty and nobility, not so much of social rank here, as of the spiritual order of classical antiquity, with the odd intrusion of early modern poets such as Milton or scientists such as Galileo. By contrast, the 'moderns' with their more realistic (i.e., everyday) styles of dress, indicate an order of representation that is tilting away from the courtly to the flags, Napoleonic laurels, fortifications, and, above all, the clutching of texts, in which representation assumes its more familiar forms of *standing in* for 'the nation,' 'state authority,' and the like. As opposed to being embodiments of the nobility of the Spirit, they are embodiments of the contemporary sciences of the state. Frontenac's courtly proceedings represent the mode of performing power of French absolutism at its height – yet in the colonial translation, already fractured, as seen from France, by the upsurge of a new, more self-conscious order of performing power. Bourassa's painting, created at the end of the new order, attempts almost ludicrously to represent the courtly style, at a time when social appearance, as manifested in posture, dress, and documents such as texts of the law, has been irredeemably altered by a different mode of power's performance.

Our two examples, then, offer illustrations of the courtly style already in the course of undergoing transformation. In part this was a result of its extension to the colonies, and New France in particular, in which the 'orders' of representative publicness are no longer the same as those of the metropole, however one might want to appear to reproduce them. Into this, the appearance of new actors, such as the Huron, prove potentially disruptive to the serious pretensions of the display of European nobility, and risk making them seem ridiculous. And this at a time, especially in courtly Europe, when fear of 'the ridiculous' was a staple of contemporary theatre, as in Molière's *Les Précieuses ridicules*, for example. In this sense, Habermas is correct in remarking that even before control of the public sphere was wrested away from courtly authority, 'there had evolved under its cover a public sphere in apolitical form' (1991: 29). For Habermas this was the literary precursor of the public sphere providing the 'training ground for ... critical public reflection.' What would later become the bourgeois avant-garde of the educated middle-class first 'learned the art of critical-rational public debate' through its contact with 'the elegant world' of courtly-noble society (29). Also, to the extent that the modern state apparatus was in the process of becoming independent of the monarch's personal sphere, courtly-noble society similarly separated itself from the court to form its counterpoise in 'the town' as the life centre of civil society, especially in the world of letters of the coffee houses and the salons (29–30), the growing centres of what Arditi terms 'informational capital' (1998: 65).

As Arditi has remarked in his *Genealogy of Manners* (1998), drawing upon Norbert Elias's conception of civility, one of the profound distinctions between France and England is that in the former 'the absolutist tendencies of the *res civile* became profoundly set' (121), and the contradiction between the affirmation and renunciation of self became ever deeper, whereas in England individuation received greater expression, resulting in the transformation of civility into etiquette, as we saw in the previous chapter. The French emphasis upon the *res civile* can best be understood as the secularization of the military element at the heart of feudal nobility, and its combination with the technologies of self-control that marked *courtoisie*, as these transformed themselves into 'the exclusive focus [o]n the civil plane of power ... and the moment of apotheosis in the affirmation of the social order through an affirmation of the person of the king' (95; also 76–9). The resulting total subordination to 'the civil plane of power' established a moral order for whom the *res civile* had become the dominant criterion by which to interpret, judge, negotiate, and relate the daily experience of men and women. While it should not be confused with the entirety of the infrastructure of social relations, it was 'constituent of that infrastructure, helping concretize its foundational tendencies, embodying the specific logic in whose terms people positioned themselves in relation to others and attributed similarity and difference among them' (95). Furthermore, this order of the *res civile* was congruent and coincident with the political order. Its greatest strength, as Arditi points out, was that the insularity of the court contributed to the perpetuation of the collective self of the nobility and served as a protective layer around its centre of power, the monarch. But its greatest weakness would also be that it left vast areas of social practice beyond the sway of monarchical hegemony (79).

From the above, we can see emerging the traits of a civil culture in a continuum not dissimilar to de Tocqueville's observations regarding the continuities of the ancien régime *by* the Revolution. These give us a civil culture characterized by the privileging of rhetorical excess (in the form of flattery or combativeness), by an *esprit de finesse* in upholding the *res civile* as the standard for making distinctions of similarity as well as difference, by the continued exclusion of women from selfhood as they remain objects of chivalrous combat or seduction in a re-emphasis on the masculine element of the definition of the civil, by the conflation of the civil with the political order, and finally by the exclusion of large areas of social practice from the above. In this sense, the Revolution can be seen not as a break with subordination to the *res civile*, but rather as its radical extension. Also, leaving the French Revolution aside for now, one can see as well that these traits would deeply imprint, in the main, the civil culture of New France, especially here in Habermas's sense of 'a public sphere in apolitical form' – but less in the sense of the literary experiments with interiority of an eventual bourgeois avant-garde, and far more literally as the absence of politics outside the very limited realm of the colonial courtly, although also far more strongly in the conflation of the realm of the civil with the political order. It will be the British, the British colonial experience in the Thirteen Colonies and the local responses to it, that introduce the political to the apolitical civil culture of the ancien régime in New France.

The King's Two Bodies: Constitutional Metaphysics

When France ceded Canada to England in the Treaty of Paris, its subjects found themselves not only with a new king, but with a new metaphysics of kingship. While French legal theory distinguished between the king and his office, the English subscribed to the more complex, and quasitheological doctrine of the 'King's Two Bodies.' The concept, developed in medieval jurisprudence, established the identity of British sovereign authority.

The King has two Capacities, for he has two Bodies, the one whereof is a Body natural, consisting of natural members as every other Man has, and in this he is subject to Passions and Death as other Men are; the other is a Body politic, and the Members thereof are his Subjects, and he and his Subjects compose the Corporation, as Southcote said, and he is incorporated with them, and they with him, and he is the Head, and they are the Members, and he has the sole Government of them. (Kantorowicz 1957: 13 citing Justice Southcote 1608)

The subtleties of this legal fiction were, of course, not immediately relevant to the king's new subjects. The mores of the ancien régime could continue beyond the cession because, at least initially, these subjects were no more participants in a political realm than they had been previously. Subjects were not citizens in the modern sense. Sovereign authority was embodied in a king and enacted through a legal-administrative apparatus. Nevertheless, the king as a body natural was not sovereign, but rather he was sovereign only as a body politic – one that he both headed and embodied, and which furthermore subsumed his body natural. As we saw in chapter 4, and will treat more conceptually here, this curious metaphysic gave rise to a style of deferral, but also to a norm of prudential administration and, somewhat paradoxically, to an obligation toward deliberative reason. As such, this doctrine, as a particularly British principle, set the stage for the constitutional conflicts that would follow.

Kantorowicz traces the concept of the king's two bodies to medieval legal scholars seeking to account for the king's authority during the twelfth and thirteenth centuries, with the emergence of secular authority and law. In both England and on the continent, this new order challenged ecclesiastical hegemony. The king did not rule by divine right nor was he inhabited by a divine spirit. The rhetorical-legal task of this new order was to develop a secular language that not only legitimated and naturalized the power institutionally conferred upon the king, as a mortal man, but also placed certain limits upon its exercise. That is to say, the very idea of kingship would be a legal one; legality would distinguish kings from tyrants. The rhetorical figuration of authority in law, rather than might, required a metaphysics of sovereignty that legal scholars found in theological reasoning. Theologians had sought to explain how God could be the law-giver and yet remain 'within' the law, how Christ could be a man and remain divine, and how God could indeed be three persons. Similarly, constitutional theory had to distinguish between kings and tyrants, account for how a king, while a man, became something greater through his kingship, and develop the relationship between king and kingdom. The answer was to figure the king as a protodivine subject.

The courtly style that animated Frontenac's spectacle, and organized the basic elements of the governance of Canada's early colonial period, emerged from two metaphysical principles that establish the king as sovereign. The first concerns the nature and the second the basis for the king's authority. First, the king was not a mere man. To be king was to embody a role within the realm, itself figured in corporate terms. King and kingdom, king and subjects, formed a corporation modelled after theological accounts of Christ's relation to the Church. The Church, the community of the faithful, was figured and indeed incorporated as the 'mystical body of Christ' (195). Thus, as Kantorowicz explains, 'Baldus, for example, defined *populus*, the people, as a mystical body. He held that a *populus* was not simply the sum of the individuals of the community, "but men assembled into one mystical body" ..., a body or corporation to be grasped intellectually, since it was not a real or material body' (210). The king, of course, was figured as this body's head, just as Christ was head of the mystical body of the Church.

This doctrine rendered king and subject consubstantial with the realm. The affection that kings would express toward their subjects parallels the love Christ expressed for his flock. King and subject are bound in a relation of mutual obligation, as are parts of a common body. As he loves and cares for his subjects, so he loves and cares for his realm, which is part of him. As they express their love for their king, subjects not only engage in a ritual form of debasement, but reenact and reanimate the bond between themselves, realm, and king. There is more, however, for a king does not share Christ's divinity. What authorizes his rule? That answer as well is developed in medieval legal theory. While not a god, the king is more than a man. He holds his place in the realm because he is the legitimate law-giver, the incarnation of law itself. For John of Salisbury, the 'king' (like God) is neither above nor below the law, but he embodies it, being the 'Image of Equity' or the 'Image of Justice' (Kantorowicz 94). His authority is legitimate. He is not a tyrant because, while his will is law, it is only so as he is a *persona publica*, a category of subject derived from Roman law. One can speculate that the king, as a private person, would be subject to the law, but that question was not at issue. The salient issue was how the king, or 'prince,' as a public person could be the law-giver, and thus 'not bound by the ties of Law,' while remaining the 'Law's servant' (95, citing Salisbury) and so subject to the law as well. Salisbury resolved the matter by figuring the 'Prince' as the 'very Idea of Justice' (96). The prince would be the law made flesh. The prince as a public person cannot violate the law because as a public person he is animated by the 'Idea of Justice,' the principle that infuses law. He is not a Nietzschean law-giver. The law is more than his will. Rather, his will is the very instantiation of the principle from which law springs. As Kantorowicz puts it, 'Not the Prince rules, but Justice rules through or in a Prince who is the instrument of Justice and, though Salisbury does not quote Justinian to that effect, is at the same time the *lex animata*' (97). This sounds tautological, and in a certain manner it is of course, except that the law itself is not singular. Law is both natural and positive, and the prince is thus between the two.

In both France and England therefore, the king's body had a transcendent character. While the king can die, the King cannot, for royal authority lives on in a new king. As such, authority takes rest in and radiates from the king's body, through what is virtually a theological mystery. This mystery structures the court, with its pomp and circumstance, but does more as well. It anchors the king's authority as the centre of the realm. As such, Frontenac's staging could be effective even in the king's absence, for that absence was a centre with the aura of a god. There is more to king than court, however. The courtly style that Hariman describes does not account for all of the king's performances. While the courtly rhetorical aesthetic maintains the king-centred hierarchical structure, '[that] hierarchy culminate[s] in silence' (Hariman 1995: 63). Monarchy is not only silent, however, for it must also govern. To do so, as we have seen in chapters 4 and 5, the courtly style has been complemented by what we term a 'monarchial style,' directed not toward courtiers, but toward subjects. King and subject are both 'addressees' of an obligation. Subjects are subject to the King's will precisely because he embodies Justice, even while the king himself, as agent, is subject to the principle that takes up residence within him and suffuses his being. Furthermore, both are subject to the well-being of the realm with which they are consubstantial. This accounts, in part, for the norms of deference and deferral that we observed in chapter 4, as manifest in particular in the complementary genres of petition and proclamation or decree. However, as we saw as well, the performance of monarchical governance was also, particularly during the British period, marked by gestures of legitimation and organized around the importance of prudence, itself linked to notions of equity. Legitimations, statements of justification, were required both because royal authority was fundamentally rhetorical, that is secured symbolically, and so dependent upon continued reanimation, and because natural law and justice had by then come to be understood as transcendental ideas consubstantial with reason itself. As Frederick II wrote to the people of Rome: 'For although our imperial majesty is free from all laws, it is nevertheless not altogether exalted from the judgment of Reason, herself the Mother of all Law' (in Kantorowicz 1957: 106).

This does not, of course, guarantee that the king's reason could be challenged. Reason is not necessarily deliberative or communicative, in Habermas's sense. Kantorowicz observes that 'the interpretation of reason might easily depend on the Prince alone. Indeed, less than a century later, this semi-divine *Ratio* will become a *ratio regis et patriae*, synonymous with Reason of State, and what formerly was a goal in itself will turn into a tool, a mere instrument of statecraft' (Kantorowicz 1957: 107). Even so, kingly will becomes reasoned will, and governance finds its rhetorical legitimation in reason-giving as an act of deferral to the principle of reason, even if not to procedures of reasoning nor the substance of the reasons themselves. Finally, prudence, the third element of the monarchial style, is a consequence of way legal authority was invested in the king's body. The monarch is the *lex animata*. Writing between 1277 and 1279, Aquinus's student, Aegidus Romanus, referring to Aristotle's *Nichomachean Ethics*, explained: 'The king or prince is a kind of Law, and the Law is a kind of king or prince. For the Law is a kind of inanimate prince; the prince, however, a king of animate Law. And in so far as the animate exceeds the inanimate the king or prince must exceed the Law' (in Kantorowicz 1957 134).

Aegidus thus concludes that 'it is better to be ruled by a king than by the Law.' Of course, this was not Aristotle's conclusion. Nevertheless, even while favouring rule by law, Aristotle recognized the need for a prudent prince or judge, who could apply the law to particular cases and so do justice to the matter at hand. In medieval legal theory, the need for a judge was a consequence of the distinction between justice as an idea and law as a rule. Kantorowicz explains:

Baldus, in one of his ethically most high-toned legal opinions, talked abut the Prince who surrenders himself to Justice. 'That is, to the Substance of what is good and right; for the person who judges may err, but Justice never errs.' And yet (Baldus pointed out) 'wanting a person, Reason and Justice act nothing'; they are incapacitated without the personator of their substance, wherefore, if controversy arises, 'wanting an official dignitary Justice is buried.' (Kantorowicz 1957: 142)

Because prudence is conceptually necessary as a mediation between abstract principle and the particularity of any case, a rhetoric and appearance of prudence was necessary for the continuing legitimation of executive authority in the absence of some other transcendent principle, such as divine right or popular sovereignty. Monarchs, in other words, were constrained to enact their authority in a manner that makes present that they are not tyrants, that they rule by right and duty, and that their will and actions make present what is best.

None of this is unique to the British Constitution. Thus, the subjects of the ancien régime could quite easily adapt themselves to the new order. What was unique to the British Constitution, however, was the doctrine of the King's Two Bodies as a peculiar adaptation of the principle of the monarch as a *persona publica* animated by the spirit of the law (446). Under that doctrine, while the king ruled, his will was not fully his own. Writing at the same time as Frederick II, Bracton also considered the king to be both above and below the law. However, while Frederick II had resolved the question regarding the limit to royal will by identifying it with natural law and reason as ideas, Bracton renders these material by locating them in the deliberative world of the king's council: '[What has pleased the Prince is Law] – that is, not what has been rashly presumed by the [personal] will of the king, but what has been rightly defined by the *consilium* of his magnates, by the king's authorization, and after deliberation and conference concerning it' (cited in Kantorowicz 1957: 152). In France, the king was understood to have all the rights of his kingdom in 'his breast,' and his council served only to give it voice. In England, the matter was reversed, as Kantorowicz elaborates. 'Contrariwise, to Bracton, the councillors do not appear as the "mouth of the Prince," but it was rather the Prince, or king, who appeared as the "mouth of the council," who promulgated laws "as he pleased" only after discussion with the magnates and on their advice; that is, the king's pleasure is Law only insofar as it is "an authoritative promulgation by the king of what the magnates declare to be the ancient custom"' (154).

This constitutional metaphysic established a very curious dynamic between the sovereign and sovereign authority. In France, the state is an apparatus, an impersonal extension of the king's will. In England, the apparatus of governance is in a sense consubstantial with the king. The monarch has two bodies, one natural, the other as king-in-council. Sovereignty rests with the king-in-council, or later with Parliament, conceived as the trinity of king, lords, and commons. This formulation has two fundamental consequences: First, it limits royal authority. The British Constitution is not absolutist because the king is not the judge of his own reason. Second, as the regal will is formed in council, prudence becomes not only a norm of governance but of government and law because the king-in-council is the *lex animata*. That is to say, the virtue of prudence that was understood to be inherent to the king as a public person now inheres to his council, his government, which remains personified. The king appears as a public person only in and through the council, which itself can only appear as his manifestation, and which therefore is expected to act and enact regally.

This doctrine had consequences. First, it gives rise to the sovereignty of Parliament, a place animated by political debate. In its most extreme form, it permitted constitutional rebellion. In 1642, Parliament battled the armies of Charles I, 'king body natural' in the 'name and by the authority of Charles I, King body politic.' As the Declaration of the Lords and Commons of 27 May 1642 made quite clear, royal authority can be exercised by the king's ministers against the king in his own person. While the British legacy to Canada is 'counter-revolutionary,' the British Constitution contains a 'republican' element that can be radical when the king does not act prudently, that is to say in accordance with the deliberative reason of his council (21). There is a fine (even if revolutionary) line between the will of the king-in-Parliament and the will of 'the people.' More modestly, the quest for responsible government can be understood as the process of developing a local king, a king-in-Canada, whose will could be counterpoised to that of the king-in- (British or Imperial) Parliament. While the Canadian people would not be sovereign in the American sense, Canada could become sovereign as a separate realm, with its own institutional embodiment of the king. Indeed, as we noted in chapter 8, David Smith argues that a characteristic of Canada's constitution is that the monarchy is furthermore subdivided because it also resides in the executive of each province, giving rise to what he terms a 'compound monarchy.' Second, and if less dramatic, still of equal importance, was the expectation that the king-in-council and its agents would act prudently. Prudence is an embodied virtue. As we saw in chapters 4 and 5, the constitutional accommodations that England provided its new subjects, and London's initial remonstration of Macdonald in the first phase of the Riel affair, were articulated in terms of the monarch's embodied concerns. However, under the principle of the king-in-council, the monarch's feelings as expressed were not exactly his own. The king-in-council, speaking for the king's body politic affected the monarchial style, a prudential and embodied style. The king-in-council, the executive as an institution, came to speak as if its words were anchored in the body natural, as if it remained the *lex animata*. Thus, as we saw, governors were explicitly instructed to act prudently, even an expectation of prudent governance suffused the rhetoric addressed to the Crown.

The transition from colonial administration to responsible government and Confederation proceeded through an interaction of these rhetorical norms and styles. There is a rhetoric of petition and proclamation based in courtly deference, with its concomitant subordination to duty, as well as a deliberative discourse of reason regarding the laws and the commonweal. Both these rhetorics are addressed to the king, as *persona publica*, whose embodied presence anchors the system, but each respectively privileges one of the two aspects of his being as *lex animata*. The first rhetoric, animated by figures of love, is addressed to the king as coloured or influenced by his body natural. The second rhetoric, which gains preeminence with the emergence of parliamentary institutions, is addressed to the king as a subject of deliberative reason and thus the law. One does not exclude the other. Thus, as we saw in our discussion of the Confederation debates, the two were complementary. Indeed, responsible government and Confederation required that king-in-council yield to a new body, or more precisely be 'split' into (at least) two bodies, one to remain in England, and the other to appear in British North America. Such an event could only be a gift, and not surprisingly, a rhetoric of affection and deferral supplemented arguments as to the prudence of refiguring the king's body itself.

The 'Monarchical Republican' Style of Contemporary Canada

We suggested in the previous chapter that one way of understanding the paradoxes that have configured Canada's civil culture was that the style of governance that came to prevail by the late twentieth century, in ways still difficult to grasp because paradoxical, was one of a fusion of monarchical principles (including the co-sovereignty of the provinces) with republican ones, especially in the form of a democratic populist rhetoric whose form would be principally manifested in parliamentary debate. As we have also said, both monarchical and republican elements remain difficult to 'see' – the former in David E. Smith's sense that the principle of the Crown is largely 'invisible' and ill-understood; and the latter because Canadian republicanism had to adopt a discursive cloaking (as the very word was tainted by association with the anarchic republic to the south).

In both cases part of the problem concerns the disjunct between public speech and private worlds, a disjunct that is especially complex in a putatively bilingual country. This theme has preoccupied us throughout this study. Smith notes, for instance, that it could be said of Canada that there is 'a public tradition' (as opposed to a re-public, but very similar to it), whose sources are English, and there are 'private traditions,' whose sources are not-English (1999: 19–22). One could just as well, as we have, argue the contrary: namely, that the source of the public tradition is, in fact, French (the *res civile*) and it is the private traditions that are English. But this sort of game of priorities can get confusing or tiresome. More important than debates over origins is the significance of the figures that did appear. It is worth noting that the figures of republicanism, while hidden in some respects, were blatantly bold-faced in others.

Two examples make our case here: In the recent collection by Ajzenstat et al., *Canada's Founding Debates*, James Johnston of the Nova Scotia House of Assembly is seen pondering, on 28 March 1864, the 'will o' the wisp' question of what makes Canadians different from Americans. He asks: 'What is it that separates us in *form of speech, or habit, or desire*, from our neighbours in the republic? Every person knows that there is a difference – we feel it ourselves' (168, emphasis added). But stating that difference is a trickier matter, especially given that 'we are almost as republican, I might say, in all our institutions.' Given, then, 'the presence of strong material influences that are continually operating' on Canadians, how are 'we' to preserve a difference that 'exists in sentiment, and not in any material or real form? ... Are we at last to be absorbed into a pure ... republicanism, or are we to remain animated by all *the feelings* that republicans enjoy, with the distinctions that are created by those sentiments that exist in older countries where monarchical and aristocratic institutions obtain?' (169, emphasis added). Johnston himself has no answer to the problems he raises: 'I take it for granted that the future of the British American provinces is at this moment, and must be, shrouded in mystery' (1999, 168–9). Our second example we draw once more from Napoléon Bourassa's *Apothéose*, that baroque unfinished fresco that literally 'figures out' the genealogy of Canada's civil culture. And here, in the procession of what we earlier termed the historical (as opposed to poetic) figures that culminate in Macdonald, Moses-like, holding the BNA Act over his heart, we also find some of the founding figures of the American Republic: William Penn, Lafayette, Washington, and Franklin. They are here, together with Papineau, Mackenzie, Balwin, and Lafontaine, the lineage of Reformers we encountered above with Romney: the decentralizers of Confederation, the Canadian Republicans.

In what sense has Canada been marked by, and still manifests, a republican moment? Not all would share Johnston's perception. Writing at the close of the following century, David E. Smith argues rather that Canada's institutions and political traditions consistently and markedly have been anti-republican. Specifically, Smith argues that in Canada, sovereignty has always rested with the Crown, rather than in an extra-legal 'people'; that government has not been conceived of as an expression of the popular will of equal individual citizens, but as the representation and management of competing groups and interests; and finally that Canada's constitutions have never been 'balanced,' as is favoured in republican theory, but have always concentrated power in the executive (1999). As such, Smith dismisses the Canadian Republicans as losers: the history of Canada can be seen as a *defeat* of republican ideas, whether expressed by Papineau and the 92 Resolutions, by William Lyon Mackenzie, or as we saw in chapter 5, by Louis Riel. Smith's argument is convincing as far as it goes: Canada remains a monarchy of sorts but, by that standard, one can question whether the Unites States is truly a republic. Certainly, as Hariman points out, the republican sentiments that animated the American founding did not result in a classical republic. Indeed, one could even argue that the Americans ditched the monarchy only to reinvent it in elected form. But perhaps Johnston was not that far off the mark if republicanism is understood as a sensibility rather than an institutional arrangement. When we broaden the idea of 'republicanism' to include rhetorical traditions and styles, the matter is quite different. As Hariman argues, political styles are not fully determined by constitutional or structural arrangements, but are a rhetorical resource that can be reanimated in performance.[1] Furthermore, from that perspective, republicanism and monarchy are not necessarily incompatible. Republicanism is not fully an institutional question, but also a style of governance based in a kind of speech.

As Fortescue observed in the fifteenth century, England, even then, was ruled 'politically,' by the body politic, in contrast to France, which was ruled 'regally,' by the king alone (Kantorowicz 1957: 223). The concept of the king-in-Parliament, fundamental to the idea of 'political' rule, favours the 'republican' style to the degree that Parliamentary debate, particularly in the House of Commons, plays a role in the forming of the 'king's' will. From this perspective, responsible government itself can be seen as a monarchical adaptation of a republican idea, and the republican style marks Parliamentary debate. While the American model did not take hold in Canada, republican sentiments animated the 1837–8 rebellions in the Canadas, which themselves rendered responsible government inevitable and necessary. This is what Bourassa suggests in his fresco. Without a republican countertradition, Canada would not have its current constitutional form, and that countertradition furthermore remains available as a means of countering central authority, as it was in Riel's time. As Smith admits, republican ideas not only animate Quebec debates over language, and are part and parcel of the sovereignty project, they also inform the Reform Party's advocacy of Senate reform and the weakening of party discipline in the House of Commons (1999: 140, 173). Furthermore, while the degree to which Canada's 1867 constitution is structurally 'republican' remains a subject of a debate, and regardless of whether James Johnston was correct to say that Canada was almost republican 'in its institutions,' G.E. Cartier's promise of a 'new nationality,' like Johnston's recognition of both an identity and difference with respect to the United States, gestured toward a polity-in-itself, a civil society, almost a 'people' seeking the monarch's recognition. These gestures reveal fundamantally republican sentiments, even if they were mediated by the Crown and the British Constitution.

In addition, one must recognize not only that there have been Canadian republicans, but that much of Canada's political discourse is marked by Hariman's 'republican' (or 'civic humanist') style. For Hariman, the republican style is not a matter of antimonarchical sentiments, but of parliamentary manners and performative norms, such as 'the appreciation of rhetorical technique, the norm of consensus, attention to the presentation and discernment of character, the equation of polity with public talk, an architectonic rule of decorum, a cultivation of liberal education, and the like' (Hariman 1995: 125). For an understanding of this style and its characteristics, Hariman examines Cicero's letters to Atticus, in which the former 'conflat[es] political activity with the compositional techniques of public address' (102). Indeed, while it might well be that republican ideas have not found materialization in constitutional arrangements, and serve only as a basis for critique, republican gestures quite commonly mark Canadian political oratory. Indeed, Wilfrid Laurier's rise to prominence is commonly attributed in large measure to his rhetorical virtue, particularly when defending Riel.

In fairness to Smith, however, one mark of republicanism is that the people can 'appear' outside of Parliament. The American Constitution, for example, makes reference to the people directly, not only as incorporated in the several states. The British Constitution, and in most respects the Canadian as well, does not grant the polity such an autonomous existence. In other words, while the republican style appears in Parliament because of the importance that the doctrine of the King's Two Bodies places upon deliberative reason, it is not granted such a place in civil society itself. It is perhaps for this reason that two aspects of the republican style identified by Hariman, the predilection for symbolic foundings, and the constitution's precariousness and dependence upon each rhetorical moment, have not found their counterpart here. Furthermore, even in Parliament, the republican ideal of spirited debate animated by civic virtue finds itself, as Smith is at pains to point out, hampered by the executive's command of a parliamentary majority. The law, and the Crown, serve to contain the excess, the noise, and also some of the sympathy and life that the republicanism style offers.

The Legal-Administrative Style

Confederation secured a Canadian king-in-council. However, it did so at the expense of the king (or queen)'s body natural and his (her) influence upon the body politic. That is to say, under Confederation both prudence and the identification of subjects, now citizens, with the realm become increasingly strained. This development also had its roots in the metaphysics of the British Constitution as it played out in Canada, and specifically the principle of the Crown. As Kantorowicz explains, a further and fundamental element of the doctrine of the king's two bodies was the idea of the invisible Crown. The Crown was a corporate entity, more abstract than either king or kingdom. There was of course a visible crown, placed upon the king's head during the coronation ceremony. The invisible Crown, however, encompassed 'all the royal rights and privileges indispensable for government of the body politic' (337). The Crown, as principle, represents the 'fundamental rights and claims of the country' (347). The Crown is more abstract than the king-in-council, for it stands as the very principle of law and sovereignty. As the principle of sovereignty itself, the Crown even today possesses inalienable property, and defends inalienable legal rights (381). The Crown was not the same as the 'state' as the concept evolved on the Continent in the sixteenth-century, however, for it incorporates all those within the realm, similar in meaning to the 'people' in American political thought. Even so, the Crown cannot be easily distinguished from the king, for if the Crown is a principle, it requires a king for its actualization. Under British constitutional law, the Crown remains a 'minor' whose guardian is the king. The wearing of the crown symbolizes the materialization of the invisible Crown's duties and prerogatives in the king, who finds his will through Parliament itself. Of course, even so, the king, in his body natural, can fail the Crown; Richard II, for example, was charged with 'crimes against the Crown' (369).

David Smith (1995) argues that the invisible Crown is the 'first principle of Canadian government.' Smith has a less metaphysical understanding of 'invisible' than the one offered by Kantorowicz. For Smith, the Crown is invisible in the sense that it is an unseen and largely unknown principle that in Canada has conferred considerable discretionary powers upon the political executive (11). We will note the implications of Smith's remarks below, particularly as they relate to executive prerogatives, patronage, and the particulars of governance. For the moment, however, we want to emphasize that Canadian Confederation resulted in a symbolic splitting of what previously could usually only be distinguished analytically. While Smith is not primarily preoccupied with the symbolic functions of the Crown, he nevertheless notes: 'There has never been in Canada the peculiarly personal relationship between [embodied] Crown and Parliament which lies at the heart of British politics and which was symbolized until 1867 in the practice of Parliament's dissolving upon the death of the sovereign' (115).[2] What Smith's observation suggests is that the king or queen's body natural came to have little significance in Canada's constitutional culture. Of course, the emergence of responsible government meant that the Crown found its expression through a king-in-council, or to be more historically precise, a queen-in-council in which neither the monarch nor her representative actually participated. More importantly from our perspective is that the origin of prudential governance, the conflation of the king's body natural with the body politic, no longer obtains. Not only is the Crown invisible, so is the king-in-council, being but the instrument and manifestation of the executive.

The Riel case, in all its complexity, testifies to the loss of monarch from the Canadian constitutional and rhetorical landscape. Macdonald's government did not approach the question of the Northwest prudentially. Its law lacked the animating principle that legitimated royal authority. While formally the doctrine of the king's two bodies could serve as a constitutional fiction legitimating the authority of the Crown, it was increasingly incapable of infusing governance with a regal ethos. The Crown was not only invisible, but also disembodied. The medieval normative ontology yielded increasingly to a modern and positive conception of law, but without a fully developed alternative 'modern' metaphysical principle to take its place. This is part of what renders Riel such a tragic figure. The Crown is not animated by Queen Victoria's obligations to her subjects. Metaphysically, but neither legally nor constitutionally, the Crown has become akin to the state, except that it still holds within itself the principle of sovereignty. Under the British Constitution, while sovereignty rested in the Crown, the Crown itself was an incorporation of the realm. Under Canadian Confederation, the Crown remained, but no longer as the incorporation of the realm, but instead only as the abstract principle of legality itself.

The Americans, as is well known, dispensed with the Crown. Their break was not so radical, however, as to eliminate the metaphysical structure in which it held a place. Rather, in lieu of the Crown, they proclaimed 'the People,' and established a balanced constitution based on the division of the legislative, executive, and judicial functions of government. The tempering influence of the monarch, the *lex animata*, was replaced at least in principle by this division, and in particular by the autonomy of the legislative branch. In Canada, the law was not so tempered institutionally. A distant monarch and the subordination of the House of Commons to the executive both favoured the loss of the *lex animata* in favour of positive law. Subsequent to Confederation, both the monarchical and republican styles found themselves subordinated by a sovereign and often unfeeling Crown. To fully appreciate this loss, we turn once again to two images.

Let us start with Charles Huot's *Esquisse de la première séance de la Chambre d'Assemblée* ca. 1910, also sometimes referred to as *le débat sur la langue*, an episode that we discussed in chapter 3. What immediately strikes the eye is that this is a scene of some obvious animation – not just because of the body language of the orator, with his arm outstretched in the classic elocutionary gesture signifying that something of great import is being said, but also by the surrounding press of bodies in the Chamber, sitting, standing, milling about, leaning in closely to hang on the words spoken by the orator, and the crowd in the packed galleries above in the upper left, and the more indistinct sense of crowded background figures in the middle rear quadrant of the painting. Something of significant public importance is indeed going on! This is a scene that could easily be mistaken for equivalent (in fact, it is almost identical to) representations of the constitutional debates at the Philadelphia Convention of 1787, or those of 4 August 1789, when the French aristocracy clamorously renounced its feudal privileges.

Contrast this excited scene of the performance of power as a deeply shared rhetorical moment with Robert Harris's 1883 cartoon for the meeting of the delegates of British North America to settle the terms of Confederation at Quebec in October, 1864. This is one of a series of similar cartoons, sketches and paintings that Harris executed of *The Fathers of Confederation*, and that since then has been replicated on postage stamps and in countless high-school history textbooks. It is, in effect, *the* representation of Confederation. But note the differences between this and Huot's celebration of parliamentary oratory. The Fathers are frozen, speechless, as if posing for one of those early photographs that required sitters not to move for some fifteen or twenty minutes or risk spoiling the take. But it is not a photograph, and though Macdonald stands in the focal centre of the drawing, he is not speaking. He is perhaps about to speak, or has just finished speaking, as he holds a text in his right hand. But other Fathers are also standing, both to his left and to his right, so Macdonald has no greater proxemic importance here relative to the others; above all, *no one* is speaking. Some of the delegates are reading; others look simply bored; some stare in the direction of Harris putatively sketching; others just gape at nothing in particular. We cannot tell what is going on here; obviously a meeting of some kind, with a touch of *gravitas*, but there are no visual clues about the reasons for the meeting or its importance. Not quite: in the middle top centre there is a cartouche written by Harris, dated December 1916, which explains that this was the original preparatory drawing for the painting *The Fathers of Confederation* that was destroyed in the fire that burned down the Parliament Buildings in Ottawa earlier that year.

The point about the Harris drawing is that while it does represent historical persons at what was a significant moment of agreement over the terms of Confederation (the Quebec Resolutions), it is, one could say, an entirely *textual* form of representation: what matters are the terms of the text of the Resolutions that perhaps Sir John A. is holding; what matters is Harris's cartouche as the other text one requires to know what the drawing is about. In itself, that is, as a visual representation, it is stunningly mute: there are no gestures, there is no speech, no body language that tells us anything other than that a meeting took place. To know more about this meeting, whether it was successful or not, whether the men shown here did more than attend a meeting together, one has to turn to other texts to find out. Huot's painting, by its depiction of the figures shown, clearly lets us know, both directly and indirectly by reference to similar moments in the art of parliamentary life, that something significant is going on, that it has to do with what is being spoken, that it is a celebration of public speech, of the rhetoric of parliamentary oratory that affects not only those foregrounded but those in the background who have come to listen to what is being said. All of these elements grow in significance once one learns that what was being debated at this first session was the use of French in the Assembly. By contrast, Harris's cartoon is visually hermetic; aside from a depiction of the physical appearance of the delegates represented, it is a reference primarily to a variety of texts: the text in Macdonald's right hand and the other texts on the table that his left hand is touching; the newspaper or proclamation that a delegate on the left is reading to himself; the books on the table at the bottom left; the book a delegate is holding open on his lap. In a word, it is an index to the open-ended textualities of Canadian constitutionalism, as the *hors-texte* that frames this drawing in particular and all the traditions of textual redaction, analysis, and interpretation, and the enormous discourse of constitutional law in the Canadian context, that both preceded the meeting depicted and has so voluminously proliferated subsequently. It is in the gap between these two representations – between rhetoric and law, between public speech and the silent secrecies of the text, between the French language and what it stands for and what its place is to be, both in public space and in the texts of Canadian constitutionalism – that develops the legal-administrative style that preoccupies us in this section, and that arises as a means of managing all the gaps just enumerated.

The answers that emerged, however, we are suggesting (especially as regards the central government and its managerial-administrative style) prepared a way to render *some dimensions* of these problems manageable: they did so by laying the groundwork of a constitutional and legal culture in the form of anti-American nation-building that degraded French-Canada to a mere cultural peculiarity. The post-Confederation legal-administrative style did attempt through the national codification of the criminal law, to establish an administration of law 'on the basis of the antecedent determination of legality in its own right,' to use Richard D. Winfield's language, although he is not talking about Canada as such, but of the principles involved (see 1995: 75). But this was achieved by overpoliticizing the administration of justice through executive control over judicial appointments (a supine Supreme Court, etc.) in a high-handed manner that, as Romney points out, culminated in Trudeau's 1982 'patriation' of the Constitution back from Westminster without Quebec's assent or signature. On the other hand, through such measures as the Royal Commission on Biculturalism and Bilingualism, by attempting to manage the French-English cultural duality, the Trudeau government did try to make Canada 'bilingual from sea to sea' – too little, too late, some might say. This legal-administrative style attempted to constitute from above a Canadian civil society in the image of the central state, in a forcing of cultural nationalism that some observers see as a perilous overinvestment in nationalism to the point of near-suicide (Goodenough 1998).

One might also say that in such endeavours as the attempt to micromanage into being a form of civil society that was really a political creation of the centralizing state of law, the weight of history was more favourable to arbitrariness and undemocratic methods than the contrary. The apolitical public sphere inherited from the French regime, the British mode of rule by parliamentary oligarchy, the fractured legal culture, part-French, part-English, that was never permitted to form a new whole – all of these institutional antecedents helped constitute a civil culture that would seem to be at best one of public antagonism, and at worst one of resentful withdrawal in the private realm, with an endless nursing of particularistic wounds and grievances. And yet, as we have tried to show, there were always other possibilities present; other and different discourses. As we saw, the apolitical public sphere allowed for the possibility of a recovery of *logos* in an alternative form of communicative sociability; the British tradition of liberty fueled more radical and more democratic versions of political existence than Loyalism and rule by oligarchy; and, as we have seen, the debates over Confederation, if Romney is correct, inspired not only a profoundly different story of Canada, but as well gave rise to new traditions of political rhetoric that presuppose not just speaking but also being able to hear and to listen. In the end, perhaps, the gap between Huot's *Esquisse* and Harris's *Fathers* is less rigid than it might first appear – if one assumes in the case of the latter that rather than standing silently, or having already said what was formalized in the texts of the law, the Fathers of Confederation captured by Harris – it is a *preparatory* sketch after all – are listening to echoes of that first session of the Quebec Assembly, just as they *too* can now begin to speak.

Law, Rhetoric, and Irony in Canada's Civil Culture

Our final figure, the one with which we terminate this study of the political-aesthetic styles that make up Canada's civil culture, is represented by Robert Houle's *Kanata* (1992), his ironic version of Benjamin West's *The Death of General Wolfe* (1770).[3] Unfortunately, a black-and-white depiction of Houle's painting flattens it out and reduces the shadings and depth of perspective that are so important to the colours of Houle's original; the English here form a ghostly background to the foregrounded thinker-figure of 'the Indian,' who maintains the inscrutability of the same figure in West's painting. But in the intervening two-and-a-quarter centuries, that 'inscrutability' has become searingly ironic.

'Well, well, General,' he might be thinking, 'whatever the thoughts of a dying man, a military leader at a battlefield who does not know if he has won or lost but does know that he himself is leaving this earth and has all the possible regrets that such knowing might entail, you've had over 200 years to think your dying thoughts, and guess what? *Nothing* has changed, General, or precious bloody little. We trusted you, we fought with and for you, and what has that gotten us? Life is, in many ways, so much worse for us now. Your death, your entry into historical monumentality, brought us nothing but tears, lies – endless lies! – as our understandings with you, the English, and whatever the historical importance of this great battle of yours is, came to nothing. Your masters over there in England did not even know what to do with our land: keep it, maybe even leave it to us, or trade it for the sugar and molasses of Guadeloupe. Well, they kept the land in the end, which meant they took it away from us, and we were left with pieces of paper, your solemn treaties and the many signs made by Your Majesties. Pieces of paper! And courts of law, over here and over there! And years and years of learned argument over the words on the pieces of paper: looking at them this way, that way; according to this authority, or that one. And all along we had given *our* word, not on some piece of paper, but before God – before God! It meant nothing at all to you, or as little as your words on pieces of paper, blown away on the tongues of lawyers, bewigged lords of the law, in court upon court, Parliaments, and Houses of Lords. Lords of the Earth! And what are we, then, in all this? Nothing, less than nothing, as I watch you die now for 222 years. But I am still alive and watching and you are still dying, General. But I am still watching and waiting and hoping that one day your words and your promises – your lies! – may still shed their skins and become at last as true as the fact that you are slowly dying, while I continue to sit and think about this, in wonderment, astonishment, and sorrow. Ah, General, whatever sorrow you may be feeling, it pales compared to mine and that of my peoples. Yet I can still sit and think and even hope, whereas you are beyond all that.'

Or words to that effect – if we could know. What we do know is that the struggle between the words of the law and the words spoken by the First Peoples over the land treaties continues, despite everything, and with some significant victories before the courts and still festering problems over fishing and other rights. And the ironies abound. A victory in the courts, for instance, brings out the racist speech and violence of the environing society. So it goes. Meanwhile, Quebec, in part as a result of the separatist Bloc Québécois presence in federal politics, has since lost the centrality as a provincial electoral bloc that made it indispensable to winning federal elections: the Quebec electoral bloc that preserved elements of the *pacte solennel* in post-Confederation national elections from 1867 to the Mulroney years of the mid-1980s has fragmented. As a result, Quebec is no longer necessary to the formation of a Canadian national government. The ensuing diminishment of Quebec's electoral centrality has given traditionally outsider provinces, especially those of the West, a far greater voice in national politics than ever before, but it has also tripled Ontario's electoral clout in the process. While the independentist governing party in the Quebec National Assembly continues to play three-card monte with the threat of yet another referendum over separation, Quebec public opinion could seemingly care less about 'the constitutional question.' And the federal government has, furthermore, managed to entangle the whole question in the murky legal language of the so-called Clarity Bill. And so too it goes, as the contest between the language of law, populist rhetorics, and the rhetoric of independence continues, finding expression not only in some of the ironies just remarked upon, but in something possibly worse: public cynicism and a latent crisis of governmentality. We looked above at Gilles Paquet's analysis of the conflict between multiple forms of social appearance and belongingness and centralizing modernist modes of governance that lag behind the so-called postmodern condition. As manifestations of yet another form of disjunct between public and private worlds, if one goes by the evidence of recent Quebec films and novels (Louis Bélanger's 1999 feature film *Postmortem*, for example), we see emerging a portrait of a deeply cynical society of meaningless public speech, where utterly privatized con artists practise necrophilia within a culture of the blues. This is, it should be noted, a miserabilist view of Quebec society that recurs fairly regularly at times of generalized social transformation.

While the rise of public cynicism, and perhaps even more in the U.S. than here, has been widely decried by no end of pundits blaming politics, the media, the decline of the family – you name it – others see in cynicism (or 'Kynicism' in Peter Sloterdijk's classic [1987] reformulation) not only a long, ironic-critical philosophical tradition going back to the figure of Diogenes, but a democratic cultural stance that grants far greater latitude to contingency than, say, the deference to elites that was part of Madison's strategy of civility. Such Kynicism is well rendered by Lyotard, as he recounts an episode where Diogenes, having been captured by pirates, is being auctioned as a slave. 'The auctioneer shouts to him, "And you, Diogenes, what do you know how to do?" Diogenes responds, "I know how to command, so sell me to Xeniades over there, he has need of a master"' (Lyotard 1993: 69). Diogenes is a truth-sayer through laughter and ironic negation, quite unlike modern cynics, marked by 'enlightened false consciousness,' who 'know what they are doing, but they do it because, in the short run, the force of circumstances and the instinct for self-preservation are speaking the same language, and they are telling them it has to be so' (Sloterdijk 1987: 5). Diogenes' kynicism is not based on silence, but is rhetorical. It is embodied, performed before others, and transparently ironic. It is also political, and indeed one could say it has a subversive republican moment, for it 'presupposes the city, together with its successes and shadows' (Sloterdijk, 4) and as such is founded in what Kenneth Burke has termed 'dialectical irony,' 'based in a sense of fundamental kinship with the enemy, as one who *needs* him, is *indebted* to him, is not merely outside him as an observer but contains him *within*, being consubtantial with him' (Burke 1969: 514). It enacts a cautious and agonistic *philia*, as it humbles those who are its address-ees and who make it make sense. As such, ironic kynicism is marked neither by modern cynicism's fatalism and bad faith, nor is it 'romantic,' based on a sense of superiority or an unwillingness to go beyond a recognition of antinomy and enter the fray. It engages the moment even as it maintains distance through a moment of ironic play.

Irony in Canada is a complex affair, for it appears as stance, as attitude, as political sensibility, and as rhetorical strategy. Futhermore, while at times clearly cynical, it is often kynical as well. Indeed, we contend that these apparently incompatible modalities have ironically depended upon each other. In this sense, irony can become a lever *into* civil discourse, allowing those who have been excluded from the public sphere (e.g., women, First Peoples, and so on) to ironize official discourse and by mocking it civilly (i.e., both nonvio-lently and playfully) forcing it to live up to its manifest content. Irony has thus been the preferred Canadian rhetorical idiom; Canadians verbally cope with the general state of affairs through strategies of ironic incorporation.

One effect of all of this, of course, has been to ironize the law. What then of constitution in irony? In a fascinating paper that draws heavily upon Schlegel's reconfiguration of irony, Adam Carter argues that Schlegel's irony 'deliberately and self-consciously juxtapos[es] and alternat[es] between the antinomies of liberal and conservative assumptions on such fundamental issues as the indi-vidual, the community, progress, and the status of reason in an attempt to delineate a politics ... that might permit both individual freedom and the recognition of one's place and duty within the wider totality of the polis' (n.d.: 3). This does not eliminate contradiction, but it does bring it to the fore. The German Romantics, like Canadian Toryism, however much the former were seduced by the French Revolution, were never revolutionaries either *à la française* or *à l'américaine*, but remained embedded within a sense of contra-diction as a process of 'continual self-creating interchange' (Carter, 4). The state and the constitution will never be perfect, but will remain instead a rhetorical agonistics, and irony represents an awareness of such situational limitations; what is important is not to withdraw into sullen, even if pointedly ironic, silence but to keep trying to speak across the abyss. As Sloterdijk puts it: 'The fully developed ability to say No is also the only valid background for Yes, and only through both does ... freedom ... take form' (cited in Chaloupka 1999: 171). So, the more contingency, the more democracy; let us try to escape the games of cynicism. It is good advice, although easier said than done. But it reminds us also, if we return to the Canadian context, that the ironic style, while it has provided protective camouflage from the other modes of the performance of power, is itself a mode of the same as well.

From the pages above, and from those works we have drawn upon in writing this book, we can see that the law, rhetoric, and irony form a constellation, the contours of which we have attempted to map out in the context of our own particular country's history, because it seems to us that such a mapping is sorely needed. We have done so, at the very least, for the sake of self-knowledge, in the belief that a better understanding of past events and past words helps orient us in the present, if not the future, and the political culture of this country is in serious need of a better sense of orientation. This may be an arrogant assumption on our part: we think not, because others have made similar attempts before. And another try, especially if it serves some useful purpose, cannot hurt. Among such useful purposes, we intend one to be a form of reassurance. The history of this country is, we believe, reassuring in the sense that we find it is no worse nor better than that of any other country; maybe worse in some subtle ways, maybe better in others. The point, of course, is not one of worse or better, or good or bad; it is that of *difference*, of a different articulation of stories. We hope, then, to have told in these pages a somewhat different story than the familiar ones, a story that says that it matters what one does, or does not do, with words; it matters a lot.

Conclusion: Law, Rhetoric, and Irony in Global Civil Culture

The specific styles of words we have looked at, then, are those constituted by the interactions of law, rhetoric, and irony. There is nothing terribly new in this. One could very well argue that the constellation of law, rhetoric, and irony has in Western discourse occupied a central figuration for a long time – since the Greeks, in fact, as McLuhan and Innis, in their different ways, first pointed out in the context of theories and histories concerning patterns of communication in Canadian history in relation to the figures ('monopolies' in Harold Innis's apt phrase for Canadian figurations) of knowledge. And influencing both Innis and McLuhan is the work of Eric Havelock, Walter Ong, and others, who have attempted to figure out the relationships between forms of knowledge and media of communication in the formation of literate societies. As Jan Swearingen notes in *Rhetoric and Irony* (1991), which draws heavily on Havelock, Ong, and Goody, among others, the constellation of law, rhetoric, and irony, and the differences between them, were central to the development of all three in that major period of media upheaval, roughly from the eighth to the fourth centuries BCE, for these were forms of answers to the problems posed by the shift from orality to literacy. Similar problems have recurred since, but are especially germane to our present age of the transition to what some scholars have termed variously 'post-literacy,' 'secondary literacies,' or some journalists 'the new century of the Internet.' And one of the sets of questions, then as now, concerns the problems of how to speak of and figure a future that has an eye for justice. Furthermore, this difficulty seems to intensify as societies become ever increasingly mediated by a proliferation of texts, words, images, and more sophisticated devices for the storage, manipulation, and recombination of multimedia data.

Against such a background emerged the long, three-cornered struggle between rhetoric and philosophy and law over which was the better means of inventing what Burke calls an 'art of living' or, what is possibly the same, engaging the aporias and ironies that seem to be an inherent dimension of the discursive regimes of all three forms of knowledge. Narrowing the discussion considerably, what we have specifically focused upon in this book is what we might term the problem of *political literacy*, in the sense of the semantic, lexical, and figural conditions for a sustained discussion of the orientation of a polity. We see this in terms of how these issues were faced by the northern part of the American continent, when the Europeans encountered both the land and its original inhabitants, the subsequent permutations of that contact in the transfer and translation of political, legal, and rhetorical discourses and styles from France and Britain to the North American context of New France, and their development in what became 'the Canadas,' and eventually Canada itself. To recapitulate our story, Canadians became politically literate by having to learn how to contend with the five styles of the performance of power and social appearance that we have discussed above, drawing out from each of these how a version of the law interacted, often ironically, with rhetorical forms and formulations. As we hope to have shown, this apprenticeship in political speech as inventional capacity has been a lengthy and difficult one, given the complex interweaving of often seemingly contradictory discursive traditions, complicated by the problems of internal and external linguistic frames.

If our analysis has some value, then all we can claim to have shown is the development of the civil culture of this particular country. If we have usefully contributed to demonstrating what, in the Canadian context, political literacy consists of, then it just remains to add: 'So go now and be more literate about, and more rhetorically adept at what you do; what exactly that will consist of is your problem, not ours; ours was in showing you what you are.' As it happens, we end this study at a time when the problems faced by 'the law,' whether domestic or international, stand before particularly fascinating sets of questions: for instance, how to better align domestic and international laws in the form of 'good government' (and not only as regards trade matters); how international law can become a more effective instrument for dealing with gross human rights abuses, punishing the leaders of domestic regimes of terror – the emerging law of 'human security'; how, in short, to advance towards the *jus humanitatis* of an increasingly global civil society. Of rhetoric, one is tempted to say that it will continue to be part of whatever we do as speakers, writers, and so on. We have tried to show that it is more than a cynically detached way of speaking down to the vulgar, and it is more than the counterpart and origin, as Swearingen has shown, of the West's claim and will to truth (1991). Rhetoric is not reducible to representation, but can stand as midwife to imagination and becoming. As Hariman observes, 'rhetorical enquiry is better appreciated as an opportunity for engagement with, rather than escape from, the problems of authority and marginality and the methods of concealment and revelation' (Hariman 1986: 51). This requires recognizing that rhetoric, like irony, the law, and the West itself, cuts both ways, and that there is much to be mined from the *marginalia* of these traditions.

For this reason, then, we risk the irony of closing with an evocation of Antigone – we might have preferred perhaps some words from Houle's warrior-thinker, but they are lost and we, at best, could only again speak for him ... Antigone then it will have to be, as she is herself the figure of a different conception of law: *Diké* or justice, as opposed to *nomos*, the law of the state (see Douzinas and Warrington 1994: 35). That is, she remains 'the Voice [that] sings from a time before the law, before the Symbolic took one's breath away and reapportioned it into language under its authority of separation' (cited in Swearingen, 254).

Notes

1: Situating Canada's Civil Culture

1 Since the publication of *A Border Within* (1997), Angus has further refined some of these ideas. In a paper given at the Brock University 'Two Days of Canada' conference in November 1999, he proposes a 'three-step development model' for thinking philosophically about Canada. The first or 'critical' step would be the attempt to reverse the biases of Eurocentrism; the second or 'post-colonial' step would be 'a philosophy that is merely *in* Canada,' a philosophy about Canada and the issues it poses; and the third step would 'involve ... a philosophy *of* Canada ... whose terms are universalizations derived from its particularity and which strain to produce ... a tradition ... which illuminates the human condition as such.' Angus sees current work in Canadian Studies as largely between the last two steps, giving as evidence of its potential 'universality' European interest in Canadian multiculturalism, multination states, and Aboriginal title, a consequence of the issues deriving from European integration (see Angus 2000).

2 Scholars as diverse as Bruno Latour and Donna Haraway have noted the centrality of the activity of translation in a sociology of scientific communication in the first case and in the morphing toward the posthuman in the second. The current transformation toward an information society has seen an explosion of translation activity on an unprecedented scale. This is the case not only for the massive in-crease in the translation of technical, scientific, administrative, and legal texts and, in the wake of growing demand, the drive to develop translation machines to handle the immense volume of non-literary materials. With the proliferation of new computer 'languages,' the growth of artificial intelligence, and thinking machines, not only have the boundaries between 'natural' and artificial languages shifted, but there has been a corresponding displacement of the limits of what it means to be human, and in this

sense a further complexity of the machine/human interface or translation has developed, with implications that are far from clear. See for example Downey 1998; Haraway 1997; Latour and Woolgar 1986; Latour, 1993. On the level of psychoanalytic theory and the analysis of the difficulties of translating Freud, the late Darius Ornston, for example, in a paper on the limitations of Strachey's translations of the Standard Edition, notes how the latter tended to 'mechanize' Freud's thought, turning such concepts as *Übertragung* (transference or translation) into the more mechanistic notion of transmission. See Ornston 1992: 10–11. Here too the implications are considerable for a more sophisticated understanding of the transferential dimensions carried by translation.

3 J.C.D. Clark, for instance, comments on the consternation of 'forward-looking Britain' committed to Blackstonian doctrine of the absolute authority of the Crown in Parliament, faced by 'backward-looking' Americans 'still obsessed' with the ideas of the seventeenth-century jurist, Sir Edward Coke. See Clark 1997: 134.

4 As Clark notes, the British acquisition of Canada, and especially the decision to retain Canada, 'is now acknowledged as "a major cause" of the American Revolution' because it was interpreted by the colonists as reflecting London's intention of greater centralization and military control. Thomas Hutchison, lieutenant-governor of Massachussetts, considered the retention of Canada by the British to be a great mistake; without it, 'none of the spirit of opposition to the Mother Country would have ... appeared' (Clark 1997: 149). The historian goes on to note that the retention of Canada was thus a necessary, although not a sufficient, cause for the American rebellion, as illustrated by the fact that there was no rebellion in Canada, and the *Canadiens'* lack of enthusiasm for the American adventure would produce from the British extraordinary measures of conciliation, including the granting of a colonial assembly.

2: 'Who Killed Canadian History?'

1 Our title is taken from historian Jack Granatstein's controversial 1998 polemic, a little book that was influential less for the sharpness of its ideas than for provoking a conservative backlash in the teaching of Canadian history, particularly at the high-school level. For discussion of Granatstein among Canadian historians, see Carr 1998; McKillop 1999; and Palmer 1999.

3: The Legitimacy of Conquest

1 'You will yourselves have the freedom to remedy your burdens, but we will forbid you any means of knowing them,' *Le Canadien* 2(32), 25 June 1808, 128–30, in the context of an exchange with one Plebeius (shades of the American

Revolution!) over the nature of constitutional authority. Reprinted in Vachon 1969.

2 The obvious exception here, of course, is the deportation of the Acadians from Nova Scotia in 1755, in the period immediately preceding the cession of New France.

3 'Since the origins of Confederation, we have lived a sort of double nationality, as Canadians and as Quebecers. This duality has become acutely painful, to the point of dividing the citizenry according to their allegiances ... Since the Conquest, there have been in Quebec not only French speakers and English speakers, but two juxtaposed societies, with their respective institutions and two sets of collective references that have never managed to reconcile themselves one with the other.'

4 Pawlisch in his *Sir John Davies and the Conquest of Ireland: A Study in Legal Imperialism* (1985) makes the case not only that 'Irish native policy' served as the prototype for English subjugation of native peoples elsewhere and particularly in the American colonies (8), but further that in the wake of the Tudor conquest of Ireland, the juridical stance elaborated by Davies regarding Gaelic property 'laid the basis for an imperial formula that was fundamental in the creation of the British empire' (14). In recent years, the prototypical model served up by Ireland as the site where the English worked out their global model for colonization has itself come under debate within Irish historiography. See unpublished conference abstracts, 'Defining Colonies,' The Third Galway Conference on Colonialism, National University of Ireland, Galway, 17–20 June 1999.

5 'À la seule expérience le développement des modes d'interaction et de collaboration ... donc voue les nouvelles règles du jeu politique à une explicitation largement coutumière.'

6 'If the transfer of Canada was part of the logic of things ... [it must be remembered that] colonization also produces very long-term mass effects.'

7 The exact titles, orthography, and publication dates of Cugnet's four so-called treatises vary from source to source in part because of the enormous length of their titles; for example, 1775b's title takes up eighteen lines of type. Compare, for example, Leland 1961: 3n1, with Dionne [1905–9] 1974:13. The most accurate reproduction of Cugnet's titles and publication dates, and even here 1775a's title is not reproduced in its entirety, would appear to be in Hamelin, Beaulieu, and Gallichan 1981: 7–8.

8 On mono-, bi- and plurijurality, see Howes 1987.

9 Some of these were published in London in 1772–3 (Huberdeau 1947: 63–4); publication in French took place in 1775 in Quebec of the three 'treatises' of 1771, 1772, and 1773, along with the extracts of French royal edicts, *ordonnances* and regulations. See Cugnet 1775a–d.

10 'Thus were abolished the laws of France with their great precision, clarity, and wisdom, and they were replaced by English laws, a confused jumble of Acts of Parliament and juridical decisions written in a [needlessly] complicated and barbaric style.'

11 'There is to this day the same confusion of French and English laws, the same uncertainty in [juridical] decisions, the same caprice in the application of the law as there was 50 to 60 years ago.'

12 'An airtight and unbridgeable barrier separates [our] two great juridical systems' and as a result there was 'no risk of seepage or absorption of one at the profit or detriment of the other.'

13 'What are the laws that guide us today? Who can say? What citizen, lawyer, or judge could say: "This is the law." The law! Why we don't have one, or rather we have so many, both old and new, so outworn and so contradictory, that even the best jurists cannot sort through the confusion.'

4: Constituting Constitutions under the British Regime

1 'His most Christian Majesty cedes and guarantees in all propriety to His afore-mentioned Britannic Majesty, Canada and its dependencies' and agrees to grant to his new subjects 'the freedom of the Catholic Religion ... insofar as the Laws of Great Britain allow it.' (Shortt and Doughty [1907] 1918: 85)

2 'The true Glory of a Victorious King consists in assuring to the vanquished the same happiness and the same tranquillity in their Religion and in the possession of their property that they enjoyed before their defeat. We have enjoyed the Tranquillity even during the War, and it has increased since the establishment of the Peace. Would that thus it had been secured to us! Deeply attached to our religion, we have sworn at the foot of the altar unalterable fidelity to Your Majesty. From it we have never swerved and we swear anew that we never will swerve therefrom, although we should be in the future as unfortunate as we have been Happy: but how could we ever even be unhappy, after those tokens of paternal affection by which Your Majesty has given the assurance that we shall never be disturbed in the Practice of our Religion ...

For four years we enjoyed the greatest tranquillity. By what sudden stroke has it been taken away through the action of four or five jurists, whose character we respect, but who do not understand our language, and expect us, as soon as they have spoken, to comprehend legal constructions which they have not yet ex-plained, but to which we should always be ready to submit, as soon as we become acquainted with them; but how can we know them, if they are not delivered to us in our own tongue?' (Shortt and Doughty [1907] 1918: 165).

3 'That we may not further encroach upon Your Majesty's Precious Time, we conclude by assuring You, that without knowing the English Constitution we
have during the past four years, enjoyed the Benefice of the Government, and we
should still enjoy it, if Messrs the English Jurors were as submissive to the wise
decisions of the Governor and his Council, as we are; if they were not seeking by
new regulations, by the introduction of which they hope to make us their slaves'
(Shortt and Doughty [1907] 1918: 165).

4 'Resolved, That His Majesty's loyal subjects, the people of this province of Lower
Canada, have shown strongest attachment for the British Empire, of which they
are a portion; that they have repeatedly defended it with courage in time of war;
that at the period which preceded the Independence of the late British colonies on
this continent, they resisted the appeal made to them by those colonies to join
their Confederation.'

5 'That this House and the people whom it represents do not wish or intend to
convey any threat; but that, relying as they do upon the principles of law and
justice, they are and ought to be politically strong enough not to be exposed to
receive [sic] insult from any man whomsoever, or bound to suffer it in silence;
that the style of the said extracts from the despatches of the Colonial Secretary, as
communicated to this House, is insulting and inconsiderate to such a degree that
no legally constituted body, although its functions were infinitely subordinate to
those of legislation, could or ought to tolerate them ...

This House would esteem itself wanting in candour to the people of England, if
it hesitated to call their attention to the fact that in less than 20 years the population of the United States of America will be as great or greater than that of Great
Britain, and that of British America will be as great or greater than that of the
former English Colonies was when the latter deemed that the time was come to
decide that the inappreciable advantage of governing themselves instead of being
governed, ought to engage them to repudiate a system of Colonial Government
which was, generally speaking, much better than that of British America now is'
(Kennedy 1930: 280).

6 'Considering ourselves no longer linked except by force to the English government, we will submit as to a government of force, and await from God, from our
proper rights, and from better circumstances, the benefits of liberty and a more
just government.'

5: The Limits of Law

1 The English version of the Declaration cited here is taken from an unsigned draft
published 7 December 1869 (Manitoba Archives, MG3 A1–6) which corresponds,

in translation to the French version voted upon and published 8 December 1869 (Manitoba Archives, MG3 A1–7, reprinted in Peel 1874, 13). The only major difference between the English draft and the final version, voted in both languages but available in the Manitoba and National archives only in French, is the addition of 'LA SEULE AUTORITE LEGITIME AUJOURD'HUI DANS LA TERRE DE RUPERT ET DU NORD-OUEST EST L'AUTORITE PROVISOIREMENT ACCORDEE PAR LE PEUPLE A NOUS SES REPRESENTANTS' (The only legitimate authority today in Rupert's Land and the North-West is the authority provisionally granted by the people to us its representatives,' translation ours.) The English version usually cited (Oliver 1915: 904–6) differs in minor respects from the English version discussed here, but also has a more 'politically correct' figuring of the Indian than here or in the French version. Instead of 'hordes of barbarians,' Oliver's version has 'neighbouring tribes of Indians.'

6: 'Impious Civility'

1 Throughout this chapter, we will employ the form 'woman's rights' rather than the more common 'women's rights' because it better corresponds to suffrage rhetoric at the beginning of the twentieth century and because the term calls attention to woman as a *category* rather than women as a group of individuals who might bear rights.

2 It is worth noting that Cleverdon, who produced the first major study on woman's suffrage in Canada, is an American. Her doctoral work at the University of Toronto was supervised by Ramsey Cook. Her nationality takes nothing away from the quality of her study, but it does account for her rhetorical flourish here. As even her own history makes clear, woman's suffrage in Canada was not inscribed within a narrative of freedom's forward march.

3 Under common law, only unmarried women could hold property. Marriage resulted in the ceding of title to the husband. The legislating of property rights for women only occurred in 1872 (the married women's property act, 1872). Common law also gave the husband full control over his children (he could even put them up for adoption) and gave the wife no claim on his estate if he died intestate. Under civil law, marriage did not dispossess women, but the right to dispose of property fell to the husband. Furthermore, and for some time to come, married women did not hold citizenship directly. In both the British Empire and the United States, women marrying a foreign national lost their citizenship and acquired his. See Altschul and Carron (1975).

4 See for example, Charlotte Gray, 'Unsung Heroes in a Vast Landscape: Challenge in Redefining Greatness,' *National Post*, 21 August 1999, B5.

7: The Dialectic of Language, Law, and Translation

1 See Latour (1993) for a provocative discussion of the impossibility of being resolutely modern.
2 The so-called Larose Commission published, in late August 2001, a report entitled 'Le français, une langue pur tout le monde,' that makes French nothing less than the basis for participation in Quebec civil society. See *La Presse*, 'Citoyenneté et constitution, 21 August 2001, A1–2, A11.
3 The term is Marc André Bernier's (1998) in the sense of the transformations of the ubiquity of Native oratory into a 'culture oratoire' ceaselessly 'called upon to nourish the ensemble of literary production and cultural life,' particularly in Quebec (106).

8: Civility, Its Discontents, and the Performance of Social Appearance

1 Recent studies, however, have shown a marked decline in deference; see notably Nevitt 1996.
2 For another such recent appeal, see also Gairdner 1996.
3 Although Cuddihy's study focuses on the problems of 'passing' as civilized as this and preoccupied a specifically Jewish intelligentsia, we might also think of these questions even more diasporically using Lyotard's definition of 'the jews' as what 'we always already are but have forgotten we are,' in David Carroll's paraphrase. See Lyotard 1990.

9: The Figures of Authority in Canadian Civil Culture

1 The death of Pierre Trudeau and in particular his lying-in-state in the Parliament Buildings in Ottawa was, especially in the way in which it was shot on television, precisely a 'republican' moment in this sense. With the camera placed just to the rear of the body of the fallen hero, whose coffin was draped in the national flag and thus representing the nation or republic, some 100,000 people over two days approached the coffin in waves of four, each wave performatively reconstituting the body of the republic. Neither was it accidental that at his father's funeral mass in Montreal, Justin Trudeau opened his eulogy with the words: 'Friends, *Romans*, Countrymen ...' (our emphasis). We are indebted to Bob Hariman for the first observation. For the text of Justin Trudeau's utterly performative eulogy, see ' "Je t'aime, Papa": The eulogy that touched a nation,' *Ottawa Citizen*, 4 October 2000, A1–A2.
2 Smith's formulation is here not quite true to British constitutional theory, for the

king as *persona publica* never 'dies.' More properly, one speaks of the 'demise' of the king's body natural, as it leaves the body politic, to be immediately replaced by a successor.

3   That West's painting, which became an icon of the British Empire, 'embraced rhetoric' (Schama 1991) and took great liberties with the historical record almost goes without saying. It was, in other words, always ripe for irony. See Schama (1991) and Stacey (1996).

Bibliography

1. Archival Sources Consulted

Archives Nationales (Paris)

Série C

C11A. Canada proprement dit (des origines à 1784)

C11A2. 1663–1710. Folio 199. 5 avril, 1666. Versailles. Lettre du ministre Colbert à Talon explique pourquoi le roi 'ne peut consentir à dépeupler son royaume pour faire du Canada un grand et puissant état ...'

C11G. Canada divers 2è série (1677–1748)

Série F

F3.4. 23 mars 1673, Règlement de police concernant la ville de Québec, fait par M. de Frontenac. Folio 109, 20 pp.

13 juin 1673, Extrait d'une lettre du ministre à M. de Frontenac. With instructions to 'anéantir insensiblement' the Estates-General according to His Majesty's wishes and to 'jamais donner cette forme au corps des habitants du pays' [Canada], and as well to 'suprimer insensiblement le syndic des habitants.' Folio 121, 1 p.

30 mai 1675, Provisions d'Intendant de justice, police et finance du Canada pour le Sieur Duchesneau. Fol. 427, 3½ p.

Langlois, M. 1958. 'Guide des archives du Parlement de Paris,' 65–160. *Guide de recherches dans les fonds judiciaires de l'Ancien Régime*. Paris: AN

Doléances des peuples coloniaux à l'assemblée nationale constituante. 1989. Paris: AN

Série G

Roussier, Paul. 1929. 'Le dépot des papiers publics des colonies,' 240–62. *Revue d'histoire moderne* 4

Perte du Canada. Archives de la Marine, série B3 (réfugiés canadiens en France après 1760)

Perte du Canada. 5 v. de minutes de notaire du Canada (1646–1759)

Bibliothèque Nationale (Paris)

Bibaud, M. 1862. *Notice historique sur l'enseignement du droit au Canada.* Montreal: L. Perrault

Brougham, Henry B. 1803. *An Inquiry into the Colonial Policy of the European Powers.* 2 vols. Edinburgh: D. Willison

De la Mare, Nicolas. 1705–38. *Traité de la police, où l'on trouvera l'histoire de son établissment, les fonctions et les prérogations de ses magistrats, toutes les loix et tous les reglemens qui la concernent.* Paris: J. and P. Cot (microfilm M-4691)

Griffin, A.P.C. 1900. *List of Books with Reference to Periodicals relating to the Theory of Colonization, Government of Dependencies, Protectorates and Related Topics.* 2nd ed. Washington: Government Printing Office

Hey, William. 1857. 'View of the Civil Government in the Province of Canada When It Was Subject to the Crown of France,' 48pp. *Lower Canada Jurist* 1, appendix

Keith, A.B. 1917. 'Ministerial Responsibility in the Dominions,' 227–32. *Journal of Comparative Legislation* 17

Martin, Olivier. 1922–30. *Histoire de la Coutume de Paris.* 3 vols. Paris: Sirey

Maxwell, W.H. 1913. *Complete List of British and Colonial Law Reports and Legal Periodicals with a Checklist of Canadian Statutes.* London: Sweet and Maxwell

Maxwell, W.H., and Maxwell, Leslie. F., comps. 1955. *A Legal Bibliography of the British Commonwealth of Nations.* 7 vols. London: Sweet and Maxwell

Petit, Emilien. 1911. *Droit public du gouvernement des colonies françaises.* Paris: Gauthier

Private Papers of British Colonial Governors, 1782–1900. 1986. London: HMSO

Ramsay, T.K. 1863–4. *Notes sur la Coutume de Paris.* Montreal: La Minerve

Roy, J. Edmond. 1911. 'Rapport sur les archives de France relatives à l'histoire du Canada,' 1093 pp. *Archives du Canada* no. 6. Ottawa: Imp. du Roi

Tautet, Victor. 1908. *Catalogue méthodique de la bibliothèque du ministère des colonies.* Melun: Cie. Admi.

Tarrins, C.J. 1893. *Chapter on the Law Relating to the Colonies.* 2nd ed. enlarged. London: Stephens and Hayns

Todd, Alpheus. 1880. *Parliamentary Government in the British Colonies.* London: Longmans, Green

Wallis, J.P. 1896. 'Early Colonial Constitutions,' 59–83. Royal Historical Society, *Transactions*, new series 10

Duke University Law Library (Durham, NC)

Hartog, Hendrik, ed. 1981. 'Law in the American Revolution and the Revolution in American Law: A Collection of Review Essays in American Legal History.' *New York University School of Law Series in Legal History* 3
Tiedeman, Christopher. 1886. *A Treatise on the Limitations of Police Power in the United States*, microform LT 26470–7

Manitoba Provincial Archives

MG3 A1–6 Declaration of the People of Rupert's Land and the North-West. 7 December 1869.
MG3 A1–7 Déclaration des habitants de la Terre de Rupert et du Nord'Ouest. 8 December 1869.

National Archives of Canada

Manuscript Groups
MG8, A5, Nouvelle France, Conseil Supérieur, Règlements de police faits par le Conseil souverain, 1676
MG21, King's MSS. 207, Reports on the State of Laws and Administration of Justice, Province of Quebec, 1769, 70 pp.

Public Archives of Canada Reports
1883 *PACR*, 'Public Records Office, London, Synopsis of Papers 1683–1791,' 18–116; also 'BN, Paris, MSS. & Documents re Canada, Synopsis, 1535–1761,' 155–9
1890 *PACR*, 'Administration of Justice, Documents 1768–1770 [Guy Carleton],' lx–lxxiv, 1–9
1904 *PACR*, 'Canadian Archives in 1787: Proceedings of the Committee Appointed to Inquire into the State of Archives and Reports 1790,' 79–189; also 'PRO, Instructions to Governors, 1793–1787,' 191–286 (see also MG11, supp. II, no. 7)
1905 *PACR*, 'PRO, Instructions to Governors' (cont'd), vol. 1, pt. 1, 1–135; vol. 1, pt. 3, 'BN. Paris, MSS & Documents re Canada, 1599–1801,' Synopses, 45–53
1909 *PACR*, 'Index to Reports of Canadian Archives from 1872 to 1908'

Rare Books Collection
Cugnet, François-Joseph. 1775a. *Traité de la loi des fiefs qui a toujours été suivie en Canada depuis son établissement* ... 71pp. Quebec: Guillaume Brown [1774 or 1775]
– 1775b. *Traité abrégé des anciennes loix, coutumes et usages de la colonie du*

Canada aujourd'hui Province de Québec, tiré de la coûtume de la prévoté et vicomté de Paris ... 188pp. Quebec: Guillaume Brown
- 1775c. *Traité de la police qui a toujours été suivie en Canada aujourd'hui Province de Québec depuis son établissment* ... 25pp. Quebec: Guillaume Brown
- 1775d. *Extrait des édits, ordonnances et règlements de sa Majesté Très Chrétienne* ... 106pp. Quebec: Guillaume Brown

Public Records Office (UK)

Colonial Office, CO42/194, General Union of the British Provinces in North America 1822 and 1823, 83pp + appendices and observations
CO42/195, Pts 1 and 2, Canada. Union of the Legislatures 1823 (petitioners for and against, 1822–4)
CO47/122–40, Blue Books of Statistics 1821–40
CO324/67 Précis of Correspondence, Canada, 1801–1813
1930 UK House of Lords and Privy Council AC. 'Henrietta Muir Edwards and Others, Appellants and Attorney General for Canada and Others, Respondents, on Appeal from the Supreme Court of Canada,' 124–42
1927 Canada. Privy Council. 2034. 19 October 1927

2. Government Publications or Documentary Reprints

Canada. Parliament. 1865. *Parliamentary Debates on the Subject of the Confederation of the British North American Provinces.* 3rd Session, 8th Provincial Parliament of Canada. Quebec
- 1885. House of Commons. *Debates*
Dionne, N.-E. [1905–9] 1974. *Inventaire chronologique des Livres, Brochures, Journaux et Revues Publiés en langue française dans la province de Québec depuis l'établissement de l'imprimerie au Canada jusqu'a nos jours, 1764–1905,* vol. 1. Quebec 1905–9, repr. New York: Burt Franklin
Government of Canada. [1839] 1966. *Debates of the House of Commons in the Year 1774.* London: Ridgway 1839; reprint
Hamelin, Jean, André Beaulieu, and Gilles Gallichan. 1981. *Brochures québécoises 1764–1972.* Quebec: Gouvernement du Québec
Lower Canada. Legislature. House of Assembly. 1834. *Les quatre-vingt-douze résolutions proposées à la Chambre par Bédard, le vendredi, 21 février 1834 [microform] : suivies d'une discussion sur l'état de la province et d'une adresse de la Chambre 'Aux honorables chevaliers, citoyens et bourgeois, les Communes du Royaume-Uni de la Grande Bretagne et d'Irlande, assemblées en Parlement.'*

Oliver, Edmund Henry. 1914–15. *The Canadian North-West: Its Early Development and Legislative Records.* Publications of the Canadian Archives, no. 9

Rapports des Archives publiques du Canada (reproducing French documents from the Archives nationales in Paris drawn principally from C11 'Canada. Série principale')

1885 (C11A, fols 1–30)

1886 (C11A, fols 31–76)

1887 (C11A, fols 77–125; C11B, fols 1–38; C11D, fols 1–10; C11E, fols 1–16; C11F)

1899 (C11G), pp. 39–191

1900, pp. 487–533

1905, pp. 1–358; 442–502

1906, pp. 1–441

Privy Council 2034, 19-10-1927

Supreme Court of Canada, Reports

1928 *SCR* 'In the Matter of Reference as to the Meaning of the Word "Persons" in Section 24 of the British North America Act, 1867,' 276–304

1985 1 *SCR* Re Manitoba Language Rights, 721, 83 pp. (http://www.droit. umontreal.ca/doc/csc-scs ... publies/1985/vol1/html/1985scr1_0721.html)

1997 3 *SCR* Delgamuukw v. British Columbia 1010, 65 pp (http://www.lexum. umontreal.ca/csc-scc/en/pub/1997/vol3/html/1997scr3_1010.html)

3. Books, Articles, and Dissertations

Abrams, Phillip. 1982. *Historical Sociology.* Shepton Mallet: Open Books

Acland, Charles R., and William J. Buxton, eds. 1999. *Harold Innis in the New Century: Reflections and Refractions.* Montreal: McGill-Queen's University Press

Adam, G. Mercer, 1885. *The Canadian North-west: Its History and Its Troubles, from the Early Days of the Fur-trade to the Era of the Railway and the Settler; with Incidents of Travel in the Region, and the Narrative of Three Insurrections.* Toronto: Rose Publishing Co.

Adorno, T.W. [1951] 1974. *Minima Moralia: Reflections from Damaged Life.* London: New Left Books

Adorno, Theodor, and Max Horkheimer. [1944] 1982. *The Dialectic of Enlightenment.* New York: Continuum

Ajzenstat, Janet. 1988. *The Political Thought of Lord Durham.* Montreal: McGill-Queen's University Press

Ajzentstat, Janet, Paul Romney, Ian Gentles, and William D. Gairdner, eds. 1999. *Canada's Founding Debates.* Toronto: Stoddart

Ajzenstat, Janet, and Peter J. Smith, eds. 1995. *Canada's Origins: Liberal, Tory, or Republican?* Ottawa: Carleton University Press

Almond, Gabriel A., and Sidney Verba. 1989. *The Civic Culture: Political Attitudes and Democracy in Five Nations.* 1963. Rev. ed. 1975. Reprint, Newbury Park, CA: Sage.

Altschul, Susan, and Christine Carron. 1975. 'Chronology of Some Legal Landmarks in the History of Canadian Women.' *McGill Law Journal* 21: 476–94

Anderson, Benedict. 1986. *Imagined Communities: Reflections on the Origin and Spread of Nationalism.* London: Verso

Anderson, Perry. 1969. 'Components of the National Culture.' Pp. 214–86 in *Student Power: Problems, Diagnosis, Action*, ed. Alexander Coburn and Robin Blackburn. 1965. Reprint, Harmondsworth: Penguin

Angus, Ian. 2000. 'Locality and Universalization: Where Is Canadian Studies?' *Journal of Canadian Studies* 35 (3): 15–32

– 1997. *A Border Within: National Identity, Cultural Plurality and Wilderness.* Montreal: McGill-Queen's University Press

'Anniversary Celebrations.' 1991–2. *Journal of Canadian Studies* 26 (winter): 5–17

Arditi, Jorge. 1998. *A Genealogy of Manners: Transformations of Social Relations in France and England from the Fourteenth to the Eighteenth Century.* Chicago: University of Chicago Press

Arendt, Hannah. 1958. *The Human Condition.* Chicago: University of Chicago Press

Arnold, Thurman W. 1935. *The Symbols of Government.* New York: Harcourt, Brace and World

Association of Métis and Non-status Indians of Saskatchewan. 1979. *Louis Riel: Justice Must Be Done.* Winnipeg: Manitoba Métis Federation Press

Atwood, Margaret. 1972. *Survival: A Thematic Guide to Canadian Literature.* Toronto: Anansi

Babe, Robert E. 2000. *Canadian Communication Thought.* Toronto: University of Toronto Press

Bacchi, Carol Lee. 1983. *Liberation Deferred? The Ideas of the English-Canadian Suffragists, 1877–1918.* Toronto: University of Toronto Press

Bagehot, Walter. [1867] 1963. *The English Constitution.* Intro. Richard Crossman. London: Fontana

Bailyn, Bernard. 1967. *The Ideological Origins of the American Revolution.* Cambridge, MA: Harvard University Press

Baker, G. Blaine. 1985. 'The Reconstitution of Upper Canadian Legal Thought in the Late-Victorian Empire.' *Law and History Review* 3: 219–92

Baldick, Chris. 1987. *The Social Mission of English Criticism, 1848–1932*. Oxford: Clarendon Press

Barrett, Harold. 1991. *Rhetoric and Civility: Human Development, Narcissism, and the Good Audience*. Albany: State University of New York Press

Baudoin, Louis. 1963. 'La réception du droit étranger en droit privé québécois.' Pp. 3–70 in *Quelques aspects du droit de la Province de Québec*, ed. Louis Baudoin et al. Paris: Editions Cujas

Bauman, Zygmunt. 1989. *Modernity and the Holocaust*. Cambridge: Polity

Beard, Charles A. [1913] 1935. *An Economic Interpretation of the Constitution of the United States*. New York: Macmillan

Beardsmore, H. Baetens. 1982. *Bilingualism: Basic Principles*. Tieto, UK: Clevendon

Beiner, Ronald. 1983. *Political Judgment*. Chicago: University of Chicago Press

Benjamin Walter. 1978. 'Critique of Violence.' Pp. 277–300 in *Reflections: Essays, Aphorisms, Autobiograpical Writings*, ed. and intro. Peter Demetz, trans. Edmund Jephcott. New York: Harvest / HBJ

Berger, Carl. 1986. *The Writing of Canadian History: Aspects of English-Canadian Historical Writing: 1900 to 1970*. 2nd ed. Toronto: Oxford University Press

– ed. 1967. *Approaches to Canadian History*. Toronto: University of Toronto Press

Berman, Harold J. 1983. *Law and Revolution: The Formation of the Western Legal Tradition*. Cambridge, MA: Harvard University Press

Bernard, Jean-Paul. 1995. 'L'historiographie canadienne récente (1964–94) et l'histoire des peuples du Canada.' *Canadian Historical Review* 76 (3): 321–53

Bernier, Gérald, and Daniel Salée. 1992. *The Shaping of Quebec Politics and Society: Colonialism, Power and the Transition to Capitalism in the 19th Century*. Washington: Crane Russak

Bernier, Marc André, ed. 1998. 'Dossier: La conquête de l'éloquence au Québec. La rhétorique et son enseignement (1712–1800).' *Canadian Journal of Rhetorical Studies* 9 (September) 97–153

Bird, Kym. 1996. 'The Politics of Early English-Canadian Women's Theatre 1876–1927.' PhD dissertation, York University

Blache, Pierre. 1994. 'La Charte canadienne: obstacle postmoderne à l'émergence d'un Québec moderne et rassembleur.' *Thémis* 28 (2–3): 335–70

Bliss, Michael. 1991. 'Privatizing the Mind: The Sundering of Canadian History, the Sundering of Canada.' Creighton Centennial Lecture, University of Toronto History Department's 100th

Bodemann, Y. Michal. 1984. 'Elitism, Fragility, and Commoditism: Three Themes in the Canadian Sociological Mythology.' Pp. 210–28 in *Models and Myths in Canadian Sociology*, ed. S.D. Berkowitz. Toronto: Butterworths

Boodman, Martin, et al. 1993. *Quebec Civil Law: An Introduction to Quebec Private Law*. Toronto: E. Montgomery

Boorstin, Daniel J. 1973. *The Mysterious Science of the Law: An Essay on Blackstone's Commentaries* ... Gloucester, MA: Peter Smith

Boyd White, James. 1990. *Justice as Translation: An Essay in Cultural and Legal Criticism.* Chicago: University of Chicago Press

Brisson, Jean-Maurice. 1986. *La formation d'un droit mixte: l'évolution de la procédure civile de 1774 à 1867.* Montreal: Ed. Thémis

Brown, George. 1912. 'Speech to Parliament June 22, 1864.' Pp. 331–5 in *Public Men and Public Life in Canada*, ed. James Young. Toronto: William Briggs

Brun, Henri. 1970. *La formation des institutions parlementaires québécoises.* Quebec: Presses de l'Université Laval

Bryant, Donald C. 1965. 'Rhetoric: Its Function and Scope.' Pp. 32–62 in *Philosophy, Rhetoric and Argumentation*, ed. Maurice Natanson and Henry W. Johnstone, Jr. University Park: Pennsylvania State University Press

Bryce, James. 1921. *Modern Democracies.* 2 vols. New York: Macmillan

Buckner, Phillip. 1985. *The Transition to Responsible Government: British Policy in British North America, 1815–1850.* Westport, CT: Greenwood

Burchell, David. 1995. 'Virtue, Manners and the Activity of Citizenship.' *Economy and Society* 24 (4): 540–58

Burke, Kenneth. 1969. *A Grammar of Motives.* Berkeley: University of California Press

Careless, J.M.S. 1969. '"Limited Identities" in Canada.' *Canadian Historical Review* 50 (1): 1–10

– 1967. 'Frontierism, Metropolitanism and Canadian History.' (1954). Pp. 63–83 in Berger

Carlson, A. Cheree. 1992. 'Creative Casuistry and Feminist Consciousness: The Rhetoric of Moral Reform.' *Quarterly Journal of Speech* 78: 16–32

Carr, Graham. 1998. 'Harsh Sentences: Appealing the Strange Verdict of *Who Killed Canadian History?*' Review essay, *American Review of Canadian Studies* 28 (2): 167–76

Carter, Adam. '"Insurgent Government": Romantic Irony and the Theory of the State.' *Romantic Circles Praxis Series* (http://www.rc.umd.edu/praxis/irony/carter/schlegel.html)

Carter, Stephen L. 1998. *Civility: Manners, Morals and the Etiquette of Democracy.* New York: Basic Books

Chaloupka, William. 1999. *Everybody Knows: Cynicism in America.* Minneapolis: University of Minnesota Press

Charland, Maurice. 1986. 'Technological Nationalism.' *Canadian Journal of Political and Social Theory* 10 (1–2): 196–220

Clark, J.C.D. 1997. 'British America: What If There Had Been No American Revolution?' Pp. 125–74 in *Virtual History: Alternatives and Counterfactuals*, ed. Niall Ferguson. London: Papermac

Cleverdon, Catherine L. 1974. *The Woman Suffrage Movement in Canada*. Toronto: University of Toronto Press

Cohen-Tanugi, Laurent. 1985. *Le droit sans l'état: sur la démocratie en France et en Amérique*. Paris: Presses universitaires de France

Cohn, Bernard S. 1996. *Colonialism and Its Forms of Knowledge: The British in India*. Princeton, NJ: Princeton University Press

Colas, Dominique. 1997. *Civil Society and Fanaticism: Conjoined Histories*. Stanford, CA: Stanford University Press

Collins, Richard. 1990. *Culture, Communication and National Identity: The Case of Canadian Television*. Toronto: University of Toronto Press

Condren, Conal. 1994. *The Language of Politics in Seventeenth-Century England*. New York: St. Martin's Press

Conklin, William E. 1996. 'The Invisible Author of Legal Authority.' *Law and Critique* 7 (2): 173–92

– 1989. *Images of a Constitution*. Toronto: University of Toronto Press

Conway, John. 1969. 'Politics, Culture, and the Writing of Constitutions.' Pp. 3–17 in *Empire and Nations: Essays in Honour of Frederic H. Soward*, ed. Harvey L. Dick and H. Peter Krosby. Toronto: University of Toronto Press

Cook, David. 1985. *Northrop Frye: A Vision of the New World*. Montreal: New World Perspectives

Coombe, Rosemary J. 2001. 'Is There a Cultural Studies of Law?' Forthcoming in *The Blackwell Companion Guide to Cultural Studies*, ed. Toby Miller. New York and Oxford: Blackwell

Corrigan, Philip, and Derek Sayer. 1985. *The Great Arch: English State Formation as Cultural Revolution*. Oxford: Blackwell

Cote, J.E. 1977. 'The Reception of English Law.' *Alberta Law Review* 29–92

Creighton, Donald G. 1967. 'Sir John Macdonald and Canadian Historians.' Pp. 50–62 in Berger

– [1937] 1956. *The Empire of the St. Lawrence*. Toronto: Macmillan

Cuddihy, John M. 1974. *The Ordeal of Civility: Freud, Marx, Lévi-Strauss and the Jewish Struggle with Modernity*. New York: Basic Books

Dargo, George. 1975. *Jefferson's Louisiana: Politics and the Clash of Legal Traditions*. Cambridge, MA: Harvard University Press

Davies, K.G. 1974. *The North Atlantic World in the Seventeenth Century*. Minneapolis: University of Minnesota Press

de Grazia, Sebastian. 1997. *A Country with No Name: Tales from the Constitution*. New York: Pantheon

Delâge, Denys. 1991. *Le pays renversé: Amérindiens et Européens en Amérique du Nord-Est, 1600–1664*. Montreal: Boréal

de Lagrave, Jean-Paul. 1993. *L'Epoque de Voltaire au Canada: Biographie politique de Fleury Mesplet (1734–1794)*. Montréal: L'Etincelle de Sousa Santos, Boaventura. 1995. *Toward a New Common Sense: Law, Science and Politics in the Paradigmatic Transition*. New York: Routledge

de Tocqueville, Alexis. [1856] 1955. *The Old Régime and the French Revolution*, trans. Stuart Gilbert. New York: Anchor

Denton, Trevor. 1966. 'The Structure of French Canadian Acculturation, 1759 to 1800.' *Anthropologica* 8 (1): 29–43

Derrida, Jacques. 1992. 'Force of Law: The "Mystical Foundation of Authority."' Pp. 3–67 in *Deconstruction and the Possibility of Justice*, ed. Drucilla Cornell, Michel Rosenfeld, and David G. Carlson. New York: Routledge

– 1986. 'Declarations of Independence.' *New Political Science* 15: 7–15

Deschênes, Jules. 1979. 'On Legal Separatism in Canada.' (1978). Pp. 31–42 in *The Sword and the Scales*. Toronto: Butterworths

Diamond, Sigmund. 1967. 'An Experiment in "Feudalism": French Canada in the Seventeenth Century.' Pp. 81–96 in *Three American Empires*, ed. John J. TePaske. New York: Harper and Row

Dickason, Olive P. 1993. 'Concepts of Sovereignty at the Time of First Contacts.' In Green and Dickason: 141–251

Dingwall, John Scott. 1978. 'Rhetoric, Logic and Politics: Parliamentary Debate in Canada.' PhD dissertation, Yale University

Dionne, N.-E. 1974. *Inventaire chronologique des livres, brochures, journaux et revues publiés en langue française dans la Province de Québec, depuis l'établissement de l'imprimerie au Canada jusqu'à nos jours, 1794–1905*. Vol. 1. New York: Burt Franklin

Doern, Russell. 1985. *The Battle over Bilingualism: The Manitoba Language Question, 1983–85*. Winnipeg: Cambridge Publishers

Doiron, Normand. 1991. 'Rhétorique jésuite de l'éloquence sauvage au XVIIe siècle: Les *Relations* de Paul Lejeune (1632–1642). *XVIIe Siècle* 43 (4): 375–402

Dolan, Frederick M. 1991. 'Hobbes and/or North: The Rhetoric of American National Security.' Pp. 191–209 in *Ideology and Power in the Age of Lenin in Ruins*, ed. Arthur Kroker and Marilouise Kroker. New York: St. Martin's Press

Doob, Jamie. 1988. 'Who Says That Canadian Culture Is Ironic?' Pp. 5–23 in *Essays in Canadian Irony*. Vol. I, ed. Linda Hutcheon. North York: York University

Dorland, Michael. 1997. '"The Expected Tradition": Innis, State Rationality and the Governmentalization of Communication.' *Topia* 1 (1): 1–16

– 1988. '"A Thoroughly Hidden Country": *Ressentiment*, Canadian Nationalism, Canadian Culture.' *Canadian Journal of Political and Social Theory* 12 (1–2): 130–64

Dosse, François. 1987. *L'Histoire en miettes: Des Annales à la 'nouvelle histoire.'* Paris: La Découverte

Douzinas, Costas, and Ronnie Warrington. 1994. *Justice Miscarried: Ethics, Aesthetics and the Law*. New York: Harvester Wheatsheaf

Dowler, Kevin. 1996. 'The Cultural Industries Policy Apparatus.' Pp. 328–46 in *The Cultural Industries in Canada: Problems, Policies and Prospects*, ed. Michael Dorland. Toronto: Lorimer

Downey, Gary Lee. 1998. *The Machine in Me: An Anthropologist Sits among Computer Engineers*. New York and London: Routledge

Dubuc, Alain. 2000. 'We Must Break This Vicious Cycle.' *Policy Options* (June): 8–28

Dumont, Fernand. 1993. *Genèse de la société québécoise*. Montreal: Boréal

Dumont, Fernand, and Yves Martin, eds. 1963. *Situation de la recherche sur le Canada français*. Quebec: Presses de l'Université Laval

Duncan, Hugh D. 1962. *Communication and Social Order*. London: Oxford University Press

Durham, John George Lambton, 1st Earl of. [1839] 1970. *Report on the Affairs of British North America*. Ed. Sir Charles Lucas. 3 vols. Oxford: Clarendon Press, 1839. Reprint, New York: A.M. Kelly

Duxbury, Neil. 1995. *Patterns of American Jurisprudence*. Oxford: Clarendon

Eccles, William J. 1969. *The Canadian Frontier, 1534–1760*. New York: Holt, Rinehart and Winston

– 1959. *Frontenac: The Courtier Governor*. Carleton Library Series. Toronto: McClelland and Stewart

Edwards, John L.J. 1964. *The Law Officers and the Crown*. London: Sweet and Maxwell

Egerton, H.E., and W.L. Grant. 1907. *Canadian Constitutional Development: Shown by Selected Speeches and Dispatches, with Introductions and Explanatory Note*. London: John Murray

Eggleston, Stephen. 1996–7. 'The Myth and Mystery of PogG.' *Journal of Canadian Studies* 31 (4): 80–96

Elder, R. Bruce. 1989. *Image and Identity: Reflections on Canadian Film and Culture*. Waterloo: Wilfrid Laurier University Press

Elias, Norbert. [1939] 1994. *The Civilizing Process: The History of Manners and State Formation and Civilization*. Oxford: Blackwell

Elkins, Stanley M. [1959] 1976. *Slavery: A Problem in American Institutional and Intellectual Life*. 3rd rev. ed. Chicago: University of Chicago Press

Enos, Theresa, ed. 1996. *Encyclopedia of Rhetoric and Composition: Communication From Ancient Times to the Information Age*. New York: Garland Publishing

Falardeau, Jean-Charles, ed. 1953. *Essais sur le Québec contemporain*. Quebec: Presses de l'Université Laval

Farr, David M.L. 1955. *The Colonial Office and Canada, 1867–1887*. Toronto: University of Toronto Press

Farrell, Thomas. 1993. *Norms of Rhetorical Culture*. New Haven: Yale University Press
– 1976. 'Knowledge, Consensus and Rhetorical Theory.' *Quarterly Journal of Speech* 62 (1): 1–14
Fecteau, Jean-Marie. 1999. 'Between Scientific Inquiry and the Search for a Nation: Quebec Historiography as Seen by Ronald Rudin.' *Canadian Historical Review* 80: 440–63
Fecteau, Jean-Marie, and Douglas Hay. 1996 '"Government by Will and Pleasure Instead of Law": Military Justice and the Legal System in Quebec, 1775–83.' Pp. 129–71 in *Canadian State Trials: Law, Politics, and Security Measures, 1608–1837*, ed. F. Murray Greenwood and Barry Wright. Toronto: Osgoode Society for Canadian Legal History / University of Toronto Press
Flaherty, David H., ed. 1981. *Essays in the History of Canadian Law*. Vol. 1. Toronto: Osgoode Society / University of Toronto Press
Flanagan, Thomas. 1988. 'Louis Riel: Insanity and Prophecy.' Pp. 208–26 in *Louis Riel: Selected Readings*, ed. Hartwell Bowsfield. Toronto: Copp Clark Pitman
Fliegelman, Jay. 1993. *Declaring Independence: Jefferson, Natural Language and the Culture of Performance*. Stanford, CA: Stanford University Press
Foucault, Michel. 1991. *The Order of Things: An Archaeology of the Human Sciences*. New York: Random House
– 1980. *Power/Knowledge: Selected Interviews and Other Writings, 1972–1977*, ed. Colin Gordon. New York: Pantheon Books
– 1970. 'Governmentality.' Pp. 87–104 in *The Foucault Effect: Studies in Governmentality*, ed. Graham Burchell, Colin Gordon, and Peter Miller. Chicago: University of Chicago Press
Fox, Edward W. 1971. *History in Geographic Perspective: The Other France*. New York: W.W. Norton
Francis, Daniel. 1997. *National Dreams: Myth, Memory and Canadian History*. Vancouver: Arsenal Pulp Press.
Friedenberg, Edgar Z. 1980. *Deference to Authority: The Case of Canada*. White Plains, NY: M.E. Sharpe
Friedman, Thomas L. 2000. *The Lexus and the Olive Tree: Understanding Globalization*. Expanded ed. New York: Anchor.
Frye, Northrop. 1971. *The Bush Garden: Essays on the Canadian Imagination*. Toronto: Anansi
Fyson, Donald. 1999. 'Changes in the Penal Law in Quebec across and after the Conquest.' Paper presented at the Annual Meeting of the American Society for Legal History, Toronto, October; available at: http://www.fl.ulaval.ca/hst/Profs/Dfyson/CrimLaw.htm
– 1993. 'A Guide to Legislation in Pre-Condeferation Quebec and Lower Canada.' Pp. 5–27 in *Class, Gender and the Law in Eighteenth and Nineteenth-Century*

Quebec: Sources and Perspectives, ed. Donald Fyson, Colin M. Coates, and
  Kathryn Harvey. Montreal: Montreal History Group also available at: http://
  www.fl.ulaval.ca/hst/Profs/Dfyson/Legis.htm
Gagnon, Serge. 1978. *Le Québec et ses historiens de 1840 à 1920*. Quebec: Presses
  de l'Université Laval
Gairdner, William D. 1996. *On Higher Ground: Reclaiming a Civil Society*. Toronto:
  Stoddart
Garner, John. 1969. *The Franchise and Politics in British North America*. Toronto:
  University of Toronto Press
Garver, Eugene. 1994. *Aristotle's Rhetoric: An Art of Character*. Chicago: University
  of Chicago Press
– 1987. *Machiavelli and the History of Prudence*. Madison, University of Wisconsin
  Press
Gellner, Ernest. 1994. *Conditions of Liberty: Civil Society and Its Rivals*. London:
  Hamish Hamilton
Gémar, Jean-Claude. 1995. *Traduire ou l'art d'interpréter: Langue, droit et société:
  éléments de jurilinguistique*. 2 vols. Sainte-Foy: Presses de l'Université du Québec
Genovese, Eugene D. 1967. *The Political Economy of Slavery: Studies in the
  Economy and Society of the Slave South*. New York: Vintage
Genovese, Eugene D., and Leonard Hochberg, eds. 1989. *Geographic Perspectives in
  History: Essays in Honor of Edward Whiting Fox*. Oxford: Basil Blackwell
Giddens, Anthony. 1995. *A Contemporary Critique of Historical Materialism*. Vol. 2
  The Nation-State and Violence. London: Macmillan
Gilman, Sander, and Carole Blai, eds. & trans. 1989. *Friedrich Nietzsche on Rhetoric
  and Language*. New York: Oxford University Press
Glasbeek, Amanda. 1998. 'Maternalism Meets the Criminal Law: The Case of
  the Toronto Women's Court.' *Canadian Journal of Women and the Law* 10:
  481–502
Glendon, Mary-Ann. 1991. *Rights Talk: The Impoverishment of Political Discourse*.
  Toronto: Collier Macmillan
Godard, Barbara. 1997. 'Writing between Cultures.' *TTR* 10 (1) special issue on
  Languages, Translation, and Post-Colonialism: 53–100
Gold, Marc. 1985. 'Constitutional Scholarship in Canada.' *Osgoode Hall Law Journal*
  23 (3): 495–518
Goldfarb, Jeffrey C. 1998. *Civility and Subversion: The Intellectual in Democratic
  Society*. Cambridge: Cambridge University Press
– 1991. *The Cynical Society: The Culture of Politics and the Politics of Culture in
  American Life*. Chicago: University of Chicago Press
Goldie, Terry, Carmen Lambert, and Rowland Lorimer, eds. 1994. *Canada: Theoretical
  Discourse / Discours théorique*. Montreal: Association for Canadian Studies

Goldsmith, Elizabeth C. 1988. *Exclusive Conversations: The Art of Interaction in Seventeenth-Century France*. Philadelphia: University of Philadelphia Press

Goodenough, Oliver. 1998. 'Defending the Imaginary to Death.' *Arizona Journal of International and Comparative Law* 15 (1): 203–53

Goodrich, Peter. 1994. 'Antirrhesis: Political Structures of Common Law Thought.' Pp. 57–102 in *The Rhetoric of Law*, ed. Austin Sarat and Thomas K. Kearns. Ann Arbor: University of Michigan Press

– 1990. *Languages of Law: From Logics of Memory to Nomadic Masks*. London: Routledge

Gordon, Daniel. 1994. *Citizens without Sovereignty: Equality and Sociability in French Thought, 1670–1789*. Princeton, NJ: Princeton University Press

Gouldner, Alvin W. 1979. *The Future of Intellectuals and the Rise of the New Class*. New York: Seabury

– 1970. *The Coming Crisis of Western Sociology*. New York: Basic Books

Granatstein, J.L. 1998. *Who Killed Canadian History?* Toronto: HarperCollins

Grant, George. 1965. *Lament for a Nation*. Toronto: Anansi

Green, L.C. 1993. 'Claims to Territory in Colonial America.' Pp. 1–40 in Green and Dickason

Green, L.C., and Olive P. Dickason. 1993. *The Law of Nations and the New World*. Edmonton: University of Alberta Press

Greenblatt, Stephen J. 1990. *Learning to Curse: Essays in Modern Culture*. New York: Routledge

Greene, Jack P. 1988. *Pursuits of Happiness: The Social Development of Early Modern British Colonies and the Formation of American Culture*. Chapel Hill: University of North Carolina Press

Greenwood, F. Murray. 1993. *Legacies of Fear: Law and Politics in Quebec in the Era of the French Revolution*. Toronto: Osgoode Society / University of Toronto Press

Greenwood, F. Murray, and Barry Wright, eds. 1996. *Canadian State Trials: Law, Politics and Security Measures, 1608–1837*. Toronto: Osgoode Society / University of Toronto Press

Greer, Allan. 1991. 'La République aux hommes: les patriotes de 1837 face aux femmes.' *Revue d'histoire de l'Amérique française* 44 (4): 507–52

Griffiths, Franklyn. 1996. *Strong and Free: Canada and the New Sovereignty*. Toronto: Stoddart

Groulx, Lionel-A. 1924. *Notre maître le passé*. Montreal: Bibliothèque de l'Action française

– 1919. *La Naissance d'une race*. Montreal: Bibliothèque de l'Action française

Guillaume, M. 1993. 'Spectralité et communications.' *Cahiers du LASA* 15–16: 74–81

– 1989. *La contagion des passions*. Paris: Plon

Habermas, Jürgen. 1996. *Between Facts and Norms: Contributions of a Discourse Theory of Law and Democracy*, trans. Wilhem Regh. Cambridge, MA: MIT Press

– 1991. *The Structural Transformation of the Public Sphere: An Inquiry into a Category of Bourgeois Society*, trans. Thomas McCarthy. Cambridge, MA: MIT Press

– 1989. *The New Conservatism: Cultural Criticism and the Historians' Debate*, trans. Shierry Weber Nicholsen, Cambridge. MA: MIT Press

– 1974. *Theory and Practice*, trans. John Viertel. Boston: Beacon Press

– 1973. *Legitimation Crisis*, trans. Thomas McCarthy. Boston: Beacon Press

Hamilton, Roberta. 1988. *Feudal Society and Colonization: The Historiography of New France*. Gananoque, ON: Langdale Press

Haraway, Donna. 1997: *Modest_Witness@Second Millenium: FemaleManc_Meets_ Onco-MouseT*. New York: Routledge

Hare, John. 1993. *Aux Origines du parlementarisme Québécois 1791–1793*. Sillery, QC: Septentrion

Hariman, Robert, ed. 1995. *Political Style: The Artistry of Power*. Chicago: University of Chicago Press

– 1990. *Popular Trials: Rhetoric, Mass Media, and the Law*. Tuscaloosa: University of Alabama Press

– 1986. 'Status, Marginality and Rhetorical Theory.' *Quarterly Journal of Speech* 72: 35–52

Harrington, Michael. *The Other America: Poverty in the United States*. Baltimore, MD: Penguin 1965

Hartz, Louis. 1964. *The Founding of New Societies*. New York: Harcourt, Brace and World

Hegel, G.W.F. 1965. *La Raison dans l'histoire*, trans. Kostas Papaioannou. Paris: 10/18. Originally published as *Die Vernunft in der Geschichte*. 5th ed. Hamburg: Hoffmeister, 1955

Hirschman, Albert O. 1977. *The Passions and the Interests: Political Arguments for Capitalism before Its Triumph*. Princeton, NJ: Princeton University Press

Horguelin, Paul A. 1977. 'Les premiers traducteurs (1760 à 1791).' *Meta* 22 (1): 15–32

Horowitz, Gad. 1966. 'Conservatism, Liberalism and Socialism in Canada: An Interpretation.' Pp. 21–44 in Ajzenstat and Smith 1995

Howard, Joseph. 1974. *Strange Empire*. Toronto: James Lewis and Samuel

Howes, David. 1987. 'From Polyjurality to Monojurality: The Transformation of Quebec Law, 1875–1929.' *McGill Law Journal* 32: 523–58

Huberdeau, Roger. 1947. 'François-Joseph Cugnet, jurisconsulte canadien: Essai historique.' MA thesis, Université de Montréal

Hubert, Henry A. 1994. *Harmonious Perfection: The Development of English Studies in Nineteenth-Century Anglo-Canadian Colleges*. East Lansing: Michigan State University Press

Hughes, Robert. 1986. *The Fatal Shore: The Epic of Australia's Founding*. New York: Vintage

Hutcheon, Linda. 1994. *Irony's Edge: The Theory and Politics of Irony*. London: Routledge

– 1992. *Double Talking: Essays on Verbal and Visual Ironies in Canadian Contemporary Art and Literature*. Toronto: ECW Press

– 1991. *Splitting Images: Contemporary Canadian Ironies*. Toronto: Oxford University Press

– 1988. *The Canadian Postmodern*. Toronto: Oxford University Press

Hutcheon, Linda, ed. 1988–9. *Essays in Canadian Irony*. 3 vols. North York, ON: York University

Innis, Harold A. 1972. *Empire and Communications*. Toronto: University of Toronto Press

– 1956. *Essays in Canadian Economic History*. Toronto: University of Toronto Press

– [1930] 1962. *The Fur Trade in Canada: An Introduction to Canadian Economic History*. Toronto: Macmillan

– 1923. *A History of the Canadian Pacific Railway*. London: P.S. King and Son

Jacoby, Russell. 1987. *The Last Intellectuals: American Culture in the Age of Academe*. New York: Basic

Janeway, Michael. 1999. *Republic of Denial: Press, Politics and Public Life*. New Haven: Yale University Press

Jenkyns, Richard. 1998. 'Cards of Identity.' Review of David Lowenthal, *The Heritage Crusades and the Spoils of History. New York Review of Books*, 23 April: 49–51

Johnston, W. Ross. 1973. *Sovereignty and Protection: A Study of British Jurisidictional Imperialism in the Late Nineteenth Century*. Durham, NC: Duke University Press

Jusdanis, Gregory. 1991. *Belated Modernity and Aesthetic Culture: Inventing National Literature*. Minneapolis: University of Minnesota Press

Kann, Mark E. 1998. *A Republic of Men*. New York: New York University Press

Kantorowicz, Ernst. 1957. *The King's Two Bodies: A Study in Mediaeval Political Theology*. Princeton: Princeton University Press

– 1955. 'Mysteries of State. An Absolutist Concept and Its Late Mediaeval Origins.' *Harvard Theological Review* 48: 65–91

– [1927] 2000. *Oeuvres*. Paris: Gallimard

Kaufer, D. 'Irony and Rhetorical Strategy.' *Philosophy and Rhetoric* 10 (1977): 90–109

Kennedy, W.P.M. 1932. *Some Aspects of the Theories and Workings of Constitutional Law: The Fred Morgan Kirby Lectures Delivered at Lafayette College 1931*. New York: Macmillan

Kennedy, W.P.M., ed. 1938. *The Constitution of Canada, 1534–1937: An Introduction to its Development Law and Custom*. 2nd ed. Toronto: Oxford University Press

– 1930. *Statutes, Treaties and Documents of the Canadian Constitution, 1713–1929*. Toronto: Oxford University Press

– 1918. *Documents of the Canadian Constitution, 1759–1915*. Toronto: Oxford University Press

Keohane, Kieran. 1997. *Symptoms of Canada: An Essay on the Canadian Identity*. Toronto: University of Toronto Press

Kilbourn, William, ed. 1970. *Canada: A Guide to the Peaceable Kingdom*. Toronto: Macmillan

Klinck, Carl F., ed. 1976. *Literary History of Canada*. 3 vols. 2nd ed. Toronto: University of Toronto Press

Knaplund, Paul. 1953. *James Stephens and the British Colonial System, 1813–1847*. Madison: University of Wisconsin Press

Kolish, Evelyn. 1987. 'The Impact of the Change in Legal Metropolis on the Development of Lower Canada's Legal System: Judicial Chaos and Legal Paralysis in the Civil Law, 1791–1838.' Pp. 318–58 in *Papers Presented at the 1987 Canadian Law in History Conference*. Ottawa: Carleton University

Kolko, Gabriel. 1968. *The Politics of War: The World and United States Foreign Policy, 1943–1945*. New York: Random House

Kulchyski, Peter, ed. 1994. *Unjust Relations: Aboriginal Rights in Canadian Courts*. Toronto: Oxford University Press

Kymlicka, Will. 1998. 'The Theory and Practice of Canadian Multiculturalism.' Paper, Queen's University (23 November). Humanities and Social Sciences Federation of Canada programs (http://www.hssfc.ca)

Lakietz, Naomi. 1999. 'Everyday Heroines Forged Own Successes.' *Calgary Herald* 19 October, 27 A

Larabbee, Leonard W. 1930. *Royal Government in America: A Study of the British Colonial System before 1783*. New Haven: Yale University Press

Laskin, Bora. 1960. *Canadian Constitutional Law: Cases, Texts and Notes on Distribution of Legislative Power*. 2nd ed. Toronto: Carswell

– 1947. '"Peace, Order and Good Government" Re-Examined.' *The Canadian Bar Review* 25: 1054–87

Larose, Gérald. 2001. 'Langue: une nouvelle approche stratégique et citoyenne.' Excerpts from the report, 'Le français, une langue pour tout le monde.' *La Presse*, Montreal: 21 August, A11.

Latouche, Daniel, ed. 1977. *Le manuel de la parole: Manifestes québécois*. Vol. 1. Sillery: Éditions du Boréal Express

Latour, Bruno. 1997. *Science in Action: How to Follow Scientists and Engineers through Society*. Cambridge, MA: Harvard University Press

– 1993. *We Have Never Been Modern*. Cambridge, MA: Harvard University Press

Latour, Bruno, and Steve Woolgar. 1986. *Laboratory Life: The Construction of Scientific Facts*. 2nd ed. Princeton, NJ: Princeton University Press

Laxer, Gordon. 1989. 'The Schizophrenic Character of Canadian Political Economy.' *Canadian Review of Sociology and Anthropology* 26 (1): 178–92

Leathes, Sonia. 1914. 'Votes for Women.' *University Magazine* 23: 68–78

Leff, Michael. 1999. 'The Habitation of Rhetoric.' Pp. 52–61 in *Contemporary Rhetorical Theory: A Reader*, ed. John L. Lucaites, Celeste M. Condit, and Sally Caudill. New York: Guilford

Legendre, Pierre. 1992. *Trésor historique de l'état en France: L'Administration classique*. Paris: Fayard

– 1988. *Le Désir politique de Dieu: Etude sur les montages de l'état et du droit*. Paris: Fayard

– 1968. *Histoire de l'administration de 1750 à nos jours*. Paris: Presses universitaires de France

Leland, Marine. 1961. 'François-Joseph Cugnet 1720–1789.' *La Revue de l'Université Laval* 16 (1): 3–13 and 16 (2): 129–39

Lemieux, Rodolphe. 1901. *Les origines du droit franco-canadien*. Montreal: C. Théoret

Lemire, Maurice, and Denis Saint-Jacques, eds. 1991–6. *La vie littéraire au Québec*. 3 vols. Sainte-Foy: Presses de l'Université Laval

Lerner, Daniel. 1958. *The Passing of Traditional Society: Modernizing the Middle East*. Glencoe, IL: Free Press

Lewis, William F. 1990. 'Power, Knowledge, and Insanity: The Trial of John W. Hinckley, Jr.' Pp. 114–32 in *Popular Trials: Rhetoric, Mass Media, and the Law*, ed. Robert Hariman. Tuscaloosa: University of Alabama Press

Liebersohn, Harry. 1988. *Fate and Utopia in German Sociology, 1870–1923*. Cambridge, MA: MIT Press

Lipset, Seymour M. 1990. *Continental Divide: The Values and Institutions of the United States and Canada*. Toronto: Canadian American Committee

Liu, Lydia H. 1999. *Tokens of Exchange: The Problem of Translation in Global Circulations*. Durham: Duke University Press

Locke, John. 1924. *Two Treatises of Civil Government*. London: J. M. Dent and Sons

Loo, Tina. 1994. *Making Law, Order and Authority in British Columbia, 1821–1871*. Toronto: University of Toronto Press

Lowenthal, David. 1998. *The Heritage Crusade and the Spoils of History*. Cambridge: Cambridge University Press

Lucaites, John Louis. 1990. 'Constitutional Argument in a National Theatre: The Impeachment Trial of Dr. Henry Sacheverell.' Pp. 31–54 in *Popular Trials: Rhetoric, Mass Media, and the Law*, ed. Robert Hariman. Tuscaloosa: University of Alabama Press

Lucaites, John Louis. 1984. 'Flexibility and Consistency in Eighteenth-Century Anglo-Whiggism: A Case Study of the Rhetorical Dimensions of Legitimacy.' PhD dissertation, University of Iowa

Luhmann, Niklas. 1985. *A Sociological Theory of Law*. London: Routledge

Lyotard, Jean-François. 1993. 'On the Strength of the Weak.' Pp. 62–72 in *Toward the Postmodern*, ed. Robert Harvey and Mark S. Roberts. Atlantic Highlands, NJ: Humanities Press International

– 1990. *Heidegger and 'The Jews,'* trans. Mark S. Roberts and Andreas Michel. Minneapolis: University of Minnesota Press

– 1988. *The Différend: Phrases in Dispute*, trans. Georges Van Den Abbeele. Minneapolis: University of Minnesota Press

– 1979. *La condition post-moderne*. Paris: Editions de Minuit

MacDonald, Kevin. 1998. *The Culture of Critique: An Evolutionary Analysis of Jewish Involvement in Twentieth-Century Intellectual and Political Movements*. Westport, CT: Praeger

Macdonald, Roderick A. 1985. 'Understanding Civil Law Scholarship in Quebec.' *Osgoode Hall Law Journal* 23 (4): 573–608

MacGregor, David. 1992. *Hegel, Marx and the English State*. Boulder, CO: Westview

Mackenzie, William Lyon. 1974. *1837: Revolution in the Canadas as Told by William Lyon Mackenzie*, ed. Greg Keilty. Toronto: NC Press

MacNutt, W.S. 1965. *The Atlantic Provinces: The Emergence of a Colonial Society 1712–1857*. Toronto: McClelland and Stewart

Macphail, Andrew. 1914. 'On Certain Aspects of Feminism.' *University Magazine* 23: 79–91

Maier, Charles S. 1988. *The Unmasterable Past: History, Holocaust and German National Identity*. Cambridge, MA: Harvard University Press

Mander, Christine. 1985. *Emily Murphy: Rebel*. Toronto: Simon and Pierre

Martin, Ged. 1995. *Britain and the Origins of Canadian Confederation, 1837–1867*. Vancouver: UBC Press

Marx, Karl, and Friedrich Engels. 1998. *The Communist Manifesto: A Modern Edition*, ed. and intro. Eric Hobsbawm. London: Verso

Massicotte, E.-Z. 1928. 'Hôtelleries, Clubs et Cafés à Montréal de 1760 à 1850.' *Transactions of the Royal Society of Canada*, 3rd ser., 22 (1): 37–61

Matthews, Richard K. 1995. *If Men Were Angels: James Madison and the Heartless Empire of Reason*. Lawrence: University Press of Kansas

Mauss, Marcel. 1970. *The Gift: Forms and Functions of Exchange in Archaic Societies*, trans. Ian Cunnison. London: Routledge and Kegan Paul

McGee, Michael Calvin. 1980a. 'The Origins of "Liberty": A Feminization of Power.' *Communication Monographs* 47: 23–45

– 1980b. 'The "Ideograph": A Link between Rhetoric and Ideology.' *Quarterly Journal of Speech* 66: 1–16

McGregor, Gaile. 1985. *The Wacousta Syndrome: Explorations in the Canadian Landscape*. Toronto: University of Toronto Press

McKillop, A.B. 1999. '"Who Killed Canadian History?" A View from the Trenches.' *Canadian Historical Review* 80: 269–99

McLean, Don. 1985. *1885: Metis Rebellion or Government Conspiracy?* Winnipeg: Pemmican Publications

McRoberts, Kenneth. 1997. *Misconceiving Canada: The Struggle for National Unity*. Toronto: Oxford University Press

Melody, William H., Liora Salter, and Paul Heyer, eds. 1981. *Culture, Communication and Dependency: The Tradition of Harold Innis*. Norwood: Ablex

Merry, Sally E. 1991. 'Law and Colonialism.' *Law and Society Review* 25 (4): 889–922

Mignolo, Walter D. 1995. *The Darker Side of the Renaissance: Literacy, Territoriality and Colonization*. Ann Arbor: University of Michigan Press

Mills, David. 1988. *The Idea of Loyalty in Upper Canada, 1784–1850*. Montreal: McGill-Queen's University Press

Milobar, David. 1995. 'Quebec Reform, the British Constitution and the Atlantic Empire, 1774–75.' Pp. 65–88 in *Parliament and the Atlantic Empire*, ed. Philip Lawson. Edinburgh: Edinburgh University Press

Moore, Christopher. 1997. *1867: How the Fathers Made a Deal*. Toronto: McClelland and Stewart

Morgan, Cecilia. 1996. *Public Men and Virtuous Women: The Gendered Languages of Religion and Politics in Upper Canada, 1791–1850*. Toronto: University of Toronto Press

Morgan, Edmund S. 1958. *The Puritan Dilemma*. Boston: Little Brown

Morin, Michel. 1997. *L'usurpation de la souveraineté autochtone: Le cas de peuples de la Nouvelle France et des colonies anglaises de l'Amérique du Nord*. Montréal: Boréal

Morse, Bradford W. 1985. *Aboriginal Peoples and the Law: Indian, Metis and Inuit Rights in Canada*. Ottawa: Carleton University Press

Morton, Desmond. 1972. *The Last War Drum: The North West Campaign of 1885*. Toronto: Hakkert

Morton, William L. [1946] 1967. 'Clio in Canada: The Interpretation of Canadian History.' Pp. 42–9 in Berger

– 1964. *The Critical Years: The Union of British North America, 1857–1873.* Toronto: McClelland and Stewart

– 1957. *Manitoba: A History.* Toronto: University of Toronto Press

Mossman, Manfred. 1988. 'The Charismatic Pattern: Canada's Riel Rebellion of 1885 as a Millenarian Protest Movement.' Pp. 227–45 in *Louis Riel: Selected Readings*, ed. Hartwell Bowsfield. Toronto: Copp Clark Pitman

Mulvaney, Charles Pelham. 1885. *The History of the North-West Rebellion of 1885.* Toronto: A.H. Hovey & Co.

Myrdal, Gunnar. [1944] 1964. *An American Dilemma.* 2 vols. New York: McGraw Hill

Naipaul, V.S. 1980. *The Return of Eva Perón.* Harmondsworth: Penguin

Naylor, R.T. 1975. *History of Canadian Business, 1867–1914.* 2 vols. Toronto: Lorimer

Neatby, Hilda M. 1937. *The Administration of Justice under the Quebec Act.* Minneapolis: University of Minnesota Press

Nelken, David, ed. 1996. *Law as Communication.* Aldershot: Dartmouth Publishing

Nevitt, Neil. 1996. *The Decline of Deference: Canadian Value-Change in Cross-National Perspective.* Peterborough, ON: Broadview Press

Nicolai, Martin L. 1992. 'Subjects and Citizens: French Officers and the North American Experience, 1755–1783.' PhD dissertation, Queen's University

Ormsby, Margaret. 1958. *British Columbia: A History.* Toronto: Macmillan

Ornston, Darius G., ed. 1992. *Translating Freud.* New Haven: Yale University Press

Osler, E.B. 1961. *The Man Who Had to Hang: Louis Riel.* Toronto: Longmans Green

Ouellet, Fernand. 1966. *Histoire économique et sociale du Québec, 1760–1850: Structures et conjonctures.* Montreal: Fides

Owram, Doug. 1977. 'Narrow Circles: The Historiography of Recent Canadian Historiography.' *National History* 1 (1): 5–21

Pagden, Anthony. 1995. *Lords of All the World: Ideologies of Empire in Spain, Britain and France, c. 1500–c. 1800.* New Haven: Yale University Press

– 1982. *The Fall of Natural Man: The American Indian and the Origins of Comparative Enthnology.* Cambridge: Cambridge University Press

Palmer, Bryan D. 1999. 'Of Silences and Trenches: A Dissident View of Granatstein's Meaning.' *Canadian Historical Review* 80: 676–86

Paquet, Gilles. 1999. *Oublier la Révolution Tranquille: Pour une nouvelle socialité.* Montréal: Liber

Paquet, Gilles, and Jean-Pierre Wallot. 1987. 'Nouvelle France / Québec: A World of Limited Identities.' Pp. 95–114 in *Colonial Identity in the Atlantic World*, ed. Nicholas Canny and Anthony Pagden. Princeton, NJ: Princeton University Press

– 1974. 'Groupes sociaux et pouvoir: Le cas canadien au tournant du XIXe siècle.' *Revue d'histoire d'Amérique française* 27 (4): 509–64

Parker, Graham. 1986. 'Canadian Legal Culture.' Pp. 3–30, in *Law and Justice in a New Land: Essays in Western Canadian Legal History*, ed. Louis A. Knafla. Toronto: Carswell

Parkman, Francis. 1887. *The Old Régime in Canada*. Boston: Little, Brown

Pawlisch, Hans S. 1985. *Sir John Davies and the Conquest of Ireland: A Study in Legal Imperialism*. Cambridge: Cambridge University Press

Peel, Bruce. 1974. *Early Printing in the Red River Settlement 1859–1870, and Its Effect on the Riel Rebellion*. Winnipeg: Peguis

Phillips, Jim. 1997. 'Recent Publications in Canadian Legal History.' *Canadian Historical Review* 78 (2): 236–57

Picard, André. 1999. 'The French Glass Is Empty. No, It's Overflowing.' *Globe and Mail*, 2 September, A 13

Pocock, J.G.A. 1976. 'The Classical Theory of Deference.' *American Historical Review* 81 (3): 516–23

– 1975. *The Machiavellian Moment: Florentine Political Thought and the Atlantic Republican Tradition*. Princeton, NJ: Princeton University Press

Pole, J.R. 1983. *The Gift of Government: Political Responsibility from the English Restoration to American Independence*. Athens: University of Georgia Press

Pollock, Frederick. 1894–5. 'Sovereignty in English Law.' *Harvard Law Review* 8: 243–51

Poulakos, John. 1984. 'Rhetoric, the Sophists and the Possible.' *Communication Monographs* 51 (3): 215–26

Presthus, Robert. 1973. *Elite Accommodation in Canadian Politics*. Toronto: Macmillan

Pue, Wesley, and DeLloyd Guth, eds. 1996. 'Canada's Legal Inheritances,' *Manitoba Law Journal* 23 (1/2)

Radforth, I.W., and Allan Greer, eds. 1992. *Colonial Leviathan: State Formation in Mid-nineteenth Century Canada*. Toronto: University of Toronto Press

Reid, Allana G. 1946. 'Representative Assemblies in New France.' *Canadian Historical Review* 27: 19–26

Revel, Jacques, and Lynn Hunt, eds. 1995. *Histories: French Constructions of the Past*. Vol. 1, *Postwar French Thought*. New York: New Press

Riel, Louis. 1985. *The Collected Writings of Louis Riel / Les écrits complets de Louis Riel*. Vol. 3. Ed. Thomas Flanagan. Edmonton: University of Alberta Press

– 1985. *The Collected Writings of Louis Riel / Les écrits complets de Louis Riel*. Vol. 4. Ed. Glen Campbell. Edmonton: University of Alberta Press

– 1974. *The Queen v Louis Riel*. With an introduction by Desmond Morton. Toronto: University of Toronto Press

– 1874. *L'Amnestie: Mémoire sur les causes des troubles du Nord-Ouest et sur les négociations qu'ont amené à leur règlement amiable*. Bureau du Nouveau Monde

Risk, Richard. 1996. 'The Scholars and the Constitution: P.O.G.G. and the Privy Council.' *Manitoba Law Journal* 23 (3): 496–523

Robbins, Bruce. 1993. *Secular Vocations: Intellectuals, Professionalism, Culture*. London: Verso

Robert, Jean-Claude. 1990. 'La recherche en histoire du Canada.' *International Journal of Canadian Studies* 1–2: 11–33

Roberts, Wayne. 1979. '"Rocking the Cradle for the World": The New Woman and Maternal Feminism, Toronto 1877–1914.' Pp. 15–45 in *A Not Unreasonable Claim: Women and Reform in Canada, 1880s–1920s*, ed. Linda Kealey. Toronto: The Women's Press

Robinson, Randall. 1999. *The Debt: What America Owes to Blacks*. New York: Dutton

Romney, Paul. 1999. *Getting It Wrong: How Canadians Forgot Their Past and Imperilled Confederation*. Toronto: University of Toronto Press

Rover, Constance. 1967. *Women's Suffrage and Party Politics in Britain: 1866–1914*. Toronto: University of Toronto Press

Rudin, Ronald. 1997. *Making History in Twentieth-Century Quebec*. Toronto: University of Toronto Press

Ryerson, Stanley B. 1968. *Unequal Union: Confederation and the Roots of Conflict in the Canadas, 1815–1873*. Toronto: Progress Books

Saul, John Ralston. 1997. *Reflections of a Siamese Twin: Canada at the End of the Twentieth Century*. Toronto: Viking

– 1995. *The Unconscious Civilization*. Toronto: Anansi and CBC

– 1993. *Voltaire's Bastards: The Dictatorship of Reason in the West*. Toronto: Penguin

Schama, Simon. 1991. *Dead Certainties: Unwarranted Speculations*. London: Granta Books

Schudson, Michael. 1998. *The Good Citizen: A History of American Civic Life*. New York: Free Press

Seery, John E. 1996. *Political Theory for Mortals: Shades of Justice, Images of Death*. Ithaca, NY: Cornell University Press

Séguin, Maurice. [1956] 1987. 'La notion d'indépendance dans l'histoire du Canada.' Pp. 213–15 in *Maurice Séguin, historien du pays québécois vu par ses contemporains*, ed. Robert Comeau. Montreal: VLB Editeur

Séguin, Robert-Lionel. 1972. *Vie libertine en Nouvelle-France au XVIIIe siècle*. 2 vols. Montreal: Léméac

Seligman, Adam B. 1992. *The Idea of Civil Society*. Princeton, NJ: Princeton University Press

Shanks, Andrew. 1995. *Civil Society, Civil Religion.* Oxford: Blackwell

Shortt, Adam, and Arthur G. Doughty, eds. [1907] 1918. *Documents Relating to the Constitutional History of Canada, 1759–1791.* (1907). Part I. Ottawa: J. de L. Taché

Shugart, H.A. 1999. 'Postmodern Irony as Subversive Rhetorical Strategy.' *Western Journal of Communication* 63: 433–55

Siegfried, André. 1907. *The Race Question in Canada.* New York: Appleton

Silver, A.I. 1982. *The French-Canadian Idea of Confederation, 1864–1900.* Toronto: University of Toronto Press

Simon, J.E.S. 1960. 'English Idioms from the Law.' Part 1. *The Law Quarterly Review* 76 (April): 283–446

Sloterdijk, Peter. 1987. *Critique of Cynical Reason.* Minneapolis: University of Minnesota Press

Smith, Allan. 1994. *Canada An American Nation? Essays on Continentalism, Identity and the Canadian Frame of Mind.* Montreal: McGill-Queen's University Press

Smith, David E. 1999. *The Republican Option in Canada, Past and Present.* Toronto: University of Toronto Press

– 1995. *The Invisible Crown: The First Principle of Canadian Government.* Toronto: University of Toronto Press

Smith, Rogers M. 1997. *Civic Ideals: Conflicting Visions of Citizenship in U.S. History.* New Haven: Yale University Press

Sombart, Werner. 1976. *Why is There No Socialism in the United States?* London: Macmillan

Somers, Margaret R. 1999. 'The Privatization of Citizenship: How to Unthink a Knowledge Culture.' Pp. 121–61 in *Beyond the Cultural Turn: New Directions in the Study of Society and Culture,* ed. Victoria E. Bonnell and Lynn Hunt. Berkeley: University of California Press

– 1995. 'What's Political or Cultural about Political Culture and the Public Sphere? Toward an Historical Sociology of Concept Formation.' *Sociological Theory* 13 (2): 113–44

Soros, George. 1998. 'Between Borders and Business' (conversation with Shimon Peres). *New Perspectives Quarterly* 15 (2): 21–9

Sparer, Michel, and Wallace Schwab. 1979. 'Loi et héritage culturel.' *Cahiers de Droit* 20: 399–431

Stacey, C.P. 1966. 'Benjamin West and "The Death of Wolfe,"' The National Gallery of Canada *Bulletin,* 4 (1): 1–5

Stanley, George F.G. 1961. *The Birth of Western Canada: A History of the Riel Rebellions.* Toronto: University of Toronto Press

Starobinski, Jean. 1989. *Le remède dans le mal: Critique et légitimation de l'artifice à l'âge des Lumières.* Paris: Gallimard

Steele, Ian K. 1986. *The English Atlantic, 1675–1740: An Exploration of Communication and Community*. New York: Oxford University Press

Stern, Fritz. 1961. *The Politics of Cultural Despair*. Berkeley: University of California Press

Stewart, Gordon T. 1986. *The Origins of Canadian Politics: A Comparative Approach*. Vancouver: UBC Press

Stewart, Susan. 1991. *Crimes of Writing: Problems in the Containment of Representation*. Durham, NC: Duke University Press

Stonechild, Blair, and Bill Waiser. 1997. *Loyal till Death*. Calgary: Fifth House

Strayer, Joseph R. 1970. *On the Medieval Origins of the Modern State*. Princeton, NJ: Princeton University Press

Swearingen, C. Jan. 1991. *Rhetoric and Irony: Western Literacy and Western Lies*. New York and London: Oxford University Press

Talmon, J.L. 1961. *The Origins of Totalitarian Democracy*. London: Heinemann

Tate, C. Neal, and Torbjörn Vallinder, eds. 1995. *The Global Expansion of Judicial Power*. New York: New York University Press

Thérien, Gilles, ed. 1995. *Figures de l'Indien*. Montréal: Typo

Thompson, E.P. 1963. *The Making of the English Working Class*. New York: Pantheon

Tierney, B. 1962. 'The Prince Is Not Bound by the Law: Accursius and the Origins of the Modern State' *Comparative Studies in Society and History* 5: 378–400

Tousignant, Pierre. 1991. 'Les aspirations libérales des réformistes canadiens-français et la séduction du modèle constitutionnel britannique, de 1789 à 1792.' Pp. 229–38 in *La Révolution Française au Canada Français*, ed. Sylvain Simard. Ottawa : Presses de l'Université d'Ottawa

– 1973. 'Problématique pour une nouvelle approche de la Constitution de 1791.' *Revue d'Histoire d'Amérique française* 27 (2): 181–234

Tousignant, Pierre, and Madeleine Dionne Tousignant. 1979. 'François-Joseph Cug-net.' In *Dictionary of Canadian Biography*, vol. 4. Toronto: University of Toronto Press

Tribe, Keith. 1988. *Governing Economy: The Reformation of German Economic Discourse, 1750–1840*. Cambridge: Cambridge University Press

Trigger, Bruce G. 1985. *Natives and Newcomers: Canada's 'Heroic Age' Reconsidered*. Montreal: McGill-Queen's University Press

Tucker, Thomas W. 1969–70. 'Sources of Louisiana's Law of Persons: Blackstone, Domat and the French Codes.' *Tulane Law Review* 44: 264–95

Underhill, Frank. 1970. 'Some Reflections on the Liberal Tradition on Canada.' In Berger 1967: 29–41

– 1960. *In Search of Canadian Liberalism*. Toronto: Macmillan

Unger, Roberto M. 1976. *Law in Modern Society: Toward A Criticism of Social Theory*. New York: Free Press

Upton, L.F.S. 1967. *The United Empire Loyalists: Men and Myths*. Toronto: Copp
Clark
Vachon, G.-André, ed. 1969. 'Une pensée incarnée: *La Gazette de Montréal / La
Gazette de Québec / Le Canadien.' Etudes françaises* 5 (3): 249–260
Valverde, Mariana. 1991. *The Age of Light, Soap and Water: The Age of Moral
Reform in English Canada, 1885–1925*. Toronto: McClelland and Stewart
Veilleux, Christine. 1990. 'Les gens de justice à Québec, 1760–1867.' PhD disserta-
tion, Université Laval
Voisy, Paul. 1975. 'The "Votes for Women" Movement.' *Alberta History* 23 (3): 10–
23
Wallace, Karl R. 1971. 'The Substance of Rhetoric: Good Reasons.' Pp. 357–70 in
Contemporary Theories of Rhetoric: Selected Readings, ed. Richard L. Johannesen.
New York: Harper and Row
Wallace, W. Stewart, ed. 1959. *The Maseres Letters, 1766–1768*. Toronto: Oxford
University Press
Wallerstein, Immanuel. 1999. *The End of the World as We Know It: Social Science for
the Twenty-First Century*. Minneapolis: University of Minnesota Press
– 1991. *Unthinking Social Science: The Limits of Nineteenth-Century Paradigms.*
Cambridge: Polity Press
Walzer, Michael. 1965. *The Revolution of the Saints*. Cambridge, MA: Harvard
University Press
Wark, Wesley. 1992. 'Security Intelligence in Canada, 1864–1945: The History of a
National Insecurity State.' Pp. 153–78 in *Go Spy the Land: Military Intelligence in
History*, ed. Keith Nelson and B.J.C. McKercher. Westport, CT: Praeger
Warkentin, Germaine. 1995. *Critical Issues in Editing Exploration Texts*. Toronto:
University of Toronto Press
Wexler, Stephen. 1984. 'The Urge to Idealize: Viscount Haldane and the Constitution
of Canada.' *McGill Law Journal* 29: 609–47
Whelan, Edward, ed. 1865. *The Union of the British Provinces: A Brief Account of
the Several Conferences Held in the Maritime Provinces and in Canada, in Sep-
tember and in October, 1864, on the Proposed Confederation of the Provinces,
together with a Report of the Speeches Delivered by the Delegates from the Prov-
inces, on Important Public Occasions*. Charlottetown: G.T. Hansard
White, Richard. 1991. *The Middle Ground: Indians, Empires and Republics in the
Great Lakes Region, 1650–1815*. Cambridge: Cambridge University Press
Williams, Raymond. 1977. *Marxism and Literature*. Oxford: Oxford University Press
Williams, Robert. 1990. *The American Indian in Western Legal Thought: The Dis-
courses of Conquest*. New York: Oxford University Press
Williams, William A. [1959] 1988. *The Tragedy of American Diplomacy*. New York
and W.W. Norton

Wills, Gary. 1999. *A Necessary Evil: A History of American Distrust of Government*. New York: Simon and Schuster

Wilson, Bruce. 1981. *As She Began: An Illustrated Introduction to Loyalist Ontario*. Toronto: Dundurn Press

Winfield, Richard Dean. 1995. *Law in Civil Society*. Lawrence: University Press of Kansas

Wise, S.F. 1993. *God's Peculiar Peoples: Essays on Political Culture In Nineteenth-Century Canada*, ed. A.B. McKillop and Paul Romney. Ottawa: Carleton University Press

Wright, Barry. 1998. 'Quiescent Leviathan? Citizenship and National Security Measures in Late Modernity.' *Journal of Law and Society* 25 (2): 213–36

Young, Brian. 1994. *The Politics of Codification: The Lower Canadian Civil Code of 1866*. Toronto: Osgoode Society for Canadian Legal History; McGill-Queen's University Press

Žižek, Slavoj. 1991. *For They Know Not What They Do: Enjoyment as a Political Factor*. London: Verso

Zweiben, Beverly. 1990. *How Blackstone Lost the Colonies: English Law, Colonial Lawyers and the American Revolution*. New York: Garland

Index

acculturation, 88–9

Act of Union (1840), 62, 100, 102, 106, 133, 143–5

American revolution, 140; impact of, on Canadians, 103–4; response to, 100

Amerindians, 154–6; legal status, British perspectives on, 154–8; rights under natural law, 154–5. *See also* Métis

Amherst, General, 156

Apothéose de Christophe Colomb (Bourassa), 10, 12, 293, 303–4

Arditi, Jorge, 268–9, 294

aristocracy, *Canadien,* 138

Aristotle, 270–6, 284, 286, 299; and civic rhetoric, 275; definition of style, 278; persuasive rhetoric, 272–7; on prudence, 125, 131; views on citizenship, 265

Bacchi, Carol Lee, 193–5, 197, 206, 211

Barrett, Harold, 270–1, 276

Benjamin, Walter, 169

Berger, Carl, 42–3, 46

Bernard, Jean-Paul, 43–6

bilingualism, 92, 102–3, 164, 233, 302, 309; degeneration of, historical, 94; in law, problems of, 77–9, 224, 236–41; in Manitoba, debates over, 225–34; in Quebec, policy of, 224–5, 234–7; relationship to multiculturalism, 254; Royal Commission on Bilingualism and Biculturalism, 77, 254, 309; understanding, 254

Blache, Pierre, 242–9, 254

Borden, Robert, 205, 218

Bourassa, Napoléon: *L'Apothéose de Christophe Colomb,* 10, 12, 293, 303–4

British North America Act (BNA Act), 5, 10, 20, 32, 37, 63–4, 119–20, 146, 148, 150, 152, 159, 176, 216, 218–19, 221–2, 261, 293, 303

Burchell, David, 265–7

Burke, Kenneth, 115, 147, 149–50, 186, 208, 210, 214, 271, 279, 312, 315; art of living, 315; casuistic stretching, 210; dialectical irony, 312; epistemology of irony, 214

Canada: and American threat, perceived, historically, 56–61; constitution of, *see* constitution; and culture of *ressentiment,* 18–19; forms of governance, early forms, 30–3; irony in, 313; legal

32–3, 37, 75, 175, 221–2, 125, 271;
under British law, 33, 175; definition
of, 3, 5; POgG clause, 5–6, 261
political culture (Canadian): problems of,
3–5
postcolonialism, 21
postmodernity, global, 21–4; and processes of breakdown, 22; and symbolic
disturbance, 22
power, 281–2, 285; conventional
accounts of, and rhetorical challenge
to, 290; feminization of, 124; implications of democratic discourse to,
281–2; performing, 290, 292–4, 298,
313, 315; —, in courtly style, 292–4,
296, 298; resistance of, 127
printing press, requests for, 31
private sphere, 262–5, 302, 312
prudence, in governing, 125–6, 130–1,
133, 144, 149, 296, 298–301, 305;
as element of monarchical style,
298–301; rhetoric of, 299
public speech, 30
public sphere, 27–31, 94, 98–100, 224,
262–4, 276–7, 294–5, 302, 309–10,
312–13; fear of, 263; French, 112–13;
of French absolutism, apolitical,
291–5; —, and courtly style, 292–3;
and symbolic order, control of, 31–4;
and woman's suffrage, 195, 202,
207–8, 259

Quebec: and *ancien régime* domination,
theory of, 20; civil culture, 20, 235;
and Confederation, 57, 62–6, 119; and
constituting Canada, 118, 120–1, 124,
126–9, 133–8; and creation of courts,
under British governance, 126–8,
130–1, 134; historiography, 79–84;
importance of language, 234–41; —,
French language, in law, 126–8;

language and legislation, 234–41; —,
Bill 63, 234; Bill 22, 234; Bill 101,
234, 236; and law, impact on, *see* law,
and civil society, in Quebec; as model
of multiculturalism, 256; modern/
postmodern status, 242–3, 245,
248–53; New France, and Conquest
(cession), problems of, 79–88; —,
social organization, 86; official
bilingualism, policy of, 224–5, 233–41,
254; sovereignty, 15; spectral socio-
economy, 251–2
Quebec Act, 65, 81, 85, 90, 94–5, 97–8,
101–2, 119, 128, 132–6, 143; criminal
law, treatment of, 134; and extension
of territory, 135; Quebec Revenue Act,
134–5; treatment of religion, 134
Quiet Revolution, 44, 224, 235, 242,
244, 248–52, 257

rebellion, 142–3. *See also* Northwest
Rebellions
religion: civil, 268–9; in constituting
Canada, rights of, 120, 123, 127–8,
131–2, 134; role in mobilizing Indians/
Métis, 172–3, 189; role in suffrage,
208–9; role in temperance movement,
206; Roman Catholic Church, 88, 95,
120
rhetoric: of accommodation, in woman's
suffrage, 194, *see also* suffrage,
woman's; Aristotelian, 272–7; —,
and contingency, 273; —, and emotions, 273–6; —, genres of, 272–3; —,
goal of, 273; —, and place of logic,
274; of Canada's constitutions, under
British regime, 119–29, 130–52; of
Canadian rebellion, 61–2; and civility,
270–2, 276, 281–3; of contingency, in
British constitution, 136–7; and cynicism, 312–13; decorum, as element of,